M000168267

First Grade
Math
with Confidence
Instructor Guide

First Grade Math
with Confidence

Instructor Guide

KATE SNOW

WELL-TRAINED MIND PRESS

PHOTOCOPYING AND DISTRIBUTION POLICY

The illustrations and all other content in this book are copyrighted material owned by Well-Trained Mind Press. Please do not reproduce any part on email lists or websites.

For families: You may make as many photocopies of this book as you need for use WITHIN YOUR OWN FAMILY ONLY. Photocopying the pages so that the book can then be resold is a violation of copyright.

Schools and co-ops MAY NOT PHOTOCOPY any portion of this book, with the exception of the blackline masters in the back of the book. For information on purchasing a school license for the Student Workbook, or for other additional information, please contact Well-Trained Mind Press: email support@welltrainedmind.com; phone 1.877.322.3445.

Publisher's Cataloging-In-Publication Data
(Prepared by The Donohue Group, Inc.)

Names: Snow, Kate (Teacher), author.
Title: First grade math with confidence. Instructor guide / Kate Snow.
Description: [Charles City, Virginia] : Well-Trained Mind Press, [2021] |
    Series: [Math with confidence] ; [5]
Identifiers: ISBN 9781952469053 (paperback) | ISBN 9781952469060 (ebook)
Subjects: LCSH: Mathematics--Study and teaching (Elementary)
Classification: LCC QA107.2 .S66 2021 (print) | LCC QA107.2 (ebook) | DDC
    372.7--dc23

No part of this work may be reproduced or transmitted in any form or by any means, electronic or mechanical, including photocopying and recording, or by any information storage or retrieval system without prior written permission of the copyright owner unless such copying is expressly permitted by federal copyright law, or unless it complies with the Photocopying and Distribution Policy above.

Address requests for permissions to make copies to: support@welltrainedmind.com
© 2021 Well-Trained Mind Press
All rights reserved.

Reprinted March 2024 by Bradford and Bigelow.

3 4 5 6 7 8 9 11 B&B 30 29 28 27 26 25 24

Table of Contents

Introduction

Welcome to *First Grade Math with Confidence*!

First Grade Math with Confidence is a complete first-grade math curriculum that will give your child a solid foundation in math. It's **playful, hands-on, and fun** with thorough coverage of all the skills your child needs to become capable and confident at math:

- reading, writing, and comparing numbers to 100
- understanding place value in numbers to 100
- mastery of the addition and subtraction facts to 20
- solving addition and subtraction word problems
- reading bar graphs, measuring length, and identifying shapes
- counting money and telling time to the half hour

The carefully-sequenced and confidence-building lessons will help your child develop a strong understanding of math, step by step. Daily review will ensure she fully masters what she has learned in previous lessons. With this blend of **deep conceptual understanding** and **traditional skill practice**, you'll give your child a thorough first-grade math education.

Fun activities like Addition Bingo, Pretend Store, and Measurement Scavenger Hunt will help your child develop a **positive attitude** toward math. You'll also find optional weekly enrichment lessons, with suggestions for delightful math picture books and real-world math activities that will help your child appreciate the importance of math in real life.

Besides this Instructor Guide, *First Grade Math with Confidence* also includes a **colorful, engaging Student Workbook** to reinforce what your child has learned. These short, straightforward workbook pages both reinforce new skills and review previous lessons so that your child remembers what he's learned.

If you're like most parents, you've probably never taught math before. You may even feel a little anxious or intimidated. But don't worry: if you can add 9 + 8 and count to 100, I promise you'll be fine! *First Grade Math with Confidence* is full of features that will help you teach math with confidence all year long:

- **Scripted, open-and-go lessons** guide you every step of the way
- **Clear goals** at the beginning of each lesson so you know exactly what you're trying to accomplish
- **Explanatory notes** help you understand more deeply how children learn math so you feel well-equipped to teach your child
- **Checkpoints** at the end of each unit give you specific guidance on whether to spend more time on the current unit or move on to the next one

In the next section, you'll learn how the program is organized and how to get your materials ready. Invest a little time reading this section now (and getting your Math Kit ready), and you'll be ready to teach math like a pro all year long.

Wishing you a joyful year of first grade math!

Kate Snow

How to Use This Book

The Goals of *First Grade Math with Confidence*

First Grade Math with Confidence aims to help children become capable and confident math students, with a deep understanding of math concepts, proficiency and fluency with fundamental skills, and a positive attitude toward math.

Deep conceptual understanding

You'll focus on one concept at a time for several weeks so your child can build deep, connected knowledge of each new topic. (Educators call this a *mastery approach* to new content.) Each new lesson builds on the previous one so your child gradually develops thorough understanding and makes connections between concepts.

Proficiency with fundamental skills

Children need lots of practice in order to master the basic skills necessary for proficiency in math. *First Grade Math with Confidence* provides continual, ongoing review of these core skills so your child fully grasps them by the end of the year. (Educators call this a *spiral approach* to review, because children periodically revisit topics, just as the curve of a spiral returns to the same point on a circle.)

Positive attitude

The lessons in *First Grade Math with Confidence* include games, movement, pretend activities, and lots of hands-on learning so your child enjoys and even looks forward to math time. Optional enrichment lessons each week (with a picture book and math extension activity) provide a break from the usual routine and help your child appreciate how math is used in real life.

Overview

First Grade Math with Confidence is organized into units, weeks, and lessons. Each section has clear goals so you know exactly what you're trying to accomplish.

Units

First Grade Math with Confidence is divided into 11 units. Each unit focuses on developing thorough understanding of one core topic, such as addition, measuring length, or place value.

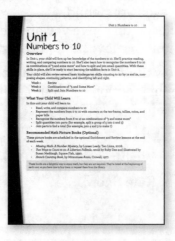

Weeks

Each unit is divided into 2–4 weeks (with a total of 32 weeks of lessons). Each week focuses on a specific topic, such as bar graphs or measuring in inches. These groups of lessons are called weeks, but you don't have to finish each one in a calendar week—it's fine to have your "week" begin on Wednesday and end on the following Friday.

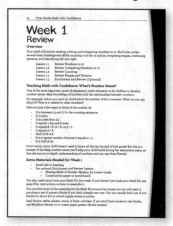

The preview for each week includes the following:

- **Overview.** A brief summary of what you'll teach your child that week, along with a list of the lessons.
- **Teaching Math with Confidence.** These notes will help you understand more deeply how children learn math so that you're well-prepared and confident as you teach your child the new concepts.
- **Extra Materials.** You'll sometimes need to supplement your regular math materials with a few everyday household items, such as small toys, tape, or scissors. This section will give you a heads-up if you need any extra materials for the week. (See below for more information on materials.)

Two Types of Lessons

Each week includes five lessons: four required core lessons and one optional enrichment lesson. The core lessons teach and review essential first-grade concepts and skills, while the enrichment lessons provide extra fun and real-life math applications.

Both types of lessons follow a consistent three-part format, with the purpose and materials listed at the top for easy reference. Plan to spend 20-25 minutes on each lesson.

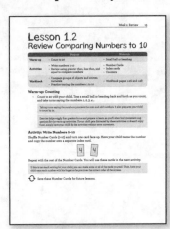 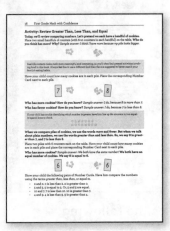 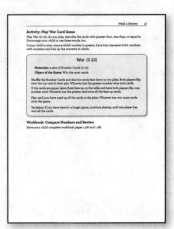

Within the lessons:

- **Bold** text indicates what you are to say.
- *Italic* text provides sample answers.
- Gray-highlighted text indicates explanatory notes.

If possible, try to plan a consistent time for teaching math each day. Many families find it best to do math first thing in the morning when everyone's fresh. If you have younger children, you might find it works better to teach math in the afternoon while your younger children are napping.

Core Lessons (Required)

Each core lesson includes several short and varied activities to help your child stay engaged and attentive.

Warm-up: counting, memory work, and review (3-5 minutes)

The warm-up provides regular, brief practice with counting and memory work. It also includes a quick review activity so your child remembers and retains what he has learned. Try to keep this part of the lessons short and sweet so your child isn't worn out before the new learning later in the lesson.

You'll find a full list of the memory work your child will memorize this year on page 499. The lessons include regular review to help your child gradually master this list over the course of the year, but feel free to adjust as needed to better fit your child. If your child already knows a particular fact, you do not need to review it every time it is listed in the instructor's guide. Or, if your child needs more practice than suggested, feel free to add it.

Hands-on activities (10-15 minutes)

These parent-directed activities are the most important part of each lesson. You'll teach your child the new concepts and skills through conversation, hands-on materials, and games. The lessons are scripted so you can just open the book and start reading, but you're welcome to rephrase the words to fit your own teaching style better.

Feel free to inject your own personality into your teaching, and personalize the lessons for your child. You might use your child's favorite objects for counting, change the names in word problems to match your family members, or take your math lesson outside to enjoy a beautiful day.

Workbook (5-10 minutes)

Your child will complete a two-sided workbook page at the end of each core lesson. (These workbook pages are included in the separate Student Workbook.) Side A gives your child written practice with the lesson's new material. Side B reviews skills your child has already learned. Most first-graders will be able to complete the worksheets independently, but many will need their parent to help read and interpret the directions. If writing is difficult for your child, feel free to have your child complete part or all of the worksheets orally rather than writing out the answers.

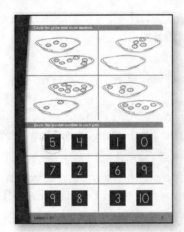
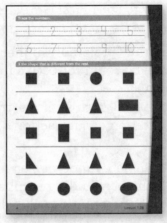

Have your child use a pencil for the workbook pages so it's easy to erase mistakes. You'll also occasionally need crayons or markers for coloring activities, so make sure you have them available. And, try to check the workbook pages as soon as your child finishes them. This immediate feedback shows your child that you value his work, and it helps prevent mistakes from becoming ingrained habits.

Enrichment Lessons (Optional)

The enrichment lessons are scheduled on the fifth day of each week. Many parents and children find that these enrichment lessons are their favorite part of the week. (Siblings often enjoy participating in them, too!) However, these enrichment lessons are completely optional. You are free to choose the ones that sound the most fun for your family, or skip them entirely if your schedule is too full.

Warm-up: counting, memory work, and review (3-5 minutes)

The enrichment lessons give your child a chance to show off her counting skills and recite all of the memory work she has learned so far. If you have time, you can also revisit one of her favorite or most challenging activities from the week.

Picture book (10 minutes)

Reading math picture books together is a fun, cozy, and delightful way to enjoy math. Most of the suggested books relate to the main concept studied that week, but some expose your child to other interesting math topics. **These picture books are not required.** You do not need to buy every book or track down every book in your library system.

Enrichment activity (varies)

The enrichment activities help your child understand and appreciate how math is used in everyday life. You'll find suggestions for art projects, field trips, physical activities, and more to make math come alive for your child.

Pacing and Checkpoints

Just as children learn to crawl, walk, and talk at different times, they are developmentally ready to learn math at different times, too. *First Grade Math with Confidence* provides lots of flexibility so your child can learn at his own pace. You know your child best, and you are always welcome to slow down or speed up the pace of the lessons based on your child's needs. Use the information below to help make decisions about pacing.

Is My Child Ready to Start *First Grade Math with Confidence*?

Most children are ready to start *First Grade Math with Confidence* when they are 6 years old. Your child is ready to begin this program if she can:

- Count to at least 10 (preferably higher).
- Write the numbers from 1 to 10. (It's fine if they're crooked or she sometimes reverses some of them.)
- Identify basic shapes, such as circle, triangle, and square.
- Solve simple addition or subtraction word problems by acting them out with concrete objects.

If your child did not complete *Kindergarten Math with Confidence*, you may find you need to spend a little extra time on building number sense with the numbers from 0 to 10 in Unit 1. The Checkpoint at the end of Unit 1 will help you decide whether to continue on to Unit 2 or spend more time solidifying these core number concepts. (See the next question for more on Checkpoints.)

How Do I Know Whether to Stick with a Lesson or Move On?

Most children need lots of exposure to a new concept or skill before they fully grasp it. Each lesson in *First Grade Math with Confidence* gently builds on the previous one, but your child doesn't need to completely master every lesson before moving on to the next. The program includes many opportunities for review and practice before your child is expected to achieve full proficiency with any topic.

As a general principle, continue teaching new lessons until you reach the end of a unit. At the end of each unit, you'll find a Checkpoint that will help you assess how your child is doing. The Checkpoints will also give you guidance on whether to move on to the next unit or give your child more practice with the current unit.

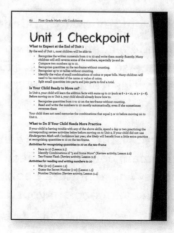

Each Checkpoint is divided into 3 parts:

- **What to Expect at the End of the Unit** This list of skills tells you what first graders typically are able to do at the end of each unit.
- **Is Your Child Ready to Move On?** This section tells you what your child needs to have mastered before moving on to the next unit.
- **What to Do if Your Child Needs More Practice** If your child isn't quite ready to move on, this section gives you options for reviewing and practicing the skills your child needs to master before the next unit. (This section is omitted if no specific skills are necessary for the next unit.)

For many units, your child does not need to master all of the material from the current unit before moving on. For example, in Unit 2, your child will learn the addition facts up to 10. But, he does not need to master the addition facts before studying shapes in Unit 3. Instead, he'll continue to practice the addition facts throughout Unit 3. That way, he'll be ready to build on them as he begins subtraction in Unit 4.

What Should I Do If My Child is Crying or Frustrated?

Extra tiredness, oncoming illness, or just plain grumpiness can make for a less-than-cheerful day of math (for both kids and parents). Don't worry if your child occasionally gets frustrated or cries during lesson time. If emotions rise during math, it's usually best to cut the lesson short and resume later in the day or the next day.

However, if your child is continually frustrated, resisting math lessons, or crying during math time, it's a clear sign you should take a break from the current topic, do some easy review, and then try the topic again in a few weeks. If your child shows these signs frequently, this book may be too challenging for his current maturity level, no matter how old he is. It may be wiser to use *Kindergarten Math with Confidence* instead. Every child's brain matures at a different rate, and you and your child will both find math time much more enjoyable when your child is developmentally ready for the book.

What Should I Do If the Lessons are Taking Too Long?

Most first-graders have a short attention span. The lessons in this program are meant to take no more than 20-25 minutes and include a variety of activities so your child can stay engaged and attentive. If you find a particular lesson takes longer than 25 minutes or if your child gets restless, stop and resume the lesson the next day. Or, break the lesson into two parts: do the hands-on activities during one part of the day, and then have your child do the workbook page at a different time. The rest of the lesson will probably go much more smoothly once your child is fresh.

What Should I Do If My Child Flies Through the Lessons?

The Unit 1 lessons are especially short as children build their attention spans and confidence during the first few weeks of the program. If you used *Kindergarten Math with Confidence*, many of the Week 1 activities may feel very familiar. Feel free to condense lessons or teach two per day if your child whizzes through the activities.

After Unit 1, the lessons become a bit longer. If you have a child who picks up math quickly, you can condense lessons or skip some of the warm-up activities or review workbook pages. If you go this route, occasionally double-check whether your child still remembers these skills. Just because she knew a skill at one point doesn't mean she still knows it, and periodic checks will help cement that information in her memory.

What You'll Need

You'll use simple household items to make math hands-on, concrete, and fun in *First Grade Math with Confidence*. Most lessons will only require materials from your Math Kit, but you'll also sometimes use everyday objects to enhance the lessons. No need for an expensive shopping trip, though! You likely already own just about everything you need.

How to Create Your Math Kit

You'll use materials from your Math Kit in every core lesson. Stick the following materials in a box or basket so that they're always ready to go, and keep them handy when you're teaching.

- **125 small counters.** Any type of small object (such as plastic tiles, Legos, blocks, plastic bears, coins, or dried beans) is fine. These work best (and fit the Blackline Masters) if they are less than .75" (or 2 cm) across. You'll occasionally need 2 colors, so make sure at least 10 of the counters are a different color than the rest.
- **Pattern blocks.** Pattern blocks are a specific set of small plastic or wooden hexagons, triangles, squares, trapezoids, and diamonds. They're generally available for about $10 online or at school supply stores. Children typically love pattern blocks and enjoy making designs from them. If you don't have access to real pattern blocks, you can photocopy and color Blackline Master 10 (page 549) instead.
- **Coins (20 pennies, 20 nickels, 10 dimes, 4 quarters).** You can use toy coins, but children often enjoy using real coins more. If you live outside the U.S., use your local currency or the generic coins on Blackline Master 11 instead. See page 28 for more details on your options.
- **Play money (10 one-dollar bills, 10 five-dollar bills, and 10 ten-dollar bills).** Play money from a toy cash register or board game works well, or you can copy and cut out the play money on Blackline Master 12.
- **2 packs of 100 blank index cards.** You'll use index cards for many different activities, such as making Number Cards for creating equations and playing games. Three-inch by five-inch blank cards are ideal, but anything similar will work. You'll have quite a few cards by the end of the year, so label 4 envelopes or zip-top bags now to make organizing the cards easier.

- **2 packs of playing cards and 2 dice.** You'll use playing cards and dice for some of the games in the book. Any standard 52-card decks and regular, six-sided dice will work fine.
- **Clock with hands.** Your clock should have clear, easy-to-read numbers, tick marks along the edge for each minute, and hands your child can easily move. If your family's clocks don't meet these criteria, you may want to buy an inexpensive plastic teaching clock (sometimes called a "Judy clock") to make these lessons easier to teach.
- **1-foot ruler.** Any type of ruler is fine, as long as it's labeled in inches. (If your family uses the metric system, you'll need a 30-centimeter ruler, labeled in centimeters, instead.)
- **Blank paper.** Any kind of paper is fine, including plain copy paper.
- **Pencils.** Keep sharp pencils on hand for lessons and workbook pages.

- **Binder with about 20 plastic page protectors. (Recommended, but not required.)** Blackline Masters and game boards are an important part of the program and are often re-used. Many pilot-test families found it easiest to keep track of these papers in plastic page protectors in a binder.

You'll find all the Blackline Masters at the back of this book. You can also download them at welltrainedmind.com/mwc.

 You will occasionally need to save items for future lessons. This symbol will alert you if you need to save anything.

Other Supplies Needed

You'll only need your Math Kit for most lessons, but occasionally you'll need a few other common household items. You'll find these items listed in three different places so you always know what you need:

- The preview for each week lists all extra household items needed.
- The top of each lesson lists all supplies you'll need to teach that lesson. These lists include items from your Math Kit as well as extra household items. (Note that nearly every lesson requires paper and pencils. To save space, they are not listed every time.)
- You'll find the complete list of household items needed throughout the year on page 504.

Don't feel you have to gather these extra household items now. Most are common things like tape, scissors, or small toys you can grab right before you begin the lesson.

Helpful Resources

You'll find an appendix of helpful resources at the back of this book:

- Scope and Sequence
- Complete Memory Work List
- Complete Picture Book List
- Materials List
- Game List (and extra copies of game boards)
- Blackline Masters

Unit 1
Numbers to 10

Overview

In Unit 1, your child will firm up her knowledge of the numbers to 10. She'll practice reading, writing, and comparing numbers to 10. She'll also learn how to recognize the numbers 6 to 10 as combinations of "5 and some more" and how to split and join small quantities. With these skills in place, she'll be ready to start learning the addition facts in Unit 2.

Your child will also review several basic kindergarten skills: counting to 20 by 1s and 2s, composing shapes, continuing patterns, and identifying left and right.

Week 1	Review
Week 2	Combinations of "5 and Some More"
Week 3	Split and Join Numbers to 10

What Your Child Will Learn

In this unit your child will learn to:

- Read, write, and compare numbers to 10
- Represent the numbers from 0 to 10 with counters on the ten-frame, tallies, coins, and paper bills
- Recognize the numbers from 6 to 10 as combinations of "5 and some more"
- Split quantities into parts (for example, split a group of 5 into 2 and 3)
- Join parts to find a total (for example, join 4 and 3 to make 7)

Recommended Math Picture Books (Optional)

These picture books are scheduled in the optional Enrichment and Review lessons at the end of each week.

- *Missing Math: A Number Mystery*, by Loreen Leedy. Two Lions, 2008.
- *Two Ways to Count to 10: A Liberian Folktale*, retold by Ruby Dee and illustrated by Susan Meddaugh. Square Fish, 1990.
- *Anno's Counting Book*, by Mitsumasa Anno. Crowell, 1977.

These books are a delightful way to enjoy math, but they are not required. They're listed at the beginning of each unit, so you have time to buy them or request them from the library.

Week 1
Review

Overview

Your child will review reading, writing, and comparing numbers to 10. She'll also review several basic kindergarten skills: counting to 20 by 1s and 2s, composing shapes, continuing patterns, and identifying left and right.

Lesson 1.1	Review Numbers to 10
Lesson 1.2	Review Comparing Numbers to 10
Lesson 1.3	Review Counting
Lesson 1.4	Review Shapes and Patterns
Lesson 1.5	Enrichment and Review (Optional)

Teaching Math with Confidence: What's Number Sense?

One of the most important goals of elementary math education is for children to develop number sense: deep knowledge of numbers and the relationships between numbers.

For example, before you read on, think about the number 16 for a moment. What can you say about it? How is it related to other numbers?

Here are just a few ways to think of the number 16:

- It is between 15 and 17 in the counting sequence.
- It is even.
- It is 4 less than 20.
- It equals 1 ten and 6 ones.
- It equals 8 + 8, 10 + 6, or 9 + 7.
- It equals 2 × 8.
- Half of 16 is 8.
- It is a square number, because it equals 4 × 4.
- It is half of 32.

Don't worry—your child doesn't need to know all this by the end of first grade! But this is a sample of the deep number sense you'll help your child build during her elementary years, so that she has an in-depth understanding of numbers and can use them fluently.

Extra Materials Needed for Week 1

- Small ball or beanbag
- For optional Enrichment and Review Lesson:
  - × *Missing Math: A Number Mystery,* by Loreen Leedy
  - × Construction paper or posterboard

You also need items from your Math Kit this week. If you haven't yet made your Math Kit, see page 8 for instructions on how to assemble it.

You can find most of the materials for the Math Kit around the house, but you will need to purchase a set of pattern blocks if you don't already own one. You can usually find a set of 100 blocks for about $10 at school supply stores or online.

Real blocks--either plastic, wood, or foam--are best. If you don't have access to real blocks, use Blackline Master 10 to create paper pattern blocks instead.

Lesson 1.1
Review Numbers to 10

	Purpose	Materials
Warm-up	• Count to 10	• None
Activities	• Set a positive tone for the year and preview what your child will learn • Review reading and sequencing numbers to 10	• Math Kit, assembled according to the directions on page 8 • Index cards
Workbook	• Put the numbers from 1 to 10 in order • Practice tracing the numbers from 1 to 10	• Workbook pages 1.1A and 1.1B

The Week 1 lessons assume that your child already knows these skills and simply needs a quick review. If your child already knows these skills well, skim through the lessons quickly (or even skip them altogether). If your child has never learned a particular skill, spend some extra time practicing it, and review it regularly until she has it mastered. You know your child best, so always feel free to adjust the amount of practice and review based on what your child needs.

Warm-up: Counting

- **Each day, we'll begin with a warm-up. Count from 1 to 20.** *1, 2, 3, …*

Activity: Number Scavenger Hunt

Today, you'll begin your new math book. Let's take a look at your workbook and see what you'll learn this year. Briefly page through the workbook with your child. **What are you most excited to learn about in math this year?** *Answers will vary.*

Math is the study of numbers, shapes, measurement, and patterns. We use math all the time in everyday life: in cooking, at the store, at home, everywhere!

I wonder how many different places you can find numbers in our house. Walk around your home and have your child look for numbers.

Activity: Introduce the Math Kit

We'll use the Math Kit to help you learn and understand math. Show your child your Math Kit and talk about the items in it. For example: **We'll use pattern blocks to build patterns and shapes. You'll learn more about telling time and counting coins this year.**

If you haven't gathered the supplies for your Math Kit yet, work with your child now to collect the necessary materials. See page 8 for the full list.

Activity: Make Number Cards

We need to make Number Cards for our Math Kit. We'll use the cards for activities and games. Write the numbers from 0 to 10 on index cards. Have your child trace each number with her finger to review the order of strokes for writing the numbers.

You'll sometimes use these cards face-down for games like Memory, so make sure you use a writing utensil that does not show through the backs of the cards.

Mix up the Number Cards and have your child put them in order from 0 to 10.

 Save the Number Cards for future lessons and add them to your Math Kit.

Workbook: Put Numbers in Order and Review

After we do some math activities together, you'll practice what you've learned on paper. Look at workbook pages 1.1A and 1.1B with your child and make sure she understands what to do in each section. Then, have your child complete the pages.

As your child traces the numbers on 1.1A, check that she starts each number at the starting dot and follows the correct sequence of strokes (indicated by the arrows).

Your child will complete 2 workbook pages at the end of every lesson (except for the optional Enrichment and Review lesson at the end of each week). Side A generally provides practice with the new skill or concept from the lesson, while Side B provides review.

First-graders often need help understanding directions and staying focused, so make sure you keep an eye on your child as she works. If you find the worksheets are too demanding for your child's fine-motor skills, either scribe her answers or have her complete the worksheets orally.

Lesson 1.2
Review Comparing Numbers to 10

	Purpose	Materials
Warm-up	• Count to 20	• Small ball or beanbag
Activities	• Write numbers 1-10 • Review using *greater than, less than,* and *equal* to compare numbers	• Number Cards • Index cards • Counters
Workbook	• Compare groups of objects and written numerals • Practice tracing the numbers 1 to 10	• Workbook pages 1.2A and 1.2B

Warm-up: Counting

• Count to 20 with your child. Toss a small ball or beanbag back and forth as you count, and take turns saying the numbers: *1, 2, 3, 4...*

> Taking turns saying the numbers previews the even and odd numbers. It also prepares your child to count by 2s.

> Exercise helps wiggly first graders focus and prepare to learn, so you'll often find movement suggestions for the warm-up activities. If your child gets distracted by these activities or doesn't enjoy them, simply have your child do the activities without extra movement.

Activity: Write Numbers 0-10

Shuffle Number Cards (0-10) and turn one card face-up. Have your child name the number and copy the number onto a separate index card.

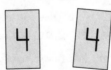

Repeat with the rest of the Number Cards. You will use these cards in the next activity.

> If this is too much writing for your child, you can make some or all of the cards yourself. Then, have your child trace each number with his finger so he practices the correct order of the strokes.

 Save these Number Cards for future lessons.

Activity: Review Greater Than, Less Than, and Equal

Today, we'll review comparing numbers. Let's pretend we each have a handful of cookies. Place two small handfuls of counters (with 6-10 counters in each handful) on the table. **Who do you think has more? Why?** *Sample answer: I think I have more because my pile looks bigger.*

Real-life contexts make math more meaningful and interesting, so you'll often find pretend activities involving food in this book. Always feel free to use a different food than the one suggested to better match your family's eating habits.

Have your child count how many cookies are in each pile. Place the corresponding Number Card next to each pile.

Who has more cookies? How do you know? *Sample answer: I do, because 8 is more than 7.*

Who has fewer cookies? How do you know? *Sample answer: I do, because 7 is less than 8.*

If your child has trouble identifying which number is greater, have him line up the counters in two equally-spaced lines to check.

When we compare piles of cookies, we use the words *more* **and** *fewer***. But when we talk about plain numbers, we use the words** *greater than* **and** *less than***. So, we say 8 is** *greater than* **7, and 7 is** *less than* **8.**

Place two piles with 6 counters each on the table. Have your child count how many cookies are in each pile and place the corresponding Number Card next to each pile.

Who has more cookies? *Sample answer: We both have the same number!* **We both have an equal number of cookies. We say 6 is** *equal to* **6.**

Show your child the following pairs of Number Cards. Have him compare the numbers using the terms *greater than, less than,* or *equal to.*

- *2 and 0. 0 is less than 2. 2 is greater than 0.*
- *5 and 5. 5 is equal to 5. Or, 5 and 5 are equal.*
- *10 and 7. 7 is less than 10. 10 is greater than 7.*
- *4 and 9. 4 is less than 9. 9 is greater than 4.*

Activity: Play War Card Game

Play War (0-10). As you play, describe the cards with *greater than*, *less than*, or *equal to*. Encourage your child to use these words, too.

If your child is ever unsure which number is greater, have him represent both numbers with counters and line up the counters to check.

War (0-10)

Materials: 2 sets of Number Cards (0-10)

Object of the Game: Win the most cards.

Shuffle the Number Cards and deal the cards face down in two piles. Both players flip over the top card in their pile. Whoever has the greater number wins both cards.

If the cards are equal, leave them face-up on the table and have both players flip over another card. Whoever has the greater card wins all the face-up cards.

Play until you have used up all the cards in the piles. Whoever has won more cards wins the game.

Variation: If you have time for a longer game, continue playing until one player has won all the cards.

Workbook: Compare Numbers and Review

Have your child complete workbook pages 1.2A and 1.2B.

Lesson 1.3
Review Counting

	Purpose	Materials
Warm-up	• Count to 20 • Review left and right	• Small ball or beanbag
Activities	• Review counting objects by 1s or by 2s • Identify numbers on the 100 Chart • Review using *greater than* and *less than* to compare numbers	• Counters • 100 Chart (Blackline Master 3)
Workbook	• Compare numbers	• Workbook pages 1.3A and 1.3B

Warm-up: Counting and Review

• Count to 20 with your child. Toss a small ball or beanbag back and forth as you count, and take turns saying the numbers: *1, 2, 3, 4...*

• Show your child her right and left hands. **Here's a trick to remember which hand is right and which is left. Left starts with L. Your left hand makes a capital L when you put it flat on the table.**

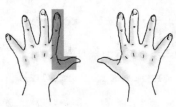

If your child is right-handed, point out your child writes with her right hand.

Activity: Review Counting by 1s and 2s

We'll review counting today. Secretly count out 18 counters and place them on the table. **How many counters do you think there are?** *Answers will vary.*

Estimating first makes counting activities more interesting and fun. Don't worry if your child's guess is far from the actual number. Her estimates will become more accurate as she gains experience with estimation and counting.

Have your child count the pile. Encourage her to move each counter to a new pile as she counts. Make sure she says only one number word for each counter and slow her down as needed. **How many counters are there?** *18.*

Moving the counters from one pile to the other helps slow your child down so that she says only one number per counter.

We can also count by 2s. Demonstrate how to count the pile by 2s: **2, 4, 6...**

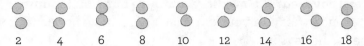

> Your child will have many more opportunities to practice counting by 1s and 2s in future lessons.

Activity: Review the 100 Chart

How high do you think you can count? *Answers will vary.* Have your child count as high as she can. Stop her if she reaches 120. **You'll learn how to count to 150 by 1s, 2s, 5s, and 10s this year.**

Show your child the 100 Chart (Blackline Master 3). **This chart is called a 100 Chart. It shows all of the numbers from 1 to 100.**

1	2	3	4	5	6	7	8	9	10
11	12	13	14	15	16	17	18	19	20
21	22	23	24	25	26	27	28	29	30
31	32	33	34	35	36	37	38	39	40
41	42	43	44	45	46	47	48	49	50
51	52	53	54	55	56	57	58	59	60
61	62	63	64	65	66	67	68	69	70
71	72	73	74	75	76	77	78	79	80
81	82	83	84	85	86	87	88	89	90
91	92	93	94	95	96	97	98	99	100

The numbers on the 100 Chart are arranged in rows and columns. The lines that go across the page are called rows. Slide your finger across the rows of the 100 Chart from left to right.

The lines that go up and down the page are called columns. Slide your finger down the columns of the 100 Chart from top to bottom.

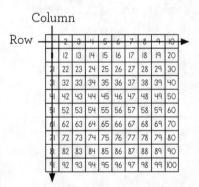

What are some patterns you notice? *Answers will vary.* Spend a few minutes looking for patterns on the 100 Chart. For example, your child might notice that all the numbers in the rightmost column contain a 0, or that all the numbers in a given column have the same number in the ones-place.

> It's fine if your child doesn't notice many patterns on the 100 Chart yet. Asking her to look for patterns in this lesson primes her to expect patterns and keep her eyes open for them in future lessons.

We'll use the top row of the 100 Chart today. Cover the bottom 9 rows of the 100 Chart so only the top row is showing.

With your child looking away, secretly cover the number 7 with a small counter. **Can you guess which number I covered?** *7*. **How did you figure out which number I covered?** *Sample answer: I know 7 comes after 6.* If your child isn't sure, have her count forward from 1 and point to each number as he says it.

| 1 | 2 | 3 | 4 | 5 | 6 | ⬤ | 8 | 9 | 10 |

Repeat with several other numbers from 1 to 10.

Activity: Play Guess the Secret Number (1-10)

Play Guess the Secret Number (1-10) several times. Once your child understands the game, reverse roles and have your child choose the secret number.

Guess the Secret Number (1-10)

Materials: 100 Chart (Blackline Master 3), counters

Object of the Game: Guess the secret number.

Secretly choose a number between 1 and 10, and write it on a slip of paper.

Place a counter on the 1 and the 10 on the 100 Chart. **My secret number is greater than 1 and less than 10.**

| ⬤ | 2 | 3 | 4 | 5 | 6 | 7 | 8 | 9 | ⬤ |

The other player guesses the secret number. If the guess is incorrect, move one counter to the number she guesses, so the secret number is still between the two counters. For example, if the secret number is 4, and your child guesses 6, move the counter from the 10 to the 6 and say: **My secret number is less than 6.**

Example of how to move the counter if the secret number is 4 and your child guesses 6.
Make sure your secret number is always between the two counters.

Have your child continue guessing. Keep moving the counters so your secret number is between the two counters. Once your child guesses correctly, reveal your written number.

You will continue to play this game throughout the year with larger numbers.

Workbook: Compare Numbers and Review

Have your child complete workbook pages 1.3A and 1.3B.

Workbook page 1.3B directs your child to color the left and right sides of the shapes. If your child doesn't enjoy coloring or finds it tiring, she can draw an X of the appropriate color instead of coloring the entire shape.

Lesson 1.4
Review Shapes and Patterns

	Purpose	Materials
Warm-up	• Count out a given number of objects • Review *left* and *right*	• Counters
Activities	• Explore pattern blocks • Review patterns • Review ordinal numbers	• Pattern blocks
Workbook	• Continue patterns	• Workbook pages 1.4A and 1.4B • Pattern blocks

Warm-up: Counting and Review

- Have your child count out 19 counters.

- Play Simon Says. **If I say "Simon says" first, then you should follow my direction. But if I don't say "Simon says," don't follow my direction.** Give your child 8-10 directions like the following:

  × **Simon says jump up and down on your right foot.** *Child jumps up and down on his right foot.*

  × **Simon says wave your left hand.** *Child waves his left hand.*

  × **Stand on one foot.** *Child doesn't do anything.* If your child stands on one foot, remind him he should only follow the direction when you say, "Simon says."

Activity: Explore Pattern Blocks

Today, we'll review shapes and patterns. Show your child the pattern blocks. Tell him the name of each shape.

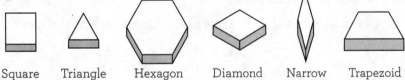

Square   Triangle   Hexagon   Diamond   Narrow Diamond   Trapezoid

Your child does not need to memorize the names of the pattern blocks.

Give your child time to explore the blocks and make designs. Use the correct names for the blocks as you discuss his creations. For example, **I see you put two trapezoids together to make a hexagon.**

Putting the pattern blocks on top of a piece of felt or a fuzzy towel helps prevent them from sliding and makes it easier to line up the sides of the blocks exactly.

Activity: Review Patterns

We can use the blocks to make patterns, too. Patterns in math must always follow a rule. If I randomly put some blocks in a row, it's not a pattern. Take a handful of about 6 pattern blocks and lay them randomly in a row from left to right.

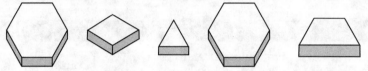

This row of blocks isn't a pattern. But if I think of a rule in my head and then follow it, I make a pattern.

Use pattern blocks to make the following patterns. Have your child add a few blocks to continue each pattern.

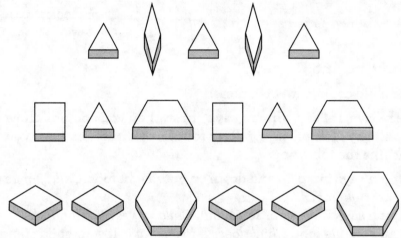

If your child has trouble continuing any of the patterns, have her first point to each element in order and say its name aloud: "triangle, diamond, triangle, diamond…" This allows her to hear the pattern as well as see it.

Activity: Review Ordinal Numbers

Place 6 pattern blocks in a line as shown. **How many blocks are in the line?** *6.*

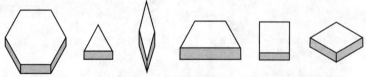

We use numbers like one, two, and three when we count and tell how many blocks there are. But we use numbers like *first*, *second*, and *third* to describe the blocks' order.

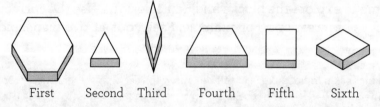

First   Second   Third   Fourth   Fifth   Sixth

Point to the hexagon. **This block is first.** Point to the triangle. **This block is second.** Continue with the rest of the blocks.

Rearrange the order of the blocks. **Now which block is first? Second? Third? Fourth? Fifth? Sixth?** *Child points to the corresponding block.*

Numbers like *first, second,* and *third* are called *ordinal numbers.* We use ordinal numbers to describe how objects or events relate to each other, as opposed to the cardinal numbers (like one, two, three, etc.) which we use to count and tell how many. Your child does not need to know these terms but simply needs to be able to use both kinds of numbers correctly in context. Later this year, he'll learn to use ordinal numbers to identify the date on a calendar.

Workbook: Continue Patterns and Review

Have your child complete workbook pages 1.4A and 1.4B. Your child does not need to write anything on the pattern block outlines at the bottom of page 1.4A.

Lesson 1.5
Enrichment and Review (Optional)

	Purpose	Materials
Warm-up	• Review counting • Review your child's favorite or most challenging activities from Week 1	• Varies, depending on the activities you choose
Picture Book	• Appreciate the many ways numbers are used in daily life	• *Missing Math: A Number Mystery,* by Loreen Leedy
Enrichment Activity	• Make a poster showing important real-life numbers	• Construction paper or poster board

Warm-up: Counting and Review

- Have your child count to 20.

- If you have time, repeat one or two of the activities from this week's lessons. Choose activities your child especially enjoyed or found challenging.

Math Picture Book: *Missing Math: A Number Mystery*

Read *Missing Math: A Number Mystery,* by Loreen Leedy. After you read the book, talk about what other problems you might have if there were no numbers.

Enrichment Activity: My Numbers Poster

Help your child make a poster that shows numbers that are important to her, such as her address, phone number, birthday, age, and the number of people in her family. Encourage her to label the numbers with words or pictures and help as needed.

The purpose of these lessons is to help your child enjoy math, develop a positive attitude toward math, and appreciate how math is used in everyday life. Feel free to adapt the enrichment activity directions to fit your family. Simplify them if you're short on time or use different materials if you don't have the exact items listed. On the other hand, if your child is particularly excited about a project, make the project more elaborate and spend more time on it.

Note there are no workbook pages for Enrichment and Review lessons.

Week 1 Answer Key

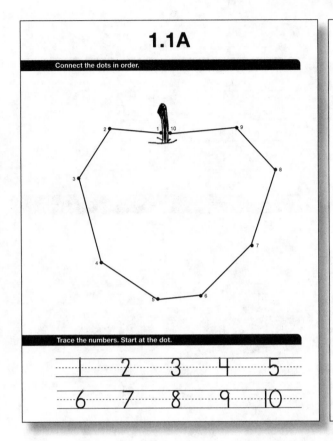

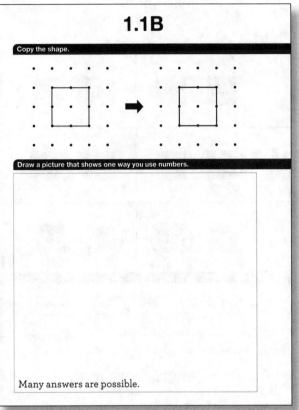

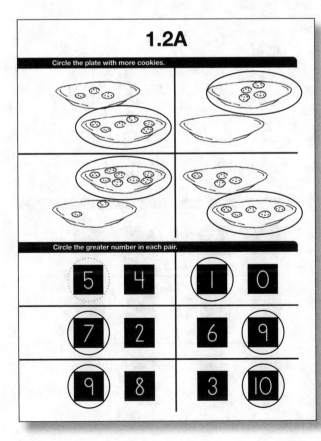

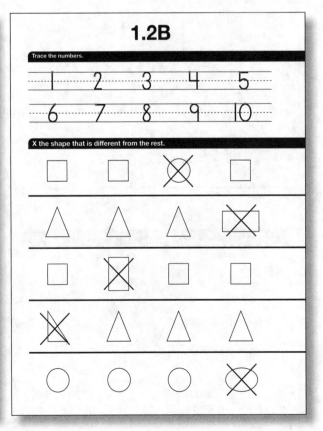

Week 1 Answer Key

1.3A

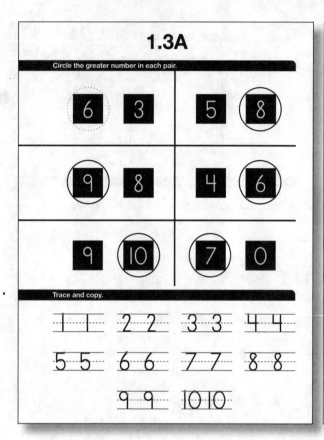

1.3B

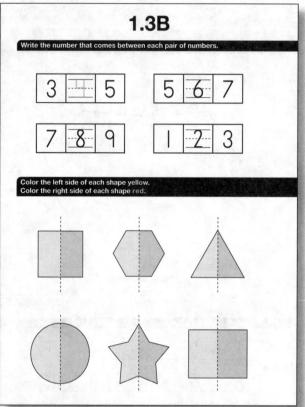

1.4A

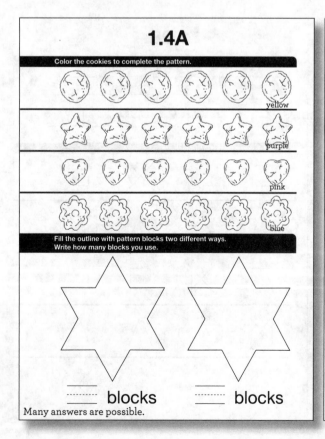

1.4B

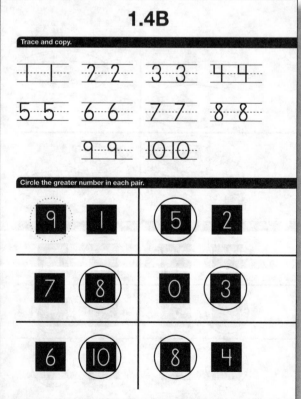

Week 2
Combinations of "5 and Some More"

Overview

Your child will represent the numbers to 10 with counters on the ten-frame, tallies, coins, and paper bills. She will especially focus on learning to recognize the numbers from 6 to 10 as combinations of "5 and some more."

Lesson 2.1   "5 and Some More" on the Ten-Frame
Lesson 2.2   "5 and Some More" with Tallies
Lesson 2.3   "5 and Some More" with Coins
Lesson 2.4   "5 and Some More" with Paper Money
Lesson 2.5   Enrichment and Review (Optional)

Teaching Math with Confidence:
Recognizing Numbers 6-10 as Combinations of "5 and Some More"

In *Kindergarten Math with Confidence*, your child learned how to recognize the numbers from 6 to 10 as combinations of "5 and some more." (For example, 7 equals 5 and 2, or 9 equals 5 and 4.) Five is an important anchor in our number system (because it is half of 10, the base for our place-value system) and so learning these combinations helps prepare your child for addition and subtraction.

This week, you'll use the ten-frame, tallies, coins, and paper money to review these combinations. As you teach the lessons, always encourage your child to look for the combinations of "5 and some more" rather than counting items one by one.

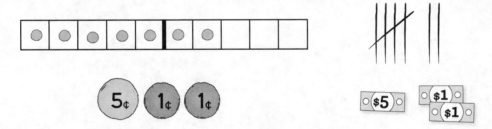

If you did not use *Kindergarten Math with Confidence*, your child may need some extra practice to master these combinations. For now, follow the lessons as written. When you reach the end of the unit, the Unit 1 Checkpoint (page 60) will give you guidance on whether your child needs more practice before you move on to Unit 2.

Extra Materials Needed for Week 2

- Real five-dollar bill and one-dollar bill
- 5 small toys
- For optional Enrichment and Review Lesson:
    × *Two Ways to Count to 10: A Liberian Folktale,* retold by Ruby Dee and illustrated by Susan Meddaugh
    × Chalk, tape, or 10 sheets of paper (for making a hopscotch course)
    × Small beanbag, stone, stick, or other hopscotch marker

Materials Note for Families Living Outside the U.S.

This book frequently uses money to practice counting, place value, and mental math. If you live outside the U.S., either use your country's coins or the generic coins on Blackline Master 11 in place of the American coins. For paper bills, use play money (from a board game or children's cash register toy) or the generic bills on Blackline Master 12.

As you teach lessons with money, simply change the language in the lessons to match whatever currency you use. You won't need to modify the worksheets, since they contain simplified coins and paper money rather than photo-realistic American coins or bills.

Lesson 2.1
"5 and Some More" on the Ten-Frame

	Purpose	Materials
Warm-up	• Estimate and count up to 20 objects • Introduce memory work • Review identifying the numbers before and after a given number	• Counters • Number Cards
Activities	• Learn to think of the numbers from 6 to 10 as combinations of "5 and some more" • Identify quantities on the ten-frame by sight	• Double ten-frames (Blackline Master 1) • Counters • Coin
Workbook	• Recognize quantities on the ten-frame by sight	• Workbook pages 2.1A and 2.1B

If your child is already familiar with ten-frames from *Kindergarten Math with Confidence*, make this a quick review lesson.

Warm-up: Counting, Memory Work, and Review

- Place about 12-15 counters on the table. **About how many counters do you think there are?** *Answers will vary.* Have your child count to find the actual number of counters, either by 1s or 2s.

- Show your child the Memory Work list on page 499. **You'll memorize these important facts this year. You'll memorize a new fact every two weeks. You'll also review the facts you've already learned.**

  This week, you'll practice left and right. Raise your left hand. Raise your right hand.

  Many children have trouble consistently identifying left and right until they are 7 or 8, so don't worry if your child needs a lot of practice.

- Have your child place the Number Cards in order from 0 to 10. Turn all the cards face-down. Flip over a card in the middle of the line. Have your child identify the numbers that come before and after the number on the card. For example, if you flip over a 7: **What number comes after 7?** *8.* **What number comes before 7?** *6.*

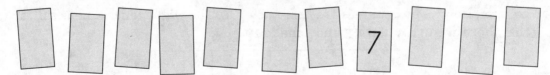

After your child answers, have her flip over the cards before and after your card to check her answers. Then, flip all the cards face-down again.

Repeat with several different cards in the line.

Activity: Introduce Combinations of "5 and Some More"

Last week, you practiced the numbers to 10. This week, you'll learn to think of the numbers from 6 to 10 as combinations of "5 and some more." Thinking of the numbers this way will help you later this year when you learn to add and subtract.

See the Week 2 **Teaching Math with Confidence** for more information on why these combinations are so important.

Show your child the ten-frames on Blackline Master 1. **Can you guess why these grids are called ten-frames?** *Sample answer: Each grid has 10 boxes.*

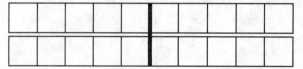

Cover the bottom ten-frame with a piece of paper so only the top one is showing. Place 5 counters on the top ten-frame.

Always fill the ten-frame from left to right, without skipping any boxes.

How many counters are there? *5.* **The dark line splits the ten-frame into two groups of 5. Since the counters fill every box up to the dark line, there must be 5.**

Add 1 counter. **How many counters are there now?** *6.* If your child begins to count one-by-one, point out there is 1 more than 5, so there must be 6. **5 and 1 make 6.**

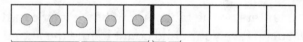

Add 1 counter. **How many counters are there now?** *7.* **5 and 2 make 7.**

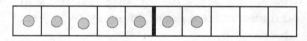

Add 1 counter. **How many counters are there now?** *8.* **5 and 3 make 8.**

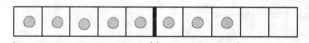

Add 1 counter. **How many counters are there now?** *9.* **5 and 4 make 9.**

Add 1 counter. **How many counters are there now?** *10.* **The whole ten-frame is full, so we know that there are 10 counters. 5 and 5 make 10.**

Using the ten-frames on Blackline Master 1 helps your child visualize numbers and develop deep number sense. These foundational skills prepare her to learn to add and subtract efficiently and accurately, without counting on her fingers.

If you've used other math programs, you may have seen ten-frames organized into 2 rows of 5 instead.

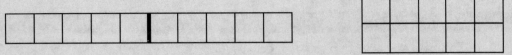

The 1×10 ten-frame used in this program.   The 2×5 ten-frame used in some other programs.

There's nothing wrong with 2×5 ten-frames, and both types help children develop deep number sense. This program uses a 1×10 ten-frame for several reasons:

1. Children find the end of the row to be a very powerful mental end point. This prepares them to think of a group of 10 as 1 unit and understand place value.
2. 1×10 ten-frames can be stacked, so that children immediately see how many boxes are full. For example, in Unit 5 you will use stacked ten-frames to teach your child place value for the numbers from 11 to 20.
3. 1×10 ten-frames prepare children to use arrays to represent multiplication in second and third grade.

Activity: Play Race to 10

Play Race to 10. As you play, encourage your child to think of the combinations of "5 and some more" as she names the number of counters on her ten-frame.

Race to 10

Materials: Double ten-frames (Blackline Master 1), coin, counters

Object of the Game: Be the first player to reach 10.

Each player chooses one ten-frame to fill.

On your turn, flip the coin. If it is heads, add one counter to your ten-frame. If it is tails, add 2 counters. After you add the counters, say the total number of counters on your ten-frame.

Take turns until one person has filled his entire ten-frame.

Workbook: Identify Quantities on the Ten-Frame and Review

Have your child complete workbook pages 2.1A and 2.1B. Encourage her to look for combinations of "5 and some more" as she matches the ten-frames and numbers (rather than counting one by one).

Lesson 2.2
"5 and Some More" with Tallies

	Purpose	Materials
Warm-up	• Estimate and count up to 20 objects by 2s • Practice memory work • Review combinations of "5 and some more" on the ten-frame	• Counters • Double ten-frames (Blackline Master 1)
Activities	• Recognize up to 10 tallies • Draw tallies	• Coin • Number Cards • Index cards
Workbook	• Recognize up to 10 tallies	• Workbook pages 2.2A and 2.2B

Warm-up: Counting, Memory Work, and Review

- Place about 10-12 counters on the table. **About how many counters do you think there are?** *Answers will vary.* Have your child count by 2s to find the actual number of counters.

- **Hop on your left leg. Hop on your right leg.**

- Arrange counters on the ten-frame as shown. For each arrangement, have your child identify the combination of "5 and some more" and the total number of counters.

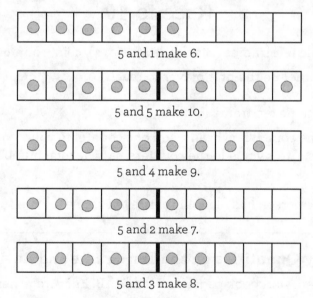

5 and 1 make 6.

5 and 5 make 10.

5 and 4 make 9.

5 and 2 make 7.

5 and 3 make 8.

Activity: Use Tallies to Record Heads and Tails

In the last lesson, you learned the combinations of "5 and some more" on the ten-frame. Today, you'll learn how to represent numbers up to 10 with tallies. You'll learn to recognize tallies as combinations of "5 and some more," too.

Because tallies are arranged in groups of 5, they provide more practice with the combinations of "5 and some more."

Have you ever seen someone use tallies or used them yourself? Discuss your child's experience with tallies.

Tallies help us keep count. We'll use tallies today to keep track of coin flips. You'll flip a coin, and then I'll make a tally to count whether the coin shows heads or tails. We'll keep going until there are 10 heads or 10 tails. I wonder whether heads or tails will win!

Make a simple chart as shown.

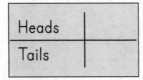

Have your child flip a coin. Mark a tally in the chart to match the flip. For example, if he flips heads, make a tally in the Heads row.

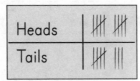

Continue until one row has 10 tallies. Draw every fifth tally horizontally across the previous 4 tallies, as shown.

Sample results

How many heads did you flip? How many tails did you flip? Did heads or tails win? *Answers will vary.*

Activity: Make Tally Cards

Have your child put 1 set of Number Cards in order from 0 to 10. For 0 through 5, have your child draw the corresponding number of tallies on blank index cards. (For 0, leave the card blank.)

Show your child how to make Tally Card 6. **5 and 1 is 6. First, I draw 5 tallies.** Draw a group of 5 tallies, with the fifth tally drawn horizontally across the previous 4 tallies. **Then, I draw 1 more, for a total of 6.**

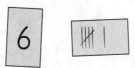

Have your child make Tally Cards for numbers 7 through 10. For number 10, show your child how to draw the final tally horizontally across the previous 4 tallies.

 Save these Tally Cards for future lessons.

Workbook: Identify Tallies and Review

Have your child complete workbook pages 2.2A and 2.2B. Before he starts, show him Blackline Master 2, Number Examples. **You can look at this if you have trouble remembering how to write any of the numbers.**

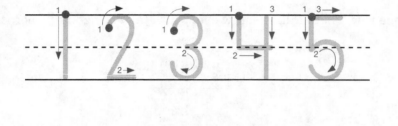

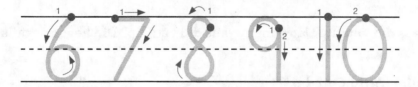

First-graders often reverse numbers, so Blackline Master 2 provides a visual model for your child to use as needed. Post it on a wall, tape it onto the table where your child usually works, or tuck it into the workbook so your child can refer to it throughout the year.

Lesson 2.3
"5 and Some More" with Coins

	Purpose	Materials
Warm-up	• Count out a given number of counters by 2s • Practice memory work • Review combinations of "5 and some more" with tallies	• Counters • Tally Cards
Activities	• Find the value of coin combinations • Represent combinations of "5 and some more" in many ways	• Coins • Number Cards • Tally Cards
Workbook	• Find the value of coin combinations	• Workbook pages 2.3A and 2.3B

If you live outside the U.S., see page 28 to learn how to modify lessons to match your local currency.

Warm-up: Counting, Memory Work, and Review

- Have your child count out 18 counters by 2s.

- **Wink your right eye. Wink your left eye.**

- Shuffle Tally Cards 6-10. Show your child one card at a time. Have her identify the combination of "5 and some more" and the total number of tallies on each card.

5 and 3 make 8.

> Some children find review activities confidence-building and affirming. Others feel insulted when asked to revisit skills they've already learned. If you have a child who hates review, focus your warm-up time on the topics your child most needs to practice and skip reviewing material that she knows well. Or, save these warm-up exercises for the end of the lesson so that her aversion to them doesn't ruin the entire session.

Activity: Introduce Pennies and Nickels

In the last lesson, you learned to draw tallies. Today, you'll learn about coins, and you'll use coins to make combinations of "5 and some more."

Have you ever used coins to buy something? Discuss your child's experiences with coins.

Show your child a penny. **This coin is called a penny. It's worth one cent.**

Show your child 3 pennies. **If 1 penny is worth 1 cent, how many cents are 3 pennies worth?** *3 cents.* **2 pennies?** *2 cents.* **4 pennies?** *4 cents.* **5 pennies?** *5 cents.*

Imagine if pennies were our only kind of money. We would need a lot of pennies just to buy a few things at the grocery store! It would take a long time to count out all those pennies every time we bought something!

That's why we use coins and paper bills worth more than just one cent. Instead of 5 pennies, we can use 1 nickel. 1 nickel is also worth 5 cents. Show your child 1 nickel.

Show your child 6 pennies. Have your child group 5 of the pennies. **1 nickel is worth 5¢. So, we can trade these 5 pennies for 1 nickel.** Have your child help you trade the 5 pennies for 1 nickel.

How much are a nickel and a penny worth together? *6¢.*

> If your child has trouble answering, remind her the nickel is worth 5¢. So, she can count on from 5 to find the answer: *5, 6.*

Show your child the following coin combinations and have her tell the value of each combination.

- 1 nickel and 2 pennies (7¢)
- 1 nickel and 3 pennies (8¢)
- 1 nickel and 4 pennies (9¢)
- 2 nickels (10¢)

Activity: "5 and Some More" Relay

Set up 3 stations around the room. Place the following supplies at each station.

- Station 1: Number Cards 5-10.
- Station 2: Tally Cards 5-10
- Station 3: Coins. Include at least 7 nickels and 10 pennies.

> This activity helps your child understand the connection between the different ways to show the combinations of "5 and some more."

Start at Station 1 with your child. Give your child one of the Number Cards. Have her run to Station 2 to pick up the corresponding Tally Card, then to Station 3 to pick up the corresponding coin combination.

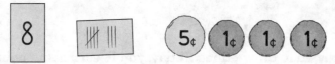

Then, she should run back to Station 1 and begin again with a new Number Card. Continue until she uses all the cards.

Workbook: Recognize Money Combinations and Review

Have your child complete workbook pages 2.3A and 2.3B. On 2.3A, point out the cents sign (¢) and explain what it means.

> Children often have trouble remembering coin names and values. To prevent frustration, the workbook uses simplified coins rather than photo-realistic images. Your child will memorize the names and values of coins as part of her Memory Work.

Lesson 2.4
"5 and Some More" with Paper Money

	Purpose	Materials
Warm-up	• Count to 20 • Practice memory work • Review identifying quantities on the ten-frame by sight	• 100 Chart (Blackline Master 3) • Counters • Double ten-frames (Blackline Master 1) • Coin
Activities	• Introduce paper money • Find the value of paper money combinations	• Real five-dollar bill and one-dollar bill • Paper play money (either from a board game or Blackline Master 12) • 5 small toys • Index cards
Workbook	• Find the value of paper money combinations	• Workbook pages 2.4A and 2.4B

If you live outside the U.S., see page 28 to learn how to incorporate your country's paper bills throughout the year.

Warm-up: Counting, Memory Work, and Review

- Have your child count to 20, pointing to each number on the 100 Chart as he says it.
- **Raise your left hand. Raise your right hand.**
- Play Race to 10. See Lesson 2.1 (page 31) for directions.

Activity: Introduce Paper Money

In the last lesson, you learned about pennies and nickels. Today, you'll learn about paper money.

Have you ever used paper bills to buy something? Discuss your child's experiences with paper bills.

Show your child a one-dollar bill. **This is a one-dollar bill. One dollar equals one hundred cents.**

Later this year, your child will memorize that a dollar equals 100 cents. He does not need to memorize it now.

Show your child a five-dollar bill. **This is a five-dollar bill. It's worth the same as 5 one-dollar bills.**

Show your child the play money in your Math Kit. **We'll use play money in math this year.** Show your child the following paper money combinations and have him tell the value of each combination.

- 4 one-dollar bills ($4)
- 2 one-dollar bills ($2)
- 1 five-dollar bill and 1 one-dollar bill ($6)
- 1 five-dollar bill and 4 one-dollar bills ($9)
- 1 five-dollar bill and 3 one-dollar bills ($8)
- 1 five-dollar bill and 2 one-dollar bills ($7)
- 2 five-dollar bills ($10)

Children learn math best and enjoy it most when the material is at their "Goldilocks" challenge level: not too hard, not too easy, but just right. You'll frequently find lists of practice problems (like the one above) in this program. The problems are generally in order from easiest to most difficult. Feel free to adjust the difficulty level based on how well your child has grasped the material. If he's struggling, focus on the easier problems, or make up some more similarly easy problems. If your child readily learns the material, skip to the harder problems, or make up some related problems that are even harder. You'll both enjoy math time more when your child is working at the appropriate challenge level.

Activity: Pretend Store with Paper Money

We are going to play store. First, let's make the price tags. Write $6 on an index card. Point to the dollar sign. **This is called the dollar sign. It looks like an S with a line through it.**

Have your child write $7, $8, $9, and $10 on index cards. Lay 5 small toys in a row and place one of the index cards next to each toy. Give your child play five-dollar bills and one-dollar bills to "buy" things with.

What would you like to buy? *Answers will vary.* Have him tell you the price and pay for the item with a five-dollar bill and the correct number of one-dollar bills. (He should use 2 five-dollar bills for the $10 item.)

Continue until your child has bought all of the items.

Workbook: Recognize Money Combinations and Review

Have your child complete workbook pages 2.4A and 2.4B.

Lesson 2.5
Enrichment and Review (Optional)

	Purpose	Materials
Warm-up	• Review counting • Review memory work • Review your child's favorite or most challenging activities from Week 2	• Varies, depending on the activities you choose
Picture Book	• Understand counting by 2s in a real-life context	• *Two Ways to Count to 10: A Liberian Folktale*, retold by Ruby Dee and illustrated by Susan Meddaugh
Enrichment Activity	• Review numbers 1-10 through active play	• Chalk, tape, or 10 sheets of paper for making a hopscotch course • Small beanbag, stone, or other hopscotch marker

Warm-up: Counting, Memory Work, and Review

- Have your child count to 20 by 1s and 2s.

- Quiz your child on the memory work through Week 2. See page 499 for the full list.

- If you have time, repeat one or two of the activities from this week's lessons. Choose activities your child especially enjoyed or found challenging.

Math Picture Book: *Two Ways to Count to 10*

Read *Two Ways to Count to 10: A Liberian Folktale*, retold by Ruby Dee and illustrated by Susan Meddaugh.

Enrichment Activity: Play Hopscotch

If you're able to play outside, draw a hopscotch board (shown below) with chalk on pavement. If you're playing inside, use tape to create the hopscotch board on a flat surface. Or, write each number on a piece of paper and tape the paper to the floor.

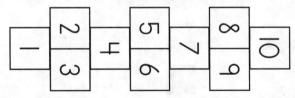

Choose from the following hopscotch activities:

- Challenge your child to hop from 1 to 10 in order, without falling over or touching a line. When he reaches 10, he should turn around and hop back to 1.
- Ask your child to hop by 2s from 2 to 10.
- Teach your child how to play traditional hopscotch: Throw a beanbag (or stone, or another marker) onto square 1. Don't hop on the square with the beanbag, then hop through every square up to 10. When you reach 10, turn around and hop back through the course. When you reach the beanbag, balance on one foot to pick it up and finish the course. Then, toss the beanbag onto square 2 and repeat. Continue tossing the beanbag onto the squares in order. See how high a number you can reach before you lose your balance or touch a line.

Week 2 Answer Key

2.1A

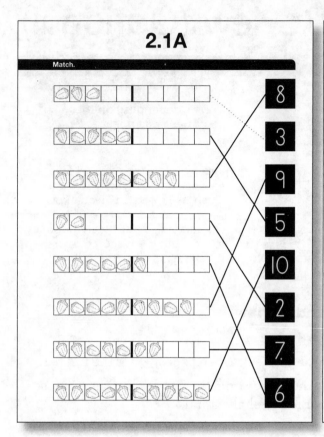

2.1B

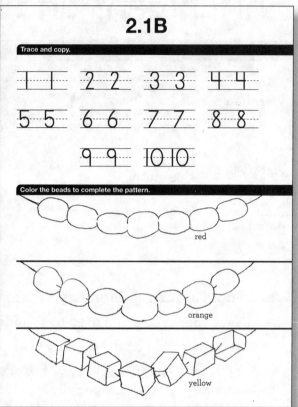

2.2A

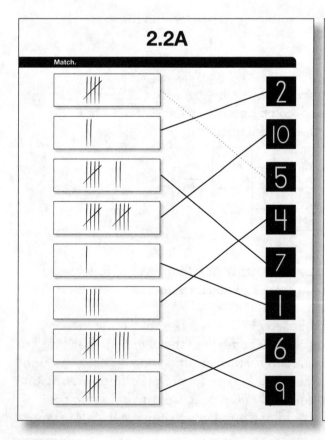

2.2B

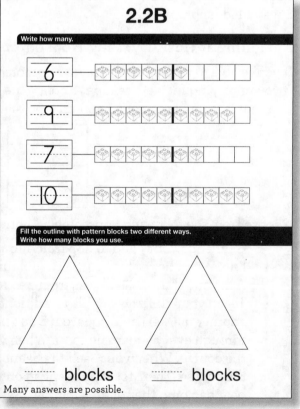

Week 2 Answer Key

2.3A

Match.

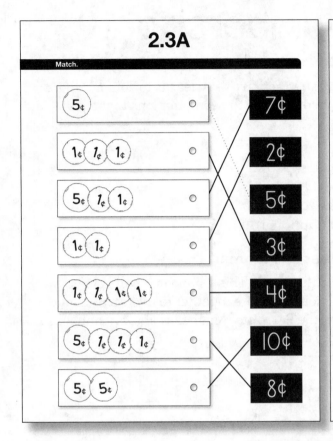

2.3B

Trace and copy.

X the shape that is different from the rest.

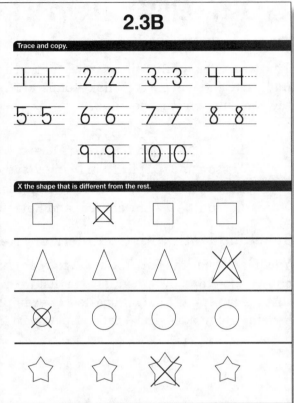

2.4A

Complete.

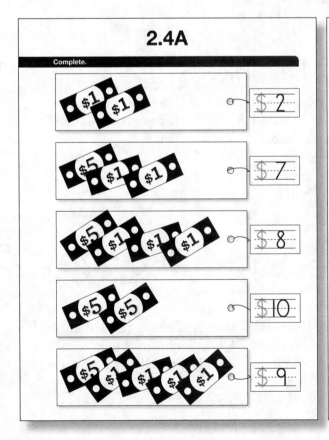

2.4B

Write how many.

Copy the shape.

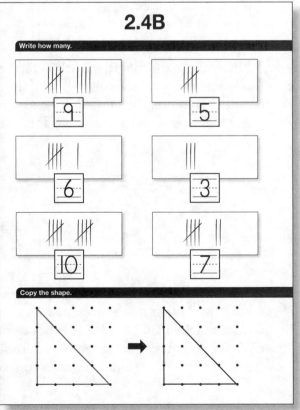

Week 3
Split and Join Numbers to 10

Overview

This week, your child will preview addition and subtraction as she learns to split numbers into parts and join parts to make totals. She'll also practice the combinations that equal 5 and the combinations that equal 10.

Lesson 3.1   Split 5 into Parts
Lesson 3.2   Join Parts to Make a Total
Lesson 3.3 · Split 10 in Many Ways
Lesson 3.4   Combinations That Make 10
Lesson 3.5   Enrichment and Review (Optional)

Teaching Math with Confidence: The Part-Total Mat

You'll introduce the Part-Total Mat to your child this week. This simple mat will help your child understand the essential idea that we can join numbers together to make a total and that we can split a total into parts. For example, the Part-Total Mat below shows 2 and 3 can be joined to make 5, and 5 can be split apart into 2 and 3.

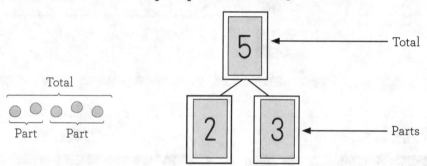

Your child will use the mat this week to record her results as she splits and joins quantities. She'll develop a deeper understanding of the relationships between these parts and totals, so that she is well-prepared for addition and subtraction. Later in the program, she'll use the Part-Total Mat to help write and solve addition and subtraction equations.

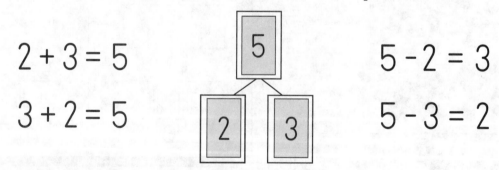

$$2 + 3 = 5$$
$$3 + 2 = 5$$

$$5 - 2 = 3$$
$$5 - 3 = 2$$

If you have used other math programs, you may have seen other versions of these diagrams. Sometimes they're made from circles or oriented horizontally, and sometimes they're called "Part-Whole" diagrams rather than "Part-Total." No matter what they're called or how they look, they all express the same fundamental concept.

Extra Materials Needed for Week 3

- Small toy
- Plastic plate, optional
- For optional Enrichment and Review Lesson:
    - × *Anno's Counting Book,* by Mitsumasa Anno

Lesson 3.1
Split 5 into Parts

	Purpose	Materials
Warm-up	• Count objects by 2s with a leftover • Practice memory work • Review finding combinations of one-dollar and five-dollar bills	• Counters • Play money
Activities	• Use the Part-Total Mat to identify parts and totals • Find combinations that make 5	• Counters • Part-Total Mat (Blackline Master 4) • Number Cards • Small toy • Play money
Workbook	• Find combinations that make 5	• Workbook pages 3.1A and 3.1B

Warm-up: Counting, Memory Work, and Review

- Secretly count out 15 counters and place them on the table. **About how many counters do you think there are?** *Answers will vary.* Help your child count by 2s to find the actual number of counters. Demonstrate how to add on the final counter: **14 and 1 more is 15.**

   If your child finds the counting activities repetitive, vary the objects you ask her to count. Food, toys, or seasonal items all make counting more fun and interesting.

- **Raise your right hand. Raise your left hand.**

- Show your child the following play money combinations. Have her tell the value of each.
   - × 3 one-dollar bills *($3)*
   - × 1 five-dollar bill *($5)*
   - × 1 five-dollar bill and 2 one-dollar bills *($7)*
   - × 1 five-dollar bill and 3 one-dollar bills *($8)*
   - × 2 five-dollar bills *($10)*

Activity: Introduce the Part-Total Mat

This week you'll learn about splitting and joining numbers. Today, you'll split a group of 5 into parts and learn how to record the parts and total on a special mat.

Place 5 counters on the table. **Let's pretend the counters are cookies for us to split.** Split the counters as shown. **If I get 2 cookies, how many do you get?** *3.*

In math this year we'll use a mat called the Part-Total Mat to show how we split and join groups. Show your child the Part-Total Mat (Blackline Master 4). **The total goes in the box at the top. The parts go in the boxes at the bottom.**

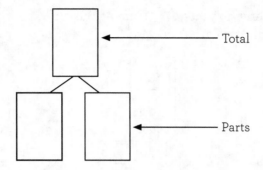

Total

Parts

We have a total of 5 cookies. Place Number Card 5 on the mat as shown. **I split the cookies into two parts. I got 2 cookies, and you got 3.** Place Number Cards 2 and 3 on the mat.

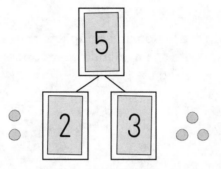

If you find the Number Cards cumbersome, place the Part-Total Mat in a plastic page protector and write the numbers with dry-erase marker instead.

See the Week 3 **Teaching Math with Confidence** for more information about the purpose of the Part-Total Mat and how to use it.

Let's split the cookies a different way. If I get 4 cookies, how many do you get? *1.* Have your child split the counters to match and show the parts and total with Number Cards on the Part-Total Mat.

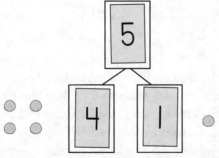

Your child can arrange the parts on the Part-Total Mat in any order. In the above example, your child can switch the 1 and 4.

If I get 0 cookies, how many do you get? *5.* Have your child split the counters to match and show the parts and total on the Part-Total Mat.

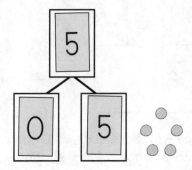

Activity: How Much More Money Do I Need?

Have your child choose a toy to use in the lesson and bring it to the table. **Let's pretend you want to buy this toy, and it costs $5.** Write $5 on an index card and place it next to the toy. **But, you only have 4 dollars.** Give your child a 4 $1-bills.

How many more dollars do you need to buy the toy? *$1.* If she's not sure, place Number Cards on the Part-Total Mat to help: **You need a total of $5, so 5 goes in box at the top. You already have $4, so 4 is one of the parts. 4 and what make 5?** *1.*

Repeat this process with the following problems. Act out each problem with play money and use the Part-Total Mat as needed to find the answers.

- **If you have $2, how many more dollars do you need to buy the toy?** *$3.*
- **If you have $1, how many more dollars do you need to buy the toy?** *$4.*
- **If you have $0, how many more dollars do you need to buy the toy?** *$5.*
- **If you have $3, how many more dollars do you need to buy the toy?** *$2.*
- **If you have $5, how many more dollars do you need to buy the toy?** *$0.*

Workbook: Combinations That Make 5 and Review

Have your child complete workbook pages 3.1A and 3.1B.

Lesson 3.2
Join Parts to Make a Total

	Purpose	Materials
Warm-up	• Count objects by 2s with a leftover • Practice memory work • Review patterns and ordinal numbers	• Counters • Pattern blocks
Activities	• Join parts to make a total • Represent parts and totals on the Part-Total Mat • Visualize quantities and totals	• Pattern blocks • Plastic plate, or piece of paper • Part-Total Mat (Blackline Master 4) • Number Cards
Workbook	• Find totals with small numbers	• Workbook pages 3.2A and 3.2B

Warm-up: Counting, Memory Work, and Review

- Have your child count out 17 counters. Ask him to count by 2s to 16, then add 1 more counter for a total of 17.

- **Hop on your right leg. Hop on your left leg.**

- Begin a pattern as shown:

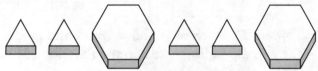

  Have your child continue the pattern. Then, briefly review ordinal numbers: **Which block did I place first? Second? Fifth? Fourth? Third?**

Activity: Join Parts to Make a Total

In the last lesson, you split a group of 5 into parts and learned how to record the parts and total on the Part-Total Mat. Today, we'll join parts to make a total.

We're going to play restaurant today. Let's pretend the pattern blocks are crackers. I'll be the customer, and you can be the server. Could you please serve me 2 triangle crackers and 3 square crackers? *Child places 2 triangles and 3 squares on a plastic plate (or blank piece of paper) and pretends to serve it to you.*

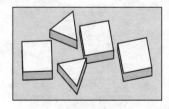

Let's put cards on the Part-Total Mat to match the crackers. There are 2 triangle crackers, so I'll put a 2 on the mat to stand for them. Place Number Card 2 on the mat as shown below. **There are 3 square crackers, so I'll put a 3 on the mat to stand for them.** Place Number Card 3 on the mat.

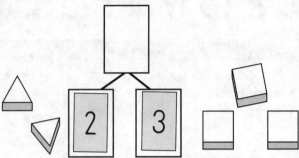

Once you join the squares and triangles, how many crackers are there in total? 5. **So, let's put a 5 in the total box.** Place Number Card 5 on the mat.

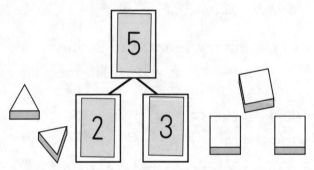

Repeat with the following orders. For each order, have your child model the problem with pattern blocks and place the corresponding cards on the Part-Total Mat.

I'd like 1 triangle cracker and 4 square crackers, please.

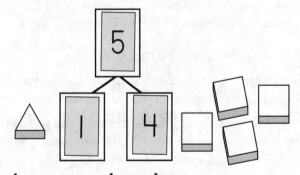

I'd like 2 triangle crackers and 2 square crackers, please.

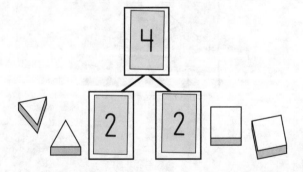

I'd like 3 triangle crackers and 0 square crackers, please.

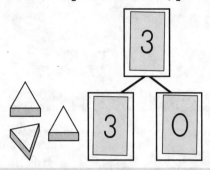

> The numbers in this lesson are small so your child focuses on making sense of the Part-Total Mat. If your child wants more of a challenge, use 6-10 total crackers instead.

Activity: Find Totals of Boys and Girls

We can also use the Part-Total Mat for real-life parts and totals. Let's use it to show the children in our family. How many boys are in our family? How many girls? *Answers will vary.*

Have your child place Number Cards on the Part-Total Mat to match the number of boys and girls in your family. For example, if you have 2 boys and 1 girl, have him place a 2 and a 1 on the mat.

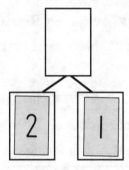

What's the total number of children in our family? *Answers will vary.* Have your child place the Number Card that matches the total on the Part-Total Mat. For example, if you have 2 boys and 1 girl, have your child place Number Card 3 at the top of the mat.

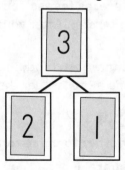

Repeat this activity with several other families you know. Try to include a larger family, as well as a family with either no boys or no girls (so your child practices finding the total when one part is 0).

> If your child has trouble finding the totals, use counters to stand for each child. Then, have your child count all the counters to find the total.

Workbook: Find Totals and Review

Have your child complete workbook pages 3.2A and 3.2B.

Lesson 3.3
Split 10 in Many Ways

	Purpose	Materials
Warm-up	• Count to 20 by 2s • Practice memory work • Review combinations of "5 and some more" on the ten-frame	• Counters • 100 Chart (Blackline Master 3) • Double ten-frames (Blackline Master 1) • Paper
Activities	• Find combinations that make 10 • Represent parts and totals on the Part-Total Mat	• Counters • Double ten-frames (Blackline Master 1) • Part-Total Mat (Blackline Master 4) • Number Cards
Workbook	• Find combinations that make 10	• Workbook pages 3.3A and 3.3B

Warm-up: Counting, Memory Work, and Review

- Have your child count by 2s to 20. Have her cover each number on the 100 Chart with a counter as she says it.

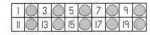

- **Wink your right eye. Wink your left eye.**

- Secretly place 9 counters on the ten-frame and cover the counters with a piece of paper.

  I'm going to show you some counters for just a second. When I lift the paper, tell me how many counters there are, as fast as you can. Lift the piece of paper for just a few seconds. **How many counters?** 9. After your child responds, lift the paper and allow her to check her answer.

  Repeat with 5, 6, 7, 8, and 10 counters, in random order. Encourage her to think about the combinations of "5 and some more" rather than counting.

Activity: How Many Ways to Split 10?

In the last lesson, we joined parts together to make totals. Today, we'll split a group of 10.

Let's pretend we have 10 candies to share. Place 10 counters on the ten-frame.

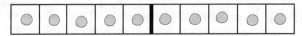

How many different ways do you think there are for us to split these 10 candies? *Answers will vary.* **Let's see how many different ways we can find. I'll make a chart to keep track.**

Draw a simple chart like the following on a piece of paper.

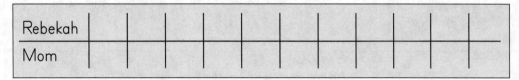

What's one way we could split the counters? Have your child place a pencil on the ten-frame to split the counters between the two of you, either evenly or unevenly. Then have your child place Number Cards on the Part-Total Mat to match. Record how many counters each of you get in the chart.

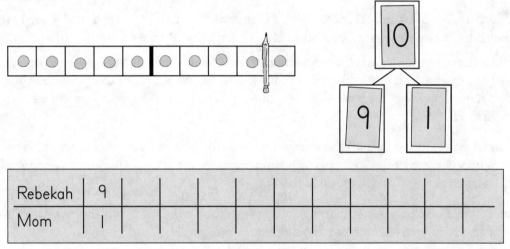

Rebekah	9									
Mom	1									

Sample answer.

Have your child find more ways to split the counters until she can't think of any more.

After she finishes, show her the chart below and discuss if there are any ways you missed.

Rebekah	9	8	7	6	5	4	3	2	1	0	10
Mom	1	2	3	4	5	6	7	8	9	10	0

The goal of this activity is for your child to understand that numbers can be split in many ways, not to teach her how to find all possible combinations. It's fine if she only finds a few ways to split the counters. Later in elementary school, she will learn how to make organized lists to keep track of all possible combinations.

Activity: Play Make 10 Go Fish

Play one round of Make 10 Go Fish.

This game is just like the classic Go Fish game, but players find pairs of cards that equal 10 rather than cards with the same number.

Make 10 Go Fish

Materials: 2 sets of Number Cards (0–10)

Object of the Game: Collect the most pairs of cards that make 10.

Shuffle two sets of Number Cards (0–10). Deal out 5 cards to yourself and 5 cards to your child. Spread the rest of the cards face down on the table to be the "fishpond."

On your turn, ask for a card that would create a total of 10 with a card already in your hand. (For example, if you have a 6, ask for a 4.) Your opponent must give you the card if she has it. If she doesn't have the card, she says, "Go fish!" and you take a card from the fishpond.

Play until you have paired all the cards. Players who run out of cards before the fishpond is used up may take 2 cards from the fishpond to continue playing. Whoever has more pairs at the end of the game is the winner.

Leave 10 counters on the ten-frame as you play. Your child can split the counters into 2 parts if she is not sure which card to ask for. For example, if she has a 6:

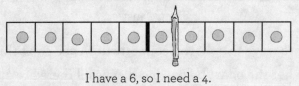

I have a 6, so I need a 4.

Games provide a fun and motivating way for your child to practice her math skills. However, they also take some time. If you don't have time for a particular game (or if your child is resistant to it), skip the game and simply practice the skill instead. For example, if you don't have time to play Make 10 Go Fish, tell your child a number from 0 to 10 and have her name the matching number that makes 10.

Workbook: Find Parts and Totals and Review

Have your child complete workbook pages 3.3A and 3.3B.

Lesson 3.4
Combinations That Make 10

	Purpose	Materials
Warm-up	• Count to 20 by 2s • Practice memory work • Review writing numbers to 10	• Counters • 100 Chart (Blackline Master 3)
Activities	• Find combinations that make 10	• Counters • Double ten-frames (Blackline Master 1) • Part-Total Mat (Blackline Master 4) • Number Cards • Playing cards
Workbook	• Find combinations that make 10	• Workbook pages 3.4A and 3.4B

Warm-up: Counting, Memory Work, and Review

- With your child looking away, place counters on the 100 Chart so that the numbers you say when you count by 2s to 20 are covered.

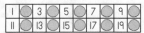

  Have your child count by 2s to 20. Have him remove each counter after he says the number underneath it.

- **Touch your left ear. Touch your right ear.**

- Say a number from 0 to 10 and have your child write the number on a piece of paper. Repeat with all of the numbers from 0 to 10, in random order.

> This informal assessment shows you how your child is doing with writing the numbers from 0 to 10. It's very common for first graders to have trouble with reversing numbers or forgetting the order of strokes, so don't worry if your child makes several mistakes.

Activity: Find Missing Parts of 10

In the last lesson, you split 10 in many ways. Today, you'll practice the combinations that make 10 some more.

Place Number Cards on the Part-Total Mat as shown. **What number is missing?** *1*.

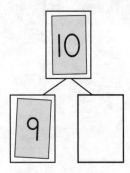

If your child isn't sure, have him place 10 counters on the ten-frame and split the counters into a group of 9 and 1. **You can split 10 into a group of 9 and a group of 1, so 1 is the missing number.**

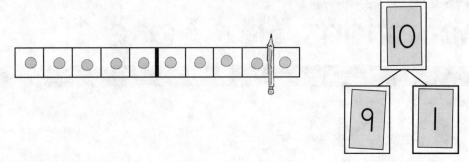

Ask your child to find the following missing numbers on the Part-Total Mat. Have him use counters on the ten-frame as needed to find the answers.

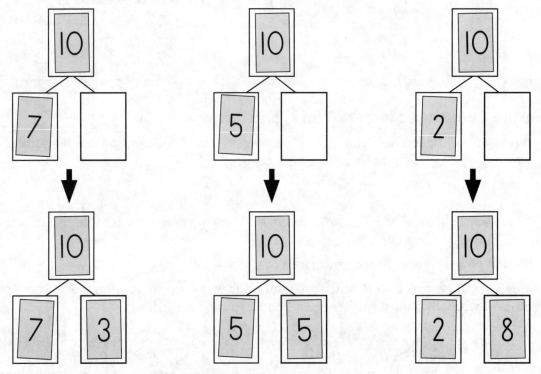

Activity: Play Make 10 Pyramid Solitaire

Have your child play one round of Make 10 Pyramid Solitaire. Allow your child to use the ten-frame and counters as needed.

If your child is still learning the pairs that make 10, Make 10 Pyramid may be too complicated. If so, play Make 10 Go Fish again instead. See Lesson 3.3 (page 52) for directions. Both games practice the same skills, so use whichever game your child enjoys more.

Make 10 Pyramid Solitaire

Materials: Deck of playing cards with face cards removed

Object of the Game: Remove as many cards as possible from the pyramid. (The best score possible is 0. Depending on how the cards are dealt, it's not always possible to remove every card.)

Shuffle the cards. Deal them out face-up in a pyramid shape. An example is shown below. Start at the top and place each new row so it slightly overlaps the previous row. Place the remaining cards in a face-down pile.

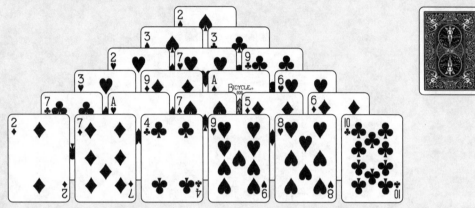

Look for pairs that make 10 in the bottom row of the pyramid. For example, in the sample game above, you could remove the 8 and 2, since they make a 10. You could also remove the 10, since it equals 10 by itself.

As more cards are uncovered, use those to make 10 as well. You can only use cards that are fully uncovered. For example, in the pyramid below, you can remove the 4 and 6; however, you cannot use the 5, 7s, or Ace in the second row from the bottom.

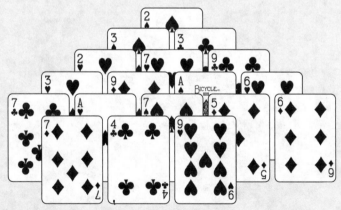

Once you have removed as many cards as possible from the pyramid, flip over the top card from the face-down pile. See if you can use it to make a 10 with a card in the pyramid. As more cards are uncovered in the pyramid, you may also find more pairs there.

Continue flipping over the top card in the pile and removing pairs that make 10 until no more are possible. (You are allowed to flip through the face-down pile as many times as you wish.) Count how many cards are left in the pyramid for the final score.

Workbook: Find Combinations That Make 10 and Review

Have your child complete workbook pages 3.4A and 3.4B. He can use the ten-frame printed at the top of 3.4A to help. If he has trouble finding any of the missing numbers, have him place his pencil on the printed ten-frame to split the counters to match the Part-Total diagram.

Many first graders have a short attention span. If your child struggles to complete the workbook pages, try breaking it into chunks throughout the day. Set a timer for 5 minutes at a time and ask your child to give his best effort for the full 5 minutes. Children are often amazed at how much they can get done in a short amount of time when they give their work their full attention.

Lesson 3.5
Enrichment and Review (Optional)

	Purpose	Materials
Warm-up	• Review counting • Review memory work • Review your child's favorite or most challenging activities from Week 3	• Varies, depending on the activities you choose
Picture Book	• Find numbers represented in many different ways	• *Anno's Counting Book,* by Mitsumasa Anno
Enrichment Activity	• Use real-life objects to represent a number in many ways	• Varies

Warm-up: Counting, Memory Work, and Review

- Have your child count to 20 by 1s and 2s.

- Quiz your child on the memory work through Week 2. See page 499 for the full list.

> New memory work is introduced every 2 weeks, so there is no new memory work on the odd-numbered weeks.

- If you have time, repeat one or two of the activities from this week's lessons. Choose activities your child especially enjoyed or found challenging.

Math Picture Book: *Anno's Counting Book*

Read *Anno's Counting Book,* by Mitsumasa Anno. As you read, discuss the many ways each number is represented on its page. For example, on the page showing the number 5, you can find 5 trees, 5 wisps of smoke, 5 flags, 5 adults, 5 children, and a clock reading 5:00 (among many others!) Point out that any of the pictures depict splitting a number into parts. For example, the 5 children are split into a group of 3 and a group of 2.

Enrichment Activity: Number Display

Have your child pick a number from 1 to 10 and create a display of real-life objects that show the number many different ways. For example, for the number 5, she might include 5 stuffed animals, 5 grains of rice, a clock set to 5:00, the number 5 circled on a calendar, a 5-dollar bill, and a die showing 5 dots.

Encourage her to use a variety of sizes in her display and point out how a given number can look quite big or quite small depending on what objects you use to model it. For example: **5 stuffed animals look a lot bigger than 5 grains of rice!**

Week 3 Answer Key

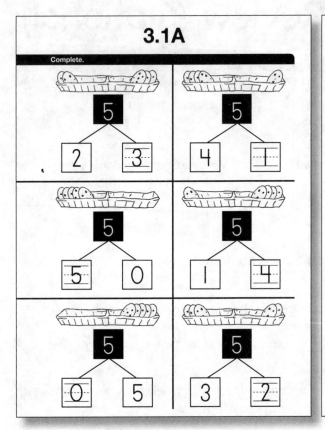

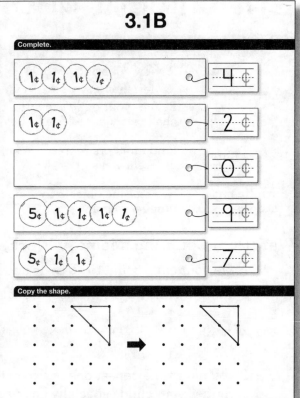

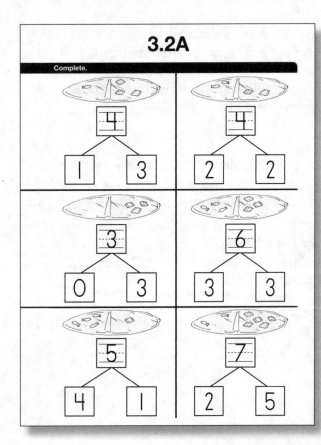

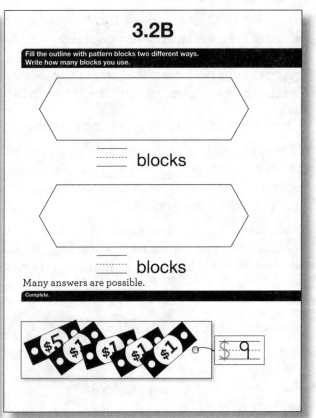

Week 3 Answer Key

3.3A

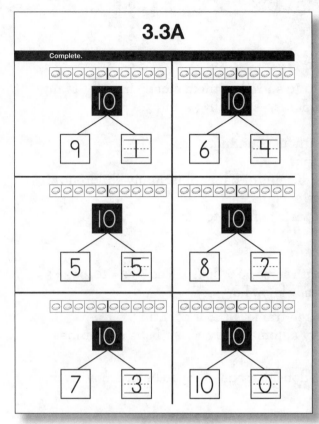

3.3B

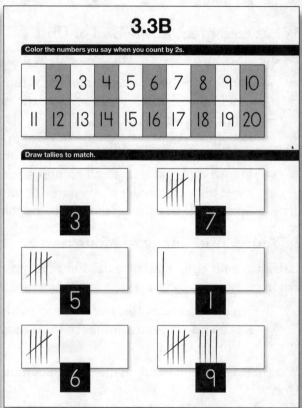

3.4A

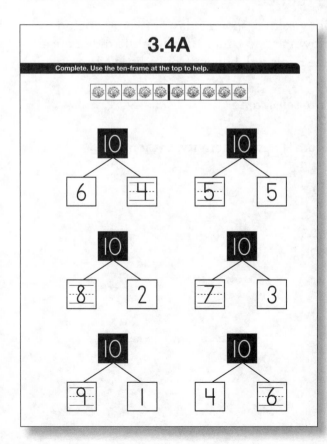

3.4B

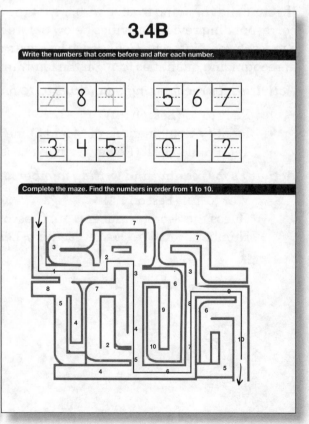

Unit 1 Checkpoint

What to Expect at the End of Unit 1

By the end of Unit 1, most children will be able to:

- Recognize the written numerals from 0 to 10 and write them mostly fluently. Many children will still reverse some of the numbers, especially 3s and 5s.
- Compare two numbers up to 10.
- Recognize quantities on the ten-frame without counting.
- Recognize up to 10 tallies without counting.
- Identify the value of small combinations of coins or paper bills. Many children will need to be reminded of the name or value of coins.
- Split small quantities into parts and join parts to find a total.

Is Your Child Ready to Move on?

In Unit 2, your child will learn the addition facts with sums up to 10 (such as 8 + 2 = 10, or 3 + 3 = 6). Before moving on to Unit 2, your child should already know how to:

- Recognize quantities from 0 to 10 on the ten-frame without counting.
- Read and write the numbers to 10 mostly automatically, even if she sometimes reverses them

Your child does not need memorize the combinations that equal 5 or 10 before moving on to Unit 2.

What to Do If Your Child Needs More Practice

If your child is having trouble with any of the above skills, spend a day or two practicing the corresponding review activities below before moving on to Unit 2. If your child did not use *Kindergarten Math with Confidence* last year, she likely will benefit from a little extra practice at recognizing quantities to 10 on the ten-frame.

Activities for recognizing quantities to 10 on the ten-frame

- Race to 10 (Lesson 2.1)
- Identify Combinations of "5 and Some More" (Review activity, Lesson 2.2)
- Ten-Frame Flash (Review activity, Lesson 3.3)

Activities for reading and writing numbers to 10

- War (0-10) (Lesson 1.2)
- Guess the Secret Number (1-10) (Lesson 1.3)
- Number Dictation (Review activity, Lesson 3.4)

Unit 2
Addition to 10

Overview

In Unit 2, your child will learn to write addition equations to match counters, pictures, and real-life situations. He'll learn several important addition properties and vocabulary words, and he'll begin to master the addition facts with sums up to 10.

Week 4   +1 and +2 Addition Facts
Week 5   +3 and +4 Addition Facts
Week 6   Sums That Equal 10

What Your Child Will Learn

In this unit your child will learn to:

- write addition equations with the + and = signs
- find answers to addition facts with sums up to 10
- identify missing addends in equations with a sum of 10 (for example, 7 + __ = 10)
- solve simple addition word problems

Recommended Math Picture Books (Optional)

These picture books are scheduled in the optional Enrichment and Review lessons at the end of each week.

- *Albert Adds Up!*, written by Eleanor May and illustrated by Deborah Melmon. Kane Press, 2014.
- *Domino Addition*, by Lynette Long. Charlesbridge, 1996.
- *Math Fables: Lessons That Count*, written by Greg Tang and illustrated by Heather Cahoon. Scholastic Press, 2004.

Week 4
+1 and +2 Addition Facts

Overview

Your child will learn to write addition equations with the + and = symbols. He'll translate simple addition situations into equations, and he'll relate these equations to the parts and totals on the Part-Total Mat. Once he understands the concept of addition, he'll begin to master the +1 and +2 addition facts.

Lesson 4.1   Addition Equations
Lesson 4.2   More Addition Equations
Lesson 4.3   Introduce +1 and +2 Facts
Lesson 4.4   Practice +1 and +2 Facts
Lesson 4.5   Enrichment and Review (Optional)

Teaching Math with Confidence: 4 Steps to Mastering the Addition Facts

In this unit, your child will learn the addition facts with sums up to 10. Many parents have bad memories of learning the math facts through anxiety-inducing timed tests or overwhelming stacks of flash cards. Don't worry—you won't find any of those here! Instead, you'll use a simple four-step process to help your child master all of the addition facts over the course of the year. All these activities are scheduled in the lessons, so you don't need to supplement or schedule time for extra practice.

1. **Target one group of facts at a time.** This book breaks the addition facts into 6 groups. The facts in each group can be solved with the same strategy. That way, your child can learn one strategy and then apply the strategy to the entire group of facts instead of memorizing every addition fact individually.

2. **Learn mental strategies for finding answers.** Your child has already learned to recognize quantities to 10 on the ten-frame. You'll build on that knowledge as you teach him simple visual strategies for finding the answers for each group of addition facts. (See the Week 5 Teaching Math with Confidence for an example).

3. **Practice one set of facts at a time.** Instead of drilling flash cards over and over, your child will practice using the visual strategies until they become automatic. Games, worksheets, and oral review will give your child ample practice with each set of addition facts.

4. **Mix up the facts and practice some more.** As your child gains more confidence with each group of addition facts, you'll find that they are mixed with other addition facts on the workbook pages. With consistent practice at applying the six strategies, your child will get faster and faster at figuring out the answers.

By the end of the year, your child will "just know" the answers and have them fully mastered. However, note that he does not need to memorize all of the addition facts with sums to 10 by the end of this unit. He'll practice them throughout the next several units, and then he'll study the rest of the addition facts in Unit 8.

Extra Materials Needed for Week 4

- Plastic plate, optional
- Small ball or beanbag
- Small toy
- For optional Enrichment and Review Lesson:
    - × *Albert Adds Up!*, written by Eleanor May and illustrated by Deborah Melmon
    - × Natural objects, such as leaves, acorns, rocks, or sticks
    - × Paper, optional
    - × Glue, optional

Lesson 4.1
Addition Equations

	Purpose	Materials
Warm-up	• Count to 30 • Practice memory work • Review using *greater than, less than,* and *equal* to compare numbers	• 100 Chart (Blackline Master 3) • Number Cards
Activities	• Understand the + sign and = sign • Write equations to match concrete objects and the Part-Total Mat	• Pattern blocks • Plastic plate or piece of paper • Part-Total Mat (Blackline Master 4) • Number Cards • Index cards
Workbook	• Complete addition equations to match pictures and the Part-Total Mat	• Workbook pages 4.1A and 4.1B

Warm-up: Counting, Memory Work, and Review

- Count in unison with your child to 30. Point to each number on the 100 Chart as you say it.

- Show your child a penny and a nickel, and have him tell the name and value of each coin.

- Play War (0-10). See Lesson 1.2 (page 17) for directions.

Activity: Introduce Addition Equations

In the last unit we reviewed the numbers to 10, and we used the Part-Total Mat to split and join numbers in many ways. Today, we begin a new unit on adding. In math, we say we add whenever we join 2 groups together.

Let's play restaurant again today and pretend the pattern blocks are crackers. I'll be the customer, and you can be the server. Could you please serve me 2 triangle crackers and 3 square crackers? *Child places 2 triangles and 3 squares on a plastic plate (or blank piece of paper) and pretends to serve it to you.*

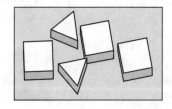

Let's use the Part-Total Mat to show how you joined the groups of crackers. Have your child place Number Cards on the Part-Total Mat to match, as shown below.

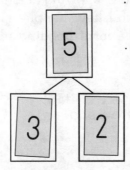

We can show how you joined the groups of crackers with a plus sign and equals sign, too. Write "+" on an index card (oriented horizontally). **This is called the plus sign. It stands for the word plus, and it means we join two groups together.**

Write "=" on an index card (oriented horizontally). **The equals sign tells us two amounts are equal to each other or are the same as each other.**

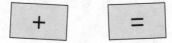

Now we can use the plus sign and equals sign to show how you joined the groups. Place the Number Cards as shown below. **We read this as *2 plus 3 equals 5*.** Point to each card as you read it.

Ask the following questions about the equation:
- **What does the 2 stand for?** *(2 triangle crackers)*
- **What does the 3 stand for?** *(3 square crackers)*
- **What does the 5 stand for?** *(5 crackers all together)*
- **What does the plus sign mean?** *(Joining the group of 2 and the group of 3.)*
- **What does the equals sign mean?** *(It means 2 + 3 is the same as or equal to 5.)*

Discuss how the numbers on the Part-Total Mat match the numbers in the equation. We add together the two parts to make a total.

2 plus 3 equals 5 **is called an equation. Listen to how the word equation starts like the word equals. That's because equations tell two amounts are equal to each other. Equations always have an equals sign.**

 Save the + sign and = sign cards with your Number Cards.

Children often mistakenly believe the equals sign means "the answer is coming." To help prevent your child from developing this misunderstanding, always emphasize the equals sign means the amounts on either side of the equals sign are the same as each other. (For example, 2 + 3 is *equal to* or is *the same as* 5.) Your child does not need to memorize the definition of equation, although it will be used throughout the book for clarity.

Activity: More Equations at the Restaurant

Play restaurant some more. Order the following amounts of "crackers" and ask your child to "serve" them to you. For each plateful, have her place Number Cards on the Part-Total Mat to match, and then have her create a corresponding addition equation with the plus sign and equals sign.

- 4 triangles and 2 squares *(4+2=6 or 2+4=6)*
- 5 triangles and 2 squares *(5+2 =7 or 2+5=7)*
- 3 triangles and 0 squares *(3+0=3 or 0+3=3)*

Your child will learn you can add numbers in any order without changing the total in Lesson 4.4.

Workbook: Complete Addition Equations and Review

Have your child complete workbook pages 4.1A and 4.1B.

Lesson 4.2
More Addition Equations

	Purpose	Materials
Warm-up	• Count to 30 • Practice memory work • Review combinations that make 10	• Small ball or beanbag • Coins • Double ten-frames (Blackline Master 1) • Counters • Index card
Activities	• Write addition equations to match simple joining situations • Model addition problems with concrete objects and solve	• Coins • Number Cards • Part-Total Mat (Blackline Master 4)
Workbook	• Solve simple addition problems with coins	• Workbook pages 4.2A and 4.2B

Warm-up: Counting, Memory Work, and Review

- Count to 30 with your child. Toss a small ball or beanbag back and forth as you count, and take turns saying the numbers: *1,* **2,** *3,* **4…**

- Show your child a penny and a nickel, and have him tell the name and value of each coin.

- Place 10 counters on the ten-frame. Cover the right-most counter with an index card. **How many counters can you see?** *9.* **How many are hidden?** *1.* Repeat the activity several times, covering up to 5 counters each time.

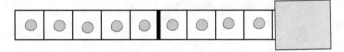

Activity: Write Equations for a Penny Scavenger Hunt

In the last lesson, we created addition equations to match plates of crackers. Today, we'll write addition equations about finding pennies. First, I need to hide some pennies for you to find!

Ask your child to briefly leave the room or close his eyes. Hide the following 8 groups of pennies around the room:

- 2 groups with 2 pennies each
- 2 groups with 3 pennies each
- 2 groups with 4 pennies each
- 2 groups with 5 pennies each

Make the groups fairly easy to find (for example, on a bookshelf or under the edge of a chair).

Have your child look around the room until he finds 2 groups of pennies. Have him place Number Cards on the Part-Total Mat to match the two groups. Then have him create a corresponding addition equation with the plus sign and equals sign.

For example, if he finds a group of 5 pennies and a group of 2 pennies:

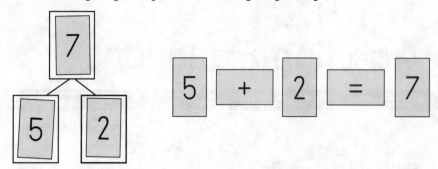

Continue until he has found all 8 groups of pennies. Have him create an equation to show the total number every time he finds 2 groups.

Activity: Model Addition Equations with Pennies

We can also use pennies to find answers to addition problems, even if there is no story.

Write "3 + 2 =" on a piece of paper. Have your child join a group of 3 pennies with a group of 2 pennies to act out the problem. **What's the total number of pennies?** *5.* **So, I'll write 5 on the other side of the equal sign, since 5 is the same as 2 plus 3.**

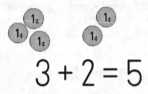

$$3 + 2 = 5$$

Writing the equation on paper prepares your child to solve written equations on the workbook page.

Repeat this process with the following equations.

- 5 + 1 = *6*
- 2 + 2 = *4*
- 8 + 0 = *8*
- 3 + 3 = *6*
- 4 + 5 = *9*
- 5 + 5 = *10*

Do not require your child to model the problems with pennies if he can easily find the answer mentally.

Workbook: Solve Addition Problems and Review

Have your child complete workbook pages 4.2A and 4.2B.

Lesson 4.3
Introduce +1 and +2 Facts

	Purpose	Materials
Warm-up	• Count up to 30 objects by 2s • Practice memory work • Review patterns	• Counters • Coins • Pattern blocks • Index card
Activities	• Use the ten-frame to add 1 or 2 • Recognize adding 0 to a number does not change it	• Double ten-frames (Blackline Master 1) • Counters
Workbook	• Practice the +1 and +2 addition facts on the ten-frame	• Workbook pages 4.3A and 4.3B

Warm-up: Counting, Memory Work, and Review

- Place about 25-30 counters on the table. **About how many counters do you think there are?** *Answers will vary.* Help your child count by 2s to find the actual number of counters. (Demonstrate how to add on the final counter as needed.)

- Show your child a penny and a nickel, and have her tell the name and value of each coin.

- Begin a pattern as shown:

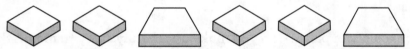

Have your child continue the pattern. Then, have her look away. Use an index card to cover one of the blocks in the pattern. Have your child guess which shape is covered and then check by removing the slip of paper. Repeat several times, covering a different block each time.

Activity: Add 1 and 2 on the Ten-Frame

In the last lesson, you solved addition problems about pennies. Today, we'll use the ten-frame to add 0, 1, or 2.

Let's pretend I had 8 pennies, and then I found 1 more. Write "8 + 1 =" on a piece of paper. Place 8 pennies on the ten-frame and 1 penny next to the ten-frame.

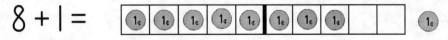

Imagine adding 1 penny. How many pennies will there be? *9.*

Imagining adding the penny helps your child begin to visualize the ten-frame in her head and "see" the answers to addition facts.

Have your child add the penny to the ten-frame, complete the written equation, and read it aloud: *8 plus 1 equals 9.*

$$8 + 1 = 9$$

If your child begins counting to find the answer, encourage her to recognize the quantity instead. Always discourage her from counting one-by-one to find totals for the addition facts.

Problems like these are called *addition facts*. They're very important facts to know so you can solve more complicated problems as you get older. We'll work on the addition facts throughout the year, so you know them all by the end!

Repeat this activity with the following problems. For each, write the problem. Then have your child place pennies on the ten-frame to find the answer and complete the written equation.

- 4 + 1 = *5*
- 9 + 1 = *10*
- 7 + 2 = *9*
- 5 + 2 = *7*
- 8 + 2 = *10*
- 6 + 1 = *7*

Don't require your child to use counters if she can find the answers mentally.

See the Week 4 **Teaching Math with Confidence** for more on how this program teaches the addition facts.

Activity: Add 0

Write "8 + 0 =" on a piece of paper. **Can you make up a penny story to match the equation?** *Sample answer: I found 8 pennies. But then I didn't find any more.*

Place 8 counters of one color on the ten-frame. **How many counters do we need to add?** *0.* **So what's 8 plus 0?** *8.* Have your child complete the written equation and read it aloud: *8 plus 0 equals 8.*

$$8 + 0 = 8$$

Why doesn't the 8 change when we add 0 to it? *Possible answer: Adding 0 means you don't add anything else to the 8.*

Workbook: Practice +1 and +2 Facts and Review

Have your child complete workbook pages 4.3A and 4.3B.

On workbook page 4.3B, your child will complete Part-Total Diagrams in which the total is 5. Children sometimes have trouble remembering which boxes represent the parts and which box represents the total. Or, they sometimes add the printed numbers together regardless of their position. If your child does this, make the exercises more concrete. Use counters to model each problem and pretend that you are splitting cookies (as in Lesson 3.1).

Lesson 4.4
Practice +1 and +2 Facts

	Purpose	Materials
Warm-up	• Count by 2s to 30 • Practice memory work • Review identifying quantities on the ten-frame	• 100 Chart (Blackline Master 3) • Small toy • Coin • Counters • Double ten-frames (Blackline Master 1)
Activities	• Discover you can add numbers in any order (for example, 3 + 2 equals 2 + 3) • Learn to start with the greater number when adding mentally	• Counters • Number Cards • Part-Total Mat • Double ten-frames (Blackline Master 1)
Workbook	• Practice the +1 and +2 addition facts	• Workbook pages 4.4A and 4.4B

Warm-up: Counting, Memory Work, and Review

- Have your child count by 2s to 30 on the 100 Chart. Have him make a small toy jump on each number as he says it.

> A small plastic animal, fun eraser, or minifigure works well for jumping on the 100 Chart. If you don't have a small toy handy, use a counter instead.

- Show your child a penny and a nickel, and have him tell the name and value of each coin.

- Play Race to 10. See Lesson 2.1 (page 31) for directions. Have your child say the matching addition fact for each play. For example, if he has 6 counters and then adds 2: *6 plus 2 equals 8.*

Activity: Can We Add in Any Order?

Sometimes, it doesn't matter what order we do things. For example, it doesn't matter if I put on my left sock first or my right sock first. But other times, the order matters a lot. It makes a big difference whether I put on my socks or my shoes first!

In the last lesson, we used the ten-frame to add 0, 1, and 2. Today, we'll explore what happens when we add numbers in different orders. We'll see whether the order makes a difference.

Let's pretend you have 7 candies. Give your child 7 counters. **Then, you get 2 more.** Give your child 2 more counters. **How many candies do you have in all?** 9.

Help your child write an equation to match. Also place Number Cards on the Part-Total Mat to match the equation.

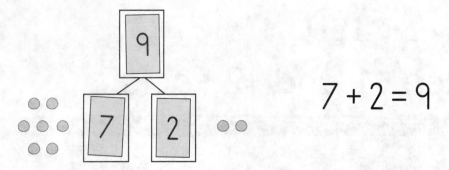

Now let's see what happens if you get the candy in a different order. Let's pretend you start with 2 candies. Give your child 2 counters. **Then, you get 7 more.** Give your child 7 more counters. **How many candies do you have in all?** *9.*

Help your child write an equation to match: 2 + 7 = 9.

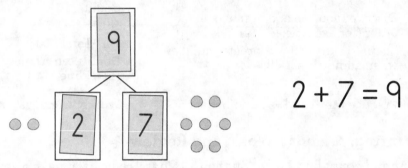

What do you notice about the answers to these problems? *They're the same!*

Does it matter what order we add the numbers? *No, you still get the same answer.*

Why do you think the two answers are the same? *Answers will vary.* If your child isn't sure, point out he joined the same groups, just in a different order.

> First-graders often have trouble putting their ideas about math into words, even when they understand the underlying concepts. Don't worry if your child has trouble articulating why the groups can be added in either order.

> The fact that we can add numbers in any order is called the commutative property of addition. Your first grader does not need to memorize the name of this property; he only needs to be able to use it.

Activity: Start with the Greater Number

We can add numbers in any order and still get the same answer. Adding in your head is usually easier if you start with the greater number and then add on the other number, no matter what order the numbers are written.

Write "2 + 6 =" on a piece of paper. **It's easier to imagine 6 + 2 on the ten-frame than 2 + 6. So, I think "What's 6 + 2?" to find the answer.** Have your child put 6 counters of one color and 2 counters of another color on the ten-frame. Then, have him complete the equation: 2 + 6 = 8.

$$2 + 6 = 8$$
$$6 + 2 = 8$$

Repeat with the following problems. Remind your child to begin with the greater addend in each problem.

- 1 + 8 = *9*
- 2 + 5 = *7*
- 1 + 6 = *7*
- 2 + 8 = *10*
- 1 + 9 = *10*
- 2 + 7 = *9*
- 1 + 7 = *8*
- 2 + 6 = *8*

Don't require your child to use the ten-frame if he can find the answers mentally.

Workbook: Practice the +1 and +2 Addition Facts and Review

Have your child complete workbook pages 4.4A and 4.4B. Allow your child to use the ten-frame and counters as needed.

Lesson 4.5
Enrichment and Review (Optional)

	Purpose	Materials
Warm-up	• Review counting • Review memory work • Review your child's favorite or most challenging activities from Week 4	• Varies, depending on the activities you choose
Picture Book	• Recognize addition in real-life contexts	• *Albert Adds Up!*, written by Eleanor May and illustrated by Deborah Melmon
Enrichment Activity	• Model addition equations with natural objects	• Natural objects, such as leaves, acorns, rocks, or sticks • Paper, optional • Glue, optional

Warm-up: Counting, Memory Work, and Review

- Have your child count to 30 by 1s and 2s.

- Quiz your child on the memory work through Week 4. See page 499 for the full list.

- If you have time, repeat one or two of the activities from this week's lessons. Choose activities your child especially enjoyed or found challenging.

Math Picture Book: *Albert Adds Up!*

Read *Albert Adds Up!*, written by Eleanor May and illustrated by Deborah Melmon. As you read the book, discuss how the printed equations match the illustrations and story.

Enrichment Activity: Addition Nature Walk

Go on an Addition Nature Walk. Have your child choose an item to collect (such as leaves, acorns, rocks, or sticks) and have him gather 10 of those objects as you walk.

Once you return home, use the natural objects to act out some simple addition equations. For example: *4 rocks plus 3 rocks equal 7 rocks*. If you'd like to extend the activity further, have your child glue some of the objects to a piece of paper and write a matching addition equation.

If the weather doesn't allow for a nature walk, have your child collect 10 craft items from around the house rather than 10 natural objects.

Week 4 Answer Key

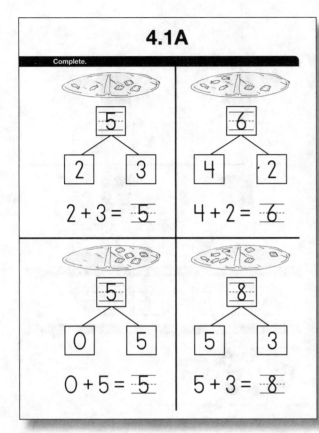

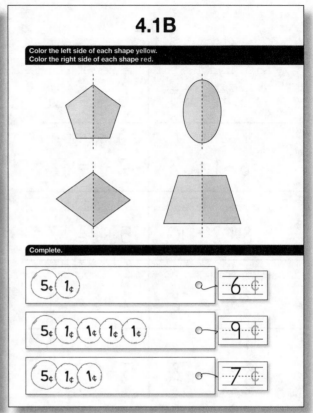

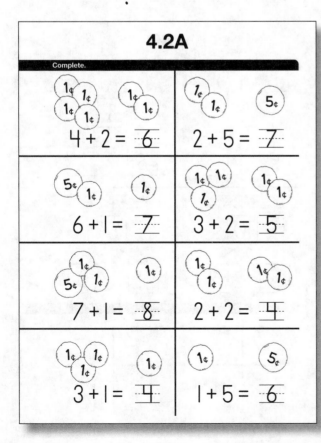

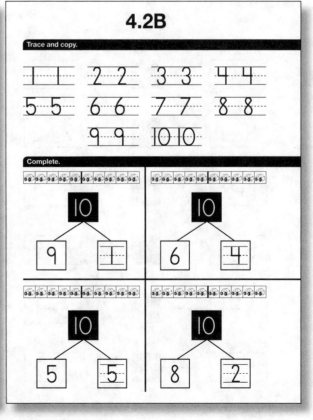

Week 4 Answer Key

4.3A

Complete.

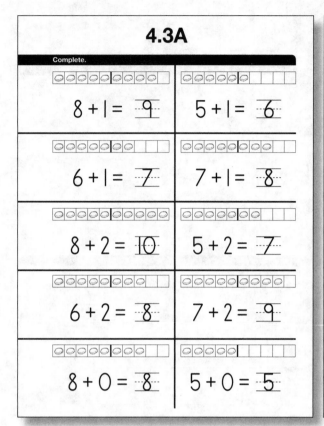

$8 + 1 = 9$ $5 + 1 = 6$

$6 + 1 = 7$ $7 + 1 = 8$

$8 + 2 = 10$ $5 + 2 = 7$

$6 + 2 = 8$ $7 + 2 = 9$

$8 + 0 = 8$ $5 + 0 = 5$

4.3B

Complete.

Many answers are possible.

Write the number that comes before and after each number.

6 7 8   2 3 4

Complete.

$7

4.4A

Match.

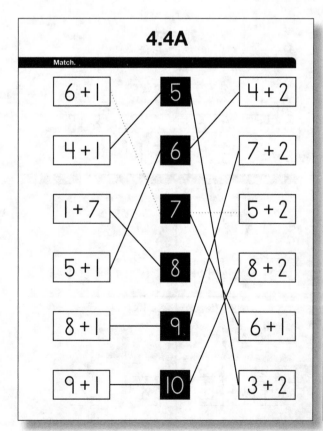

4.4B

Complete.

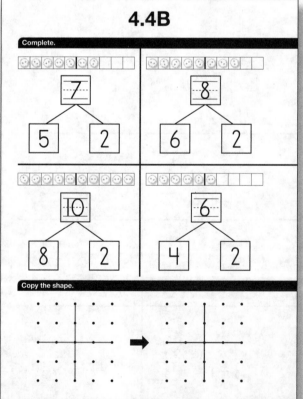

Copy the shape.

Week 5
+3 and +4 Addition Facts

Overview

Your child will learn the +3 and +4 addition facts with sums up to 10. She'll continue to use the ten-frame to visualize the problems and find answers without counting. She'll also learn the terms sum and addend.

Lesson 5.1	Introduce +3 and +4 Facts
Lesson 5.2	Practice +3 and +4 Facts
Lesson 5.3	Visualize +3 and +4 Facts
Lesson 5.4	*Sum* and *Addend*
Lesson 5.5	Enrichment and Review (Optional)

Teaching Math with Confidence:
Why Visualize Addition Facts Instead of Counting?

When children first learn addition, they usually count to find the answers. For example, to add 6 + 2, a typical first grader would count out a pile of 6 counters and a pile of 2 counters. Then, she would combine the piles and count to find that the total is 8.

$$6 + 2 = 8$$

It's fine for children to find answers in this way when they're first making sense of addition. But in the long run, counting is slow, inefficient, and error prone. That's why you'll teach your child to visualize addition facts on the ten-frame (instead of counting) to find the answers.

This week, you'll focus on the +3 and +4 addition facts with sums up to 10. Each of these sums contains a number close to 5, so your child will use the dividing line in the middle of the ten-frame as a mental reference point. For example, to solve 4 + 3, your child will add in two steps. First, she'll add 1 to the 4 to make a 5. Then, she'll add the remaining 2.

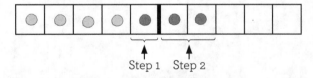

Step 1   Step 2

At first, your child will probably need to consciously think through this process. But as she practices the strategy more, it will gradually become automatic. By the end of the week, she may even "just know" the answers to these problems.

If you find your child counting one-by-one to find the answers to these problems, stop her immediately and have her place counters on the ten-frame instead (or visualize counters, as you'll teach her in Lesson 5.3). Even though it may take longer than counting right now, you'll be glad in the long run that you took the time to help your child develop more efficient strategies for the addition facts.

Extra Materials Needed for Week 5

- Small ball or beanbag
- Small toy
- For optional Enrichment and Review Lesson:
    - *Domino Addition,* by Lynette Long
    - Dominoes, optional
    - Classic card game (like Skip-Bo or Uno), optional
    - Playing cards, optional

Lesson 5.1
Introduce +3 and +4 Facts

	Purpose	Materials
Warm-up	• Count to 40 • Practice memory work • Review tallies	• 100 Chart (Blackline Master 3) • Coins • Tally Cards
Activities	• Introduce the +3 and +4 addition facts	• Counters • Double ten-frames (Blackline Master 1) • Addition Climb to the Top game board (from workbook page 5.1A) • 2 decks of playing cards
Workbook	• Practice +3 and +4 addition facts	• Workbook pages 5.1A and 5.1B

Warm-up: Counting, Memory Work, and Review

- Count in unison with your child to 40. Point to each number on the 100 Chart as you say it.

- Show your child a penny and a nickel, and have her tell the name and value of each coin.

- Shuffle Tally Cards 0-10. Show your child one card at a time. Have her identify the number of tallies on the card as quickly as she can.

Activity: Introduce +3 and +4 Addition Facts

Last week, you learned the +1 and +2 addition facts. This week, you'll learn the +3 and +4 addition facts.

Let's pretend you collect eggs on a farm, and the ten-frame is the carton for the eggs. Briefly discuss your child's experience with farms and chickens. **One day you find 5 white eggs and 4 brown eggs.**

Place 5 counters of one color and 4 counters of another color on the table. Write "5 + 4 =" on a piece of paper.

Let's put them in the carton to see how many eggs there are in all. Have your child place the counters on the ten-frame as shown.

How many eggs are there? *9.* If your child starts to count the counters one-by-one, encourage her to recognize the quantity instead: *Try to tell how many there are without counting.* **There's just one empty box, so how many must be full?** *9.*

Have your child complete the written equation: 5 + 4 = 9.

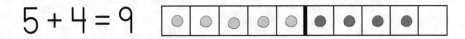

See the Week 5 **Teaching Math with Confidence** for more on why it's so important for your child to recognize quantities (and not count) as she learns the addition facts.

Repeat with the addition facts below. Keep encouraging your child to recognize the totals on the ten-frame instead of counting one-by-one.

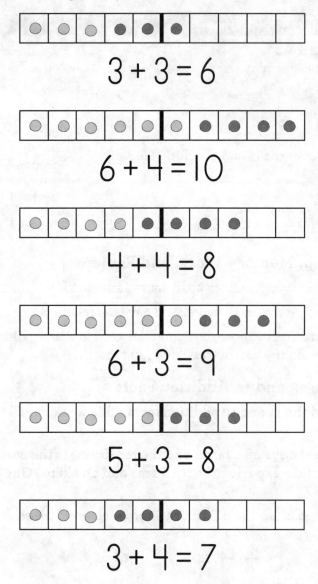

$$3 + 3 = 6$$

$$6 + 4 = 10$$

$$4 + 4 = 8$$

$$6 + 3 = 9$$

$$5 + 3 = 8$$

$$3 + 4 = 7$$

Activity: Play Addition Climb to the Top

Play one round of Addition Climb to the Top. Have your child use counters and the ten-frame to find the sums as she plays.

Addition Climb to the Top

Materials: Addition Climb to the Top game boards (Workbook page 5.1A); 3s, 4s, 5s, and 6s from two decks of cards (32 cards total); counters

Object of the Game: Be the first player to fill in an entire column and reach the top of the game board.

Shuffle the cards and place the stack face down on the table. Have each player choose one of the game boards on the workbook page. On your turn, turn over the top 2 cards and find the sum of the cards. Place a counter on the lowest empty box in the column that matches the sum. For example, if you draw a 5 and a 3, place a counter in the first empty box above the 8.

Place a counter in the box above the sum that matches your cards.

Sums greater than 10 are wild, and you can choose which column to place the counter in.

Take turns until one player fills an entire column and reaches the top.

If your counters do not fit on the game board, you can place the game board in a plastic page protector and mark your plays with dry-erase marker instead.

Workbook: Practice +3 and +4 Facts and Review

Have your child complete workbook page 5.1B. If your child counts to find the answers to the addition problems, remind her to recognize the totals on the ten-frames instead.

 Save the Addition Climb to the Top game board (workbook page 5.1A) with your math materials so you can play again.

Lesson 5.2
Practice +3 and +4 Facts

	Purpose	Materials
Warm-up	• Count to 40 • Practice memory work • Review coin combinations	• Small ball or beanbag • Coins
Activities	• Learn to visualize the second addend for +3 and +4 facts • Practice +3 and +4 addition facts	• Counters • Double ten-frames (Blackline Master 1) • Addition Climb to the Top game board (from workbook page 5.1A) • 2 decks of playing cards
Workbook	• Practice +3 and +4 addition facts	• Workbook pages 5.2A and 5.2B

Warm-up: Counting, Memory Work, and Review

- Count to 40. Toss a small ball or beanbag back and forth as you count, and take turns saying the numbers: **1**, 2, **3**, 4…

- **Tap your head with your left hand. Tap your head with your right hand.**

- Have your child tell the value of the following coin combinations.

  × 1 penny *(1¢)*
  × 1 nickel *(5¢)*
  × 1 nickel and 2 pennies *(7¢)*
  × 1 nickel and 4 pennies *(9¢)*
  × 1 nickel and 1 penny *(6¢)*
  × 1 nickel and 3 pennies *(8¢)*
  × 2 nickels *(10¢)*

Activity: Imagine the Second Addend in 2 Steps

In the last lesson, you started learning the +3 and +4 facts. Today, you'll practice these addition facts some more.

This lesson is very similar to Lesson 5.1, but with one crucial difference. Instead of placing both groups of eggs on the ten-frame right away, your child will imagine placing the second group of eggs before he actually adds them to the ten-frame. This will help him begin to memorize the answers to the +3 and +4 addition facts.

Let's pretend again that you collect eggs on a farm, and the ten-frame is the carton for the eggs. One day you find 4 white eggs and 3 brown eggs. Place 4 counters of one color and 3 counters of another color on the table. Write "4 + 3 =" on a piece of paper.

$$4 + 3 = \quad \substack{\bullet \ \bullet \\ \bullet \ \bullet} \qquad \substack{\bullet \\ \bullet \ \bullet}$$

I'll put the 4 white eggs in the carton. Put the 4 counters on the ten-frame. Place the 3 other counters next to the ten-frame.

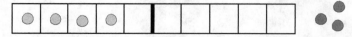

Let's imagine adding the 3 eggs to the carton in 2 steps. First, you would put 1 egg in the carton to complete the group of 5. Point to the 5th box on the ten-frame.

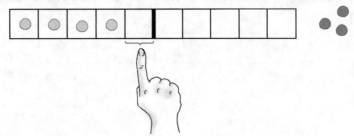

Then, you would still have 2 eggs to put in the carton. Point to the 6th and 7th boxes on the ten-frame. How many eggs will there be in all? 7.

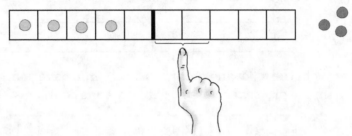

> If your child starts to count the boxes one-by-one, encourage him to recognize the quantity instead, as in Lesson 5.1.

Have your child add the 3 loose counters to the ten-frame and complete the written equation: 4 + 3 = 7.

$$4 + 3 = 7$$

Repeat this process with the following problems. Encourage your child to imagine adding the counters in 2 steps and to use the dark line in the middle of the ten-frame as a visual anchor to help him "see" the answers.

$$3 + 3 = 6$$

$$4 + 4 = 8$$

Activity: Imagine the Second Addend in 1 Step

One day you find 5 white eggs and 3 brown eggs. Place 5 counters of one color and 3 counters of another color on the table. Write "5 + 3 =" on a piece of paper.

$$5 + 3 =$$

I'll put the 5 white eggs in the carton. Put the 5 counters on the ten-frame. Place the 3 other counters next to the ten-frame.

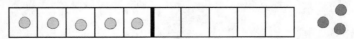

The carton's first group of 5 is already complete. So, we can just imagine putting all 3 brown eggs in the carton in one step. Point to the last box you'll fill. *Child points to 8th box on the ten-frame.*

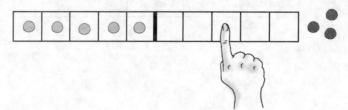

How many eggs will be in the carton then? *8.* Have your child add the 3 loose counters to the ten-frame and complete the written equation: 5 + 3 = 8.

$$5 + 3 = 8$$

Repeat this process with the following problems. Each time have your child imagine adding the second number in the problem before he actually adds counters to the ten-frame.

$$5 + 4 = 9$$

$$6 + 4 = 10$$

$$6 + 3 = 9$$

Activity: Play Addition Climb to the Top

Play Addition Climb to the Top again. See Lesson 5.1 (page 81) for directions.

Keep the ten-frame and counters available as you play. As your child plays, have him place counters to match the larger number on the ten-frame. Then, ask him to imagine adding the second number in the problem before adding real counters.

Paper game boards sometimes have a way of disappearing, so you'll find black-and-white versions of every game board used in this program in the back of this Instructor Guide (beginning on page 506). You will only need these if one of your full-color game boards from the workbook goes missing.

Workbook: Practice the +3 and +4 Facts and Review

Have your child complete workbook pages 5.2A and 5.2B. Keep the ten-frame and counters available for your child to use as needed.

Workbook page 5.2A directs your child to color the math facts that match a given number. If your child doesn't like to color (or takes a long time), he can X the correct math facts, highlight them with a highlighter, or simply show them to you rather than coloring.

Lesson 5.3
Visualize +3 and +4 Facts

	Purpose	Materials
Warm-up	• Count by 2s to 40 • Practice memory work • Review using *greater than* and *less than* to compare numbers	• Counters • Coins • 100 Chart (Blackline Master 3)
Activities	• Practice the +3 and +4 addition facts	• Counters • Double ten-frames (Blackline Master 1) • Addition Climb to the Top game board (from workbook page 5.1A) • 2 decks of playing cards
Workbook	• Practice +3 and +4 addition facts	• Workbook pages 5.3A and 5.3B

Warm-up: Counting, Memory Work, and Review

- Place about 35-40 counters on the table. **About how many counters do you think there are?** *Answers will vary.* Help your child count by 2s to find the actual number of counters. (Help her add on the final counter as needed.)

- Show your child a penny and a nickel, and have her tell the name and value of each coin.

- Play Guess the Secret Number. See Lesson 1.3 (page 20) for directions.

Activity: Imagine Both Addends

You have been learning the +3 and +4 facts. Today, you'll practice these addition facts some more.

Write "6 + 3 =" on a piece of paper. Place 6 counters of one color and 3 counters of another color on the table.

In the last lesson, we put one group of counters on the ten-frame. Then, you imagined adding the other group. Put the 6 counters on the ten-frame. Place the 3 other counters next to the ten-frame.

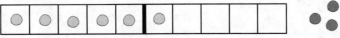

Imagine adding the 3 counters to the ten-frame. How many will there be? 9. Have your child add the 3 loose counters to the ten-frame and complete the written equation: 6 + 3 = 9.

$$6 + 3 = 9$$

Clear the ten-frame and write "4 + 3 =" on a piece of paper. **I have a new challenge for you today. Let's see if you can solve this equation without any counters at all. First, imagine 4 counters on the ten-frame.** *Child looks at ten-frame and imagines 4 counters on it.*

$$4 + 3 =$$

Next, imagine adding 3 counters. *Child looks at ten-frame and imagines adding 3 more counters.* **How many counters would be on the ten-frame?** *7.* Have your child complete the written equation.

$$4 + 3 = 7$$

If your child struggles to visualize the counters, allow her to use physical counters (as in Lesson 5.2).

Repeat this process with the other +3 and +4 addition facts. Encourage your child to imagine placing counters on the ten-frame to solve each problem.

- $3 + 3 = 6$
- $6 + 4 = 10$
- $4 + 4 = 8$
- $5 + 4 = 9$
- $5 + 3 = 8$
- $3 + 4 = 7$

You do not need to require your child to visualize the problems if she knows the answers immediately.

Activity: Play Addition Climb to the Top

Play Addition Climb to the Top. See Lesson 5.1 (page 81) for directions.

Keep the ten-frame available as you play. Encourage your child to visualize the numbers on the blank ten-frame to find the answers.

Parents often wonder how quickly their child should be able to recall the answers to the math facts. As a general rule, aim for no more than 3 seconds per fact, and less if possible. But, the ideal time depends on your child. Children who process information very quickly may rattle off an answer in less than 1 second, while children who are slower processors may always need a few seconds. You're the parent and know your child best, so adjust your expectations to your individual child.

Workbook: Practice the +3 and +4 Facts

Have your child complete workbook pages 5.3A and 5.3B. Keep the ten-frame and counters available for your child to use as needed.

Lesson 5.4
Sum and Addend

	Purpose	Materials
Warm-up	• Count to 40 by 2s • Practice memory work • Review left and right	• 100 Chart (Blackline Master 3) • Small toy
Activities	• Introduce the terms *sum* and *addend* • Practice +3 and +4 addition facts	• Counters • Double ten-frames (Blackline Master 1) • Addition Climb to the Top game board (on Workbook page 5.1A) • 2 decks of playing cards
Workbook	• Practice addition facts	• Workbook pages 5.4A and 5.4B

Warm-up: Counting, Memory Work, and Review

- Have your child count by 2s to 40. Have him make a small toy jump on each number on the 100 Chart as he says it.

- **Tap your right foot. Tap your left foot.**

- Play Simon Says. Give your child 8-10 directions involving left and right. See Lesson 1.4 for more detailed directions.

Activity: Introduce Sum and Addend

In the last lesson, you practiced the +3 and +4 addition facts. Today, you'll practice those facts and learn two important math words.

Write 5 + 4 = 9 on a piece of paper. **We call the numbers we add together the addends.** Write "addend" below the 5 and 4. **Here's how to remember this word: we add the addends.**

$$5 + 4 = 9$$
$$\underset{\text{addends}}{\uparrow\quad\uparrow}$$

We call the total of the two addends the sum. Write "sum" below the 9. **Sum sounds like the word some, but it's spelled a different way and it has a different meaning.** Write "some" on a scrap of paper to show your child the difference between the two words.

$$5 + 4 = 9$$
$$\underset{\text{addends}}{\uparrow\quad\uparrow}\quad\underset{\text{sum}}{\uparrow}$$

sum
some

Write 3 + 2 = 5 on the paper. **Which numbers are the addends?** *3 and 2.* **Which number is the sum?** *5.*

$$3 + 2 = 5$$

Have your child make up his own addition equation and identify the addends and sum.

Teaching your child math vocabulary like *sum* and *addend* makes it easier to discuss math together. But keep in mind that learning the vocabulary is far less important than learning the mathematical concepts and skills! Your child will gradually master the meaning of these words as he hears you use them in context.

Activity: Play Addition Climb to the Top

Play Addition Climb to the Top. See Lesson 5.1 (page 81) for directions. As you play, use the words *sum* and *addends* to describe the game. For example: **My addends are 6 and 3, so my sum is 9.**

Keep the ten-frame available as you play. Encourage your child to visualize the numbers on the blank ten-frame to find the answers.

Workbook: Practice Addition Facts

Have your child complete workbook pages 5.4A and 5.4B. Keep the ten-frame and counters available for your child to use as needed.

Lesson 5.5
Enrichment and Review (Optional)

	Purpose	Materials
Warm-up	• Count to 40 by 1s and 2s • Review memory work • Review your child's favorite or most challenging activities from Week 5	• Varies, depending on the activities you choose
Picture Book	• Understand addition equations in the context of dominos	• *Domino Addition*, by Lynette Long
Enrichment Activity	• Use numbers in classic games	• Dominoes, optional • Classic card game (like Skip-Bo or Uno), optional • Playing cards, optional

Warm-up: Counting, Memory Work, and Review

- Have your child count to 40 by 1s and 2s.

- Quiz your child on the memory work through Week 4. See page 499 for the full list.

- If you have time, repeat one or two of the activities from this week's lessons. Choose activities your child especially enjoyed or found challenging.

Math Picture Book: *Domino Addition*

Read *Domino Addition*, by Lynette Long. As you read, have your child answer the questions posed in the book. Also talk about how the equations match the dots on the dominoes.

> This book includes vertical addition equations. For now, simply explain it's another way to write addition equations. Your child will learn to write equations this way in second grade.

Enrichment Activity: Play a Classic Game

Play a classic game that uses numbers to help your child connect what she's learning in math with her everyday play. Choose one of the following options, depending on what you have available in your house:

- Play dominoes (to connect with the picture book).
- Play a classic card game that uses the numbers to 10, such as Uno, Skip-Bo, or Spit.
- Play Make 10 Go Fish or Make 10 Pyramid.

Week 5 Answer Key

5.1A

See *Instructor Guide* for directions on how to play.
Save these game boards for future lessons.

Addition Climb to the Top
Game Boards

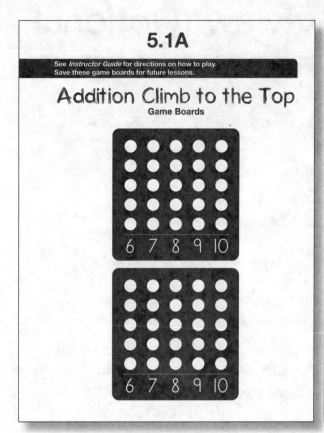

5.1B

Complete.

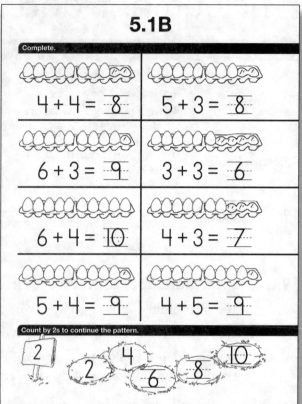

$4 + 4 = 8$

$5 + 3 = 8$

$6 + 3 = 9$

$3 + 3 = 6$

$6 + 4 = 10$

$4 + 3 = 7$

$5 + 4 = 9$

$4 + 5 = 9$

Count by 2s to continue the pattern.

2   2   4   6   8   10

5.2A

Complete.

$3 + 5 = 8$ $4 + 4 = 8$

$3 + 3 = 6$ $4 + 5 = 9$

$6 + 3 = 9$ $6 + 4 = 10$

Color the addition facts that equal the number in the star.

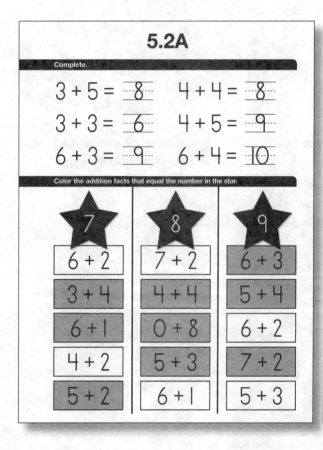

5.2B

Complete.

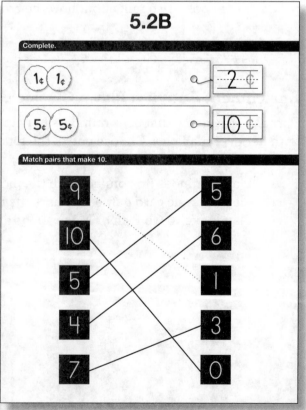

1¢ 1¢ → 2¢

5¢ 5¢ → 10¢

Match pairs that make 10.

Week 5 Answer Key

5.3A

Complete.

$4 + 4 =$ __8__ $5 + 3 =$ __8__

$5 + 4 =$ __9__ $3 + 6 =$ __9__

$3 + 3 =$ __6__ $3 + 4 =$ __7__

$6 + 1 =$ __7__ $4 + 4 =$ __8__

Use the key to color the leaves.

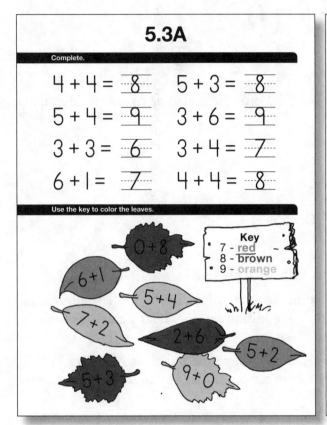

Key
7 - red
8 - brown
9 - orange

5.3B

Circle the greater number in each pair.

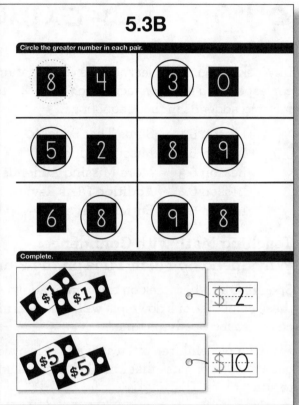

Complete.

$ 2

$ 10

5.4A

Match.

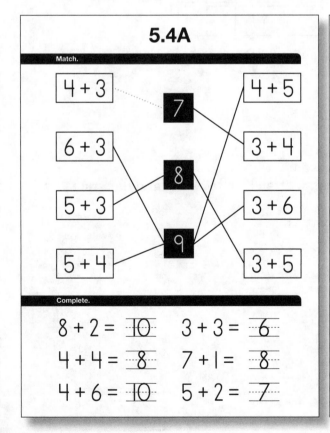

Complete.

$8 + 2 =$ __10__ $3 + 3 =$ __6__

$4 + 4 =$ __8__ $7 + 1 =$ __8__

$4 + 6 =$ __10__ $5 + 2 =$ __7__

5.4B

Write how many.

8   6   5

9   10   7

X the shape that doesn't belong.

Week 6
Sums That Equal 10

Overview

In Week 3, your child learned the combinations that make 10. This week, he will learn the corresponding addition facts (such as 6 + 4 = 10, or 5 + 5 = 10). He'll also learn how to identify missing addends in these equations.

Lesson 6.1   Sums That Equal 10
Lesson 6.2   Missing Addends
Lesson 6.3   More Missing Addends
Lesson 6.4   Addition Facts Review
Lesson 6.5   Enrichment and Review (Optional)

Teaching Math with Confidence:
Why Spend So Much Time on the Pairs That Make 10?

Spending another week on the combinations that make 10 may feel like overkill. But having these combinations down pat will make learning the addition facts with larger sums much easier, so it's worth the time.

For example, children often struggle to learn 8 + 5. But when your child already knows 8 + 2 equals 10, he can use that knowledge to quickly figure out 8 + 5. "8 plus 2 is 10, so I just need to add 3 more. That's 13!"

You'll teach your child these addition facts with sums greater than 10 in Unit 8.

Extra Materials Needed for Week 3

- Printed wall calendar
- Small toy
- Small ball or beanbag
- For optional Enrichment and Review Lesson:
    × *Math Fables: Lessons That Count*, written by Greg Tang and illustrated by Heather Cahoon
    × 10 plastic cups or empty water bottles
    × Small ball

Lesson 6.1
Sums That Equal 10

	Purpose	Materials
Warm-up	• Count to 40 by 2s • Learn the days of the week • Review pattern blocks and develop your child's spatial skills	• Printed wall calendar • Counters • Pattern blocks
Activities	• Introduce addition facts with sums of 10 • Practice finding pairs that make 10	• Counters • Double ten-frames (Blackline Master 1) • Number Cards
Workbook	• Write addition equations that equal 10	• Workbook pages 6.1A and 6.1B

Warm-up: Counting, Memory Work, and Review

• Have your child count by 2s to 40. Have her march in place as she counts.

• **Today, you'll learn the names of the days of the week. Every week has 7 days.** Point to the days of the week on the printed calendar and read them aloud to your child: **Sunday, Monday, Tuesday, Wednesday, Thursday, Friday, Saturday.**

 Say a few days at a time and then have your child repeat them: **Sunday, Monday, Tuesday.** *Sunday, Monday, Tuesday.* **Wednesday, Thursday.** *Wednesday, Thursday.* **Friday, Saturday.** *Friday, Saturday.*

> If your child already knows the days of the week, simply ask her to recite them.

• Make a simple design with 4-7 pattern blocks (you can use the design shown below or create your own). Then, have your child copy it.

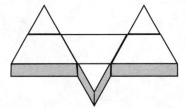 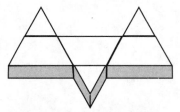

> Copying pattern block designs develops your child's spatial skills. First-graders' spatial skills vary widely, so adjust the difficulty level for your individual child. If 4-7 blocks cause frustration, use only 2-3 blocks instead. Or, if your child needs more challenge, make a design, show your design to your child, cover it with a piece of paper, and then challenge him to recreate it from memory.

Activity: Find Sums That Equal 10

In Week 5, you learned the +3 and +4 addition facts. Today, you'll learn some more addition facts.

Write "8 + 2 =" on a piece of paper. Have your child model the problem with counters on the ten-frame and complete the equation.

$$8 + 2 = 10$$

Repeat with the other addition facts with sums that equal 10.

- 7 + 3 = 10
- 9 + 1 = 10
- 6 + 4 = 10
- 5 + 5 = 10

If your child doesn't notice all the equations equal 10, ask: **What's the same about all of these problems?** *They all have a sum of 10.*

See the Week 6 **Teaching Math with Confidence** for more on why these combinations that make 10 are so important for children to master.

Activity: Play Make 10 Go Fish

Play Make 10 Go Fish. See Lesson 3.3 (page 52) for directions. As you play, use addition equations to describe the game. For example: **I have a 7. 7 plus 3 equals 10, so I need a 3.**

Workbook: Write Equations That Equal 10 and Review

Have your child complete workbook pages 6.1A and 6.1B.

Lesson 6.2
Missing Addends

	Purpose	Materials
Warm-up	• Count to 40 by 2s • Practice memory work • Review finding combinations that make 10	• Counters • Playing cards
Activities	• Introduce addition equations with missing addends • Use part-total thinking to find missing addends • Practice finding combinations that make 10	• Index card or slip of paper • Counters • Double ten-frames (Blackline Master 1) • Number Cards • Part-Total Mat (Blackline Master 4)
Workbook	• Find missing addends in equations that equal 10	• Workbook pages 6.2A and 6.2B • Pattern blocks

Warm-up: Counting, Memory Work, and Review

- Have your child count out 40 counters. Have him count them by 2s: 2, 4, 6…

- Say the days of the week in unison. Then alternate saying the days with your child: **Sunday,** *Monday,* **Tuesday,** *Wednesday,* **Thursday,** *Friday,* **Saturday. How many days are in a week?** *7.*

- Ask your child the following addition facts. Encourage him to visualize the ten-frame in his head to find the answers, but allow him to use the ten-frame as needed.

    ×   3 + 3 = *6*
    ×   6 + 4 = *10*
    ×   4 + 4 = *8*
    ×   6 + 3 = *9*
    ×   4 + 3 = *7*
    ×   5 + 4 = *9*
    ×   5 + 3 = *8*
    ×   3 + 4 = *7*

Activity: Introduce Equations with a Missing Addend

In the last lesson, you learned the addition facts with sums that equal 10. Today, you'll learn about equations where one of the addends is hidden or missing.

Write 9 + 1 = 10 on a piece of paper. **Which number is the sum in this equation?** *10.* **Which numbers are the addends?** *9 and 1.*

$$9 + \underset{\text{addends}}{1} = \underset{\text{sum}}{10}$$

Secretly cover the 1 with a slip of paper.

$$9 + \boxed{} = 10$$

What number did I cover? *1.* **How do you know?** *Sample answer: 9 and 1 make 10.*

Secretly write 8 + 2 = 10 and cover the 2 with a slip of paper. **8 and what make 10?** *2.*

If your child isn't sure, place 8 counters on the ten-frame. **How many more counters do I need to make 10?** *2.*

So, what number did I hide? *2.* Remove the slip of paper to reveal the complete equation.

Activity: X-Ray Vision with Missing Addends

Let's pretend you have X-ray vision and can see right through paper. I'm going to write an equation and hide one addend. Use your X-ray vision to tell me the missing addend.

Have your child use his "X-ray vision" to identify the hidden number in the following equations with missing addends.

$$5 + 5 = 10 \qquad 7 + 3 = 10 \qquad 4 + 6 = 10$$

$$10 + 0 = 10 \qquad 8 + 2 = 10$$

Use counters on the ten-frame as needed to help your child find the answers.

Activity: Play Make 10 Pyramid

Have your child play a round of Make 10 Pyramid. See Lesson 3.4 (page 55) for directions.

You can play Make 10 Go Fish instead if your child prefers that game. See Lesson 3.3 (page 52) for directions.

Workbook: Find Missing Addends and Review

Have your child complete workbook pages 6.2A and 6.2B. Your child can use the ten-frame at the top of 6.2A to help complete the equations. For example, to find the missing addend in __ + 7 = 10, he can place his pencil on the ten-frame to split the counters into a group of 7 and a group of 3.

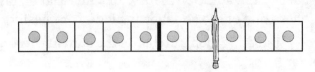

Lesson 6.3
More Missing Addends

	Purpose	Materials
Warm-up	• Count to 50 • Practice memory work • Review finding combinations of one-dollar and five-dollar bills	• 100 Chart (Blackline Master 3) • Play money
Activities	• Solve missing addend word problems • Practice finding combinations that make 10	• Small toy • Play money • Number Cards, optional • Part-Total Mat (Blackline Master 4), optional • Playing cards • Counters, optional • Double ten-frames (Blackline Master 1), optional
Workbook	• Find missing addends in equations equal to 10	• Workbook pages 6.3A and 6.3B

Warm-up: Counting, Memory Work, and Review

- Count in unison with your child to 50. Point to each number on the 100 Chart as you say it.

- Say the days of the week in unison with your child. Then alternate saying the days with your child: **Sunday,** *Monday,* **Tuesday,** *Wednesday,* **Thursday,** *Friday,* **Saturday. How many days are in a week?** *7.*

- Have your child tell the value of the following play money combinations.

    × 4 one-dollar bills *($4)*
    × 1 five-dollar bill and 1 one-dollar bills *($6)*
    × 1 five-dollar bill and 4 one-dollar bills *($9)*
    × 2 five-dollar bills *($10)*
    × 1 five-dollar bill and 3 one-dollar bills *($8)*

Activity: Solve Missing Addend Word Problems

In the last lesson, you found missing addends in addition equations. Today, we'll write missing addend equations about money.

Have you ever wanted to buy something but didn't have enough money? *Answers will vary.* Have your child choose a toy to use in the lesson and bring it to the table. **Let's pretend you want to buy this toy, and it costs $10.** Write $10 on an index card and place it next to the toy. **But, you only have $7.** Give your child a $5-bill and 2 $1-bills.

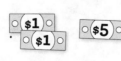

Let's write a matching addition equation. Write 7 + ___ = 10 on a piece of paper.

$$7 + \underline{} = 10$$

Ask the following questions about the equation:

- **What does the 7 stand for?** *(The $7 that I have.)*
- **What does the 10 stand for?** *(The cost of the toy.)*
- **What does the blank stand for?** *(The number of dollars I still need.)*

How many more dollars do you need to buy the toy? *$3.* If she's not sure, encourage her to think of the pairs that make 10: **7 and what make 10?** *3.* **7 and 3 make 10, so you need $3 more.**

If your child isn't sure, place 7 counters on the ten-frame. **How many more counters do I need to make 10?** *3.* Discourage her from counting to find the answers.

Repeat this process with the following problems. For each, write a matching missing addend equation and have your child find the answer.

- **Let's pretend the toy costs $10 and you have $5. How many more dollars do you need?** *5 + ___ = 10. I need $5.*
- **Let's pretend the toy costs $10 and you have $9. How many more dollars do you need?** *9 + ___ = 10. I need $1.*
- **Let's pretend the toy costs $10 and you have $2. How many more dollars do you need?** *2 + ___ = 10. I need $8.*
- **Let's pretend the toy costs $10 and you have $10. How many more dollars do you need?** *10 + ___ = 10. I need $0, so I have enough!*

Activity: Play Make 10 Go Fish

Play one round of Make 10 Go Fish. See Lesson 3.3 (page 52) for directions.

Workbook: Find Missing Addends and Review

Have your child complete workbook pages 6.3A and 6.3B. Allow your child to use the ten-frame and counters as needed.

Lesson 6.4
Addition Facts Review

	Purpose	Materials
Warm-up	• Count to 50 • Practice memory work • Review coin combinations	• Small ball or beanbag • Coins
Activities	• Practice addition facts	• 2 decks of playing cards • Counters, optional • Double ten-frames (Blackline Master 1), optional
Workbook	• Practice addition facts	• Workbook pages 6.4A and 6.4B

Warm-up: Counting, Memory Work, and Review

- Count to 50 with your child. Toss a small ball or beanbag back and forth as you count, and take turns saying the numbers: *1, **2**, 3, **4**…*

- Have your child say the days of the week. **How many days are in a week?** *7.*

- Show your child 1 nickel and 5 pennies. **How much are all the coins worth?** *10¢.* Hide 1 penny under your hand. **How many cents are hidden?** *1¢.* **How many cents can you see?** *9¢.*

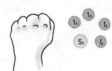

Continue in the same way, hiding a different number of pennies each time. (Always leave the nickel visible.)

Activity: Play Addition War (1-5)

Today, you'll practice the addition facts you've learned so far with a card game called Addition War. Play two rounds of Addition War (1-5). Allow your child to use the ten-frame as needed.

Addition War (1-5)

Materials: Aces, 2s, 3s, 4s, and 5s from two decks of cards (40 cards total)

Object of the Game: Win the most cards.

Shuffle the cards together and deal out all the cards into 2 face-down piles.

To play, flip over the top 2 cards in your pile. Find the sum of the 2 cards. For example, if you flip over a 3 and a 2, say, "3 plus 2 equals 5." Then, the other player turns over two cards and announces their sum. Whoever's sum is greater wins all 4 cards. If the sums are equal, play again. The player whose sum is greater wins all 8 cards.

Play until both players use up all the cards they were dealt. The player with more cards wins the game.

This game informally assesses how well your child knows the addition facts to 10. See the Unit 2 Checkpoint for more information on how to assess your child's progress.

Workbook: Practice Addition Facts and Review

Have your child complete workbook pages 6.4A and 6.4B.

Lesson 6.5
Enrichment and Review (Optional)

	Purpose	Materials
Warm-up	• Review counting • Review memory work • Review your child's favorite or most challenging activities from Week 6	• Varies, depending on the activities you choose
Picture Book	• See totals split into parts in multiple ways	• *Math Fables: Lessons That Count,* written by Greg Tang and illustrated by Heather Cahoon
Enrichment Activity	• Practice the combinations that make 10 in a kinesthetic way	• 10 plastic cups or empty water bottles • Small ball

Warm-up: Counting, Memory Work, and Review

- Have your child count to 50 by 1s and to 40 by 2s.

- Quiz your child on the memory work through Week 6. See page 499 for the full list.

- If you have time, repeat one or two of the activities from this week's lessons. Choose activities your child especially enjoyed or found challenging.

Math Picture Book: *Math Fables: Lessons That Count*

Read *Math Fables: Lessons That Count,* written by Greg Tang and illustrated by Heather Cahoon. As you read, discuss how the illustrations and text match. Point out how many different ways there are to split each group into parts.

Enrichment Activity: Make 10 Bowling

Set up 10 plastic cups or empty water bottles in a triangle on a hard surface, as in a bowling alley. Have your child stand about 10 feet away and roll a ball at the cups. After each roll, tell him how many are still standing. Have him use that information to figure out how many cups he knocked down. For example: *There are 2 cups still standing. 2 and 8 make 10, so I must have knocked down 8 cups.*

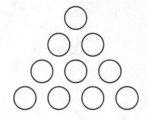

Week 6 Answer Key

6.1A

Complete the equations to match the ten-frames.

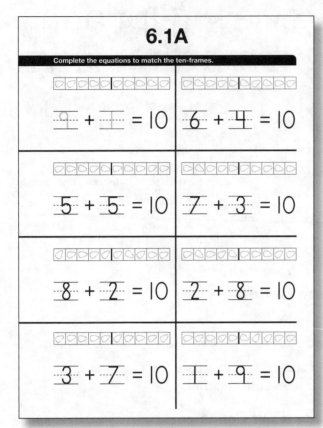

$9 + 1 = 10$ $6 + 4 = 10$

$5 + 5 = 10$ $7 + 3 = 10$

$8 + 2 = 10$ $2 + 8 = 10$

$3 + 7 = 10$ $1 + 9 = 10$

6.1B

Color the numbers you say when you count by 2s.

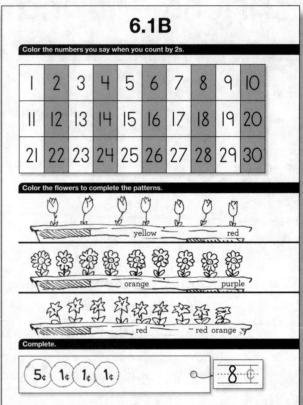

Color the flowers to complete the patterns.

yellow   red

orange   purple

red   red orange

Complete.

5¢ 1¢ 1¢ 1¢   8 ¢

6.2A

Complete. Use the ten-frame at the top to help.

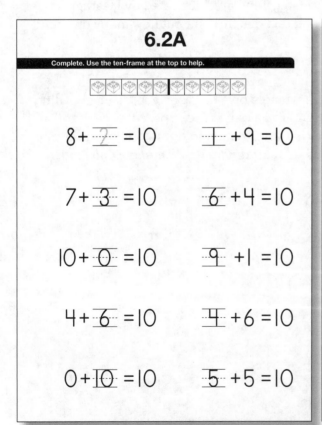

$8 + 2 = 10$ $1 + 9 = 10$

$7 + 3 = 10$ $6 + 4 = 10$

$10 + 0 = 10$ $9 + 1 = 10$

$4 + 6 = 10$ $4 + 6 = 10$

$0 + 10 = 10$ $5 + 5 = 10$

6.2B

Complete.

$6 + 4 = 10$ $1 + 8 = 9$
$5 + 5 = 10$ $5 + 1 = 6$
$4 + 2 = 6$ $7 + 3 = 10$

Fill the outline with pattern blocks. Write how many blocks you use.

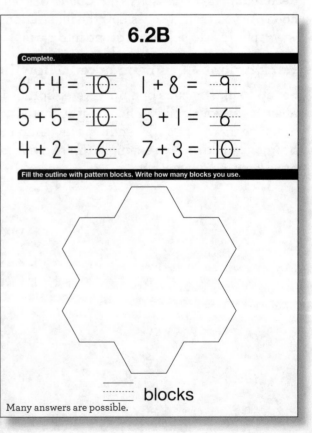

_____ blocks

Many answers are possible.

Week 6 Answer Key

6.3A

Complete.

$6 + 4 = \underline{10}$ $1 + 8 = \underline{9}$

$5 + 5 = \underline{10}$ $5 + 1 = \underline{6}$

$4 + 2 = \underline{6}$ $7 + 3 = \underline{10}$

Color the addition facts that equal the number in the star.

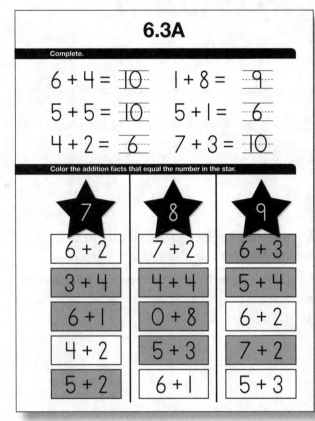

6.3B

Count by 2s to continue the pattern.

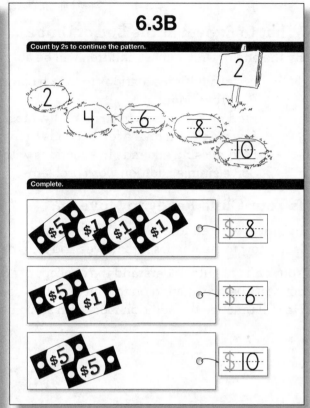

Complete.

6.4A

Match.

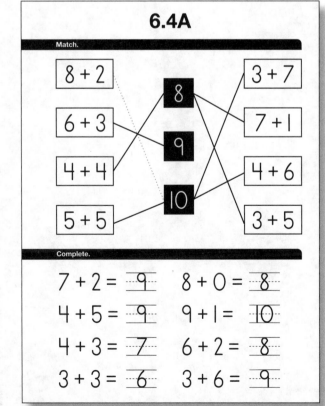

Complete.

$7 + 2 = \underline{9}$ $8 + 0 = \underline{8}$

$4 + 5 = \underline{9}$ $9 + 1 = \underline{10}$

$4 + 3 = \underline{7}$ $6 + 2 = \underline{8}$

$3 + 3 = \underline{6}$ $3 + 6 = \underline{9}$

6.4B

Connect the numbers in order from 1 to 10.

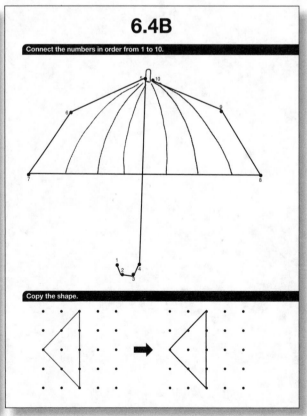

Copy the shape.

Unit 2 Checkpoint

What to Expect at the End of Unit 2

By the end of Unit 2, most children will be able to:

- Write addition equations to match counters, real-life situations, and numbers on the Part-Total Mat.
- Find most sums up to 10 mentally. Most children will know the +1 and +2 facts well. Many will still take a few seconds to figure out the +3 and +4 facts.
- Find missing addends in equations with a sum of 10.
- Solve simple addition word problems.

Is Your Child Ready to Move on?

In Unit 3, your child will learn to identify, describe, and categorize basic shapes. He will also learn how to cut shapes into halves and fourths and recognize these fractional parts.

Your child should understand the concept of addition and be able to represent equations with counters before moving on to Unit 3, but he does not need to fully master the addition facts. He will practice the addition facts with sums up to 10 throughout Unit 3.

Unit 3
Shapes

Overview

Your child will shift her focus from numbers to shapes as she learns to identify, sort, describe, and construct circles, triangles, rectangles, and squares. She will also learn to identify halves and fourths, draw lines of symmetry, and match congruent shapes.

Throughout the unit, your child will continue to practice the addition facts she learned in Unit 2. Alternating arithmetic units with topics like shape or measurement gives your child time to become more fluent with the math facts without focusing on them so intensely.

Week 7	Shapes
Week 8	Equal Parts and Congruent Shapes

What Your Child Will Learn

In this unit your child will learn to:

- identify, describe, and categorize circles, triangles, rectangles, and squares
- divide shapes into halves and fourths
- find lines of symmetry in shapes
- recognize pairs of congruent shapes

Recommended Math Picture Books (Optional)

These picture books are scheduled in the optional Enrichment and Review lessons at the end of each week.

- *The Greedy Triangle*, written by Marilyn Burns and illustrated by Gordon Silveria. Scholastic Paperbacks, 2008.
- *Captain Invincible and the Space Shapes*, written by Stuart J. Murphy and illustrated by Rémy Simard. HarperCollins, 2001.

Week 7
Shapes

Overview

Your child will learn to identify circles, triangles, rectangles, and squares. She'll sort the shapes into categories and construct them from a variety of materials.

Lesson 7.1	Circles
Lesson 7.2	Triangles
Lesson 7.3	Rectangles
Lesson 7.4	Squares
Lesson 7.5	Enrichment and Review (Optional)

Teaching Math with Confidence: Individual Shapes vs. Categories

Your child has created mental categories for objects ever since she was a baby. As she learned to tell the difference between a dog and cat, or between a bulldozer and an excavator, she developed mental categories for each type of object. This week, you'll teach your child to extend this skill to shapes.

In each lesson this week, you and your child will sort a set of Shape Cards into categories. (You'll find the Shape Cards on Blackline Master 5 on page 535.) Sorting the cards helps your child understand that names like square, triangle, rectangle, and circle describe entire categories of shapes, not just individual forms.

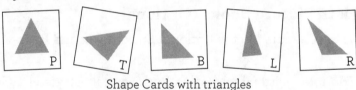

Shape Cards with triangles

By identifying similarities and differences within each category, your child will learn to focus on the most important attributes of each shape and also develop her critical thinking skills.

Extra Materials Needed for Week 4

- Small toy
- Ruler
- Scissors
- For optional Enrichment and Review Lesson:
    - *The Greedy Triangle*, written by Marilyn Burns and illustrated by Gordon Silveria
    - Toothpicks, craft sticks, or narrow strips of paper

You also need Blackline Master 5 (Shape Cards) this week. Cut them apart on the dotted lines and store them in a zip-top bag or envelope so you're ready for Lesson 7.1.

Lesson 7.1
Circles

	Purpose	Materials
Warm-up	• Count to 50 by 2s • Practice memory work • Review the meaning of *sum* and *addend*	• 100 Chart (Blackline Master 3) • Small toy • Coins • Counters
Activities	• Understand shapes can be sorted into categories • Identify circles • Identify curved and straight lines	• Paper • Shape Cards (Blackline Master 5), cut apart on the dotted lines • Ruler
Workbook	• Identify circles • Draw curved and straight lines	• Workbook pages 7.1A and 7.1B

Warm-up: Counting, Memory Work, and Review

- Have your child count by 2s to 50. Have her make a small toy jump on each number on the 100 Chart as she says it.

- Show your child a penny and a nickel, and have her tell the name and value of each coin.

- Write 3 + 4 = 7 on a piece of paper. Review addition equation vocabulary with the following questions:

  × **Which number is the sum?** *7.*
  × **Which numbers are the addends?** *3 and 4.*
  × Point to the + sign. **What is this sign called?** *The plus sign.*
  × Point to the = sign. **What is this sign called?** *The equals sign.*

$$3 + 4 = 7$$

Activity: Play Guess My Category with Circles

You will learn about shapes in this new unit. Spread the Shape Cards (Blackline Master 5, cut apart on the dotted lines) on the table. **Do you know the names of any of these shapes?** *Answers will vary.*

Let's play a game called Guess My Category. I will choose a category. Some of the shapes belong to my category, and some don't. Write "Yes" at the top of one piece of paper and "No" at the top of another piece.

Have your child choose a Shape Card. If it is a circle, place it on the "Yes" paper. If it is not a circle, place it on the "No" paper.

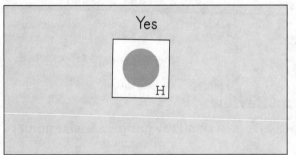
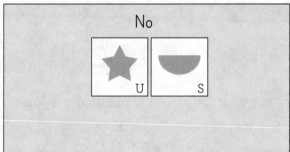

Continue until she thinks she knows the category. If she guesses correctly, have her sort the remaining cards onto the papers. If she doesn't guess correctly, have her keep choosing cards until they are all sorted.

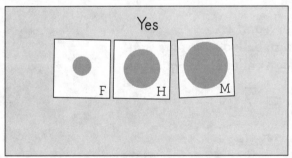
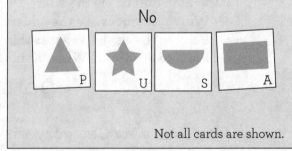

Not all cards are shown.

Point to the "Yes" paper. **These shapes are called circles. What do all the circles have in common?** *Sample answer: They are all round.* **What's different about them?** *Sample answer: They have different sizes.*

Circles are round all the way around, like a wheel. Have your child trace each circle with her finger.

The mathematical definition of a circle is a two-dimensional shape consisting of points an equal distance from its center. This is too abstract for first graders to understand, so instead this lesson emphasizes circles' overall look.

 Save the Yes/No sorting mats.

Activity: Draw Curved and Straight Lines

Circles are made from curved lines. Draw a few curved lines. **These are curved lines. When I draw a curved line, my pencil goes one way and then another.** Have your child trace each line with her finger to feel how the line changes direction.

Then, have your child draw several of her own curved lines on a piece of paper.

We can also draw straight lines. It's hard to draw straight lines freehand, so I'll use a ruler. Demonstrate how to draw several straight lines with a ruler. **When I draw a straight line, my pencil always moves in the same direction.** Have your child trace each line with her finger.

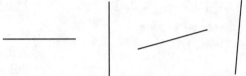

Have your child draw several straight lines with a ruler. Show her how to hold the ruler with her non-dominant hand and to run her pencil along the edge of the ruler so it just touches the edge.

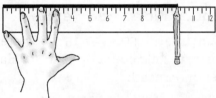

First graders often find rulers both fascinating and frustrating. If your child has trouble, hold the ruler yourself so she can focus on sliding her pencil along the edge. Keep the activity fun and low-stress, and don't worry if your child struggles to draw straight lines.

Workbook: Identify Circles, Curved Lines, and Straight Lines and Review

Have your child complete workbook pages 7.1A and 7.1B. At the bottom of 7.1A, your child can draw the straight lines freehand or use a ruler.

Lesson 7.2
Triangles

	Purpose	Materials
Warm-up	• Count by 5s to 50 • Practice memory work • Review +3 and +4 addition facts	• 100 Chart (Blackline Master 3) • Counters • Addition Climb to the Top game board (on Workbook page 5.1A) • 2 decks of playing cards
Activities	• Understand what *side* and *angle* mean • Learn triangles have 3 sides • Identify and create triangles	• Shape Cards • Yes/No Sorting mats (from Lesson 7.1) • Paper • Scissors • Ruler
Workbook	• Identify triangles • Draw triangles	• Workbook pages 7.2A and 7.2B

Warm-up: Counting, Memory Work, and Review

- Demonstrate how to count by 5s to 50: 5, 10, 15... Cover each number on the 100 Chart as you say it. Then, have your child count by 5s to 50. Have him remove each counter after he says the number underneath it.

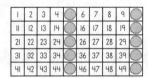

- Have your child say the days of the week. **How many days are in a week?** *7.*

- Play Addition Climb to the Top. See Lesson 5.1 (page 81) for directions.

Activity: Play Guess My Category with Triangles

Yesterday you learned about circles. Spread the Shape Cards (Blackline Master 5, cut apart on the dotted lines) on the table, as well as the sorting mats you made in Lesson 7.1. **Which ones are circles?** *Child points to cards with circles.*

Today, you'll learn about a different category of shapes. Let's play Guess My Category again and see if you can figure out my new category. Have your child choose a Shape Card. If it is a triangle, place it on the "Yes" paper. If it is not a triangle, place it on the "No" paper.

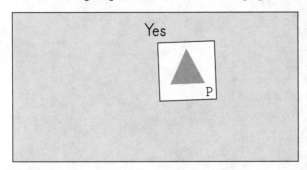
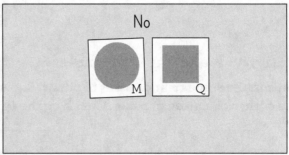

Continue until he thinks he knows the category. If he guesses correctly, have him sort the remaining shapes onto the paper. If he doesn't guess correctly, have him keep choosing cards until they are all sorted.

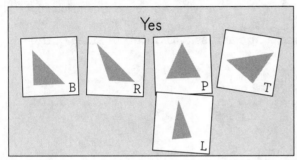
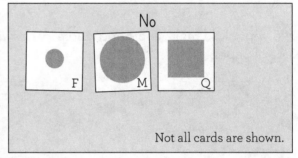

Point to the "Yes" paper. **These shapes are called triangles. What do these shapes have in common?** *Sample answer: All the triangles are pointy and have three sides.* **What's different about them?** *Sample answer: Some of the triangles look squashed, and some of them don't.*

Triangles have 3 sides and 3 angles. We call the outside edges of a shape its sides. Use your finger to trace the sides of one of the triangles. Count each side as you trace it: 1, 2, 3.

The sides meet to form angles. Point to one of the triangle's angles. **Triangles also have 3 angles.** Point out the triangle's 3 angles.

Have your child identify the 3 sides and 3 angles on the other triangle Shape Cards.

Children often have trouble counting sides, because they lose track of which sides they have already counted. To prevent this, have your child place his finger on one angle as a starting point. Have him trace his other finger around the triangle, count each side as he traces it, and stop when he reaches his starting place.

Look together at the shapes on the "No" paper, and discuss why a few of the shapes are not triangles. For example: **This shape is pointy, but it has 4 sides. So, it's not a triangle.**

Activity: Make Paper Triangles

Let's make some triangles out of paper. Show your child how to draw a straight line across the corner of a piece of paper. Cut along the line to make a triangle.

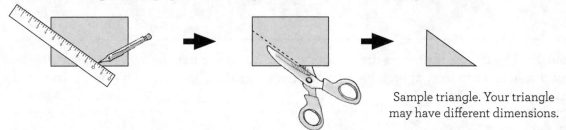

Sample triangle. Your triangle may have different dimensions.

Help your child make another triangle by drawing a line across two different sides of the piece of paper.

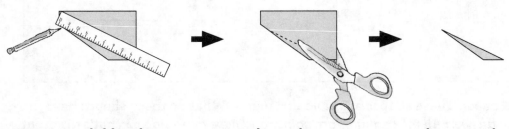

Have your child make 3-5 more triangles in this way. Encourage him to make a variety of triangles. For example, he might make some large and some small, or some that include the corner of the paper and some that don't. Use more paper as needed.

Help as needed with drawing the lines and cutting out the triangles.

Spread the paper triangles on the table. Discuss the similarities and differences between the shapes, but emphasize they all are triangles. For example: **Some of your shapes are very big, and some are very small. But all of them have 3 sides and 3 angles, so they're all triangles!**

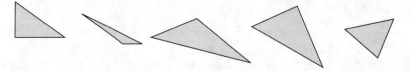

See the Week 7 **Teaching Math with Confidence** for more details on how children learn to perceive shapes as part of a category rather than individual figures.

Workbook: Identify and Draw Triangles and Review

Have your child complete workbook pages 7.2A and 7.2B. At the bottom of 7.2A, your child can draw the straight lines freehand or use a ruler.

Lesson 7.3
Rectangles

	Purpose	Materials
Warm-up	• Count by 5s to 50 • Practice memory work • Review addition facts	• 100 Chart (Blackline Master 3) • Counters • 2 decks of playing cards
Activities	• Learn rectangles have 4 sides and 4 right angles • Create and identify rectangles	• Shape Cards • Yes/No Sorting mats (from Lesson 7.1) • Paper • Scissors
Workbook	• Identify rectangles • Build rectangles with pattern blocks	• Workbook pages 7.3A and 7.3B • Pattern blocks

Warm-up: Counting, Memory Work, and Review

- With your child looking away, place counters on the 100 Chart so that the numbers you say when you count by 5s to 50 are covered.

  Have your child count by 5s to 50. Have her remove each counter after she says the number underneath it.

- **Raise your left hand. Raise your right hand.**

- Play Addition War with the aces, 2s, 3s, 4s, and 5s from two decks of cards. See Lesson 6.4 (page 100) for directions.

Activity: Play Guess My Category with Rectangles

In the last lesson, you learned about triangles. Spread the Shape Cards and Yes/No sorting mats on the table. **Which ones are triangles?** *Child points to cards with triangles.*

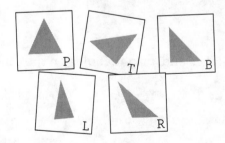

Today, you'll learn about a different category of shapes. Let's play Guess My Category again and see if you can figure out my new category. Have your child choose a Shape Card. If it is a rectangle, place it on the "Yes" paper. If it is not a rectangle, place it on the "No" paper.

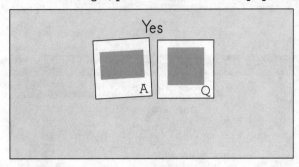

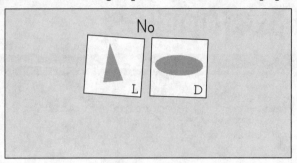

Squares are a special type of rectangle, so cards with squares go on the "Yes" paper. You will explore this idea more in Lesson 7.4.

Continue until she thinks she knows the category. If she guesses correctly, have her sort the remaining shapes onto the paper. If she doesn't guess correctly, have her keep choosing cards until they are all sorted.

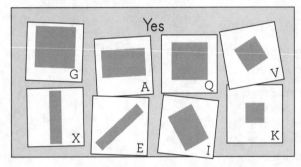

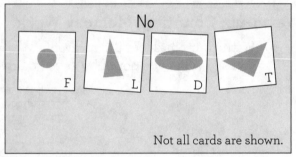

Not all cards are shown.

Point to the "Yes" paper. **We call shapes like these rectangles. What do all the rectangles have in common?** *Sample answer: They all have 4 sides. They all have corners like a piece of paper.* **What's different about them?** *Sample answer: They're different sizes and shapes. Some are long and skinny, and some aren't.*

How many sides does each rectangle have? *4.* **How many angles does each rectangle have?** *4.*

Rectangles have 4 sides. Rectangles also have angles that look like the corners on a piece of paper. These are called right angles. Tear off the corner of a piece of paper. Place the corner inside each of the angles of one of the rectangle Shape Cards to demonstrate.

Have your child identify the 4 sides and 4 right angles on the other rectangle Shape Cards.

If your child is confused by Shape Cards E and V, tilt the cards so your child can see their right angles more easily.

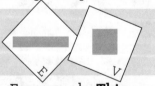

Discuss why a few of the shapes on the "No" paper are not rectangles. For example: **This shape has only 2 right angles, so it's not a rectangle.**

Your child does not need to memorize the term *right angle*. When children hear a new term used in context, they usually learn its meaning quickly. But that doesn't mean that they'll be able to use that same word or phrase correctly while speaking. Use the correct geometry terms yourself, but it's fine if your child calls right angles "corners like a piece of paper."

Activity: Make Paper Rectangles

Show your child a piece of paper. **What shape is the piece of paper?** *A rectangle!*

Let's make some more paper rectangles. Fold a piece of paper as shown. (Make sure to match the top and bottom edges so you end up with right angles.) Cut along the fold line.

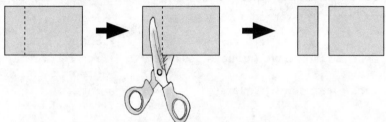

When I cut the paper, I get two rectangles! I can cut these rectangles up to make even more rectangles. Take the smaller rectangle and fold it as shown.

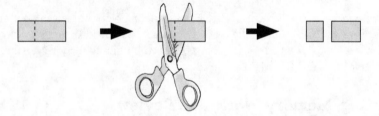

Have your child make 3-5 more rectangles in this way. Use more paper as needed.

Help as needed with folding the paper and cutting on the fold lines.

Spread the paper rectangles on the table. Discuss the similarities and differences between the shapes, but emphasize they all are rectangles. For example: **Some of your shapes are very big, and some are very small. But all of them have 4 sides and 4 right angles, so they're all rectangles!**

Workbook: Identify and Build Rectangles and Review

Have your child complete workbook pages 7.3A and 7.3B. On the bottom of 7.3A, have your child use square pattern blocks to fill in the outlines. For extra challenge, ask her to predict how many blocks she will need for each outline before she puts the blocks on the paper.

Lesson 7.4
Squares

	Purpose	Materials
Warm-up	• Count up to 50 objects by 5s • Practice memory work • Review writing equations to solve addition word problems	• Counters • Play money
Activities	• Learn squares have 4 equal sides and 4 right angles • Create and identify squares	• Shape Cards • Yes/No sorting mats (from Lesson 7.1) • Paper • Scissors
Workbook	• Identify squares • Build squares with pattern blocks	• Workbook pages 7.4A and 7.4B • Pattern blocks

In this lesson, you'll introduce the challenging idea that an item can belong to two categories at the same time. Some first graders are not developmentally ready to understand this idea, and it's okay if the concept goes right over your child's head. If that's the case, focus on teaching him to recognize squares and to understand they have four equal sides and four right angles.

Warm-up: Counting, Memory Work, and Review

- Place 40-50 counters on the table. **About how many counters do you think there are?** *Answers will vary.* With your child, organize the counters into groups of 5. Then, help your child count by 5s to find the actual number of counters. (Demonstrate how to add on the final few counters as needed.)

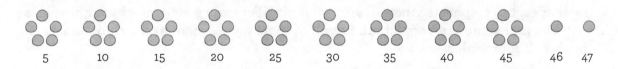

| 5 | 10 | 15 | 20 | 25 | 30 | 35 | 40 | 45 | 46 | 47 |

- Have your child say the days of the week. **How many days are in a week?** *7.*

- Ask your child the following money word problems. Act out each problem with play money, then ask your child to write and solve an equation to match.

    × **Let's pretend you had $3. Then, you earned $2 more. How much money would you have then?** *(3+2=5)*
    × **Let's pretend you had $6. Then, you earned $4 more. How much money would you have then?** *(6+4=10)*
    × **Let's pretend you had $7. Then, you earned $2 more. How much money would you have then?** *(7+2=9)*

Activity: Play Guess My Category with Squares

Yesterday you learned about rectangles. Today, you'll learn about a special shape that belongs to two categories at once.

Before we look at the shapes, let's talk about some more familiar categories. Are you an adult or a child? *A child.* **Are you a boy or a girl?** *Answers will vary.*

If your child's a girl: **So, are you a child or a girl?** *Both.*

If your child's a boy: **So, are you a child or a boy?** *Both.*

You belong to two categories at once, just like the shapes you're going to learn about today.

Spread the Shape Cards and Yes/No sorting mats on the table. **Which ones are rectangles?** *Child points to the cards with rectangles.*

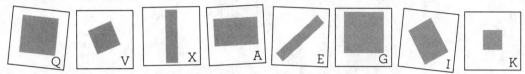

Rectangles have 4 sides and 4 right angles. Have your child identify the 4 sides and 4 right angles on one of the rectangle Shape Cards.

Let's play Guess My Category again. We'll only use the rectangle cards today. Put the rest of the Shape Cards away.

Have your child choose one of the rectangle Shape Cards. If it is a square, place it on the "Yes" paper. If it is not a square, place it on the "No" paper. Continue until he thinks he knows the category. If he guesses correctly, have him sort the remaining shapes onto the paper. If he doesn't guess correctly, have him keep choosing cards until they are all sorted.

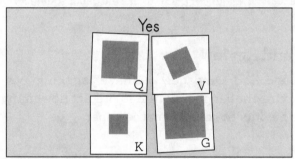
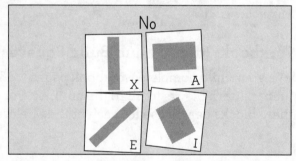

Point to the "Yes" paper. **All these shapes are rectangles, but they also have another name. We call special rectangles like these squares. Squares have 4 sides and 4 right angles, and their sides all have the same length.** Have your child trace around the sides of each square with his finger so he can feel that the sides are equal.

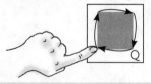

If your child is confused by Shape Card V, tilt the card so that it looks more like the other squares.

Activity: Make Paper Squares

Later this year, you'll learn how to measure length with a ruler. Today, I'll show you how to make a square with 4 equal sides without a ruler.

Place a piece of paper on the table (oriented horizontally as shown). Fold the paper's left edge up so that it aligns with the top edge.

Draw a line as shown.

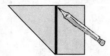

Unfold the paper and cut along the line.

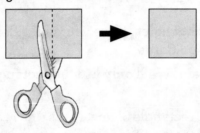

Allow your child to make his own paper square if he'd like.

If you know how to fold origami or cut out paper snowflakes, show your child how to use the paper square for one of these crafts.

Workbook: Identify and Build Squares and Review

Have your child complete workbook pages 7.4A and 7.4B. On page 7.4A, have your child use square pattern blocks to fill in the outlines. For extra challenge, ask him to predict how many square blocks he will use for each outline before he puts the blocks on the paper.

Lesson 7.5
Enrichment and Review (Optional)

	Purpose	Materials
Warm-up	• Review counting • Review memory work • Review your child's favorite or most challenging activities from Week 7	• Varies, depending on the activities you choose
Picture Book	• Introduce the names of shapes with different numbers of sides	• *The Greedy Triangle*, written by Marilyn Burns and illustrated by Gordon Silveria
Enrichment Activity	• Make shapes with different numbers of sides	• Toothpicks, craft sticks, or narrow strips of paper

Warm-up: Counting, Memory Work, and Review

- Have your child count to 50 by 1s, 2s, or 5s. (Choose whichever counting sequence your child needs to practice the most.)

- Quiz your child on the memory work through Week 6. See page 499 for the full list.

- If you have time, repeat one or two of the activities from this week's lessons. Choose activities your child especially enjoyed or found challenging.

Math Picture Book: *The Greedy Triangle*

Read *The Greedy Triangle*, written by Marilyn Burns and illustrated by Gordon Silveria.

Enrichment Activity: Make Shapes with Different Numbers of Sides

Have your child use toothpicks, craft sticks, or narrow strips of paper to make the following shapes. Tell her the name of each shape as she makes it.

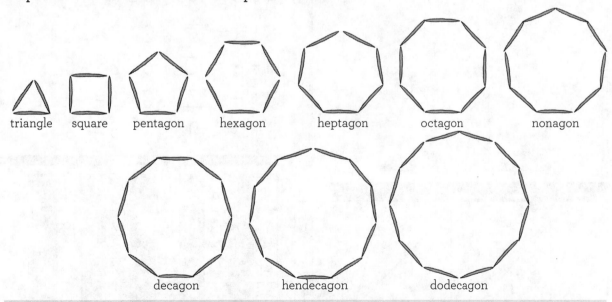

Your child does not need to memorize the names of all these shapes. If you are studying ancient history this year, she may be interested to know these names come from ancient Greek and Latin.

Week 7 Answer Key

7.1A

Color the circles. X the shapes that are not circles.

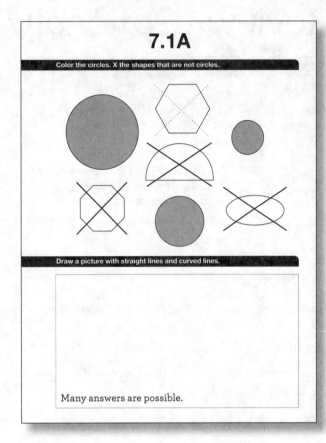

Draw a picture with straight lines and curved lines.

Many answers are possible.

7.1B

Complete.

$6 + 0 = \underline{6}$ $1 + 8 = \underline{9}$

$3 + 2 = \underline{5}$ $5 + 4 = \underline{9}$

$4 + 6 = \underline{10}$ $2 + 7 = \underline{9}$

$4 + 2 = \underline{6}$ $5 + 1 = \underline{6}$

$1 + 6 = \underline{7}$ $7 + 0 = \underline{7}$

Write the number that comes before and after.

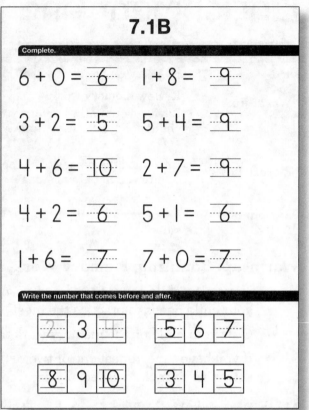

2	3	4

5	6	7

8	9	10

3	4	5

7.2A

Color the triangles. X the shapes that are not triangles.

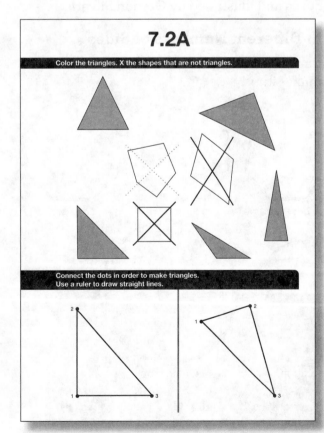

**Connect the dots in order to make triangles.
Use a ruler to draw straight lines.**

7.2B

Complete.

$5 + 4 = \underline{9}$ $9 + 1 = \underline{10}$

$3 + 3 = \underline{6}$ $2 + 7 = \underline{9}$

$4 + 6 = \underline{10}$ $6 + 2 = \underline{8}$

$3 + 4 = \underline{7}$ $3 + 6 = \underline{9}$

$8 + 1 = \underline{9}$ $3 + 5 = \underline{8}$

Color the numbers you say when you count by 2s.

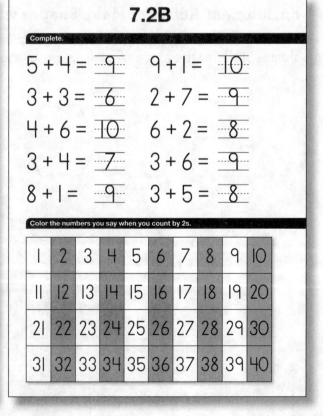

1	2	3	4	5	6	7	8	9	10
11	12	13	14	15	16	17	18	19	20
21	22	23	24	25	26	27	28	29	30
31	32	33	34	35	36	37	38	39	40

Week 7 Answer Key

7.3A

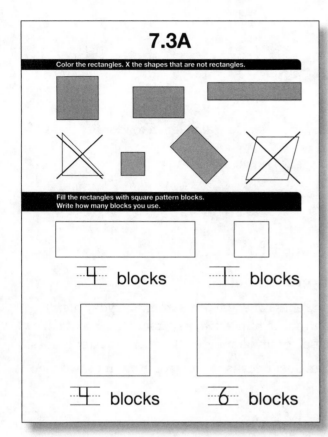

Color the rectangles. X the shapes that are not rectangles.

Fill the rectangles with square pattern blocks. Write how many blocks you use.

4 blocks   1 blocks

4 blocks   6 blocks

7.3B

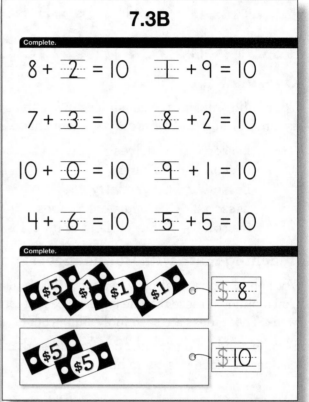

Complete.

$8 + 2 = 10$ $1 + 9 = 10$

$7 + 3 = 10$ $8 + 2 = 10$

$10 + 0 = 10$ $9 + 1 = 10$

$4 + 6 = 10$ $5 + 5 = 10$

Complete.

$8

$10

7.4A

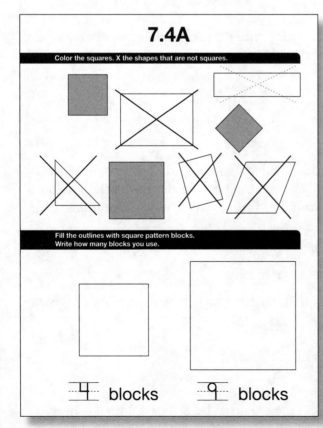

Color the squares. X the shapes that are not squares.

Fill the outlines with square pattern blocks. Write how many blocks you use.

4 blocks   9 blocks

7.4B

Complete.

$4 + 4 = 8$ $2 + 8 = 10$
$7 + 3 = 10$ $6 + 0 = 6$
$4 + 6 = 10$ $5 + 5 = 10$
$1 + 5 = 6$ $2 + 3 = 5$
$8 + 1 = 9$ $2 + 5 = 7$

Color the numbers you say when you count by 5s.

1	2	3	4	5	6	7	8	9	10
11	12	13	14	15	16	17	18	19	20
21	22	23	24	25	26	27	28	29	30
31	32	33	34	35	36	37	38	39	40
41	42	43	44	45	46	47	48	49	50

Week 8
Equal Parts and Congruent Shapes

Overview

Your child will learn to cut shapes into halves and fourths. He'll also learn to identify lines of symmetry and find pairs of congruent shapes.

Lesson 8.1   Halves
Lesson 8.2   Fourths
Lesson 8.3   Symmetry
Lesson 8.4   Congruent Shapes
Lesson 8.5   Enrichment and Review (Optional)

Teaching Math with Confidence: Fraction Foundations

Your child probably already has some informal awareness of equal parts from everyday life. You'll build on these real-life experiences as you introduce him to two key fraction concepts this week. These ideas are seemingly simple but essential for understanding fractions in later grades.

First, *fractional parts must be equal* to each other. Just because an object is cut into two pieces doesn't mean it is cut in half.

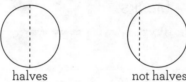

halves   not halves

Second, *the number of equal parts must match the fractional piece described*. For halves, there must be 2 equal parts. For fourths, there must be 4 equal parts.

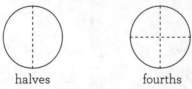

halves   fourths

Both of these concepts may feel obvious, but children need lots of hands-on experiences to fully grasp them. You'll use familiar contexts and spoken fraction words this week to help your child begin this process. In second grade, your child will learn to write fractions to represent these parts.

Extra Materials Needed for Week 8

- Small toy
- Food items that can easily be broken or torn in half or fourths, such as a banana, cookie, or slice of bread
- Scissors
- Round object for tracing (such as a cup or small bowl)
- 5 small plastic zip-top bags
- For optional Enrichment Cand Review Lesson:
    × *Captain Invincible and the Space Shapes*, written by Stuart J. Murphy and illustrated by Rémy Simard

Lesson 8.1
Halves

	Purpose	Materials
Warm-up	• Count to 50 by 5s • Practice memory work • Review finding combinations that make 10	• 100 Chart (Blackline Master 3) • Small toy • Playing cards
Activities	• Learn halves must be equal to each other • Cut shapes into halves	• Food item that can easily be broken or torn in half, such as a banana, cookie, or slice of bread • Index cards • Scissors
Workbook	• Recognize halves • Split shapes into halves	• Workbook pages 8.1A and 8.1B • Pattern blocks, optional

Warm-up: Counting, Memory Work, and Review

- Have your child count by 5s to 50. Have her make a small toy jump on each number on the 100 Chart as she says it.

- **How many sides does a triangle have?** *3.* **A square?** *4.* **A rectangle?** *4.*

- Have your child play a round of Make 10 Pyramid. See Lesson 3.4 (page 55) for directions.

Activity: Introduce Halves

Today, you'll learn about halves. Show your child a food item that can easily be cut or broken in half, like a banana, cookie, or slice of bread. **Let's pretend we want to share this food. Can you split it so we both get the same amount?** *Child breaks food item in half.*

You split the food into 2 halves. Each of us gets 1 half. When we cut something in half, we get 2 parts that are equal to each other.

See the Week 8 **Teaching Math with Confidence** for more on teaching fraction foundations.

Activity: Cut Index Cards into Halves

Give your child an index card and scissors. **Let's pretend this index card is a brownie, and we want to share it equally. Try to cut it so we both get half of the brownie.** Have your child cut the card in half. Many ways are possible.

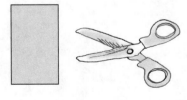

Compare the sizes of the two pieces and discuss whether they are equal. Emphasize that halves must always be equal to each other, even if your child's pieces didn't turn out exactly even.

Give your child two more index cards. **Can you cut each of these cards in half a different way?** If your child is stumped, demonstrate the following ways.

3 possible ways to cut the index card in half

There are many other possible ways to cut the index card in half. Accept your child's answer as long as the 2 pieces are equal to each other.

Cut an index card into 2 unequal pieces. **Did I cut the card in half? Why or why not?** *Sample answer: No, because the two parts aren't equal.*

Cut an index card into 4 equal pieces. **Did I cut the index card in half? Why or why not?** *Sample answer: No, because halves are 2 equal pieces, not 4.*

When we cut something into 4 equal pieces, the parts are called fourths. You'll learn more about fourths in the next lesson.

Workbook: Recognize Halves and Review

Have your child complete workbook pages 8.1A and 8.1B.

If you have time, have your child place pattern blocks on the outlines at the bottom of page 8.1A so that each outline is split into halves.

Lesson 8.2
Fourths

	Purpose	Materials
Warm-up	• Count nickels by 5s • Practice memory work • Review +3 and +4 addition facts	• Coins • Counters • Addition Climb to the Top game board (on Workbook page 5.1A) • 2 decks of playing cards
Activities	• Learn fourths must be equal to each other • Cut shapes into fourths	• Food item that can easily be broken or torn in fourths, such as a banana, cookie, or slice of bread • Index cards • Scissors
Workbook	• Recognize fourths • Split shapes into fourths	• Workbook pages 8.2A and 8.2B

Warm-up: Counting, Memory Work, and Review

- Place 9 nickels on the table. **Each nickel is worth 5¢. So, we can count the nickels by 5s to find out how much they are worth.** Have your child count by 5s to find the total value. **How many cents are the nickels worth?** *45¢.*

- **How many sides does a triangle have?** *3.* **A square?** *4.* **A rectangle?** *4.*

- Play Addition Climb to the Top. See Lesson 5.1 (page 81) for directions.

Activity: Introduce Fourths

In the last lesson, we cut food and index cards into halves. Today, we'll cut food and index cards into fourths.

Show your child a food item that can easily be cut or broken into pieces, like a banana, cookie, or slice of bread. **Let's pretend we wanted to split this food among four people.**

To help your child understand the context, name specific people. For example: **Let's pretend you, Grandpa, Aunt Louise, and I wanted to share the food.**

Can you split it into four equal parts? *Child breaks food item into four equal parts.*

You split the food into 4 fourths. When we cut something into fourths, we must get 4 parts that are equal.

Fourths are sometimes called quarters. This book uses fourths, because it makes it easier for children to remember fourths are cut into *four* pieces.

Activity: Cut Index Cards into Halves and Fourths

Let's pretend this index card is a brownie, and we want to share it equally with 4 people. Let's cut it into fourths so we get 4 equal pieces.

It's often easier to cut things into fourths if you cut them in half first. Have your child use scissors to cut the card in half. Then, have him cut each part in half again, for a total of 4 equal pieces.

Compare the sizes of the 4 pieces and discuss whether they are equal. Emphasize that fourths must always be equal, even if your child's pieces didn't turn out exactly even.

Give your child two more index cards. **Can you cut each of these cards into fourths in a different way?** Encourage him to first cut the card in half, and then cut each half into 2 equal pieces. If your child is stumped, demonstrate the following ways.

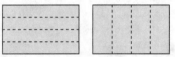

Your child can cut the index card into fourths in many ways. Accept your child's answer as long as the 4 pieces are equal.

Cut an index card into 4 unequal pieces. **Did I cut the index card into fourths? Why or why not?** *Sample answer: No, because the 4 parts aren't equal.*

Cut an index card into 3 equal pieces. Did I cut the index card into fourths? Why or why not? *Sample answer: No, because fourths are 4 equal pieces, not 3.*

Workbook: Recognize Fourths and Review

Have your child complete workbook pages 8.2A and 8.2B.

Lesson 8.3
Symmetry

	Purpose	Materials
Warm-up	• Count nickels by 5s • Practice memory work • Review pairs that make 10	• Coins • Playing cards
Activities	• Review the concept of symmetry • Find lines of symmetry in simple shapes	• Paper • Scissors • Round object for tracing (such as a cup or small bowl)
Workbook	• Draw lines of symmetry	• Workbook pages 8.3A and 8.3B

Warm-up: Counting, Memory Work, and Review

• Place 10 nickels on the table. Have your child count by 5s to find the total value. **How many cents are the nickels worth?** *50¢.*

Arrange the nickels in pairs. **How much are 2 nickels worth?** *10¢.* Demonstrate how to count the pairs of nickels by 10s: **10, 20, 30, 40, 50.**

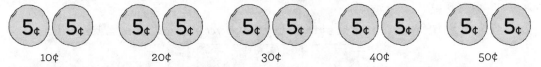

10¢   20¢   30¢   40¢   50¢

• **How many sides does a triangle have?** *3.* **A square?** *4.* **A rectangle?** *4.*

• Play one round of Make 10 Go Fish. See Lesson 3.3 (page 52) for directions.

Activity: Introduce Lines of Symmetry

In kindergarten, you learned about symmetric shapes. Do you remember what makes a shape symmetric? *Possible answers: The two sides line up with each other. The two sides are a mirror image of each other.*

Don't worry if your child doesn't remember what symmetry means (or if you didn't use the kindergarten program). You will revisit symmetry in the rest of the lesson.

Fold a piece of paper in half and then open it up again.

Shapes are symmetric if they have two halves that exactly mirror each other. Fold the paper along the original fold line so your child can see how the two halves match up with each other exactly.

Point to the fold line on the paper. **This line is called the line of symmetry. It splits the paper into two matching halves.**

line of symmetry

This piece of paper has another line of symmetry, too. Can you find another way to fold the paper so the two sides match each other exactly? Have your child experiment with folding the paper.

Watch what happens if I fold this piece of paper along the diagonal. Fold the piece of paper along the diagonal. **Do the two sides line up with each other?** *No.*

The two sides are equal, so each side is half of the paper. But the two sides don't line up, so this diagonal fold line is not a line of symmetry. Just because a line divides a shape in half doesn't mean it's a line of symmetry.

> Don't worry if the distinction between lines of symmetry and lines that divide a shape in half goes right over your child's head.

Activity: Find Lines of Symmetry in a Square and a Circle

Let's see how many different lines of symmetry you can find in a square. Cut a square out of paper (as in Lesson 7.4). Have your child try folding the paper in different ways to see if the two sides match up.

Squares have 4 different lines of symmetry. Give your child hints to help him find all 4.

Now let's see how many different lines of symmetry we can find in a circle. Have your child trace the bottom of a circular object (like a cup or bowl) on a piece of paper and cut it out (help as needed). Have her try folding the circle in different ways to see if the two sides match up.

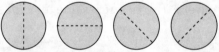

After she has found a few different lines of symmetry, ask: **How many different lines of symmetry do you think there are in a circle?** *Answers will vary.* **Every time you fold the circle in half, you always find a line of symmetry! There are too many to count. We say there are infinitely many lines of symmetry in a circle.**

> Children are often fascinated by the idea of infinity, but your child does not need to memorize this term.

 Save the paper rectangle, square, and circle for Lesson 8.4.

Workbook: Draw Lines of Symmetry and Review

Have your child complete workbook pages 8.3A and 8.3B. Your child only needs to draw one line of symmetry for each object, although multiple lines of symmetry are possible for some.

Lesson 8.4
Congruent Shapes

	Purpose	Materials
Warm-up	• Count to 50 by 10s • Practice memory work • Review missing addends	• Counters • 5 small plastic zip-top bags • Index card or small slip of paper
Activities	• Identify congruent shapes • Develop spatial skills by creating designs	• Paper rectangle, square, and circle from Lesson 8.3 • Scissors • Simplified Tangram (Blackline Master 6), cut apart on the lines
Workbook	• Match congruent shapes	• Workbook pages 8.4A and 8.4B

Warm-up: Counting, Memory Work, and Review

- Have your child count out 50 counters. After he counts each group of 10, place the 10 counters in a zip-top bag (so that you end up with 5 bags with 10 counters each). Demonstrate how to count the bags by 10s: **10, 20, 30, 40, 50.**

10   20   30   40   50

 Leave the counters in the zip-top bags. You will use them again in future lessons.

- **How many sides does a triangle have?** *3.* **A square?** *4.* **A rectangle?** *4.*

- Have your child use "X-ray vision" to identify the hidden number in the following equations. Secretly write each equation on a piece of paper and then hide the addend indicated. Allow your child to use the ten-frame as needed.

$$5 + \boxed{4} = 9 \qquad \boxed{6} + 0 = 6 \qquad 8 + \boxed{2} = 10$$

$$7 + \boxed{1} = 8 \qquad 3 + \boxed{4} = 7$$

Activity: Introduce Congruent Shapes

In the last lesson, you learned that lines of symmetry split shapes into two halves that mirror each other exactly. Show your child the paper rectangle, square, and circle you made in Lesson 8.3. Point to some of the lines of symmetry your child found.

Today, you'll learn a new word to describe shapes that are the same size and same shape as each other. Have your child cut the paper rectangle, square, and circle in half along one of the lines of symmetry.

Each half is the same size and shape as the other half. If two shapes are the same size and shape, we say they are *congruent.*

Activity: Explore Congruent Shapes with a Tangram Puzzle

Show your child the Simplified Tangram Puzzle (Blackline Master 6), cut into pieces. **These are pieces of a puzzle.** Have your child identify each shape as a triangle or rectangle.

Tangram puzzles originated in China and were brought to Europe in the early 1800s. This tangram puzzle is simpler than traditional tangrams to emphasize congruent shapes.

Congruent shapes have the same size and same shape. Can you find some pairs of congruent shapes in the puzzle pieces?

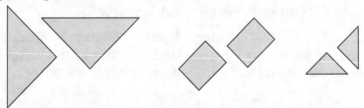

People have used puzzle pieces like these for hundreds of years to make pictures. Show your child the following ways to arrange the pieces into pictures. Give him time to make some pictures of his own, too.

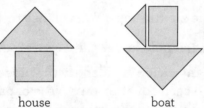

house   boat

For an extra challenge, have your child put all the pieces together to make the original large square.

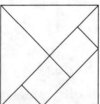

Workbook: Match Congruent Shapes and Review

Have your child complete workbook pages 8.4A and 8.4B.

Lesson 8.5
Enrichment and Review (Optional)

	Purpose	Materials
Warm-up	• Review counting • Review memory work • Review your child's favorite or most challenging activities from Week 8	• Varies, depending on the activities you choose
Picture Book	• Learn the names of 3-dimensional shapes	• *Captain Invincible and the Space Shapes*, written by Stuart J. Murphy and illustrated by Rémy Simard
Enrichment Activity	• Find and identify everyday 3-dimensional shapes	• None

Warm-up: Counting, Memory Work, and Review

- Have your child count to 50 by 1s, 2s, 5s, or 10s. (Choose whichever counting sequence your child needs to practice the most.)

- Quiz your child on the memory work through Week 8. See page 499 for the full list.

- If you have time, repeat one or two of the activities from this week's lessons. Choose activities your child especially enjoyed or found challenging.

Math Picture Book: *Captain Invincible and the Space Shapes*

Read *Captain Invincible and the Space Shapes*, written by Stuart J. Murphy and illustrated by Rémy Simard.

Enrichment Activity: Shape Scavenger Hunt

Explain to your child that solid, 3-dimensional shapes have special names, too. Show your child the pictures below and tell him the name of each shape.

sphere   cube   cylinder   cone

Have your child look for a real-life example of each solid shape around the house.

sphere   cube   cylinder   cone

Week 8 Answer Key

8.1A

Circle the sandwiches that are split in half.
X the sandwiches that are not split in half.

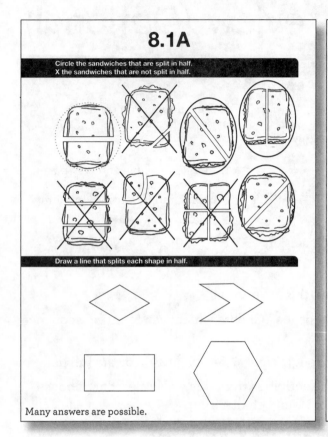

Draw a line that splits each shape in half.

Many answers are possible.

8.1B

Complete.

$4 + 4 = \underline{8}$ $6 + 2 = \underline{8}$

$6 + 3 = \underline{9}$ $5 + 5 = \underline{10}$

$6 + 4 = \underline{10}$ $2 + 2 = \underline{4}$

$1 + 4 = \underline{5}$ $4 + 3 = \underline{7}$

$3 + 3 = \underline{6}$ $2 + 8 = \underline{10}$

Draw a picture that has a square, circle, and triangle in it.

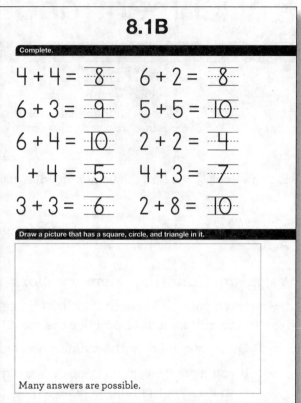

Many answers are possible.

8.2A

Circle the pizzas that are split into fourths.
X the pizzas that are not split into fourths.

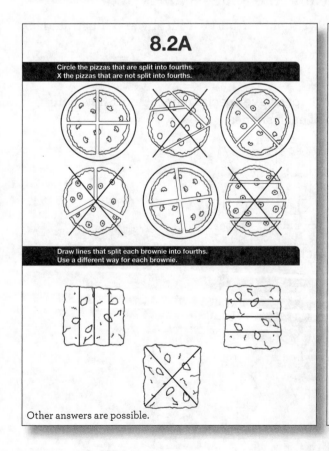

Draw lines that split each brownie into fourths.
Use a different way for each brownie.

Other answers are possible.

8.2B

Complete.

$4 + 1 = \underline{5}$ $1 + 9 = \underline{10}$

$5 + 4 = \underline{9}$ $2 + 7 = \underline{9}$

$2 + 5 = \underline{7}$ $1 + 7 = \underline{8}$

$6 + 3 = \underline{9}$ $5 + 5 = \underline{10}$

$2 + 1 = \underline{3}$ $3 + 5 = \underline{8}$

Match.

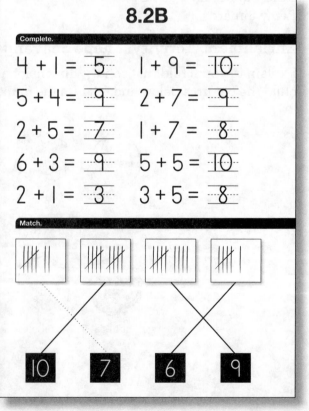

Week 8 Answer Key

8.3A

Draw a line of symmetry for each object.

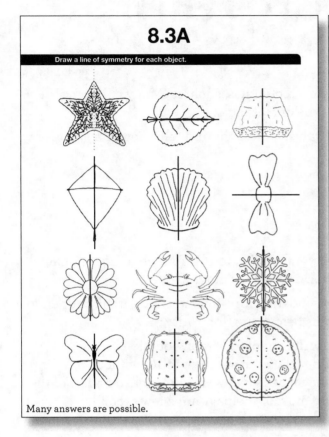

Many answers are possible.

8.3B

Complete.

1 + 1 = 2	0 + 2 = 2
2 + 2 = 4	2 + 4 = 6
3 + 3 = 6	4 + 6 = 10
4 + 4 = 8	3 + 5 = 8
5 + 5 = 10	2 + 8 = 10

X the shape that doesn't belong in each row.

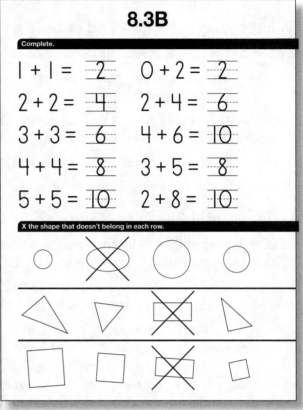

8.4A

Match the congruent shapes.

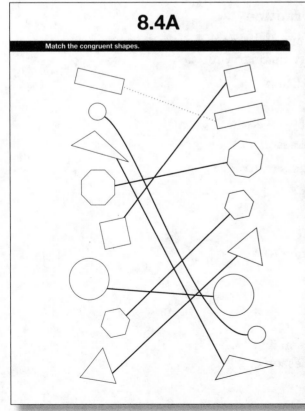

8.4B

Complete.

5 + 4 = 9	6 + 2 = 8
4 + 3 = 7	3 + 3 = 6
3 + 7 = 10	3 + 5 = 8
2 + 5 = 7	4 + 4 = 8
6 + 3 = 9	2 + 7 = 9

Complete.

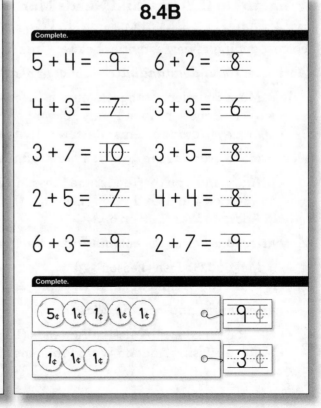

Unit 3 Checkpoint

What to Expect at the End of Unit 3

By the end of Unit 3, most children will be able to:

- Recognize and categorize circles, triangles, rectangles, squares. Many children will not quite understand how a square is a type of rectangle.

- Divide simple shapes into approximate halves or fourths and tell whether a shape is divided into halves or fourths.

- Find lines of symmetry in simple shapes.

- Tell whether two shapes are congruent.

Is Your Child Ready to Move on?

In Unit 4, your child will learn to subtract small numbers (up to 10). Your child does not need to have mastered all the shape vocabulary from Unit 3 before moving on.

However, since addition provides an essential foundation for learning subtraction, your child should have already mastered the following skills before starting Unit 4:

- Understand the concept of addition and write simple addition equations.
- Know the answers to most of the addition facts (with sums up to 10) without counting on fingers or counting one by one. It's fine if she is still working to master a few of the facts, but she should know the answers to most of them within a few seconds.
- Know the combinations that equal 10 without counting.
- Find missing addends in equations equal to 10.

What to Do If Your Child Needs More Practice

If your child is having trouble with any of the above skills, spend a few days practicing the corresponding review activities below before moving on to Unit 4.

Activities for understanding the concept of addition

- More Equations at the Restaurant (Lesson 4.1)
- Write Equations for a Penny Scavenger Hunt (Lesson 4.2)
- Money Word Problems (Review activity, Lesson 7.4)

Activities to practice the addition facts with sums to 10

- Add 1 and 2 on the Ten-Frame (Lesson 4.3)
- Addition Climb to the Top (Lesson 5.1)
- Addition War (Lesson 6.4)

Activities to practice the combinations that make 10

- Make 10 Go Fish (Lesson 3.3)
- Make 10 Pyramid Solitaire (Lesson 3.4)

Activities for finding missing addends

- X-Ray Vision with Missing Addends (Lesson 6.2)
- Solve Missing Addend Word Problems (Lesson 6.3)

Unit 4
Subtraction to 10

Overview

In Unit 4, your child will learn the subtraction facts to 10. He'll use the Part-Total Mat to understand the connection between addition and subtraction, and he'll learn to use related addition facts to solve subtraction problems.

Week 9	–1 and –2 Subtraction Facts
Week 10	–3 and –4 Subtraction Facts
Week 11	Subtraction Facts to 10

What Your Child Will Learn

In this unit your child will learn to:

- write subtraction equations with the – and = signs
- use related addition facts to solve subtraction problems
- write addition and subtraction fact families
- find answers to subtraction facts in which both numbers are 10 or less
- solve simple subtraction word problems

Recommended Math Picture Books (Optional)

These picture books are scheduled in the optional Enrichment and Review lessons at the end of each week.

- *Handa's Surprise,* by Eileen Browne. Candlewick Press, 1999.
- *Splash!,* by Ann Jonas. Greenwillow Books, 1995.
- *Applesauce Season,* written by Eden Ross Lipson and illustrated by Mordicai Gerstein. Roaring Brook Press, 2009.

Week 9
-1 and -2 Subtraction Facts

Overview

Your child will learn to write subtraction equations with the – and = symbols and begin to master the –1 and –2 facts. She'll use the Part-Total Mat to understand how subtraction and addition are connected, and she'll use missing addend equations to subtract from 10.

Lesson 9.1   Introduce Subtraction and –1 and –2 Facts
Lesson 9.2   Practice –1 and –2 Facts
Lesson 9.3   Subtract from 10
Lesson 9.4   Use Missing Addends to Subtract
Lesson 9.5   Enrichment and Review (Optional)

Teaching Math with Confidence: 2 Essential Subtraction Strategies

You'll teach your child two different subtraction strategies this week. First, you'll introduce subtraction and teach your child to take away counters on the ten-frame to solve the –1 and –2 facts.

The take-away subtraction strategy.

Thinking of subtraction as "taking away" works well for subtracting small numbers, but children find it difficult to imagine removing more than a few counters at a time. They need a different mental strategy to solve problems like 10 – 6 or 9 – 8, so you'll also teach your child how to use related addition facts to solve subtraction problems.

Understanding the connection between addition and subtraction can be challenging for first graders, so you'll introduce this strategy with the familiar Part-Total Mat and pairs that make 10. For example, here's how you'll model 10 – 6 on the Part-Total Mat.

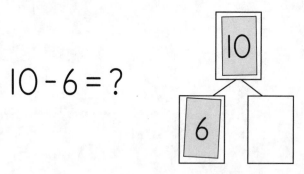

How to model 10 – 6 on the Part-Total Mat.

The Part-Total Mat makes clear how to think of this subtraction problem as a missing addend problem instead: 6 plus what equals 10? Now, your child can use the related addition fact (6 + 4 = 10) to figure out that 10 – 6 = 4.

$$10 - 6 = 4$$

6 + 4 = 10, so 10 – 6 must equal 4.

You'll introduce this strategy this week, but don't worry if your child doesn't fully understand the link between addition and subtraction right away. She'll explore it more and develop a deeper understanding as she masters more subtraction facts in Weeks 10 and 11.

Extra Materials Needed for Week 9

- Small ball or beanbag
- For optional Enrichment and Review Lesson:
  - × *Handa's Surprise*, by Eileen Browne
  - × 10 blocks, boxes, or rolls of toilet paper
  - × String
  - × Can

Lesson 9.1
Introduce Subtraction and
-1 and -2 Facts

	Purpose	Materials
Warm-up	• Count by 10s to 50 • Practice memory work • Review *sum* and *addend*	• 100 Chart (Blackline Master 3) • Counters
Activities	• Write subtraction equations with the – and = signs • Use the ten-frame to subtract 1 or 2	• Counters • Number Cards • Blank index card • Double ten-frames (Blackline Master 1)
Workbook	• Use the ten-frame to subtract 1 or 2	• Workbook pages 9.1A and 9.1B

Warm-up: Counting, Memory Work, and Review

- Demonstrate how to count by 10s to 50: **10, 20, 30…** Cover each number on the 100 Chart as you say it. Then, have your child count by 10s to 50. Have her remove each counter after she says the number underneath it.

1	2	3	4	5	6	7	8	9	◯
11	12	13	14	15	16	17	18	19	◯
21	22	23	24	25	26	27	28	29	◯
31	32	33	34	35	36	37	38	39	◯
41	42	43	44	45	46	47	48	49	◯

- Show your child a penny and a nickel, and have her tell the name and value of each coin.

- Write 5 + 4 = 9 on a piece of paper and have your child identify the sum and addends.

$$5 + 4 = 9$$

addends   sum

Activity: Introduce Subtraction

You have already learned how to add. What do we do when we add two groups together? *Sample answers: We put the groups together. We join them.*

Have your child act out the following story with counters and write an addition equation to match: **Let's pretend you have 4 pieces of candy. Then you get 1 more. How many do you have now?** *5.*

$$4 + 1 = 5$$

Why do we use a plus sign in this equation? *We joined the two groups.*

Today, you'll learn how to subtract. Subtracting is the opposite of adding.

When we add, we join two parts to make a total. Pantomime joining two groups together.

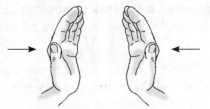

When we subtract, we split a total into parts. Pantomime splitting a group apart.

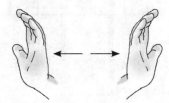

Gestures help children understand math concepts kinesthetically and concretely. Use these hand motions whenever you discuss the difference between addition and subtraction throughout the unit.

Let's pretend you have 4 pieces of candy. Then you eat 1. Place 4 counters on the table. Remove 1 counter and place it to the side. **How many do you have left?** *3.*

Write "–" on an index card. **This is called the minus sign. We use it to show when we subtract, just like we use the plus sign to show when we add.**

Here's the subtraction equation that matches the story. Arrange Number Cards as shown. To read this equation, we say 4 minus 1 equals 3.

Always read the subtraction sign as *minus* rather than *take away*, since we use subtraction for more than just take-away situations in everyday life. See the Week 11 **Teaching Math with Confidence** for more on the multiple contexts in which we use subtraction.

Ask the following questions about the equation:

- **What does the 4 stand for?** *The number of candies I started with.*
- **What does the 1 stand for?** *The candy I ate.*
- **What does the 3 stand for?** *The number of candies I have left.*
- **What does the minus sign mean?** *(Subtracting [or taking away] the 1.)*
- **What does the equals sign mean?** *(It means 4 – 1 is the same as 3.)*

Remember, the equals sign doesn't tell us to do something. It tells us two amounts are equal to each other.

Activity: Introduce –1 and –2 Subtraction Facts

Today, you'll start learning the –1 and –2 subtraction facts. Knowing the subtraction facts will help you solve more complicated problems as you get older, just like the addition facts. We'll work on the addition and subtraction facts all year long so you know them well by the end of the year!

Write 7 – 1 = on a piece of paper. Place 7 counters on the ten-frame. **If you subtract 1 counter, how many will be left?** *6.* Have your child complete the written equation and read it aloud: *7 minus 1 equals 6.*

$$7 - 1 = 6$$

> As with the addition facts, discourage your child from counting one-by-one to find the answers. Instead, encourage her to use the structure of the ten-frame to recognize the quantity.

Repeat this activity with the following problems.

- 8 – 1 = 7
- 10 – 1 = 9
- 5 – 1 = 4
- 9 – 1 = 8
- 7 – 2 = 5
- 10 – 2 = 8
- 9 – 2 = 7
- 8 – 2 = 6

> Don't require your child to use counters to solve these problems if she can easily solve them in her head.

Workbook: Practice –1 and –2 Subtraction Facts and Review

Have your child complete workbook pages 9.1A and 9.1B.

Lesson 9.2
Practice -1 and -2 Facts

	Purpose	Materials
Warm-up	• Count dimes by 10s • Practice memory work • Review symmetry	• Coins • Pattern blocks
Activities	• Recognize subtracting 0 from a number does not change it • Recognize subtracting a number from itself always equals 0 • Practice the –1 and –2 subtraction facts	• Double ten-frames (Blackline Master 1) • Counters • Coin
Workbook	• Practice the –1 and –2 subtraction facts	• Workbook pages 9.2A and 9.2B

Warm-up: Counting, Memory Work, and Review

- Place 5 dimes on the table. **Each dime is worth 10¢. So, we can count the dimes by 10s to find out how much they are worth.** Have your child count by 10s to find the total value. **How many cents are the dimes worth?** *50¢.*

  How many sides does a triangle have? *3.* **A square?** *4.* **A rectangle?** *4.*

- Fold a piece of paper in half. Open the paper and trace the fold line to make it more visible. **Let's make a symmetric pattern block design. This line on the paper will be the line of symmetry.**

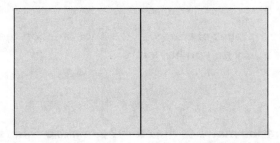

Have your child create a symmetric design with pattern blocks on the paper. If he's not sure how to start, suggest he place one block on the right side of the paper and then place a matching block on the left side of the paper.

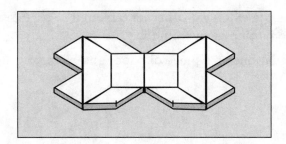

Your child can make her design as simple or complex as she likes.

Activity: Subtract a Number from Itself

In the last lesson, you worked on the –1 and –2 facts. Today, you'll practice these subtraction facts more. We'll also explore two special subtraction situations: subtracting a number from itself and subtracting 0.

Let's pretend you have 8 pieces of candy. Place 8 counters on the table. **Then, you eat all 8 pieces of candy.** Have your child pretend to eat the 8 counters. **How many do you have left?** *0.*

What subtraction equation matches the story? *8 minus 8 equals 0.* Write the equation on a piece of paper.

$$8 - 8 = 0$$

Write the following equations on a piece of paper and have your child complete them.

- 9 – 9 = *0*
- 10 – 10 = *0*
- 6 – 6 = *0*
- 4 – 4 = *0*

Use counters to model the problems only if your child doesn't know the answers immediately.

What do all these problems have in common? *Possible answer: They all have 0 as the answer.* **Why do they all have 0 as an answer?** *Possible answer: We subtract all the counters that we start with!*

Activity: Subtract 0

Let's pretend you have 7 pieces of candy. Place 7 counters on the table. **Then, you don't eat any of the candy. How many do you have left?** *7.*

What subtraction equation matches the story? *7 minus 0 equals 7.* Write the equation on a piece of paper.

$$7 - 0 = 7$$

Why doesn't the 7 change when we subtract 0 from it? *Possible answer: Subtracting 0 means you don't take anything away from the 7.*

Write the following equations on a piece of paper and have your child complete them.

- 9 – 0 = *9*
- 10 – 0 = *10*
- 6 – 0 = *6*
- 4 – 0 = *4*

Activity: Play Race to 0

We're going to play a game called Race to 0. It's the opposite of Race to 10. Instead of adding counters to fill the ten-frame, the goal is to subtract all of the counters. Play two rounds of this quick game.

Race to 0

Materials: Double ten-frames (Blackline Master 1), coin, counters

Object of the Game: Remove all counters from your ten-frame.

Each player chooses a ten-frame on Blackline Master 1 and fills it with 10 counters.

On your turn, flip a coin. If it is heads, remove one counter from your ten-frame. If it is tails, remove two counters from your ten-frame. Say the matching subtraction fact as you remove the counters. For example, if you have 10 counters and remove 2, say, "Ten minus 2 equals 8."

Always remove the counters from right to left, so it's easy to see how many counters remain on the ten-frame.

Play then passes to the other player. The first player to remove all the counters wins the game.

As you play, make sure your child says the subtraction equation that matches each move.

Workbook: Practice –1 and –2 Facts and Review

Have your child complete workbook pages 9.2A and 9.2B.

Lesson 9.3
Subtract from 10

	Purpose	Materials
Warm-up	• Count to 60 • Practice memory work • Review properties of rectangles	• 100 Chart (Blackline Master 3) • Shape Cards (Blackline Master 5)
Activities	• Model subtraction on the Part-Total Mat • Use the pairs that make 10 to subtract from 10	• Counters • Part-Total Mat (Blackline Master 4) • Number Cards
Workbook	• Subtract from 10	• Workbook pages 9.3A and 9.3B

Warm-up: Counting, Memory Work, and Review

- Count to 60 in unison with your child. Point to each number on the 100 Chart as you say it.

- Have your child say the days of the week. **How many days are in week?** *7.*

- Show your child Shape Cards A and E. Use these questions to compare and contrast the shapes.

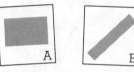

- × **What's different about the two shapes?** *Possible answers: One is longer and skinnier than the other shape. One shape is tilted on the card.*
- × **What do the shapes have in common?** *Possible answers: They both have 4 sides and 4 right angles.*
- × **What category do both shapes belong to?** *Rectangle.*

Activity: Use the Part-Total Mat to Model Subtraction

In the last lesson, you practiced the -1 and -2 facts. Today, you'll learn how to subtract numbers from 10.

Let's pretend I have 10 cookies, and I give you 6. Take 10 counters. Give your child 6 of the counters. Cover the remaining counters.

How many do I have left? *4.* **How do you know?** *Answers will vary.* If your child isn't sure, encourage her to think of the pairs that make 10: **6 and what make 10?** *4.* **So, I must have 4.** Reveal your remaining counters so your child can check.

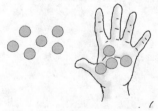

What subtraction equation matches the story? *10 minus 6 equals 4*. Have your child write the equation on paper.

$$10 - 6 = 4$$

Have your child place Number Cards on the Part-Total Mat to match how you split the cookies. If needed, prompt her with questions such as: **What was the total number of cookies that I started with?** *10*. **How many cookies are in each part?** *6 and 4*.

$$10 - 6 = 4$$

Your child can arrange the Part-Total Mat in any order. In the above example, your child could switch the 6 and the 4. She will use the Part-Total Mat to explore the connection between addition and subtraction more in future lessons. See the Week 9 **Teaching Math with Confidence** for more on this important link.

Repeat with the following cookie stories. Act out each story with counters. Then, have your child write an equation and place Number Cards on the Part-Total Mat to match.

- **I have 10 cookies, and I give you 2. How many do I have left?** *8*.

$$10 - 2 = 8$$

- **I have 10 cookies, and I give you 5. How many do I have left?** *5*.

$$10 - 5 = 5$$

- **I have 10 cookies, and I give you 7. How many do I have left?** *3.*

$$10 - 7 = 3$$

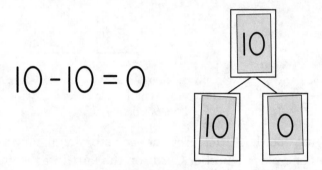

- **I have 10 cookies, and I give you 10. How many do I have left?** *0.*

$$10 - 10 = 0$$

At this point, your child should be fully fluent with the pairs that make 10. If your child has trouble, place 10 counters on the ten-frame and allow her to refer to the counters as she answers these questions. Then, spend some extra time practicing these pairs so that she memorizes them completely.

Activity: Play Subtract from 10 Memory

Play Subtract from 10 Memory. Encourage your child to think of the pairs that make 10 to solve the subtract-from-10 equations.

Subtract from 10 Memory

Materials: 2 sets of Number Cards (0-10)

Object of the Game: Collect the most pairs of cards.

Shuffle the cards together and place them face-down in a grid.

On your turn, first flip over 1 card. Subtract the number on the card from 10. For example, if you flip over a 7: 10 minus 7 equals 3.

10 – 7 = 3, so I'm looking for a 3.

Make sure your child says the equation aloud so that she practices these subtract-from-10 subtraction equations.

Flip over a second card. If the second card matches the answer to the subtraction equation, keep both cards.

10 – 7 = 3, so I get to keep the pair.

If the second card does not match the answer to the subtraction equation, turn both cards back over. Take turns until you cannot match any more cards. Whoever collects more pairs wins.

Workbook: Subtract from 10 and Review

Have your child complete workbook pages 9.3A and 9.3B. Encourage your child to think of the pairs that make 10 to complete the part-total diagrams and equations on 9.3A.

Lesson 9.4
Use Missing Addends to Subtract

	Purpose	Materials
Warm-up	• Count to 60 • Practice memory work • Review tallies	• Small ball or beanbag • Tally Cards
Activities	• Compare and contrast addition and subtraction • Write missing addend problems to match subtraction problems • Practice subtracting from 10	• Counters • Part-Total Mat (Blackline Master 4) • Number Cards
Workbook	• Practice subtracting from 10	• Workbook pages 9.4A and 9.4B

Warm-up: Counting, Memory Work, and Review

- Count to 60 with your child. Toss a small ball or beanbag back and forth as you count, and take turns saying the numbers: **1,** *2,* **3,** *4…*

- **How many sides does a triangle have?** *3.* **A square?** *4.* **A rectangle?** *4.*

- Shuffle Tally Cards 0-10. Show your child one card at a time. Have him identify the number of tallies on the card as quickly as he can.

Activity: Compare and Contrast Addition and Subtraction

In the last lesson, you learned how to subtract from 10. Today, you'll learn how to use missing addend equations to solve subtraction problems.

First, I'm going to tell you two different cookie stories. Listen for what the two stories have in common and for how they are different from each other.

Here's the first story: I have 9 cookies. Take 9 counters. **Then I get 1 more.** Take 1 more counter. **How many do I have now?** *10.* Have your child write an equation and place Number Cards on the Part-Total Mat to match.

$$9 + 1 = 10$$

Here's the second story: I have 10 cookies. Take 10 counters. **Then, I give you 1.** Give your child 1. **How many do I have now?** *9.* Have your child write an equation to match.

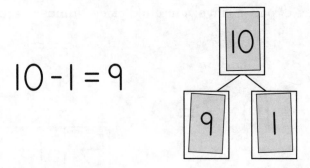

$10 - 1 = 9$

Use the following questions to help your child see that both problems involve the same parts and total:

What do these stories have in common? *Sample answer: Both are about cookies. Both have the same numbers in the equations and on the Part-Total Mat.*

How are these stories different from each other? *Sample answer: You get 1 cookie in one story, and you give away 1 cookie in the other story.*

When we add, we join two groups. We know the two parts and want to find the total. What were the two parts in the first story? *9 and 1.* **What was the total?** *10.*

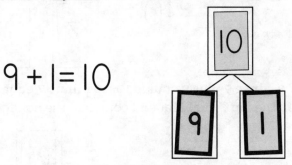

$9 + 1 = 10$

When we add, we know the two parts.

When we subtract, we split a total into parts. We know the total and one part, and we want to find the other part. In the second story, what was the total number of cookies? *10.* **What was the part we knew?** *1.* **What was the part you figured out?** *9.*

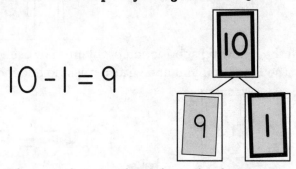

$10 - 1 = 9$

When we subtract, we know the total and one part.

Activity: Use Missing Addends to Subtract

Let's pretend I have 10 cookies again. This time, I give you 7. Take 10 counters. Give your child 7. Cover the remaining counters.

Write 10 − 7 = on a piece of paper. Have your child place Number Cards on the Part-Total Mat to match.

$$10 - 7 =$$

The Part-Total Mat shows how you can think of this subtraction problem as a missing addend problem: 7 plus what equals 10? Write 7 + ____ = 10 below 10 − 7 = on the piece of paper.

$$10 - 7 =$$
$$7 + \underline{} = 10$$

7 plus what equals 10? *3*. **Since 7 plus 3 equals 10, 10 minus 7 equals 3.** Have your child place Number Card 3 on the Part-Total Mat and complete the equations. Reveal the 3 covered counters.

$$10 - 7 = 3$$
$$7 + \underline{3} = 10$$

Repeat this activity with the following subtraction problems. For each problem, have your child place Number Cards on the Part-Total Mat and write a missing addend problem to match.

$$10 - 5 =$$
$$5 + \underline{} = 10$$

$$10 - 5 = 5$$
$$5 + \underline{5} = 10$$

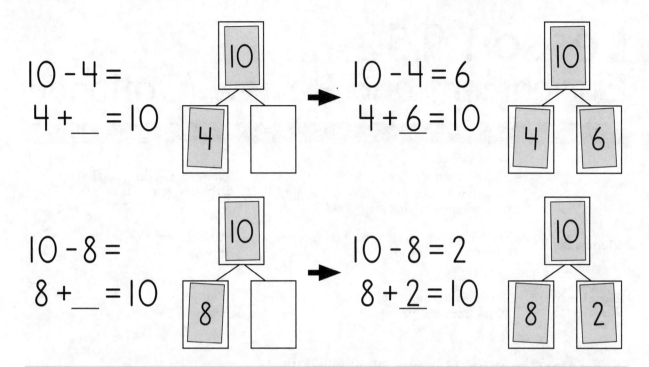

Make sure your child finds these missing addend equations, even if he knows the answers to the subtraction problems. This will help cement the connection between addition and subtraction so he is ready to use this strategy for more difficult subtraction problems. However, you can skip putting Number Cards on the Part-Total Mat if he does not need this support.

Activity: Play Subtract from 10 Memory

Play a round of Subtract from 10 Memory. See Lesson 9.3 (page 147) for directions.

Workbook: Subtract from 10 and Review

Have your child complete workbook pages 9.4A and 9.4B.

Lesson 9.5
Enrichment and Review (Optional)

	Purpose	Materials
Warm-up	• Review counting • Review memory work • Review your child's favorite or most challenging activities from Week 9	• Varies, depending on the activities you choose
Picture Book	• Recognize subtraction in a real-life context	• *Handa's Surprise*, by Eileen Browne
Enrichment Activity	• Practice the –1 and –2 subtraction facts in a kinesthetic way	• 10 blocks, boxes, or rolls of toilet paper • String • Can

Warm-up: Counting, Memory Work, and Review

- Have your child count to 60 by 1s, 2s, 5s, or 10s. (Choose whichever counting sequence your child needs to practice the most.)

- Quiz your child on the memory work through Week 8. See page 499 for the full list.

- If you have time, repeat one or two of the activities from this week's lessons. Choose activities your child especially enjoyed or found challenging.

Math Picture Book: *Handa's Surprise*

Read *Handa's Surprise*, by Eileen Browne. In the book, animals secretly steal fruit from Handa's basket. As you read, have your child make up a subtraction equation to describe what happens with the fruit on each page. For example, when the zebra swipes 1 orange from the basket with 5 pieces of fruit: 5 – 1 = 4.

Enrichment Activity: Wrecking Ball!

Have your child make a tower with 10 blocks, cardboard boxes, or rolls of toilet paper. Tie a piece of string around a can and have her knock down 1 or 2 objects at a time. Each time have your child say the subtraction equation that matches what just happened. For example, if there are 8 rolls of toilet paper, and your child knocks down 2: *8 minus 2 equals 6.*

Week 9 Answer Key

9.1A

Complete.

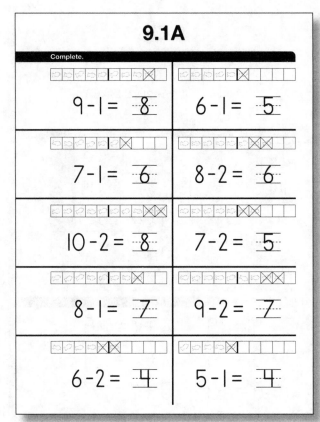

9 – 1 = 8   6 – 1 = 5

7 – 1 = 6   8 – 2 = 6

10 – 2 = 8   7 – 2 = 5

8 – 1 = 7   9 – 2 = 7

6 – 2 = 4   5 – 1 = 4

9.1B

Match pairs that make 10.

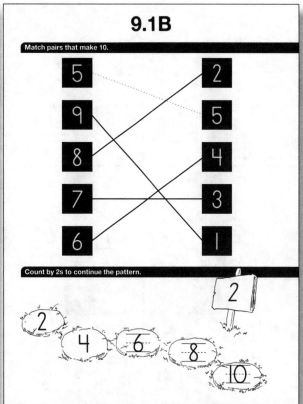

Count by 2s to continue the pattern.

2   4   6   8   10

9.2A

Match.

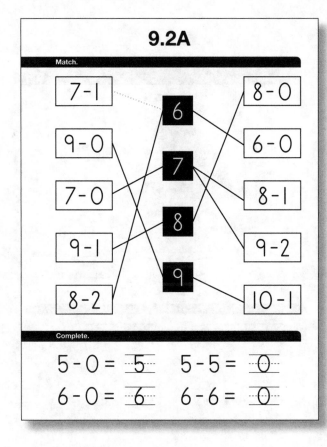

Complete.

5 – 0 = 5   5 – 5 = 0

6 – 0 = 6   6 – 6 = 0

9.2B

Match the congruent shapes.

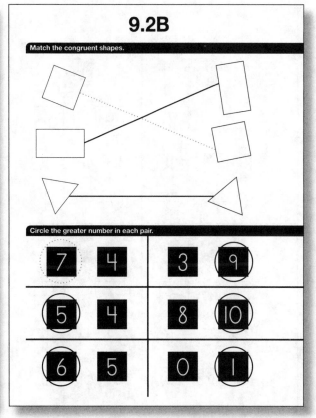

Circle the greater number in each pair.

7   4   3   9

5   4   8   10

6   5   0   1

Week 9 Answer Key

9.3A

Complete the Part-Total Diagrams and equations.

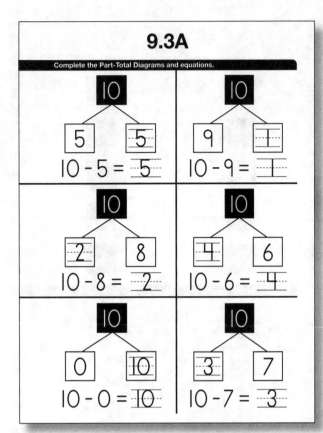

10 − 5 = 5

10 − 9 = 1

10 − 8 = 2

10 − 6 = 4

10 − 0 = 10

10 − 7 = 3

9.3B

Draw a line of symmetry for each shape.

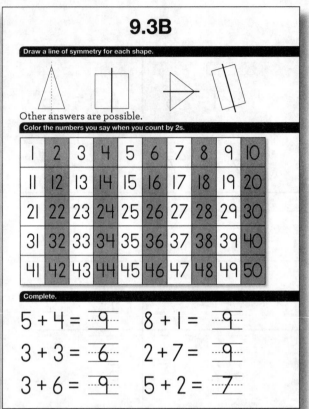

Other answers are possible.

Color the numbers you say when you count by 2s.

1	2	3	4	5	6	7	8	9	10
11	12	13	14	15	16	17	18	19	20
21	22	23	24	25	26	27	28	29	30
31	32	33	34	35	36	37	38	39	40
41	42	43	44	45	46	47	48	49	50

Complete.

5 + 4 = 9   8 + 1 = 9

3 + 3 = 6   2 + 7 = 9

3 + 6 = 9   5 + 2 = 7

9.4A

Complete the Part-Total Diagrams and equations.

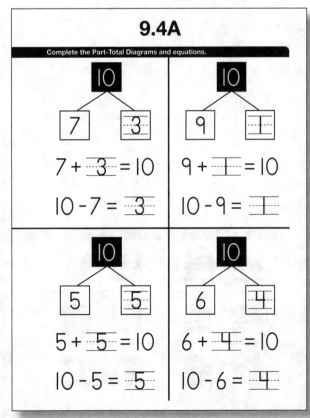

7 + 3 = 10

9 + 1 = 10

10 − 7 = 3

10 − 9 = 1

5 + 5 = 10

6 + 4 = 10

10 − 5 = 5

10 − 6 = 4

9.4B

Color the triangles red.
Color the rectangles green.
Color the circles blue.

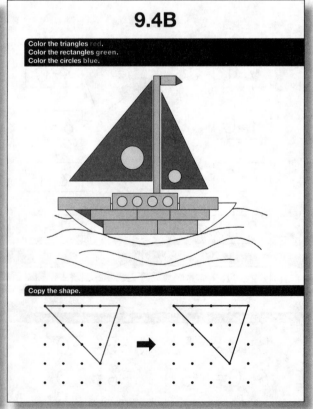

Copy the shape.

Week 10
-3 and -4 Subtraction Facts

Overview

Your child will learn the -3 and -4 subtraction facts. He'll use the ten-frame to visualize the problems and find answers without counting. He'll also learn to write fact families and use the term *difference*.

Teaching Math with Confidence: Fact Families

Last week, you used the Part-Total Mat to show your child the connection between addition and subtraction. This week, you'll teach your child to write fact families to match the Part-Total Mat.

A *fact family* is a set of equations that describes the relationships between 3 numbers. In first grade, your child will create addition and subtraction fact families. For example, here is the fact family for 3, 6, and 9:

$$6 + 3 = 9$$
$$3 + 6 = 9$$
$$9 - 3 = 6$$
$$9 - 6 = 3$$

Fact families provide a concrete way for your child to understand the link between addition and subtraction. As you teach your child about fact families, don't make the mistake of simply teaching your child to slot the numbers into the correct spots. Instead, make sure to emphasize the underlying relationships between the parts and the totals so that your child deeply grasps this important connection between addition and subtraction.

Extra Materials Needed for Week 10

- Printed wall calendar
- Small plastic zip-top bag
- For optional Enrichment and Review Lesson:
    × *Splash!,* by Ann Jonas
    × 5 small toys or household items for a pretend store

Lesson 10.1
Introduce -3 and -4 Facts

	Purpose	Materials
Warm-up	• Count by 5s to 60 • Learn the months of the year • Review halves and fourths	• 100 Chart (Blackline Master 3) • Counters • Printed wall calendar
Activities	• Introduce the -3 and -4 subtraction facts	• Counters • Double ten-frames (Blackline Master 1) • Subtraction Tic-Tac-Toe game board (on Workbook page 10.1A) • Playing cards
Workbook	• Practice the -3 and -4 subtraction facts on the ten-frame	• Workbook pages 10.1A and 10.1B

Warm-up: Counting, Memory Work, and Review

- Demonstrate how to count by 5s to 60: **5, 10, 15...** Cover each number on the 100 Chart as you say it. Then, have your child count by 5s to 60. Have her remove each counter after she says the number underneath it.

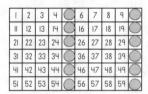

- **Today, you'll learn the months. Every year has 12 months.** Point to the names of the months on a printed calendar and read them aloud to your child. Then, have your child recite the names of the months in unison with you.

- Draw a circle, rectangle, and square on a piece of paper. Have your child draw a line that splits each shape in half.

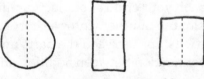

Many answers are possible.

Draw another circle, rectangle, and square. Have your child draw lines that split each shape into fourths.

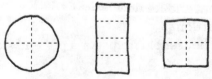

Many answers are possible.

Activity: Introduce -3 and -4 Subtraction Facts

In the last lesson, you learned how to use missing addends to subtract from 10. Today, you'll learn to subtract 3 or 4.

Write 7 – 3 = on a piece of paper and place 7 counters on the ten-frame. **Imagine if I subtracted 3 counters. First, I'd take away the 2 counters on the right side of the dark line.** Point to these 2 counters.

$$7-3=$$

Then, I'd still need to take away 1 more counter on the other side of the dark line. Point to this counter. **How many counters would be left?** *4.*

$$7-3=$$

Remove the 3 counters. Have your child complete the written equation and read it aloud: *7 minus 3 equals 4.*

$$7-3=4$$

Have your child use similar reasoning to complete the following subtraction equations. Encourage your child to use the dark line in the middle of the ten-frame as a visual anchor to help her "see" the answers rather than counting each counter one-by-one.

- 6 – 3 = *3*
- 5 – 4 = *1*
- 6 – 4 = *2*
- 8 – 3 = *5*
- 9 – 4 = *5*
- 8 – 4 = *4*
- 7 – 4 = *3*
- 9 – 3 = *6*
- 10 – 3 = *7*

Your child may use related addition facts (rather than this "take-away" strategy) to solve these problems. For example, to find 7 – 3, she might think "3 plus what equals 7?" However, if you your child counts one-by-one to find the answers, encourage her to use the ten-frame to "see" the answers instead. You'll teach her more about visualizing the -3 and -4 facts in Lesson 10.2.

Activity: Play Subtraction Tic-Tac-Toe

Play one round of Subtraction Tic-Tac-Toe. Allow your child to use the ten-frame and counters nearby to find the answers as needed.

Subtraction Tic-Tac-Toe

Materials: Subtraction Tic-Tac-Toe game board (Workbook page 10.1A); 6s, 7s, 8s, 9s, and 10s from a deck of playing cards (20 cards total); 5 counters of 2 different colors

Object of the Game: Be the first player to fill three boxes in a row, either horizontally, vertically, or diagonally.

Shuffle the cards and place the stack face down on the table. On your turn, flip over the top card. Subtract either 3 or 4 from the card and place one of your counters on the box that matches the difference. For example, if you draw a 9, you can subtract 3 from 9 and place a counter on a box with a 6. Or, you can subtract 4 from 9 and place a counter on a box with a 5.

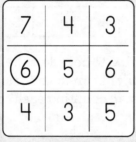 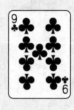

One possible play if you draw a 9. Since 9 – 3 = 6, you can cover a 6.

Another possible play if you draw a 9. Since 9 – 4 = 5, you can cover a 5.

If you draw a card you can't play, draw another card.

Play then passes to the other player. Continue until one player has completed an entire row, column, or diagonal.

Workbook: Practice –3 and –4 Subtraction Facts

Have your child complete workbook page 10.1B.

 Save the Subtraction Tic-Tac-Toe game board (workbook page 10.1A) with your math materials so you can play again.

Lesson 10.2
Practice -3 and -4 Facts

	Purpose	Materials
Warm-up	• Count nickels by 5s • Practice memory work • Review properties of rectangles and triangles	• Coins • Shape Cards (Blackline Master 5)
Activities	• Practice the -3 and -4 subtraction facts	• Counters • Double ten-frames (Blackline Master 1) • Subtraction Tic-Tac-Toe game board (on Workbook page 10.1A) • Playing cards
Workbook	• Practice subtraction facts	• Workbook pages 10.2A and 10.2B

Warm-up: Counting, Memory Work, and Review

- Place 11 nickels on the table. **Each nickel is worth 5¢. So, we can count the nickels by 5s to find out how much they are worth.** Have your child count by 5s to find the total value. **How many cents are the nickels worth?** *55¢.*

- Say the months in unison with your child. Then alternate saying the months in order with your child: **January,** *February,* **March,** *April,* etc. **How many months are in a year?** *12.*

- Show your child Shape Cards A and B. Compare and contrast the shapes with the following questions.

- × **What's the name of each shape?** *Rectangle and triangle.*
- × **How many sides does each shape have?** *4 and 3.*
- × **What's different about the two shapes?** *Possible answers: The rectangle has more sides than the triangle. The rectangle has all right angles, and the triangle has some pointy angles. The rectangle looks bigger than the triangle.*
- × **What do the shapes have in common?** *Possible answers: They are both made out of straight lines. They both have a right angle.*

Accept any reasonable answer from your child for these questions. If he doesn't notice both shapes have a right angle, point it out to review this term.

Activity: Visualize –3 and –4 Facts

In the last lesson, you subtracted 3 or 4. Today, you'll practice imagining these subtraction facts so you can "see" the answers in your head.

Write 9 – 4 = on a piece of paper. Put 9 counters on the ten-frame.

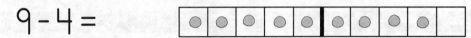

Imagine taking away 4 counters. How many would be left? 5. Encourage your child to visualize removing the counters, without physically taking them away. Then, have him complete the written equation.

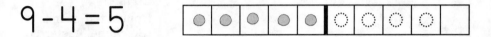

If your child has trouble visualizing removing the counters, have him physically remove the counters and revisit this activity in a few days instead.

Write 7 – 3 = on a piece of paper. Put 7 counters on the ten-frame.

7 - 3 =

Try to take a picture of the ten-frame and see it in your mind. Make sure you include the dark line in the middle in your picture. Have your child "take a picture" of the 7 counters on the ten-frame. With his eyes closed, ask: **Imagine taking away 3 of the counters. How many would be left?** 4. **Complete the written equation.**

If your child finds this difficult or frustrating, allow him to look at the ten-frame instead.

Repeat with the following –3 and –4 subtraction facts. For each problem, place counters on the ten-frame and encourage your child to "take a picture" of the counters. Then, have him imagine removing the correct number counters.

- 6 – 3 = 3
- 6 – 4 = 2
- 8 – 3 = 5
- 9 – 4 = 5
- 8 – 4 = 4
- 7 – 4 = 3
- 9 – 3 = 6
- 10 – 3 = 7

It's fine if your child prefers to think of these as missing addend problems (rather than visualizing the ten-frame), as long as he can find the answers quickly and efficiently.

Activity: Play Subtraction Tic-Tac-Toe

Play two rounds of Subtraction Tic-Tac-Toe. See Lesson 10.1 (page 158) for directions. Encourage your child to continue to visualize the ten-frame to find the answers as he plays.

Workbook: Practice Subtraction Facts and Review

Have your child complete workbook pages 10.2A and 10.2B. Allow your child to use counters and the ten-frame to find the answers as needed.

Lesson 10.3
Fact Families

	Purpose	Materials
Warm-up	• Count to 60 by 10s • Practice memory work • Review coin combinations	• Counters • Small plastic zip-top bag • 5 bags of 10 counters assembled in Lesson 8.4 • Coins
Activities	• Introduce fact families • Understand the connection between addition and subtraction • Practice the –3 and –4 subtraction facts	• Number Cards • Part-Total Mat (Blackline Master 4) • Counters • Subtraction Tic-Tac-Toe game board (on Workbook page 10.1A) • Playing cards
Workbook	• Complete fact families • Practice subtraction facts	• Workbook pages 10.3A and 10.3B

Warm-up: Counting, Memory Work, and Review

- Have your child count out 10 counters and place the counters in a zip-top bag. Add this bag to the bags you previously assembled. Demonstrate how to count the bags by 10s: **10, 20, 30, 40, 50, 60.**

    10   20   30   40   50   60

- Say the months in unison with your child. Then alternate saying the months in order with your child: **January,** *February,* **March,** *April,* **May,** *June,* etc. **How many months are in a year?** *12.*

- Have your child tell the value of the following coin combinations.

    × 1 nickel and 3 pennies *(8¢)*
    × 1 nickel *(5¢)*
    × 4 pennies *(4¢)*
    × 1 nickel and 4 pennies *(9¢)*
    × 1 nickel and 3 pennies *(8¢)*
    × 2 nickels *(10¢)*

Activity: Introduce Fact Families

You have learned that addition and subtraction are related to each other. Today, you'll learn more about the connection between addition and subtraction as you learn about fact families.

Draw a simple family tree of your immediate family. Discuss the different ways to describe your family members' relationships. For example: **We can describe how we're related in many ways. We say that I'm your** *mother* **and that you're my** *daughter*. **We say that you are James'** *sister* **and that he's your** *brother*.

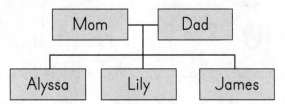

Fact families describe how numbers are related.

Place Number Cards 6, 3, and 9 on the Part-Total Mat as shown. **We can use addition to describe how the numbers are related.** Have your child write the two addition equations that match the Part-Total Mat: 3 + 6 = 9 and 6 + 3 = 9.

$$6 + 3 = 9$$
$$3 + 6 = 9$$

We can also use subtraction to describe how the numbers are related. Have your child write the two subtraction equations that match the Part-Total Mat: 9 − 6 = 3 and 9 − 3 = 6.

$$6 + 3 = 9$$
$$3 + 6 = 9$$
$$9 - 3 = 6$$
$$9 - 6 = 3$$

If your child writes the numbers in the subtraction equation in the wrong order, model the equation with counters and ask whether the equation is true: For example, if your child writes 3 − 9 = 6, place 3 counters on the table and pretend to try to subtract 9. Does 3 minus 9 really equal 6? You'll discuss why subtraction equations must begin with the total, not one of the parts, in Lesson 10.4.

Point to the list of equations. **This group of addition and subtraction facts is a fact family. The fact family shows the relationships between the numbers.**

See the Week 10 **Teaching Math with Confidence** for more on fact families.

Place Number Cards 8, 2, and 10 on the Part-Total Mat. Have your child write the matching fact family.

$$8 + 2 = 10$$
$$2 + 8 = 10$$
$$10 - 2 = 8$$
$$10 - 8 = 2$$

Use counters as needed to model the equations and concretely show the relationships between the numbers.

Activity: Play Subtraction Tic-Tac-Toe

Play two rounds of Subtraction Tic-Tac-Toe. See Lesson 10.1 (page 158) for directions. Encourage your child to continue to visualize the ten-frame to find the answers as he plays.

Workbook: Practice Subtraction Facts and Review

Have your child complete workbook pages 10.3A and 10.3B. Allow your child to use counters and the ten-frame as needed.

Lesson 10.4
Difference

	Purpose	Materials
Warm-up	• Count by 10s to 60 • Practice memory work • Review left and right	• 100 Chart (Blackline Master 3) • Counters
Activities	• Understand that subtraction equations must be written in a certain order • Introduce the term difference • Understand that some fact families have only 2 equations	• Number Cards • Part-Total Mat (Blackline Master 4) • Counters • Subtraction Tic-Tac-Toe game board (on Workbook page 10.1A) • Playing cards
Workbook	• Practice subtraction facts • Find a fact family with 2 equations	• Workbook pages 10.4A and 10.4B

Warm-up: Counting, Memory Work, and Review

- With your child looking away, place counters on the 100 Chart so that the numbers you say when you count by 10s to 60 are covered.

Have your child count by 10s to 60. Have him remove each counter after he says the number underneath it.

- Have your child say the months. **How many months are in a year?** *12.*

- Play Simon Says. Give your child 8-10 directions involving left and right. See Lesson 1.4 for more detailed directions.

Activity: Start Subtraction Equations with the Total

In the last lesson, you learned about fact families. Today, you'll learn more about subtraction equations and learn an important subtraction word.

Place Number Cards 5, 4, and 9 on the Part-Total Mat. Have your child write the matching addition equations.

$$5 + 4 = 9$$
$$4 + 5 = 9$$

When we add, we know both parts. It doesn't matter which order we join the parts, so we can write the parts in the addition equations in any order.

Subtraction is different. When we subtract, we know the total and one part. Mathematicians have agreed that we always start subtraction problems with the total, so that it is clear which number is the total and which number is the part.

> Avoid saying that subtraction equations must always begin with the greater (or "bigger") number. While true for positive numbers, this rule breaks down once children encounter negative numbers later.

In this case, 9 is the total, so it must be the first number in both subtraction equations. Have your child write the matching subtraction equations.

$$5 + 4 = 9$$
$$4 + 5 = 9$$
$$9 - 5 = 4$$
$$9 - 4 = 5$$

Activity: Introduce Difference

Point to 5 + 4 = 9. **Which numbers are the addends?** *5 and 4.* **Which number is the sum?** *9.*

$$5 + 4 = 9$$

addends   sum

We call the answer to a subtraction problem the *difference*. Point to 9 − 5 = 4. **In this equation, the difference is 4.**

$$9 - 5 = 4$$

difference

> The other numbers in subtraction equations also have special names. The first number in the equation is called the *minuend*, and the second number is called the *subtrahend*.
>
> $$9 - 5 = 4$$
>
> minuend   subtrahend
>
> This book will occasionally use these names for clarity's sake, but your child does not need to memorize them.

Activity: Find Fact Families with 2 Equations

All of the fact families you've found so far have 4 equations. Some fact families have fewer than 4 equations.

Place Number Cards 4, 4, and 8 on the Part-Total Mat. **What addition and subtraction equations can you write about these numbers?** *4 + 4 = 8 and 8 – 4 = 4.*

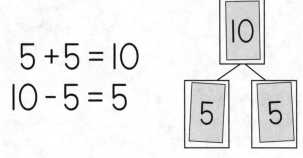

$$4 + 4 = 8$$
$$8 - 4 = 4$$

If the parts are the same, the fact family has only two equations.

Place Number Cards 5, 5 and 10 on the Part-Total Mat. Have your child write the matching fact family.

$$5 + 5 = 10$$
$$10 - 5 = 5$$

Activity: Play Subtraction Tic-Tac-Toe

Play Subtraction Tic-Tac-Toe. See Lesson 10.1 (page 158) for directions.

Workbook: Practice Subtraction Facts and Review

Have your child complete workbook pages 10.4A and 10.4B. Allow your child to use counters and the ten-frame as needed.

Lesson 10.5
Enrichment and Review (Optional)

	Purpose	Materials
Warm-up	• Review counting • Review memory work • Review your child's favorite or most challenging activities from Week 10	• Varies, depending on the activities you choose
Picture Book	• Make up addition or subtraction equations to match real-life contexts	• *Splash!*, by by Ann Jonas
Enrichment Activity	• Practice subtraction in the context of spending money	• 5 index cards or small slips of paper • 5 small toys or household items for a pretend store • Play money

Warm-up: Counting, Memory Work, and Review

- Have your child count to 60 by 1s, 2s, 5s, or 10s. (Choose whichever counting sequence your child needs to practice the most.)

- Quiz your child on the memory work through Week 10. See page 499 for the full list.

- If you have time, repeat one or two of the activities from this week's lessons. Choose activities your child especially enjoyed or found challenging.

Math Picture Book: *Splash!*

Read *Splash!*, by Ann Jonas. As you read, have your child make up addition or subtraction equations to describe how many animals enter or leave the pond. For example, when 1 turtle jumps in to join the 6 fish: *1 + 6 = 7* or *6 + 1 = 7.*

Enrichment Activity: Pretend Store

Set up a pretend store by laying five small toys in a row. Write $1, $2, $3, $4, $5 on 5 index cards and place an index card in front of each item.

Give your child ten one-dollar bills to use to pretend to buy things. After he buys each item, have him subtract to figure out how much money he has left. (For example: *I had 10 dollars, and I spent 3 dollars. 10 minus 3 equals 7, so I have 7 dollars left.*)

Have him continue to "buy" items until he has spent all his money. If you have time, give him the 10 one-dollar bills again and have him play again with a different set of items.

Week 10 Answer Key

10.1A

See *Instructor Guide* for directions on how to play.
Save this game board for future lessons.

Tic-Tac-Toe
Game Board

4	3	5
6	5	6
7	4	3

10.1B

Complete.

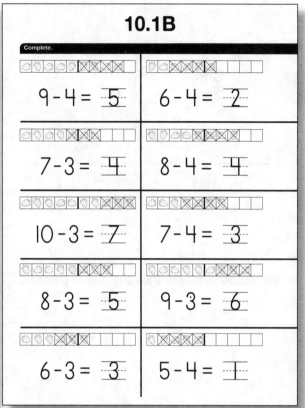

$9 - 4 = 5$ $6 - 4 = 2$

$7 - 3 = 4$ $8 - 4 = 4$

$10 - 3 = 7$ $7 - 4 = 3$

$8 - 3 = 5$ $9 - 3 = 6$

$6 - 3 = 3$ $5 - 4 = 1$

10.2A

Complete.

$7 - 3 = 4$ $10 - 5 = 5$

$8 - 8 = 0$ $6 - 4 = 2$

$9 - 4 = 5$ $7 - 2 = 5$

Color the subtraction facts that equal the number in the star.

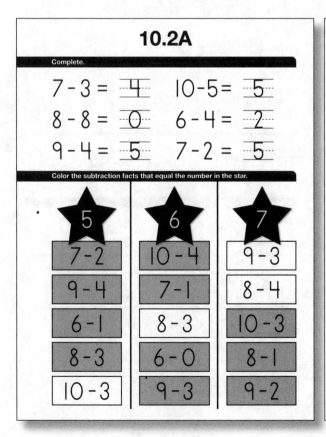

★ 5	★ 6	★ 7
7 - 2	10 - 4	9 - 3
9 - 4	7 - 1	8 - 4
6 - 1	8 - 3	10 - 3
8 - 3	6 - 0	8 - 1
10 - 3	9 - 3	9 - 2

10.2B

Color the rectangles. X the shapes that are not rectangles.

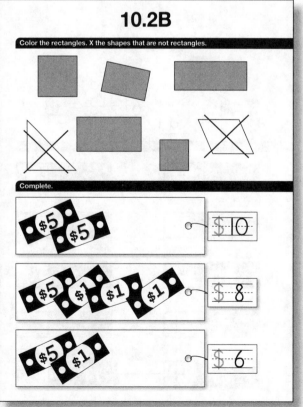

Complete.

$5 + $5 = 10

$5 + $1 + $1 + $1 = 8

$5 + $1 = 6

Week 10 Answer Key

10.3A

Complete the fact families to match.

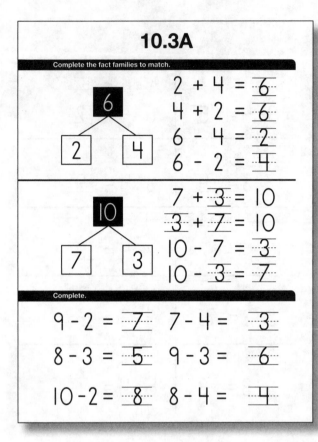

6
2   4

2 + 4 = 6
4 + 2 = 6
6 - 4 = 2
6 - 2 = 4

10
7   3

7 + 3 = 10
3 + 7 = 10
10 - 7 = 3
10 - 3 = 7

Complete.

9 - 2 = 7   7 - 4 = 3

8 - 3 = 5   9 - 3 = 6

10 - 2 = 8   8 - 4 = 4

10.3B

Color the numbers you say when you count by 5s.

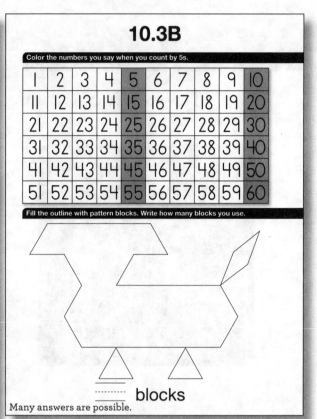

1	2	3	4	5	6	7	8	9	10
11	12	13	14	15	16	17	18	19	20
21	22	23	24	25	26	27	28	29	30
31	32	33	34	35	36	37	38	39	40
41	42	43	44	45	46	47	48	49	50
51	52	53	54	55	56	57	58	59	60

Fill the outline with pattern blocks. Write how many blocks you use.

_____ blocks

Many answers are possible.

10.4A

Complete the fact family to match,

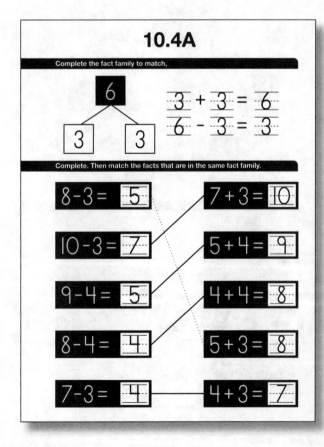

6
3   3

3 + 3 = 6
6 - 3 = 3

Complete. Then match the facts that are in the same fact family.

8 - 3 = 5   7 + 3 = 10

10 - 3 = 7   5 + 4 = 9

9 - 4 = 5   4 + 4 = 8

8 - 4 = 4   5 + 3 = 8

7 - 3 = 4   4 + 3 = 7

10.4B

Color the leaves to complete the patterns.

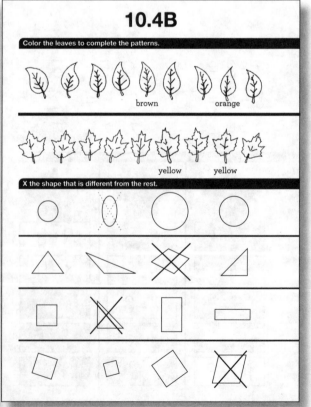

brown   orange

yellow   yellow

X the shape that is different from the rest.

Week 11
Subtraction Facts to 10

Overview

Your child will learn the last few subtraction facts in which both numbers are 10 or less. (She'll work on the subtraction facts in the teens in Unit 10.) She'll continue to use related addition facts to solve these problems. She will also learn to apply subtraction to real life, including both "take-away" and "take-apart" situations.

Teaching Math with Confidence: Three Ways to Interpret Subtraction

Last week, your child used the Part-Total Mat as she wrote fact families and began to grasp the connection between addition and subtraction. This helped make clear the underlying structure of subtraction problems: we know the total and one part, and we want to find the other part.

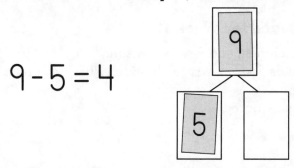

If you ask a group of adults what subtraction means, they'll likely say it means to remove or take away some items. This is true, but "take-away" is just one possible way to interpret subtraction problems. We commonly use subtraction in three different types of real-life situations: take-away, take-apart, and comparison situations.

- Take-away situations occur whenever items are consumed, removed, or used up. For example, if you buy 9 apples for your family, and your kids eat 5 of them, you can subtract $9 - 5$ to find that there are 4 left.

Take-away situation. The total is split into two parts, and one part is removed.

- Take-apart situations occur when we separate a larger group into two smaller groups without removing anything. For example, say you make cupcakes, and you already frosted some of them. If you made 9 cupcakes and already frosted 5 of them, you can subtract 9 – 5 to find you still need to frost 4 of them.

Take-apart situation. The total is split into two parts, but neither is removed.

- Comparison situations occur when we find the difference between two numbers. For example, say you made 9 peanut butter sandwiches and 5 ham sandwiches. You can subtract 9 – 5 to find you have 4 more peanut butter sandwiches than ham sandwiches.

Comparison situation.

This week, you'll teach your child how to apply subtraction to both take-away and take-apart situations. You'll introduce comparison situations later this year after your child already has a firm grip on these easier-to-understand meanings.

Extra Materials Needed for Week 11

- For optional Enrichment and Review Lesson:
  - × *Applesauce Season*, written by Eden Ross Lipson and illustrated by Mordicai Gerstein
  - × Applesauce ingredients

Lesson 11.1
Introduce Final Subtraction Facts to 10

	Purpose	Materials
Warm-up	• Count dimes by 10s • Practice memory work • Review comparing numbers	• Coins • 100 Chart (Blackline Master 3) • Counters
Activities	• Introduce the final subtraction facts up to 10 • Practice the final subtraction facts to 10	• Number Cards • Part-Total Mat (Blackline Master 4) • Subtraction Climb to the Top game board (Workbook page 11.1A) • Playing cards • Counters
Workbook	• Practice subtraction facts	• Workbook pages 11.1A and 11.1B

Warm-up: Counting, Memory Work, and Review

- Place 6 dimes on the table. Have your child count by 10s to find the total value. **How many cents are the coins worth?** *60¢.*

- **Tap your left elbow. Tap your right elbow.**

- Play several rounds of Guess the Secret Number with the numbers from 1 to 10. See Lesson 1.3 (page 20) for directions.

Activity: Introduce Final Subtraction Facts to 10

You have learned nearly all the subtraction facts up to 10! Only a few are left to learn. Today, you'll use missing addend equations to find answers to them.

Write 8 – 7 = on a piece of paper. Have your child place Number Cards on the Part-Total Mat to match.

$$8 - 7 =$$

The Part-Total Mat shows how to think of this subtraction problem as a missing addend problem: 7 plus what equals 8? Write 7 + ___ = 8 below 8 – 7 = on the piece of paper.

$$8 - 7 =$$
$$7 + \underline{} = 8$$

7 plus what equals 8? *1.* **Since 7 plus 1 equals 8, 8 minus 7 equals 1.** Have your child place Number Card 1 on the Part-Total Mat and complete the equations.

$$8 - 7 = 1$$
$$7 + \underline{1} = 8$$

Have your child solve the following subtraction problems. Encourage her to think of them as missing addend problems. Use the Part-Total Mat and write out the missing addend problems only if she needs the extra help.

- 7 – 6 = *1*
- 9 – 7 = *2*
- 8 – 6 = *2*
- 9 – 5 = *4*
- 8 – 7 = *1*
- 9 – 8 = *1*
- 9 – 6 = *3*
- 8 – 5 = *3*

Use counters to model the missing addend problems if your child cannot immediately identify the missing number. For example, for 9 – 5, place 5 counters on the ten-frame. **How many more counters would you need to have 9?** *4.* **So, 5 plus what equals 9?** *4.*

$$9 - 5 =$$
$$5 + \underline{} = 9$$

Activity: Play Subtraction Climb to the Top

Play a round of Subtraction Climb to the Top. As you play, encourage your child to think of the problems as missing addend problems. Allow her to use the ten-frame and counters as needed.

Subtraction Climb to the Top

Materials: Subtraction Climb to the Top game board (Workbook page 11.1A; 5s, 6s, 7s, 8s, 9s, and 10s from a deck of playing cards (24 cards total); counters

Object of the Game: Be the first player to fill an entire column and reach the top of the game board.

Shuffle the cards and place the stack face down on the table.

On your turn, flip over the top two cards. Subtract the lesser number from the greater number to find the difference between the two cards. Place a counter on the lowest empty box in the column that matches the difference. For example, if you draw a 9 and a 5, place a counter in the box above the 4, since 9 − 5 = 4.

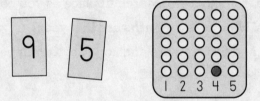

If the two cards are the same, you may place the counter in any column.

Play then passes to the other player. Continue until one player has filled in an entire column and reached the top.

Workbook: Practice Subtraction Facts and Review

Have your child complete workbook pages 11.1A and 11.1B. Encourage your child to think of the problems as missing addend problems and allow her to use the ten-frame and counters as needed.

Your child has now learned strategies for all of the subtraction facts with minuends up to 10. She will continue to practice the subtraction facts throughout the next unit so she becomes faster and more fluent with them.

Lesson 11.2
Take-Away Subtraction

	Purpose	Materials
Warm-up	• Count to 70 • Practice memory work • Review triangles	• Play money • Shape Cards (Blackline Master 5)
Activities	• Draw pictures and write equations to match take-away subtraction stories • Practice the final subtraction facts to 10	• Counters • Subtraction Climb to the Top game board (Workbook page 11.1A) • Playing cards
Workbook	• Practice subtraction facts	• Workbook pages 11.2A and 11.2B

Warm-up: Counting, Memory Work, and Review

· Count in unison with your child from 50 to 70. March in place as you count.

· Have your child say the months. **How many months are in a year?** *12.*

· Show your child Shape Cards L and O. Compare and contrast the shapes with these questions.

× **How many sides does each shape have?** *3 sides; 4 sides.*
× **How many angles does each shape have?** *3 angles; 4 angles.*
× **What's different about the two shapes?** *Sample answer: They have a different number of sides and angles.*
× **What's the same about the two shapes?** *Sample answer: They both look pointy.*
× Point to the triangle. **What do we call a shape with 3 sides?** *Triangle.*

Activity: Draw Pictures to Illustrate Take-Away Subtraction

You have learned a lot about subtraction in this unit. Today, you'll draw pictures to illustrate take-away subtraction problems.

Tell your child the following word problems. Have your child draw a simple picture to illustrate each story. Also have him write and solve an equation to match.

Let's pretend you have 6 balloons. Then, 1 balloon pops. How many do you have now? *5.*

$6 - 1 = 5$

Let's pretend you have 8 crackers. Then, you eat 5 crackers. How many do you have now? *3.*

$$8 - 5 = 3$$

Let's pretend you have 6 popsicles. Then, 3 of the popsicles melt. How many do you have now? *3.*

$$6 - 3 = 3$$

> Telling these subtraction stories and drawing matching pictures helps your child understand that "taking away" in subtraction can take many different forms: eating, popping, melting, and more.

Look at the drawings and equations with your child. **What do all these stories have in common?** *Sample answer: They're all about things going away.*

When we subtract, we split a total into two parts. In all these stories, one of the parts went away. In the next lesson, you'll draw pictures for a different kind of subtraction situation.

 Save these pictures for Lesson 11.3.

Activity: Play Subtraction Climb to the Top

Play two rounds of Subtraction Climb to the Top. See Lesson 11.1 (page 175) for directions. If your child has trouble remembering the answer to a subtraction fact, encourage him to think of it as a missing addend problem.

Workbook: Practice Subtraction Facts and Review

Have your child complete workbook pages 11.2A and 11.2B. Allow him to use the ten-frame and counters as needed.

Lesson 11.3
Take-Apart Subtraction

	Purpose	Materials
Warm-up	• Count to 70 by 5s • Practice memory work • Review combinations of one-dollar and five-dollar bills	• 100 Chart (Blackline Master 3) • Small toy • Play money
Activities	• Draw pictures and write equations to match take-apart subtraction stories • Practice the final subtraction facts to 10	• Counters • Subtraction Climb to the Top game board (Workbook page 11.1A) • Playing cards
Workbook	• Practice subtraction facts	• Workbook pages 11.3A and 11.3B

Warm-up: Counting, Memory Work, and Review

- Have your child count by 5s to 70. Have her make a small toy jump on each number on the 100 Chart as she says it.

- Have your child say the days of the week. **How many days are in a week?** *7.*

- Have your child tell the value of the following play money combinations.

    × 2 one-dollar bills *($2)*
    × 2 five-dollar bills *($10)*
    × 1 five-dollar bill and 2 one-dollar bills *($7)*
    × 1 five-dollar bill and 4 one-dollar bills *($9)*

Activity: Draw Pictures to Illustrate Take-Apart Subtraction

In the last lesson, you drew pictures about take-away subtraction stories. Show your child the pictures she drew in Lesson 11.2 and briefly review what happened in each picture.

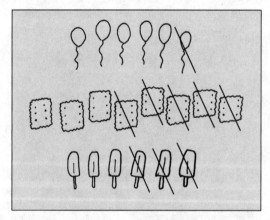

All these pictures show take-away subtraction. The total was split into two groups, and then one group was removed or taken away. The balloons popped, someone ate the crackers, and the popsicles melted.

Today, you'll draw pictures about a different kind of subtraction situation: take-apart subtraction. In take-apart subtraction, we take the total apart into smaller groups, but we don't take away any of the groups.

See the Week 11 **Teaching Math with Confidence** for more on the difference between take-away and take-apart subtraction.

Imagine this word problem as I read it. You have 6 balloons. 1 balloon is red, and the rest are blue. How many are blue?

Have your child draw the outline of 6 balloons on a piece of paper and color 1 balloon red. **If 1 balloon is red, how many must be blue?** *5.* Have your child color the remaining 5 balloons blue and write the matching subtraction equation: 6 – 1 = 5.

$$6 - 1 = 5$$

Discuss the picture and equation with these questions:

- **Which part of the picture matches the 6 in the equation?** *The total number of balloons.*
- **Which part of the picture matches the 1 in the equation?** *The 1 red balloon.*
- **Which part of the picture matches the 5 in the equation?** *The 5 blue balloons.*

No one takes away any balloons in this story. Instead, we split the balloons into two parts and use subtraction to find the part we don't know.

Repeat this process with the following take-apart subtraction stories. For each story, have your child draw a simple picture and write an equation to match.

- **You have 8 crackers. 5 crackers have seeds on them, and the rest are plain. How many are plain?** *3.*

$$8 - 5 = 3$$

- **You have 6 popsicles. 3 are orange, and the rest are red. How many are red?** *3.*

$$6 - 3 = 3$$

When we subtract, we split a total into two groups. In these stories, the total gets split into two parts. We know one part, so we use subtraction to find the other part.

Compare these drawings with your child's drawings from Lesson 11.2. Discuss the similarities and differences between the drawings.

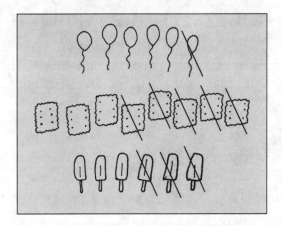 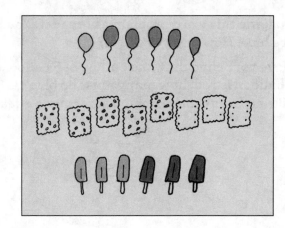

Activity: Play Subtraction Climb to the Top

Play Subtraction Climb to the Top. See Lesson 11.1 (page 175) for directions.

Workbook: Practice Subtraction Facts and Review

Have your child complete workbook pages 11.3A and 11.3B. Encourage your child to think of the problems as missing addend problems and allow her to use the ten-frame and counters as needed.

Lesson 11.4
Practice Subtraction Facts to 10

	Purpose	Materials
Warm-up	• Count by 10s to 70 • Practice memory work • Review patterns	• Counters • Small plastic zip-top bag • 6 bags of 10 counters assembled in previous lessons • Pattern blocks
Activities	• Solve addition and subtraction word problems • Compare and contrast addition and subtraction word problems • Practice subtraction facts to 10	• Counters • Double ten-frames (Blackline Master 1) • Number Cards • Part-Total Mat (Blackline Master 4) • Subtraction Climb to the Top game board (on Workbook page 11.1A) • Playing cards
Workbook	• Practice subtraction facts	• Workbook pages 11.4A and 11.4B

Warm-up: Counting, Memory Work, and Review

- Have your child count out 10 counters and place the counters in a zip-top bag. Add this bag to the bags you previously assembled and demonstrate how to count the bags by 10s: **10, 20, 30, 40, 50, 60, 70.**

10	20	30	40	50	60	70

- Have your child say the months. **How many months are in a year?** *12.*

- Begin a pattern as shown:

Have your child add several blocks to continue the pattern. Then, have your child look away. Use an index card to cover one of the blocks in the pattern. Have your child guess which shape is covered and then check by removing the slip of paper. Repeat several times, covering a different block each time.

Activity: Solve Take-Away and Take-Apart Subtraction Problems

In the last lesson, you learned about take-apart subtraction. Today, we'll review both take-apart and take-away subtraction.

Ask your child the following word problems. Have your child illustrate each story and write a matching subtraction equation.

- **You have 9 candies. Then you eat 7. How many do you have left?** *2.*

$$9 - 7 = 2$$

- **You have 9 candies. 7 are red and the rest are green. How many are green?** *2.*

$$9 - 7 = 2$$

What do these stories have in common? *Sample answers: Both are about candy. Both have 9 and 7 in them. Both are about splitting the candy into two groups.* If your child doesn't mention it, point out that both problems have the same numbers and are about splitting the candy into two parts.

How are these stories different from each other? *Sample answers: In one story, the candy is eaten up. In the other story, the candy is two different colors.*

> Comparing and contrasting word problems helps children look beyond surface-level commonalities and differences and think more deeply about the underlying structure of the problems. You'll continue to do this throughout the book.

Activity: Play Subtraction Climb to the Top

Play Subtraction Climb to the Top. See Lesson 11.1 (page 175) for directions.

> If your child already knows the subtraction facts covered in Subtraction Climb to the Top, choose a different subtraction game to play instead.

Workbook: Practice Subtraction Facts and Review

Have your child complete workbook pages 11.4A and 11.4B. Encourage your child to think of the problems as missing addend problems and allow him to use the ten-frame and counters as needed.

Lesson 11.5
Enrichment and Review (Optional)

	Purpose	Materials
Warm-up	• Review counting • Review memory work • Review your child's favorite or most challenging activities from Week 11	• Varies, depending on the activities you choose
Picture Book	• Understand numbers in the context of cooking	• *Applesauce Season,* written by Eden Ross Lipson and illustrated by Mordicai Gerstein
Enrichment Activity	• Read and understand numbers in a recipe	• Applesauce ingredients

Warm-up: Counting, Memory Work, and Review

- Have your child count to 70 by 1s, 2s, 5s, or 10s. (Choose whichever counting sequence your child needs to practice the most.)

- Quiz your child on the memory work through Week 10. See page 499 for the full list.

- If you have time, repeat one or two of the activities from this week's lessons. Choose activities your child especially enjoyed or found challenging.

Math Picture Book: *Applesauce Season*

Read *Applesauce Season,* written by Eden Ross Lipson and illustrated by Mordicai Gerstein. As you read, discuss the numbers the family uses as they buy apples from the farmer's market and make applesauce.

Enrichment Activity: Make Applesauce

Use the recipe in Applesauce Season (or your favorite recipe) to make applesauce. Before you begin, read over the recipe with your child and discuss the numbers in the recipe. Then, have your child help as much as possible so she can concretely understand the meaning of the numbers from the recipe. For example, you might have your child count out and wash the apples, measure the sugar, or set the timer.

Week 11 Answer Key

11.1A

See *Instructor Guide* for directions on how to play.
Save this game board for future lessons.

Subtraction Climb to the Top
Game Boards

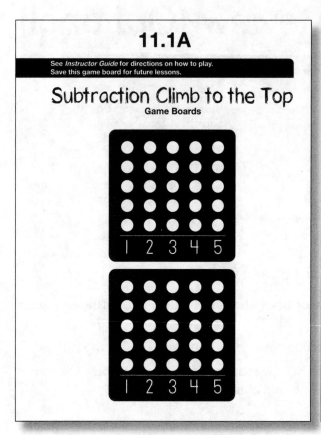

11.1B

Complete.

$9 - 7 = 2$ $8 - 5 = 3$

$8 - 6 = 2$ $10 - 8 = 2$

$10 - 9 = 1$ $9 - 6 = 3$

$8 - 7 = 1$ $9 - 8 = 1$

$9 - 5 = 4$ $7 - 6 = 1$

Draw a line that splits each cake in half.

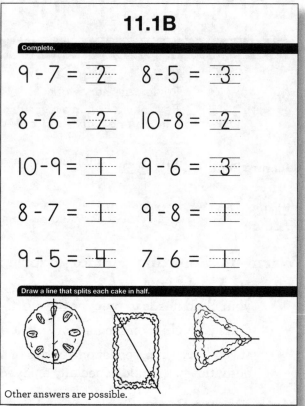

Other answers are possible.

11.2A

Match.

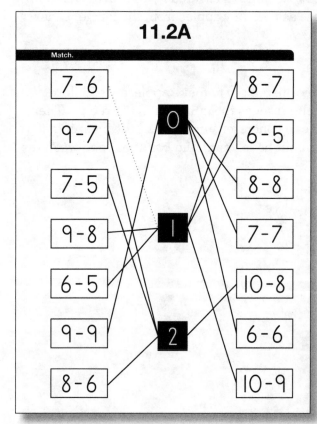

11.2B

Write the number that comes before and after.

| 7 | 8 | 9 |

| 3 | 4 | 5 |

| 8 | 9 | 10 |

| 4 | 5 | 6 |

Complete the fact family to match the Part-Total Diagram.

7
4   3

$4 + 3 = 7$
$3 + 4 = 7$
$7 - 4 = 3$
$7 - 3 = 4$

Draw lines that split each cake into fourths.

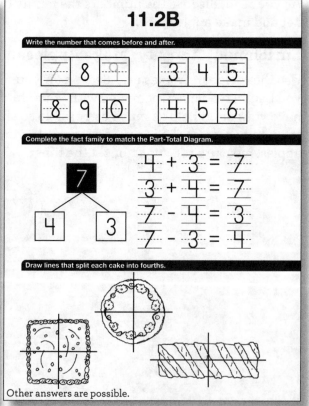

Other answers are possible.

Week 11 Answer Key

11.3A

Complete.

10 - 5 = 5　　9 - 6 = 3

8 - 5 = 3　　10 - 6 = 4

10 - 7 = 3　　9 - 5 = 4

8 - 6 = 2　　9 - 7 = 2

6 - 4 = 2　　7 - 5 = 2

Use the key to color the mittens.

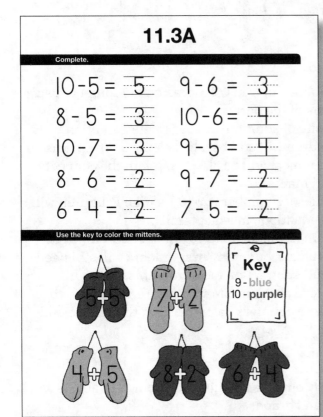

Key
9 - blue
10 - purple

11.3B

Color the numbers you say when you count by 10s.

1	2	3	4	5	6	7	8	9	10
11	12	13	14	15	16	17	18	19	20
21	22	23	24	25	26	27	28	29	30
31	32	33	34	35	36	37	38	39	40
41	42	43	44	45	46	47	48	49	50
51	52	53	54	55	56	57	58	59	60

Match.

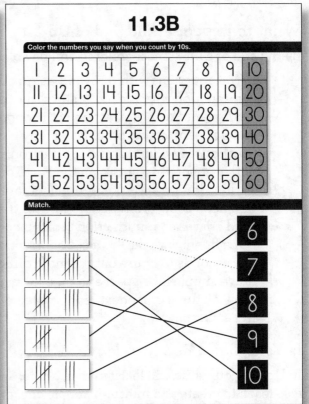

11.4A

Complete.

9 - 8 = 1　　10 - 8 = 2

10 - 9 = 1　　7 - 6 = 1

8 - 7 = 1　　6 - 4 = 2

9 - 5 = 4　　8 - 4 = 4

7 - 5 = 2　　8 - 5 = 3

Complete the fact family to match the Part-Total Diagram.

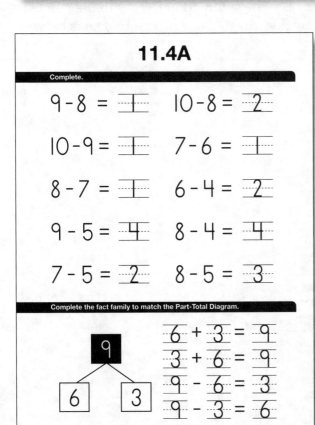

6 + 3 = 9

3 + 6 = 9

9 - 6 = 3

9 - 3 = 6

11.4B

Complete.

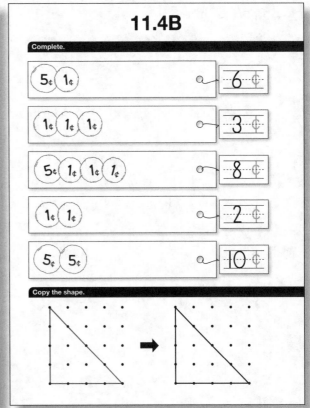

Copy the shape.

Unit 4 Checkpoint

What to Expect at the End of Unit 4

By the end of Unit 4, most children will be able to:

- Write equations with the - and = signs. Some children will occasionally forget to begin the equation with the total rather than one of the parts.
- Understand that subtraction is the opposite of addition and use related addition facts to solve subtraction problems. Many children will still be a little hazy on the precise link between addition and subtraction, but most will be able to explain the connection with a concrete example on the Part-Total Mat.
- Write addition and subtraction fact families for numbers up to 10. Many children will still need some prompting to find all the equations in a fact family.
- Find answers to subtraction problems with numbers up to 10. Most children will be quite fluent with the -1 and -2 subtraction facts, but many first graders will still need a few seconds to figure out the more difficult subtraction facts from this unit.
- Solve simple take-apart and take-away word problems. Many children will need to draw pictures or model these problems with counters before writing the corresponding equation.

Is Your Child Ready to Move on?

In Unit 5, your child will learn to read, write, and compare the numbers from 11 to 20. He will also learn to create and interpret simple charts and graphs.

Throughout Unit 5, your child will continue to practice the subtraction facts with the numbers up to 10. Your child does not need to be completely fluent with these subtraction facts before moving on to Unit 5.

Unit 5
Numbers to 20

Overview

Your child will learn to read, write, and compare numbers to 20. She'll also preview place value as she learns to recognize numbers in the teens as combinations of "10 and some more." Finally, she will create and interpret simple tally charts and bar graphs.

Many families find this unit a refreshing break after the intense focus on the subtraction facts. Your child will continue to practice both addition and subtraction facts during warm-ups and on worksheets so that she doesn't forget them.

Week 12   Place Value with Numbers to 20
Week 13   Compare Numbers to 20
Week 14   Tally Charts and Bar Graphs

What Your Child Will Learn

In this unit your child will learn to:

- Read, write, and compare numbers to 20
- Understand numbers from 11 to 20 as combinations of "ten and some more"
- Identify even and odd numbers to 20
- Identify combinations that make 20 (for example, 13 and 7)
- Create and interpret simple tally charts and bar graphs

Recommended Math Picture Books (Optional)

These picture books are scheduled in the optional Enrichment and Review lessons at the end of each week.

- *Can You Count to a Googol?*, by Robert E. Wells. INDPB, 2000.
- *Missing Mittens*, written by Stuart J. Murphy and illustrated by G. Brian Karas. HarperCollins, 2000.
- *The Best Vacation Ever*, written by Stuart J. Murphy and illustrated by Nadine Bernard Westcott. HarperCollins, 1997.

Week 12
Place Value with Numbers to 20

Overview

Your child will learn to read and write the numbers from 11 to 20. He will learn to recognize these numbers as combinations of "10 and some more" and begin to grasp the idea that the digit in the tens-place stands for the number of groups of 10.

Lesson 12.1   Write Numbers to 20
Lesson 12.2   Read Numbers to 20
Lesson 12.3   Sums of "10 and Some More"
Lesson 12.4   Numbers to 20 with Money
Lesson 12.5   Enrichment and Review (Optional)

Teaching Math with Confidence: Introducing Place Value

Place value is the fundamental principle of our number system: each digit's place in a number determines its value. For example, 41 and 14 both contain the same digits. But they represent different amounts because the 1 and 4 are in different places. In 41, the 4 is the tens-place. It stands for 4 tens, and it has a value of 40. In 14, the 4 is in the ones-place. It stands for 4 ones, and it has a value of only 4.

Place value is a very abstract and difficult concept for first graders to grasp. The first hurdle is for your child to learn to think of 10 objects as a 1 group of 10 rather than 10 individual objects. You'll help your child begin to understand this concept as you teach him to think of the numbers from 11 to 20 as combinations of "10 and some more" this week. You'll also gently introduce him to the tens-place and ones-place.

This week's lessons lay the groundwork for understanding place value. Your child will build on this foundation as he learns the numbers to 100 in Unit 6.

Extra Materials Needed for Week 12

- Small toy
- Small ball or beanbag
- 20 blank index cards
- For optional Enrichment and Review Lesson:
  - × *Can You Count to a Googol?*, by Robert E. Wells

You will introduce your child to dimes and ten-dollar bills this week, so make sure you have both in your Math Kit.

Lesson 12.1
Write Numbers to 20

	Purpose	Materials
Warm-up	• Count by 10s to 70 • Practice memory work • Review subtracting from 10	• 100 Chart (Blackline Master 3) • Counters • Number Cards
Activities	• Introduce place value • Understand the numbers from 11 to 20 as combinations of "10 and some more" • Write numbers 11-20	• Counters • Double ten-frames (Blackline Master 1) • 20 blank index cards
Workbook	• Trace numbers to 20	• Workbook pages 12.1A and 12.1B

This unit will help your child understand the connections between place value, the Part-Total Mat, and addition. If you used *Kindergarten Math with Confidence,* your child may find the Week 12 and Week 13 lessons quite easy. Feel free to condense lessons or teach two per day if your child whizzes through the activities.

Warm-up: Counting, Memory Work, and Review

- Demonstrate how to count by 10s to 70: **10, 20...** Cover each number on the 100 Chart with a counter as you say it. Then, have your child count by 10s to 70. Have her remove each counter after she says the number underneath it.

- **How many sides does a triangle have?** *3.* **A square?** *4.* **A rectangle?** *4.*
- Play Subtract from 10 Memory. See Lesson 9.3 (page 147) for directions.

Activity: Introduce Place Value

In Unit 1, you learned how to recognize combinations of "5 and some more" on the ten-frame. In this unit, you'll learn to think of the numbers from 11 to 20 as combinations of "10 and some more." You'll also learn to read and write these numbers.

Let's pretend you collect eggs on a farm, and the ten-frames are cartons for the eggs. One day you find 14 eggs. Have your child count out 14 counters.

Let's put them in the ten-frame cartons. Do you think we'll fill up an entire ten-frame? *Answers will vary.* Do you think we'll fill up both ten-frames? *Answers will vary.*

This estimation question introduces the idea that quantities can be organized into groups of 10. Don't worry if her answers are incorrect, as she'll develop a more sophisticated understanding of the numbers to 20 throughout this unit.

Help your child arrange the 14 counters on the double-ten-frames. Discuss whether your child was correct about how many ten-frames the 14 counters would fill.

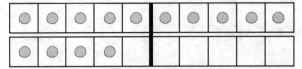

Write 14 on a piece of paper. **We call the 1 and 4 the digits in the number 14. The number 14 has 2 digits, so we call it a two-digit number. The value of the digits depends on their place in the number.**

14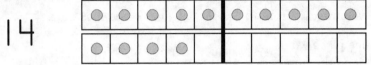

Point to the 1 in 14. **This 1 doesn't stand for just 1 counter! It stands for 1 group of ten counters.** Point to the matching group of 10 on the top ten-frame. **This place is called the tens-place, because it tells how many groups of ten there are.**

14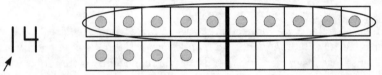

Point to the 4 in 14. **This 4 stands for the 4 extra counters.** Point to the matching 4 counters on the bottom ten-frame. **This place is called the ones-place, because it tells how many extra ones you have after you fill up as many tens as possible.**

14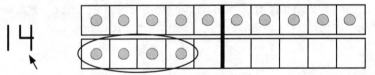

Your child does not need to master place value immediately. She will gradually become more comfortable with terms like *digit*, *ones-place*, or *tens-place* as she works with larger numbers.

Let's write number 14 on 2 index cards so we can use the cards in a game. Write 14 on an index card and have your child copy it on a separate card.

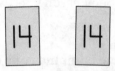

See the Week 12 **Teaching Math with Confidence** for more details on place value.

Activity: Make Number Cards for Numbers 11-20

Let's make Number Cards for the rest of the numbers from 11 to 20. Place 11 counters on the ten-frames. How many counters are on the top ten-frame? *10.* **How many counters are on the bottom ten-frame?** *1.* **How many counters are there in all?** *11.*

Write 11 on an index card and have your child copy it. **10 and 1 make 11.** Point to the 1 in the tens-place as you say "10" and the 1 in the ones-place as you say "1" to emphasize what each digit means.

10 and 1 make 11.

Continue in the same way with the rest of the numbers up to 20. Emphasize that the 1 in the tens-place stands for 1 group of 10. Also discuss the connection between the name of the number and the digit in the ones-place:

- 10 and 2 make *twelve*. **One way to remember this is to think about the words** *twice* **and** *twelve.* **If you add a counter to 10 twice, you get twelve counters.**
- 10 and 3 make *thirteen.* **One way to remember this is to think about the words** *third* **and** *thirteen.* **The** *third* **counter after 10 is number** *thirteen.*
- 10 and 4 make *fourteen.* (Add a counter and discuss 14, but you do not need to make more Number Cards for 14.)
- 10 and 5 make *fifteen.* **The fifth counter after 10 is number fifteen.**
- 10 and 6 make *sixteen.*
- 10 and 7 make *seventeen.*
- 10 and 8 make *eighteen.*
- 10 and 9 make *nineteen.*
- 2 tens make twenty. **The 2 stands for the 2 groups of 10. The 0 means you have 0 extra ones after you make the 2 groups of 10.**

If your child doesn't have the stamina for so much writing, you can write the cards yourself instead.

 Save these new Number Cards for the next activity and future lessons.

Workbook: Trace Numbers and Review

Have your child complete workbook pages 12.1A and 12.1B.

Many children won't be ready to write the teen numbers independently, so workbook page 12.1A includes tracing rather than writing numbers. Your child will practice writing the numbers 11-20 in the next few lessons.

Lesson 12.2
Read Numbers to 20

	Purpose	Materials
Warm-up	• Count to 80 • Practice memory work • Review take-apart subtraction	• Counters
Activities	• Learn to chant the combinations of "10 and some more" from 11 to 20 • Read numbers from 11 to 20	• Number Cards
Workbook	• Read numbers to 20	• Workbook pages 12.2A and 12.2B

Warm-up: Counting, Memory Work, and Review

- Count in unison with your child from 60 to 80.

- **Stomp your right foot. Stomp your left foot.**

- Ask your child the following word problems. Have your child model each problem with counters and then write and solve an equation to match.

    × **There are 9 kids on a soccer team. 6 are boys and the rest are girls. How many are girls?** *3*.

    $$9 - 6 = 3$$

    × **There are 9 kids on a soccer team. 4 are boys and the rest are girls. How many are girls?** *5*.

    $$9 - 4 = 5$$

    × **There are 9 kids on a soccer team. 2 are boys and the rest are girls. How many are girls?** *7*.

    $$9 - 2 = 7$$

Activity: Learn the "10 and Some More" Chant

In the last lesson, you learned how to think of the numbers from 11 to 20 as combinations of "10 and some more." Let's practice naming these combinations with a "10 and Some More" chant. Arrange Number Cards 11-20 in order on the table.

Say the following chant rhythmically. Encourage your child to join in as much as he can. As you chant, point to the corresponding digits on the Number Cards to emphasize what each digit means.

"10 and Some More" Chant

10 and 1. **Eleven!**
10 and 2. **Twelve!**
10 and 3. **Thirteen!**
10 and 4. **Fourteen!**
10 and 5. **Fifteen!**
10 and 6. **Sixteen!**
10 and 7. **Seventeen!**
10 and 8. **Eighteen!**
10 and 9. **Nineteen!**
2 tens. **Twenty!**

10 and 5. Fifteen!

Chanting these combinations helps your child connect the combinations of "10 and some more" with the written digits.

Activity: Play Memory (11-20)

Now we'll play Memory to practice reading the numbers from 11 to 20. Play one round of Memory. If your child has trouble reading a number, point to the digits on the card and encourage her to think of the "10 and Some More" Chant. For example: **This number is 10 and 7. What number is 10 and 7?** *17.*

Memory (11-20)

Materials: 2 sets of Number Cards (11-20), 20 cards total

Object of the Game: Find the most pairs of matching numbers.

Shuffle together 2 sets of Number Cards (11-20) and lay them face down on the table in a grid.

On your turn, flip over 2 cards. Say the name of the number on each card. If the cards are the same, keep the pair. If the cards aren't the same, turn them back over.

Play then passes to the other player. Continue until you have found pairs for all the cards. Whoever finds the most pairs wins.

Workbook: Read Numbers to 20 and Review

Have your child complete workbook pages 12.2A and 12.2B.

Don't be concerned if you find that your child has trouble recalling the subtraction facts on the workbook pages in this unit. It can be frustrating when it feels like your child has already "forgotten" a topic that you just taught, but it's all part of the learning process. As he continues to practice the subtraction facts throughout the next few units, he'll gradually cement them in his memory.

Lesson 12.3
Sums of "10 and Some More"

	Purpose	Materials
Warm-up	• Count to 80 • Practice memory work • Review +3 and +4 addition facts	• Small ball or beanbag • Number Cards • Counters • Addition Climb to the Top game board (on Workbook page 5.1A) • 2 decks of playing cards
Activities	• Write addition equations for combinations of "10 and some more" • Identify missing addends in combinations of "10 and some more"	• Counters • Double ten-frames (Blackline Master 1) • Number Cards • Part-Total Mat (Blackline Master 4) • Index card or small slip of paper
Workbook	• Complete missing addends with combinations of "10 and some more"	• Workbook pages 12.3A and 12.3B

Warm-up: Counting, Memory Work, and Review

- Count from 50 to 80 with your child. Toss a small ball or beanbag back and forth as you count, and take turns saying the numbers: **50,** *51,* **52,** *53...*

- Arrange Number Cards 11-20 in order on the table. Rhythmically say the "10 and Some More" Chant with your child. Point to the corresponding digits on the Number Cards as you chant to emphasize what each digit means. See Lesson 12.2 (page 193) for the full chant.

- Play Addition Climb to the Top. See Lesson 5.1 (page 81) for directions.

Activity: Write Addition Equations for Combinations of "10 and Some More"

You have learned how to think about the numbers to 20 as combinations of "10 and some more." Today, you'll learn how to put those combinations on the Part-Total Mat and write addition equations that match.

Let's pretend you collect eggs on a farm again, and the ten-frames are the cartons for the eggs.

Arrange 16 counters on the double ten-frames. **How many eggs are in the top ten-frame?** *10.* **How many eggs are in the bottom ten-frame?** *6.* **So, how many eggs are there in all?** *16.*

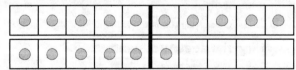

Let's put Number Cards on the Part-Total Mat to match.

- **The top ten-frame has 10.** Place a 10 on the Part-Total Mat.
- **The bottom ten-frame has 6.** Place a 6 on the Part-Total Mat.

- **There are 16 in total.** Place a 16 on the Part-Total Mat.

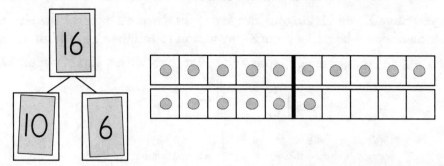

Have your child write an addition equation to match the Part-Total Mat: 10 + 6 = 16 or 6 + 10 = 16.

$$10 + 6 = 16$$

Repeat this process with 17, 14, and 20 counters.

$$10 + 7 = 17$$

$$10 + 4 = 14$$

$$10 + 10 = 20$$

Writing these equations helps your child make connections between addition, parts and totals, the numbers from 11 to 20, and place value.

Activity: X-Ray Vision with Missing Addends

Let's pretend you have X-ray vision and can see right through paper. I'll write an addition equation and hide one number. Use your X-ray vision to tell me the hidden number.

Secretly write 10 + 3 = 13 on a piece of paper and cover the 3 with a slip of paper. **What number did I hide?** *3.*

$$10 + 3 = 13$$

If your child isn't sure, encourage her to think about the combinations of "10 and some more": 10 and what make 13? Use the ten-frames or Part-Total Mat as needed.

Have your child use her "X-ray vision" to identify the hidden numbers in the following equations.

$$10 + 2 = 12 \qquad 10 + 9 = 19$$

$$10 + 5 = 15 \qquad 10 + 1 = 11$$

Workbook: Find Combinations of "10 and Some More" and Review

Have your child complete workbook pages 12.3A and 12.3B.

Lesson 12.4
Numbers to 20 with Money

	Purpose	Materials
Warm-up	• Count by 5s to 80 • Practice memory work • Review subtraction facts	• 100 Chart (Blackline Master 3) • Small toy • Subtraction Tic-Tac-Toe game board (on Workbook page 10.1A) • Playing cards • Counters
Activities	• Learn the value of ten-dollar bills and dimes • Find the value paper money and coin combinations	• Play money • Coins
Workbook	• Find the value of paper money and coin combinations	• Workbook pages 12.4A and 12.4B

Warm-up: Counting, Memory Work, and Review

- Have your child count by 5s to 80. Have him make a small toy jump on each number on the 100 Chart as he says it.

- Say the "10 and Some More" Chant with your child.

- Play Subtraction Tic-Tac-Toe. See Lesson 10.1 (page 158) for directions.

Activity: Introduce Ten-dollar Bills

You have learned about one-dollar bills, five-dollar bills, pennies, and nickels already this year. Today, you'll learn about ten-dollar bills and dimes.

Show your child a play ten-dollar bill and discuss what you can buy with it. **This is a ten-dollar bill. It's worth the same amount as 10 one-dollar bills.**

Pretend to "pay" your child the following paper money combinations and have him find the value of each combination. Remind him to use his knowledge of the combinations of "10 and some more" to find the values.

- 1 ten-dollar bill and 2 one-dollar bills (*$12*)
- 1 ten-dollar bill and 4 one-dollar bills (*$14*)
- 1 ten-dollar bill and 6 one-dollar bills (*$16*)
- 1 ten-dollar bill and 9 one-dollar bills (*$19*)
- 2 one-dollar bills (*$2*)
- 2 ten-dollar bills (*$20*)

Activity: Introduce Dimes

Show your child a dime. **This coin is a dime. It's worth 10 cents. What do you notice about how the dime looks?** *Sample answers: it's silver; it's round; it's smaller than a nickel.*

Place a penny and a nickel next to the dime. **Even though the dime is smaller than the penny and the nickel, it's worth more than either of them!**

A dime is worth 10 cents. How many pennies make 10 cents? *10.* Count out 10 pennies and trade them for 1 dime.

Each nickel is worth 5¢. How many nickels do you need to equal 10¢? *2.* Count out 2 nickels and trade them for 1 dime.

Have your child find the value of the following coin combinations.

- 1 dime and 3 pennies *(13¢)*
- 1 dime and 1 penny *(11¢)*
- 7 pennies *(7¢)*
- 1 nickel and 3 pennies *(8¢)*
- 1 dime *(10¢)*
- 2 dimes *(20¢)*
- 1 dime and 1 nickel *(15¢)*
- 1 dime, 1 nickel, and 2 pennies *(17¢)*

Workbook: Identify Money Combinations and Review

Have your child complete workbook pages 12.4A and 12.4B.

Lesson 12.5
Enrichment and Review (Optional)

	Purpose	Materials
Warm-up	• Review counting • Review memory work • Review your child's favorite or most challenging activities from Week 12	• Varies, depending on the activities you choose
Picture Book	• Marvel at the fact that the counting numbers continue infinitely	• *Can You Count to a Googol?*, by Robert E. Wells
Enrichment Activity	• Find numbers to 20 in real life	• None

Warm-up: Counting, Memory Work, and Review

- Have your child count to 70 by 1s, 2s, 5s, or 10s. (Choose whichever counting sequence your child needs to practice the most.)

- Quiz your child on the memory work through Week 12. See page 499 for the full list.

- If you have time, repeat one or two of the activities from this week's lessons. Choose activities your child especially enjoyed or found challenging.

Math Picture Book: *Can You Count to a Googol?*

Read *Can You Count to a Googol?*, by Robert E. Wells.

Enrichment Activity: Numbers to 20 Pantry Scavenger Hunt

See how many numbers from 11 to 20 you can find in your kitchen or pantry. You'll likely find these numbers on many non-perishable foods. Canned products often come in 16-ounce sizes, and many pastas, cereals, and crackers come in 11- to 20-ounce sizes.

Week 12 Answer Key

12.1A

Trace the numbers.

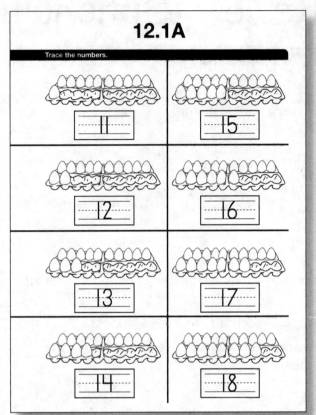

11   15

12   16

13   17

14   18

12.1B

Match.

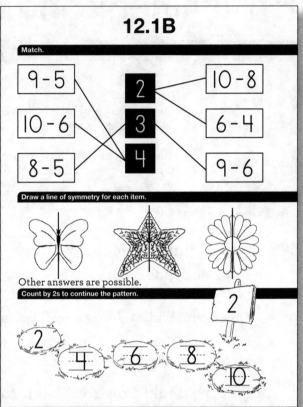

9 - 5   2   10 - 8

10 - 6   3   6 - 4

8 - 5   4   9 - 6

Draw a line of symmetry for each item.

Other answers are possible.

Count by 2s to continue the pattern.

2   4   6   8   10

12.2A

Match.

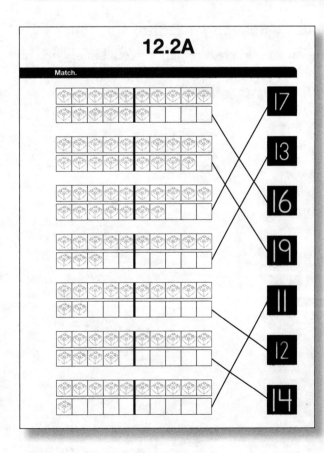

17

13

16

19

11

12

14

12.2B

Match the congruent shapes.

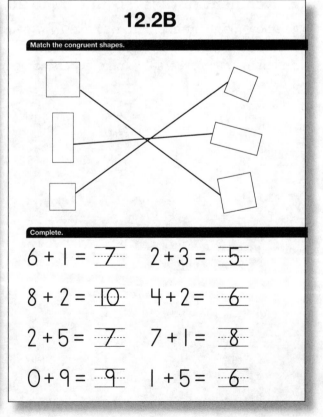

Complete.

6 + 1 = 7   2 + 3 = 5

8 + 2 = 10   4 + 2 = 6

2 + 5 = 7   7 + 1 = 8

0 + 9 = 9   1 + 5 = 6

Week 12 Answer Key

12.3A

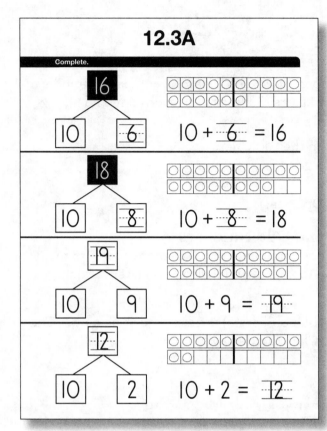

Complete.

16
10   6
10 + 6 = 16

18
10   8
10 + 8 = 18

19
10   9
10 + 9 = 19

12
10   2
10 + 2 = 12

12.3B

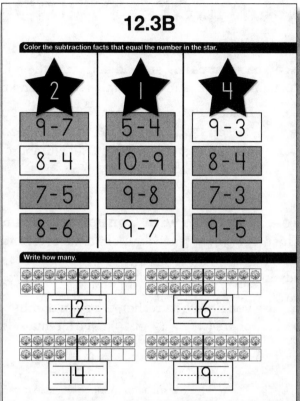

Color the subtraction facts that equal the number in the star.

⭐ 2   ⭐ 1   ⭐ 4

9 - 7	5 - 4	9 - 3
8 - 4	10 - 9	8 - 4
7 - 5	9 - 8	7 - 3
8 - 6	9 - 7	9 - 5

Write how many.

12   16

14   19

12.4A

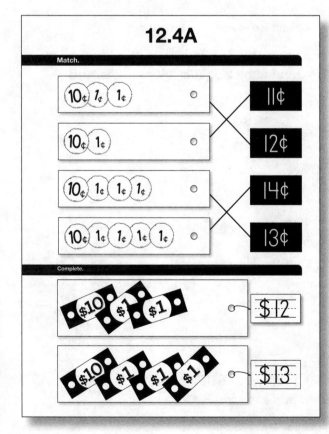

Match.

10¢ 1¢ 1¢ ○   ■ 11¢

10¢ 1¢ ○   ■ 12¢

10¢ 1¢ 1¢ 1¢ ○   ■ 14¢

10¢ 1¢ 1¢ 1¢ 1¢ ○ ■ 13¢

Complete.

$10 $1 $1 ○ $12

$10 $1 $1 $1 ○ $13

12.4B

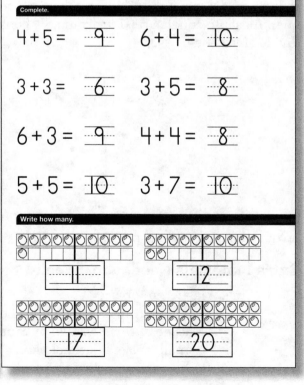

Complete.

4 + 5 = 9   6 + 4 = 10

3 + 3 = 6   3 + 5 = 8

6 + 3 = 9   4 + 4 = 8

5 + 5 = 10   3 + 7 = 10

Write how many.

11   12

17   20

Week 13
Compare Numbers to 20

Overview

Now that your child can read and write the numbers to 20, she'll learn to compare numbers to 20, identify even and odd numbers to 20, and find pairs that make 20 (such as 15 and 5).

Teaching Math with Confidence: Even and Odd Numbers

This week, you'll teach your child the even and odd numbers to 20. The main goal is to memorize the sequences of even and odd numbers up to 20, but you'll also preview several more advanced topics, like division and remainders.

In case you need a refresher, the even numbers (like 2, 6, or 20) are evenly divisible by 2. The odd numbers (like 7, 13, or 19) have a remainder when divided by 2.

6 is an even number because it can be divided evenly into 2 groups of 3.

7 is an odd number because it cannot be divided evenly into 2 groups.

In later grades, your child will learn how to use fractions and decimals to split odd-number quantities into equal parts. For example, 7 cookies divided by 2 equals 3 ½ cookies, and $7 divided by 2 equals $3.50.

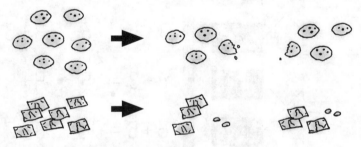

For now, you'll use the familiar context of splitting children evenly into 2 teams so that there's no question of fractional parts.

Extra Materials Needed for Week 13

- Small plastic zip-top bag
- For optional Enrichment and Review Lesson:
  - *Missing Mittens*, written by Stuart J. Murphy and illustrated by G. Brian Karas
  - 5 small toys or household items for a pretend store

Lesson 13.1
Compare Numbers to 20

	Purpose	Materials
Warm-up	• Count by 5s to 75 • Practice memory work • Review fact families and sum and difference	• Coins • Part-Total Mat (Blackline Master 4) • Number Cards
Activities	• Use *greater than*, *less than*, and *equal* to compare numbers up to 20	• Number Cards • Counters, optional • Double ten-frames (Blackline Master 1), optional
Workbook	• Compare numbers up to 20 on ten-frames	• Workbook pages 13.1A and 13.1B

Warm-up: Counting, Memory Work, and Review

- Place 15 nickels on the table. Have your child count by 5s to find the total value. **How many cents are the nickels worth?** *75¢.*

- Have your child rhythmically say the "10 and Some More" Chant. See Lesson 12.2 (page 193) for the full chant.

- Place Number Cards 5, 3, and 8 on the Part-Total Mat. Have your child write the matching fact family.

$$5 + 3 = 8$$
$$3 + 5 = 8$$
$$8 - 3 = 5$$
$$8 - 5 = 3$$

What do we call the answer to an addition problem? *The sum.*

What do we call the answer to a subtraction problem? *The difference.*

Activity: Compare Numbers to 20

You have learned how to read and write the numbers to 20. Today, we'll use *greater than, less than,* and *equal* to compare numbers to 20.

Let's pretend that I collected 17 shells at the beach, and you collected 14 shells. Write 17 and 14 on a piece of paper.

17   14

Who collected more shells? *You did.* **Which number is greater?** *17.*

Model both numbers with counters on the double ten-frames. Point out these combinations can help her know which number is greater: **17 is 10 and 7. But 14 is 10 and 4. 7 is greater than 4, so 17 is greater than 14.**

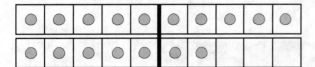 

Have your child use *greater than*, *less than*, or *equal* to compare the following number pairs. If she has trouble, encourage her to think about the combinations of "10 and some more."

- 13 and 15. *13 is less than 15. 15 is greater than 13.*
- 20 and 17. *17 is less than 20. 20 is greater than 17.*
- 12 and 12. *12 is equal to 12. Or, 12 and 12 are equal.*
- 19 and 11. *11 is less than 19. 19 is greater than 11.*

Activity: Play War (11-20)

Play 2 rounds of War with Number Cards 11-20. Have your child say the numbers aloud as she plays to practice reading them.

War (11-20)

Materials: 2 sets of Number Cards (11-20)

Object of the Game: Win the most cards.

Shuffle the Number Cards and deal the cards face down in two piles. Both players flip over the top card in their pile. Whoever has the greater number wins both cards.

If the cards are equal, leave them face-up on the table and have both players flip over another card. Whoever has the greater card wins all the face-up cards.

Play until you have used up the original piles of cards. Whoever has won more cards wins the game.

Variation: You can also continue playing until one player has won all the cards. You can play this way if you have time, but it may take a while!

Workbook: Compare Numbers to 20 and Review

Have your child complete workbook pages 13.1A and 13.1B.

Lesson 13.2
Compare Numbers to 20
on the 100 Chart

	Purpose	Materials
Warm-up	• Count by 10s to 80 • Practice memory work • Review tallies and combinations of "10 and some more"	• Counters • Small plastic zip-top bag • 7 bags of 10 counters assembled in previous lessons • Coins • Tally Cards
Activities	• Identify numbers to 20 on the 100 Chart • Compare numbers to 20 on the 100 Chart	• Counters • 100 Chart (Blackline Master 3)
Workbook	• Compare numbers to 20	• Workbook pages 13.2A and 13.2B

Warm-up: Counting, Memory Work, and Review

- Have your child count out 10 counters and place the counters in a zip-top bag. Add this bag to the bags you previously assembled and demonstrate how to count the bags by 10s: 10, 20, 30, 40, 50, 60, 70, 80.

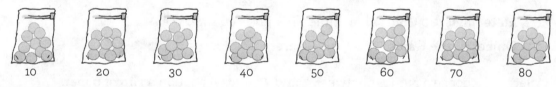

- Show your child a penny, nickel, and dime, and have him tell the name and value of each coin.

- Show your child the following pairs of Tally Cards. Have him identify the total number of tallies on both cards.

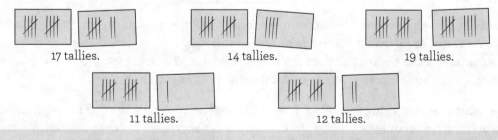

17 tallies.   14 tallies.   19 tallies.

11 tallies.   12 tallies.

Encourage your child to use the combinations of "10 and some more" to find the total tallies.

Activity: Find Numbers to 20 on the 100 Chart

In the last lesson, you learned how to compare numbers to 20. Today, we'll use *greater than* and *less than* to talk about numbers to 20 on the 100 Chart.

Show your child the 100 Chart and review the terms *row* and *column*. Cover the bottom part of the 100 Chart with paper so only the top 2 rows are showing.

1	2	3	4	5	6	7	8	9	10
11	12	13	14	15	16	17	18	19	20

Point to the following numbers on the 100 Chart (one at a time) and have your child identify them: 8, 18, 12, 20, 1, 10, 11.

Ask your child to point to the following numbers on the 100 Chart (one number at a time): 4, 14, 9, 19, 3, 13.

Pointing to the numbers in this order emphasizes that the ones-place in the numbers in each column remains the same. 14 is directly below 4, 19 is directly below 9, and so on. Your child will explore this pattern further in Unit 6.

Activity: Play Guess the Secret Number (1-20)

Play Guess the Secret Number (1-20) several times. Once your child understands the game, reverse roles and have your child choose the secret number.

Guess the Secret Number (1-20)

Materials: 100 Chart (Blackline Master 3), counters

Object of the Game: Guess the secret number.

Secretly choose a number between 1 and 20 and write it on a slip of paper.

Place a counter on the 1 and the 20 on the 100 Chart. **My secret number is greater than 1 and less than 20.**

○	2	3	4	5	6	7	8	9	10
11	12	13	14	15	16	17	18	19	○

The other player guesses the secret number. If the guess is incorrect, move one counter to the number he guesses, so the secret number is still between the two counters. For example, if the secret number is 12, and your child guesses 5, move the counter from the 1 to the 5 and say: **My secret number is greater than 5.**

Have your child continue guessing. Keep moving the counters so your secret number is between the two counters. Once your child guesses correctly, reveal your written number.

Workbook: Compare Numbers to 20 and Review

Have your child complete workbook pages 13.2A and 13.2B.

Lesson 13.3
Even and Odd Numbers to 20

	Purpose	Materials
Warm-up	• Count dimes by 10s • Practice memory work • Review subtraction facts	• Coins • Subtraction Climb to the Top game board (Workbook page 11.1A) • Playing cards • Counters
Activities	• Begin to learn the even numbers and odd numbers to 20	• Number Cards • Counters • 2 blank index cards
Workbook	• Identify even and odd numbers on the 100 Chart	• Workbook pages 13.3A and 13.3B

Warm-up: Counting, Memory Work, and Review

- Place 8 dimes on the table. Have your child count by 10s to find the total value. **How many cents are the coins worth?** *80¢.*

- Have your child rhythmically say the "10 and Some More" Chant. See Lesson 12.2 (page 193) for the full chant.

- Play Subtraction Climb to the Top. See Lesson 11.1 (page 175) for directions.

Activity: Introduce Even and Odd Numbers

In the last lesson, you compared numbers to 20. Today, you'll learn about two special names we have for numbers: even and odd.

Let's pretend 6 children are playing a game and want to split into 2 equal teams. We'll use counters to stand for the children. Place 6 counters on the table and have your child split them into two equal groups. **How many children are on each team?** *3.*

When we can split a number evenly into 2 groups, we call it an even number. So, 6 is an even number.

Let's pretend there are 7 children. Have your child try to split 7 counters into 2 equal groups. **How many children are on each team?** *3, but 1 is leftover.*

There's no way to split 7 children equally into 2 teams. What do you think the children might do? *Possible answers: They might take turns sitting out. They might just put the extra child on one of the teams.*

When a number can't be split evenly into 2 groups, we call it an odd number. So, 7 is an odd number.

See the Week 13 **Teaching Math with Confidence** for more information on even and odd numbers.

Activity: Sort Even and Odd Numbers

Let's sort the numbers from 1 to 20 into evens and odds. Have your child place Number Cards 1-20 in order on the table. Write Even and Odd on 2 index cards.

Give your child 1 counter. **Can you split 1 child into 2 equal teams?** *No.* **So, 1 is an odd number.** Place Number Card 1 next to the Odd card.

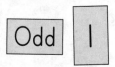

Give your child 2 counters. **Can you split 2 children into 2 equal teams?** *Yes.* **So, 2 is an even number.** Place Number Card 2 next to the Even card.

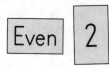

Continue in the same way to 20. For each number, give your child the matching number of counters and ask whether she can split the counters into 2 equal groups. Then, place its Number Card in the correct category.

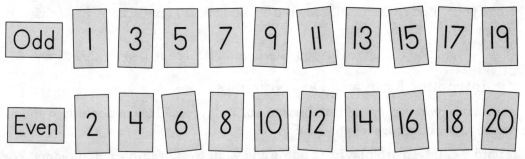

If your child notices the evens and odds alternate, work through the rest of the numbers quickly to verify the pattern continues to 20.

Activity: Discuss the Even Numbers

Have your child read the even numbers in order. **What do you notice about the even numbers?** *Possible answers: Each number is 2 more than the number before it. They're the same numbers we say when we count by 2s.*

With your child looking away, turn over the 6, 10, and 18.

Have her identify each missing number and flip over the card to check. Repeat with different numbers until your child has practiced identifying all the even numbers.

Activity: Discuss the Odd Numbers

Have your child read the odd numbers in order. **What do you notice about the odd numbers?** *Possible answers: Each number is 2 more than the number before it. They're the numbers we skip when we count by 2s.*

With your child looking away, turn over the 5, 11, and 17.

Have her identify each missing number and flip over the card to check. Repeat with different numbers until your child has practiced identifying all the odd numbers.

Leave out the sorted cards for your child to refer to as she completes the front side of the workbook page.

Workbook: Identify Even and Odd Numbers and Review

Have your child complete workbook pages 13.3A and 13.3B. Allow your child to look at the sorted Number Cards (from the previous activity) as she completes the front side of the page.

Lesson 13.4
Pairs That Make 20

	Purpose	Materials
Warm-up	• Count from 70 to 100 • Practice memory work • Review writing numbers from 11 to 20	• 100 Chart (Blackline Master 3)
Activities	• Find combinations that make 20	• Counters • Double ten-frames (Blackline Master 1) • Number Cards • Part-Total Mat (Blackline Master 4)
Workbook	• Find combinations that make 20	• Workbook pages 13.4A and 13.4B

Warm-up: Counting, Memory Work, and Review

- Count in unison with your child from 70 to 100. Point to each number on the 100 Chart as you say it.

- Have your child say the months. **How many months are in a year?** *12*.

- Name the numbers from 11 to 20 in random order. Have your child write each number on a piece of paper.

> This activity informally assesses how fluently your child can write the numbers to 20.

Activity: Find Missing Parts of 20

You've already learned the combinations that make 10. Today, you'll use what you know about the pairs that make 10 to find the pairs that make 20.

Let's pretend we have 20 candies to share. Place 20 counters on the double ten-frames.

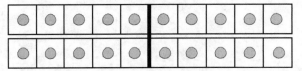

Let's pretend that you get 19. Place a pencil on the ten-frames to split the 20 counters into a group of 19 and a group of 1. **You already know 9 and 1 make 10. So, 19 and what make 20?** *1*.

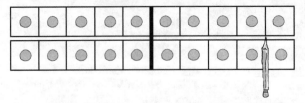

Have your child place Number Cards on the Part-Total Mat to match the counters.

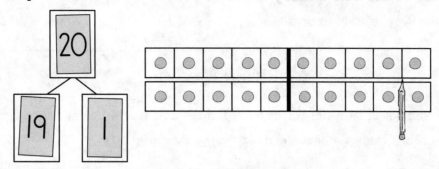

Repeat with the following questions. Encourage your child to think about the pairs that make 10 to help find the answers. For example: **7 and 3 make 10. So, 17 and what make 20?** *3*.

Let's pretend you get 17 candies. How many do I get? *3*.

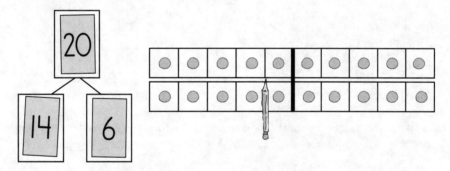

Let's pretend you get 14 candies. How many do I get? *6*.

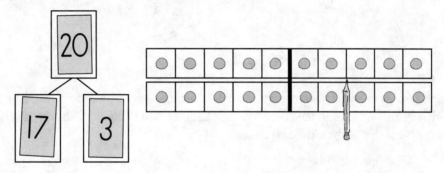

Let's pretend you get 10 candies. How many do I get? *10*.

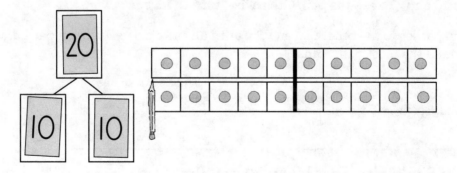

Activity: Play Make 20 Memory

Play one round of Make 20 Memory.

Make 20 Memory

Materials: 1 set of Number Cards (0-20) plus 1 additional 10-card, 22 cards total

Object of the Game: Collect the most pairs that equal 20.

Split the cards into two groups. Place Number Cards 0-9 in one group and Number Cards 11-20 in another group. Add a 10-card to each group so each has 11 cards.

Shuffle each group separately and arrange it in a face-down grid on the table. Place the grid with Number Cards 10-20 on the left side of the table and the grid with Number Cards 0-10 on the right side of the table.

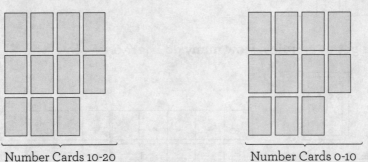

Number Cards 10-20   Number Cards 0-10

Children usually find it easier to identify the combinations that make 20 when they begin with the greater number. Arranging the cards like this ensures your child always starts with a number 10 or greater.

On your turn, flip over 2 cards (1 from each grid). If the cards have a sum of 20 (like 19 and 1, or 16 and 4), keep the pair. Otherwise, turn them back over.

Play then passes to the other player. Play until all the cards have been paired. Whoever has found the most pairs wins.

If your child isn't sure which card he needs to make a pair, have him place 20 counters on the ten-frame and split them to see which card he needs.

Workbook: Find Pairs That Make 20 and Review

Have your child complete workbook pages 13.4A and 13.4B.

Lesson 13.5
Enrichment and Review (Optional)

	Purpose	Materials
Warm-up	• Review counting • Review memory work • Review your child's favorite or most challenging activities from Week 13	• Varies, depending on the activities you choose
Picture Book	• Understand even and odd numbers in the context of mittens	• *Missing Mittens*, written by Stuart J. Murphy and illustrated by G. Brian Karas
Enrichment Activity	• Practice the numbers to 20 in the context of spending money	• 5 index cards or small slips of paper • 5 small toys or household items for a pretend store • Play money

Warm-up: Counting, Memory Work, and Review

- Have your child count to 80 by 1s, 2s, 5s, or 10s. (Choose whichever counting sequence your child needs to practice the most.)

- Quiz your child on the memory work through Week 12. See page 499 for the full list.

- If you have time, repeat one or two of the activities from this week's lessons. Choose activities your child especially enjoyed or found challenging.

Math Picture Book: *Missing Mittens*

Read *Missing Mittens*, written by Stuart J. Murphy and illustrated by G. Brian Karas. As you read, discuss the pictures of the even and odd numbers of mittens.

Enrichment Activity: Pretend Store

Set up a pretend store by laying five small toys in a row. Write $12, $14, $15, $19, $20 on 5 index cards and place an index card in front of each item.

Give your child some play ten-dollar bills, five-dollar bills, and one-dollar bills to use to pretend to buy things. Encourage her to think about the combinations that make 10 as she pays for each item. For example: *10 and 4 make 14, so I need 1 ten-dollar bill and 4 one-dollar bills.*

Week 13 Answer Key

13.1A

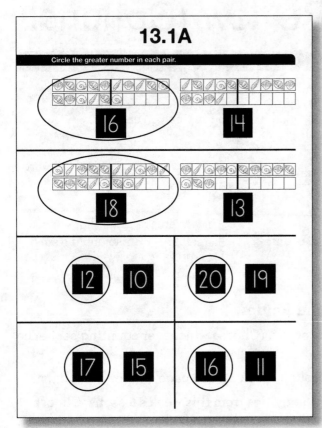

13.1B

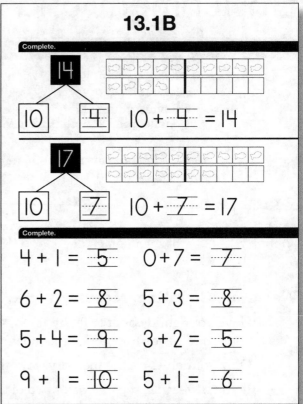

13.2A

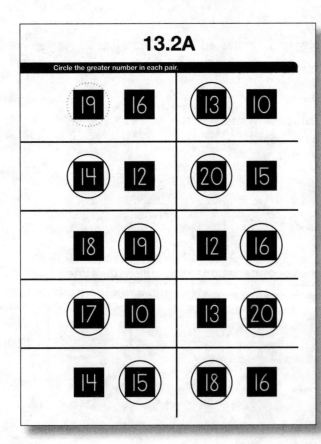

13.2B

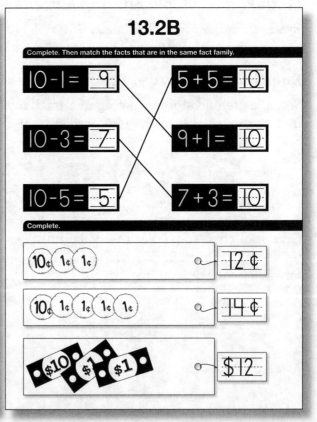

Week 13 Answer Key

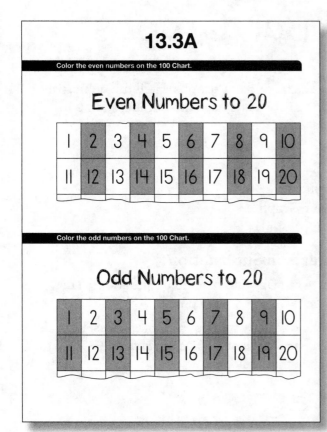

13.3A

Color the even numbers on the 100 Chart.

Even Numbers to 20

1	2	3	4	5	6	7	8	9	10
11	12	13	14	15	16	17	18	19	20

Color the odd numbers on the 100 Chart.

Odd Numbers to 20

1	2	3	4	5	6	7	8	9	10
11	12	13	14	15	16	17	18	19	20

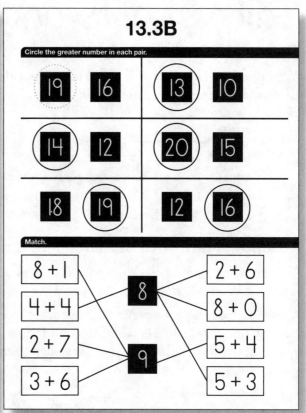

13.3B

Circle the greater number in each pair.

19   16   13   10

14   12   20   15

18   19   12   16

Match.

8 + 1   2 + 6
4 + 4   8   8 + 0
2 + 7   5 + 4
3 + 6   9   5 + 3

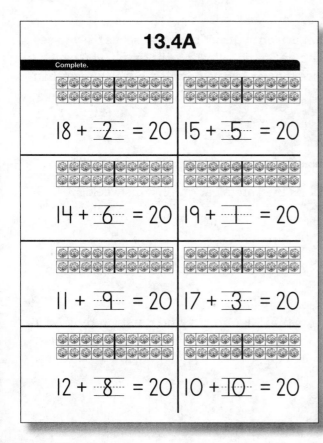

13.4A

Complete.

$18 + 2 = 20$ $15 + 5 = 20$

$14 + 6 = 20$ $19 + 1 = 20$

$11 + 9 = 20$ $17 + 3 = 20$

$12 + 8 = 20$ $10 + 10 = 20$

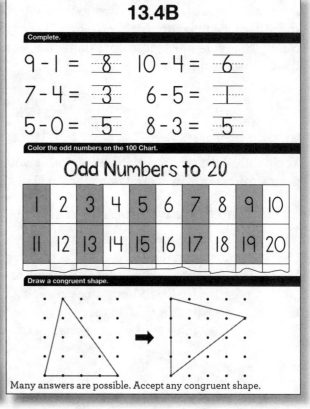

13.4B

Complete.

$9 - 1 = 8$ $10 - 4 = 6$
$7 - 4 = 3$ $6 - 5 = 1$
$5 - 0 = 5$ $8 - 3 = 5$

Color the odd numbers on the 100 Chart.

Odd Numbers to 20

1	2	3	4	5	6	7	8	9	10
11	12	13	14	15	16	17	18	19	20

Draw a congruent shape.

Many answers are possible. Accept any congruent shape.

Week 14
Tally Charts and Bar Graphs

Overview

Your child will learn to make and interpret tally charts and bar graphs. He'll flip coins, roll dice, and organize information about families you know as he uses the numbers to 20 in real-life contexts.

Lesson 14.1   Make a Tally Chart
Lesson 14.2   Introduce Bar Graphs
Lesson 14.3   Make a Real-Life Bar Graph
Lesson 14.4   Make Another Real-Life Bar Graph
Lesson 14.5   Enrichment and Review (Optional)

Teaching Math with Confidence: Comparison Subtraction

Your child has already learned how to subtract in take-away and take-apart situations. This week, he'll learn how to subtract to find the difference between two numbers.

Comparison situations occur when we want to find how many more or how many less. For example, say one child has 6 crackers and another child has 4 crackers. You can subtract 6 – 4 = 2 to find that the first child has 2 more crackers than the other child.

6 – 4 = 2. 6 is 2 more than 4.

Bar graphs provide a natural way to introduce comparison subtraction, because it's easy to see the difference in length between two bars. For example, in the following bar graph, you can clearly see there are 3 more boys than girls, because the bar for the boys is 3 boxes longer than the bar for the girls.

7 – 4 = 3. There are 3 more boys than girls.

You'll introduce comparison subtraction as your child interprets bar graphs this week. He'll practice comparison subtraction more in Unit 10.

Extra Materials Needed for Week 11

- Small sticky notes or slips of paper
- Tape, optional
- For optional Enrichment and Review Lesson:
    × *The Best Vacation Ever*, written by Stuart J. Murphy and illustrated by Nadine Bernard Westcott
    × Small sticky notes or slips of paper

Lesson 14.1
Make a Tally Chart

	Purpose	Materials
Warm-up	• Count to 100 by 5s • Practice memory work • Review pairs that make 20	• 100 Chart (Blackline Master 3) • Small toy • Number Cards
Activities	• Make and interpret a tally chart	• Coin
Workbook	• Interpret a tally chart	• Workbook pages 14.1A and 14.1B

Warm-up: Counting, Memory Work, and Review

- Have your child count by 5s to 100. Have her make a small toy jump on each number on the 100 Chart as she says it.

- **Name the even numbers in order to 20.** *2, 4, 6, 8, 10, 12, 14, 16, 18, 20.* **Name the odd numbers in order to 19.** *1, 3, 5, 7, 9, 11, 13, 15, 17, 19.*

> If your child has trouble, have her point to each number on the 100 Chart as she says it.

- Play Make 20 Memory. See Lesson 13.4 (page 212) for directions.

Activity: Make a Heads and Tails Tally Chart

This week, we're going to make charts and graphs. Have you ever seen a chart or graph? *Possible answers: I saw a chart of temperatures on the TV news. The doctor showed me a graph with my height on it.*

We use charts to organize information. Often, it's easier to understand information in a chart than it is to read every number.

> Technically, a graph shows the relationship between two sets of numerical data, while a chart is any visual way to show data. We usually use these words interchangeably in everyday conversation, so this book doesn't distinguish between the two. Your child doesn't need to understand this distinction.

Today, we'll make a Heads and Tails Tally Chart. Draw a simple chart like the one below. Point out the title to your child. **The title describes the information in the chart.**

Heads and Tails Tally Chart	
Heads	
Tails	

First, flip a coin. Then, make a tally to match whether the coin shows heads or tails. Keep going until you have either 10 heads or 10 tails.

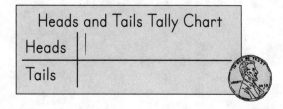

Heads and Tails Tally Chart	
Heads	||
Tails	

Have your child flip a coin and make tallies until one row has 10 tallies. Remind her to draw every fifth tally horizontally across the previous 4 tallies.

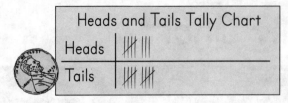

Activity: Interpret the Heads and Tails Tally Chart

Use the following questions to discuss your chart. (These sample answers are based on the sample chart above, but your child's answers should be based on her chart.)

- **How many heads did you flip?** *Sample answer: 8.*
- **How many tails did you flip?** *Sample answer: 10.*
- **How many times did you flip the coin in all?** *Sample answer: 18.* **How do you know?** *Sample answer: There were 10 tails and 8 heads. 10 and 8 make 18.*

Show your child how to write an addition equation to match.

$$10 + 8 = 18$$

Sample equation for the total number of flips.

- **Did you flip more heads or tails?** *Sample answer: Tails.* **How many more?** *Sample answer: 2.* **How do you know?** *Possible answers: 10 is 2 more than 8. I see there are 2 more tallies for tails. 10 minus 8 equals 2.*

Show your child how to write a subtraction equation that shows the difference between the number of heads and number of tails. Start your equation with the greater number.

$$10 - 8 = 2$$

Sample subtraction equation comparing the number of heads and tails.

See the Week 14 **Teaching Math with Confidence** for more on using subtraction in comparison situations. Don't worry if your child finds this subtraction equation confusing. She'll get more experience with comparison subtraction later this week and in Unit 10.

Workbook: Interpret a Tally Chart and Review

Have your child complete workbook pages 14.1A and 14.1B. Read the questions aloud as needed.

Lesson 14.2
Introduce Bar Graphs

	Purpose	Materials
Warm-up	• Count by 10s to 100 • Practice memory work • Review addition facts	• 100 Chart (Blackline Master 3) • Counters • 2 decks of playing cards
Activities	• Make and interpret a bar graph	• Workbook page 14.2A • Die
Workbook	• Review previously learned material	• Workbook page 14.2B

Warm-up: Counting, Memory Work, and Review

- Demonstrate how to count by 10s to 100: **10, 20...** Cover each number on the 100 Chart as you say it. Then, have your child count by 10s to 100. Have him remove each counter after he says the number underneath it.

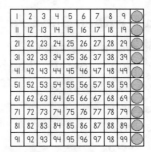

- **Name the even numbers in order to 20.** *2, 4, 6, 8, 10, 12, 14, 16, 18, 20.* **Name the odd numbers in order to 19.** *1, 3, 5, 7, 9, 11, 13, 15, 17, 19.*

- Play Addition War. See Lesson 6.4 (page 100) for directions.

Activity: Make a Number Race Bar Graph

In the last lesson, you made a Heads and Tails Tally Chart. Today, you'll make a bar graph. Bar graphs are like tally charts, but they use bars to show the same information.

We'll make the bar graph on your workbook page. Show your child Workbook page 14.2A.

1				
2				
3				
4				
5				
6				

Can you find the title? *Child points to title.* Read the title to your child.

To make the graph, roll the die and color in a matching square. So, if you roll a 6, color in the first empty square next to the 6. I wonder which row you will fill first!

Have your child roll the die and color the matching square until one row is completely full. Make sure he colors in the boxes from left to right, without skipping any boxes.

Sample final Number Race Bar Graph.

Activity: Interpret the Number Race Bar Graph

Use the following questions to discuss your chart. (These sample answers are based on the sample chart above, but your child's answers should be based on his chart.)

- **How many 1s did you roll?** *Sample answer: 4.*
- **How many 2s?** *Sample answer: 2.*
- **How many 3s?** *Sample answer: 2.*
- **How many 4s?** *Sample answer: 5.*
- **How many 5s?** *Sample answer: 1.*
- **How many 6s?** *Sample answer: 4.*
- **Which number did you roll the least?** *Sample answer: 5.*
- **Which number did you roll the most?** *Sample answer: 4.*
- **Did you roll any of the numbers the same number of times?** *Sample answer: I rolled 2s and 3s the same number of times.*
- **How many times did you roll the die in all?** *Sample answer: 18.* If your child is not sure, suggest he count the number of boxes he colored.

Also show your child how to write an addition equation that matches the total number of rolls.

$$4 + 2 + 2 + 5 + 1 + 4 = 18$$

Sample equation showing the total number of rolls.

Writing this equation helps your child understand how to use addition to find the total number of rolls, but he is not expected to be able to add these 6 numbers. He can simply count the number of colored boxes instead.

- **Were there more 1s or 2s?** *Sample answer: 1s.* **How many more?** *Sample answer: 2 more.* Suggest that your child look at the difference between the lengths of the bars to answer.

  Also show your child how to write a subtraction equation that shows this difference. Start your equation with whichever number is greater and subtract the lesser number from it.

$$4 - 2 = 2$$

Sample equation based on the sample tally chart above.

Workbook: Review

Have your child complete workbook page 14.2B.

Lesson 14.3
Make a Real-Life Bar Graph

	Purpose	Materials
Warm-up	• Count by 10s to 100 • Practice memory work • Review pairs that make 20	• Counters • 2 small plastic zip-top bags • 8 bags of 10 counters assembled in previous lessons • Number Cards
Activities	• Make a bar graph based on real-life data • Interpret a bar graph	• Small sticky notes or slips of paper • Paper • Tape, optional
Workbook	• Interpret a bar graph	• Workbook pages 14.3A and 14.3B

Warm-up: Counting, Memory Work, and Review

- Have your child count out 2 groups of 10 counters and place each group of 10 in a zip-top bag. Add these bags to the bags you previously assembled and demonstrate how to count the bags by 10s: **10, 20, 30, 40, 50, 60, 70, 80, 90, 100.**

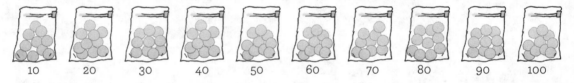

| 10 | 20 | 30 | 40 | 50 | 60 | 70 | 80 | 90 | 100 |

- **Name the even numbers in order to 20.** *2, 4, 6, 8, 10, 12, 14, 16, 18, 20.* **Name the odd numbers in order to 19.** *1, 3, 5, 7, 9, 11, 13, 15, 17, 19.*

- Play Make 20 Memory. See Lesson 13.4 (page 212) for directions.

Activity: Make a Family Bar Graph

In the last lesson, you made a Number Race Bar Graph. Today, you'll make a bar graph about some families we know.

First, we'll label sticky notes with the names of some children we know. We'll use these sticky notes to make the bars in our graph. Have your child write her name on a small sticky note or slip of paper. Also have her write the names of the other children in your family, each on its own sticky note.

Help your child with the writing as needed.

Have your child choose 3 other families with children. Write the name of each child in the families on a separate sticky note.

Choose families with different numbers of children to make the final graph more interesting.

Yesterday, we made a bar graph with horizontal bars. Today, we'll make a bar graph with vertical bars. Draw a line at the bottom of the paper and write the last name of each family below the line. Have your child stack the matching sticky notes above each last name. Add another sheet of paper with tape if you need more room.

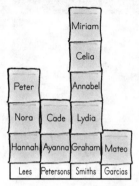

What is a good title for our bar graph? *Sample answer: Children in Families We Know.* Accept any reasonable answer and write the title (or have your child write the title) at the top of the paper.

Activity: Interpret the Bar Graph

Use the following questions to discuss your chart (these sample answers are based on the sample chart above, but your child's answers should be based on her chart).

- **How many children are in each family?** *Sample answer: Our family has 3 children. The Petersons have 2 children. The Smiths have 5 children. The Garcias have 1 child.*
- **Which family has the least number of children? Sample answer:** *The Garcias.*
- **Which family has the greatest number of children? Sample answer:** *The Smiths.*
- **Do any of the families have the same number of children?** *Sample answer: No.*
- **If we had a picnic with all these families, how many children would come?** *Sample answer: 11.* If your child is not sure how to find the answer, suggest she count all of the sticky notes.

    Show your child how to write an addition equation that matches the total number of children.

$$3 + 2 + 5 + 1 = 11$$

Sample equation, based on the bar graph above.

You can also ask your child to find the difference between the number of children in 2 families and write a corresponding subtraction equation.

 Save this graph for Lesson 14.4. You will reuse the sticky notes to make another bar graph.

Workbook: Interpret a Bar Graph and Review

Have your child complete workbook pages 14.3A and 14.3B. Read the questions aloud as needed.

Lesson 14.4
Make Another Real-Life Bar Graph

Warm-up	• Count dimes by 10s • Practice memory work • Review subtraction facts	• Coins • Subtraction Climb to the Top game board (Workbook page 11.1A) • Playing cards • Counters
Activities	• Understand information can be sorted and graphed in multiple ways • Make and interpret a bar graph	• Graph and small sticky notes from Lesson 14.3 • Paper • Tape, optional
Workbook	• Interpret a bar graph	• Workbook pages 14.4A and 14.4B

Warm-up: Counting, Memory Work, and Review

- Place 9 dimes on the table. Have your child count by 10s to find the total value. **How many cents are the coins worth?** *90¢.*

- **Name the even numbers in order to 20.** *2, 4, 6, 8, 10, 12, 14, 16, 18, 20.* **Name the odd numbers in order to 19.** *1, 3, 5, 7, 9, 11, 13, 15, 17, 19.*

- Play Subtraction Climb to the Top. See Lesson 11.1 (page 175) for directions.

Activity: Make a Boys and Girls Bar Graph

In the last lesson, you sorted children by family to make a bar graph. Show your child the bar graph from Lesson 14.3.

Today, you'll make a new bar graph about the same children. Instead of sorting them by family, we'll sort them by boys and girls.

Draw a line at the bottom of a piece of paper and write "Boys" and "Girls" below the line. Have your child stack the corresponding sticky notes above each word. Add more paper with tape if you need more room.

What is a good title for our bar graph? *Sample answer: Boys and Girls.* Accept any reasonable answer and write the title (or have your child write the title) at the top of the paper.

Activity: Interpret the Bar Graph

Use the following questions to discuss your bar graph. (These sample answers are based on the sample bar graph above.)

- **How many boys are there?** *Sample answer: 4.*
- **How many girls are there?** *Sample answer: 7.*
- **Are there more boys or girls?** *Sample answer: Girls.* **How many more?** *There are 3 more girls than boys.* Your child can look at the difference between the lengths of the bars to answer this question.

  Show your child how to write a subtraction equation that shows the difference between the number of boys and the number of girls. Start your equation with whichever number is greater.

$$7 - 4 = 3$$

Sample equation showing the difference between the number of boys and number of girls.

- **How many children are there in all?** *Sample answer: 11.* Write an addition equation that matches the total number of children.

$$4 + 7 = 11$$

Sample equation showing the total number of children.

Workbook: Interpret a Bar Graph and Review

Have your child complete workbook pages 14.4A and 14.4B. Read the questions to your child as needed.

Lesson 14.5
Enrichment and Review (Optional)

	Purpose	Materials
Warm-up	• Review counting • Review memory work • Review your child's favorite or most challenging activities from Week 14	• Varies, depending on the activities you choose
Picture Book	• Read and interpret charts in a real-life context	• *The Best Vacation Ever*, written by Stuart J. Murphy and illustrated by Nadine Bernard Westcott
Enrichment Activity	• Take a poll and create a graph of the results	• Small sticky notes or slips of paper • Paper

Warm-up: Counting, Memory Work, and Review

- Have your child count to 100 by 1s, 2s, 5s, or 10s. (Choose whichever counting sequence your child needs to practice the most.)

- Quiz your child on the memory work through Week 14. See page 499 for the full list.

- If you have time, repeat one or two of the activities from this week's lessons. Choose activities your child especially enjoyed or found challenging.

Math Picture Book: *The Best Vacation Ever*

Read *The Best Vacation Ever,* written by Stuart J. Murphy and illustrated by Nadine Bernard Westcott. As you read, point out the charts in the book and discuss them.

Enrichment Activity: Take a Poll

Have your child choose an opinion question and poll about 10 friends or family members on the question. This will work best if your child picks a question with 2-4 well-defined options. For example:

- Do you like ice cream or cake better?
- What's your favorite season?
- Which activity do you like best: ice-skating, sledding, or skiing?

Have your child write each person's name on a sticky note and then make a simple bar graph of the results. Use the bar graph in Lesson 14.2 as a model.

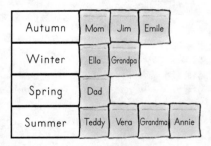

Week 14 Answer Key

14.1A

Use the chart to answer the questions.

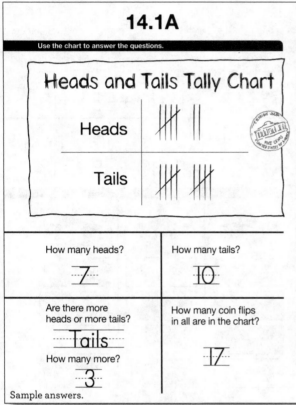

Heads and Tails Tally Chart

Heads — |||| ||

Tails — |||| ||||

How many heads?	How many tails?
7	10
Are there more heads or more tails?	How many coin flips in all are in the chart?
Tails	17
How many more?	
3	

Sample answers.

14.1B

Complete.

$10 - 8 = 2$ $9 - 7 = 2$

$9 - 3 = 6$ $4 - 0 = 4$

$8 - 2 = 6$ $7 - 4 = 3$

$8 - 6 = 2$ $9 - 5 = 4$

Match.

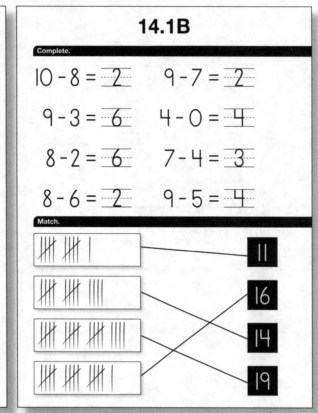

14.2A

See the *Instructor Guide* for directions on how to complete the bar graph.

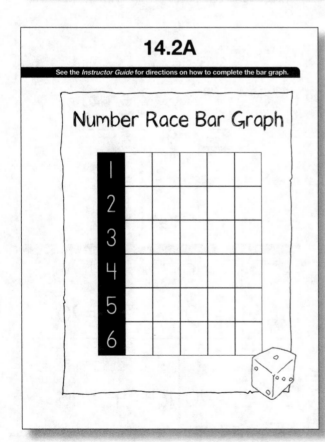

Number Race Bar Graph

1
2
3
4
5
6

14.2B

Match.

Use the key to color the hats.

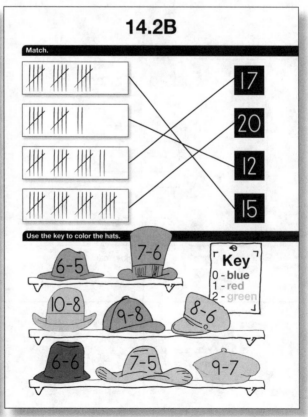

6-5   7-6

10-8   9-8   8-6

6-6   7-5   9-7

Key
0 - blue
1 - red
2 - green

Week 14 Answer Key

14.3A

Use the chart to answer the questions.

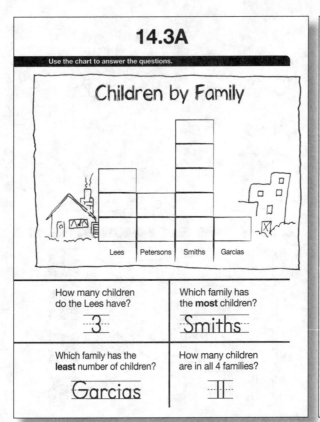

Children by Family

Lees   Petersons   Smiths   Garcias

How many children do the Lees have?	Which family has the **most** children?
3	Smiths
Which family has the **least** number of children?	How many children are in all 4 families?
Garcias	11

14.3B

Complete.

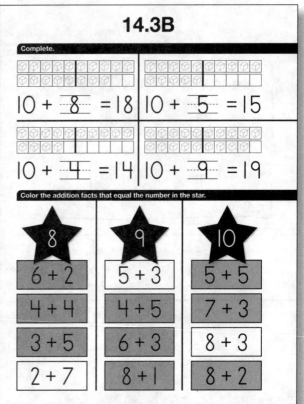

$10 + 8 = 18$ $10 + 5 = 15$

$10 + 4 = 14$ $10 + 9 = 19$

Color the addition facts that equal the number in the star.

⭐ 8   ⭐ 9   ⭐ 10

6 + 2	5 + 3	5 + 5
4 + 4	4 + 5	7 + 3
3 + 5	6 + 3	8 + 3
2 + 7	8 + 1	8 + 2

14.4A

Use the chart to answer the questions.

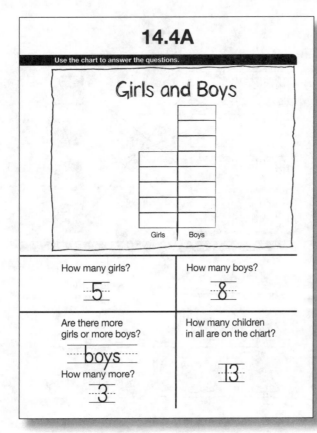

Girls and Boys

Girls   Boys

How many girls?	How many boys?
5	8
Are there more girls or more boys?	How many children in all are on the chart?
boys	13
How many more?	
3	

14.4B

Complete.

$6 - 5 = 1$ $7 - 2 = 5$

$7 - 6 = 1$ $9 - 8 = 1$

$10 - 9 = 1$ $8 - 7 = 1$

$6 - 6 = 0$ $10 - 8 = 2$

Complete.

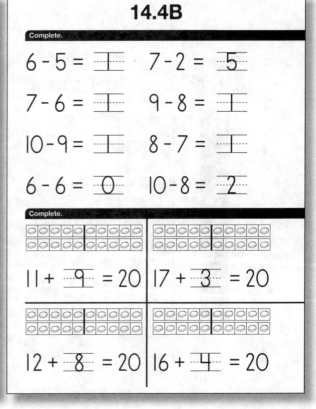

$11 + 9 = 20$ $17 + 3 = 20$

$12 + 8 = 20$ $16 + 4 = 20$

Unit 5 Checkpoint

What to Expect at the End of Unit 5

By the end of Unit 5, most children will be able to:

- Recognize the written numerals from 11 to 20 and write them mostly fluently. Some children will still confuse the order of the digits. (For example, they might write 51 instead of 15.)
- Confidently use *greater than*, *less than*, or *equal* to compare numbers to 20.
- Recognize quantities from 11 to 20 on the ten-frame without counting one-by-one. Most will be able to recognize combinations of "10 and some more," but some will still count on from 10.
- Recite the even and odd numbers up to 20.
- Identify the value of combinations of ten-dollar and one-dollar bills (or dimes and pennies), either by recognizing combinations of "10 and some more" or counting on from 10.
- Identify some of the combinations that make 20 (for example, 19 and 1). Many children will still be working on this.
- Make simple tally charts and graphs (with guidance) and answer questions about them.

Is Your Child Ready to Move on?

In Unit 6, your child will learn how to read, write, and compare numbers to 100. She will also learn more about place value. Before moving on to Unit 6, your child should know the following skills:

- Recognize quantities from 11 to 20 on the ten-frame without counting.
- Read and write numbers to 20 mostly automatically. It's fine if your child occasionally reverses the digits, but she should be able to read them accurately.
- Compare numbers to 20.

Your child does not need to fully memorize the combinations that make 20 or the even and odd numbers before moving on to Unit 6.

What to Do If Your Child Needs More Practice

If your child is having trouble with any of the above skills, spend a few days practicing the corresponding review activities below before moving on to Unit 6.

Activities for recognizing quantities from 11 to 20 on the ten-frame without counting

- "10 and Some More Chant" (Lesson 12.2)
- Write Addition Equations to Match Combinations of "10 and Some More" (Lesson 12.3)

Activities for reading and writing numbers to 20

- Memory (11-20) (Lesson 12.2)
- X-Ray Vision with Missing Addends (Lesson 12.3)
- Find Numbers to 20 on the 100 Chart (Lesson 13.2)
- Number Dictation (Lesson 13.4, Review)

Activities for comparing numbers to 20

- War (11-20) (Lesson 13.1)
- Guess the Secret Number (11-20) (Lesson 13.2)

Unit 6
Numbers to 100

Overview

In Unit 5, your child began to understand numbers in the teens as combinations of "10 and some more." In Unit 6, he'll build on this knowledge as he learns to understand two-digit numbers as combination of tens and ones. He will also learn to read, write, and compare numbers to 100.

Week 15	Place Value, Part 1
Week 16	Place Value, Part 2
Week 17	Compare Numbers to 100

What Your Child Will Learn

In this unit your child will learn to:

- Read, write, and compare numbers to 100
- Understand place value in two-digit numbers
- Add 1 or 10 to two-digit numbers
- Add and subtract multiples of 10 (for example, 30+40 or 50–20)

Recommended Math Picture Books (Optional)

These picture books are scheduled in the optional Enrichment and Review lessons at the end of each week.

- *Let's Count to 100!,* by Masayuki Sebe. Kids Can Press, 2011.
- *Chicka Chicka, 1, 2, 3,* written by Bill Martin Jr. and Michael Sampson and illustrated by Lois Ehlert. Simon & Schuster Books for Young Readers, 2004.
- *Only One,* written by Marc Harshman and illustrated by Barbara Garrison. Scholastic, 1993.

Week 15
Place Value, Part 1

Overview

Your child will learn to read and write the multiples of 10 up to 100: 10, 20, 30, 40, 50, 60, 70, 80, 90, and 100. She will also add and subtract these numbers and find pairs of them that equal 100.

Lesson 15.1   Read and Write Multiples of 10
Lesson 15.2   Add Multiples of 10
Lesson 15.3   Subtract Multiples of 10
Lesson 15.4   Pairs That Make 100
Lesson 15.5   Enrichment and Review (Optional)

Teaching Math with Confidence:
Groups of 10 as a Cornerstone for Place Value

In Unit 5, your child began to think of 10 objects as 1 group of 10 rather than 10 individual objects. This week, your child will work exclusively with groups of 10 to solidify this essential concept. These numbers (10, 20, 30, 40, 50, 60, 70, 80, 90, 100) are called the multiples of 10 up to 100. Your child doesn't need to memorize this term, but it will be used for clarity's sake in the instructor guide.

Your child already knows how to count by 10s to 100, but now she will learn how to read and write these numbers. Through hands-on practice and a chant, she'll learn to connect the spoken number names, written numbers, and hands-on representations of the multiples of 10.

Three ways to represent 40.

She will also begin to understand the meaning of the tens-place in written numbers. For example, she'll learn that the 4 in 40 stands for 4 tens.

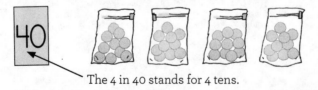

The 4 in 40 stands for 4 tens.

Once your child fully grasps the idea that a collection of 10 objects can be treated as a group rather than 10 individual objects, she'll be ready to reason more abstractly about place value. In Week 16, your child will dive deeper into place value and learn how to read and write two-digit numbers that are not multiples of 10, like 27 or 84.

Extra Materials Needed for Week 15

- 16 blank index cards
- For optional Enrichment and Review Lesson:
    - × *Let's Count to 100!*, by Masayuki Sebe
    - × 100 small craft items, such as stickers, pompoms, dried beans, beads, or small paper squares
    - × Paper, preferably construction paper
    - × Tape, optional
    - × Glue

Lesson 15.1
Read and Write Multiples of 10

	Purpose	Materials
Warm-up	• Count to 100 by 10s • Practice memory work • Review coin combinations up to 20¢	• 100 Chart (Blackline Master 3) • Small toy • Coins
Activities	• Learn to write multiples of 10 to 100 (30, 40, 50, 60, 70, 80, 90, 100) • Read written numbers for the multiples of 10	• 10 bags of counters assembled in previous lessons • 16 blank index cards
Workbook	• Identify quantities arranged in groups of 10 • Read written numbers for the multiples of 10	• Workbook pages 15.1A and 15.1B

Most children need explicit, incremental instruction to make sense of the abstract concept of place value. This unit is designed to provide gradual, clear, and step-by-step teaching so that your child has plenty of time to make sense of this tricky topic. If your child grasps place value quickly, feel free to condense lessons or skip unneeded review activities.

Warm-up: Counting, Memory Work, and Review

- Have your child count by 10s to 100. Have her make a small toy jump on each number on the 100 Chart as she says it.

- Have your child rhythmically say the "10 and Some More" Chant: **10 and 1. Eleven! 10 and 2. Twelve!** etc. See Lesson 12.2 (page 193) for the full chant.

- Have your child tell the value of the following coin combinations.

  - × 1 penny (*1¢*)
  - × 1 nickel (*5¢*)
  - × 1 nickel and 2 pennies (*7¢*)
  - × 1 dime (*10¢*)
  - × 1 dime and 1 penny (*11¢*)
  - × 1 dime, 1 nickel, and 1 penny (*16¢*)
  - × 2 dimes (*20¢*)

Activity: Make Number Cards for Multiples of 10

You have learned how to read and write numbers from 0 to 20. In Unit 6, you will learn how to read and write numbers up to 100.

The numbers you say when you count by 10s to 100 are very important, so we'll spend this week getting to know these numbers well. We call these numbers multiples of 10.

See the Week 15 **Teaching Math with Confidence** for more on why these numbers are so important.

Your child will learn more about multiples in later grades. She does not need to memorize this term, as it's used here simply for clarity.

We've already made Number Cards for 10 and 20. Now we need to make Number Cards for the rest of the multiples of 10 up to 100. We'll make 2 Number Cards for each number so we can use them for games.

With your child, make 2 Number Cards for each of the multiples of 10 from 30 to 100. (Write one card yourself and have your child use yours as a model for the other card.) Model each number with bags of counters as you write it.

- **_Three_ groups of 10 make _thirty_. _Thirty_ starts like _thirteen_ and _third_. That can help you remember the _third_ group of 10 makes _thirty_.**

- **_Four_ groups of 10 make _forty_.**

- **_Five_ groups of 10 make _fifty_. _Fifty_ starts like _fifteen_ and _fifth_. That can help you remember the _fifth_ group of 10 makes _fifty_.**

- **_Six_ groups of 10 make _sixty_.**

- **_Seven_ groups of 10 make _seventy_.**

- **_Eight_ groups of 10 make _eighty_.**

- *Nine* groups of 10 make *ninety*.

- **Ten groups of 10 make 100.**

 Save these new Number Cards for future lessons.

Activity: Learn the Tens Chant

Take one set of the Multiples of 10 Number Cards and arrange them in order on the table.

Let's practice naming these combinations with a Tens Chant. Demonstrate the following chant. Point to the tens-place on each card as you name the number of tens. Say each combination rhythmically and encourage your child to join in as much as she can.

Tens Chant

1 ten. Ten!
2 tens. Twenty!
3 tens. Thirty!
4 tens. Forty!
5 tens. Fifty!
6 tens. Sixty!
7 tens. Seventy!
8 tens. Eighty!
9 tens. Ninety!
10 tens. One hundred!

Activity: Play Multiples of 10 Memory

Play one round of Multiples of 10 Memory. If your child has trouble, prompt him to look at the digit in the tens-place. **This number has a 7 in the tens-place. Think back to the Tens Chant. 7 tens equals what?** *70.*

Multiples of 10 Memory

Materials: 2 sets of Multiples of 10 Number Cards (10, 20, 30, etc. up to 100), 20 cards total

Object of the Game: Find the most pairs of matching numbers.

Shuffle together the Number Cards and lay them face down on the table.

On your turn, flip over 2 cards. Say the name of the number on each card. If the cards are the same, keep the pair. If the cards aren't the same, turn them back over.

Play then passes to the other player. Continue until you have found pairs for all the cards. Whoever finds the most pairs wins.

Workbook: Read Numbers for Multiples of 10 and Review

Have your child complete workbook pages 15.1A and 15.1B. As your child works on 15.1A, encourage her to think about the connection between the number of groups of 10, the spoken number, and the number's tens-place digit. ***Nine* groups of 9 make *ninety*. So, you should match those groups to the number with a 9 in the tens-place.**

Lesson 15.2
Add Multiples of 10

	Purpose	Materials
Warm-up	• Count dimes by 10s • Practice memory work • Review the Tens Chant	• Coins • Number Cards
Activities	• Begin to understand the meaning of the tens-place in two-digit numbers • Use place-value thinking to add multiples of 10	• Number Cards • Counters
Workbook	• Add multiples of 10	• Workbook pages 15.2A and 15.2B

Most children need explicit, incremental instruction to make sense of the abstract concept of place value. This unit is designed to provide gradual, clear, and step-by-step teaching so that your child has plenty of time to make sense of this tricky topic. If your child grasps place value quickly, feel free to condense lessons or skip unneeded review activities.

Warm-up: Counting, Memory Work, and Review

• Place 10 dimes on the table. Have your child count by 10s to find the total value. **How many cents are the coins worth?** *100¢.*

• **Name the even numbers in order to 20.** *2, 4, 6, 8, 10, 12, 14, 16, 18, 20.* **Name the odd numbers in order to 19.** *1, 3, 5, 7, 9, 11, 13, 15, 17, 19.*

• Have your child put Number Cards 10, 20, 30, 40, 50, 60, 70, 80, 90, and 100 in order. Rhythmically say the Tens Chant with your child and have him point to the matching card as he chants each number. See Lesson 15.1 (page 236) for the full Tens Chant.

Activity: Discuss Place Value in the Number 40

In the last lesson, you learned how to read and write the numbers you say when you count by 10s to 100. Today, you'll learn to add these numbers.

Show your child Number Card 40. **How many digits are in this number?** *2.* **What are the digits?** *4 and 0.*

40

Remember, the value of each digit depends on its place. Point to the 4 on the card. **This spot is called the tens-place. What digit is in the tens-place?** *4.* **The 4 in 40 doesn't stand for 4 counters! It stands for 4 groups of 10 counters.** Place 4 bags of 10 counters next to the Number Card.

Point to the 0 on the card. **This spot is called the ones-place. What digit is in the ones-place?** *0.* **This means there are 0 extra ones.**

All of the numbers we say when we count by 10s have a 0 in the ones-place. You'll learn how to read and write numbers with a different digit in the ones-place in Week 16.

Activity: Add Groups of 10

In this unit, we're going to play Cookie Store during some of the lessons. We'll pretend you work at the Cookie Store, and that I'm a customer. We'll pretend the counters are cookies, and you sell them individually or in bags of 10. Discuss your child's experience with bakeries and buying cookies.

Teaching place value in the context of the Cookie Store gives your child a concrete way to understand the difference between "ones" and "tens." Feel free to modify these activities depending on your child's interests. If your child loves to pretend, he can choose a name for his store, make a sign, and wear an apron while filling your cookie orders. But if he dislikes pretend games or finds them babyish, you can simply use bags of counters and loose counters to teach these lessons, without emphasizing the Cookie Store context.

I'd like 2 bags of chocolate chip cookies and 3 bags of sugar cookies, please. How many total bags is that? *5.* Have your child model the problem with bags of counters and write an equation to match: 2 + 3 = 5.

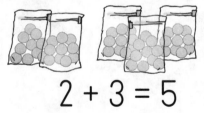

$$2 + 3 = 5$$

Now, let's write an addition equation about the cookies instead of the bags.

I have 2 bags of chocolate chip cookies, so how many chocolate chip cookies is that? *20.*

I have 3 bags of sugar cookies, so how many sugar cookies is that? *30.* Write 20 + 30 = on a piece of paper.

$$2 + 3 = 5$$
$$20 + 30 = 50$$

This looks like a tough addition problem! But if you use what you know about 2 + 3 and groups of 10, it's not so hard.

2 plus 3 equals 5. So, 2 groups of 10 plus 3 groups of 10 equals how many groups of 10? *5.*
What do 5 groups of 10 equal? *50.* **So, how many cookies do I get in all?** *50.* Have your child complete the equation.

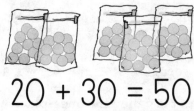

$$20 + 30 = 50$$

Repeat this process with the following addition equations. Have your child model each problem with bags of counters.

- 2 + 2 = 4; 20 + 20 = *40*
- 5 + 1 = 6; 50 + 10 = *60*
- 4 + 3 = 7; 40 + 30 = *70*
- 7 + 2 = 9; 70 + 20 = *90*
- 2 + 5 = 7; 20 + 50 = *70*

It's easy for children to simply parrot the words "tens-place" and "ones-place" without really understanding them. But when your child uses place-value concepts to add and subtract, he starts to understand place value at a deeper level. Make sure to keep the focus on these place-value concepts as you work through the addition equations with your child.

Workbook: Add Multiples of 10 and Review

Have your child complete workbook pages 15.2A and 15.2B. If your child has trouble with any of the problems on 15.2A, have him model them with bags of counters.

Lesson 15.3
Subtract Multiples of 10

	Purpose	Materials
Warm-up	• Count backward from 20 • Practice memory work • Review subtraction facts	• 100 Chart (Blackline Master 3), optional • Subtraction Tic-Tac-Toe game board (on Workbook page 10.1A) • Playing cards • Counters
Activities	• Use place-value thinking to subtract multiples of 10	• Number Cards • Counters
Workbook	• Subtract multiples of 10	• Workbook pages 15.3A and 15.3B

Warm-up: Counting, Memory Work, and Review

- Have your child count backwards from 20 to 1. Encourage her to try to do this from memory. If she has trouble, have her point to each number on the 100 Chart as she says it. *20, 19, 18, …*

- Have your child say the days of the week. **How many days are in a week?** *7.*

- Play Subtraction Tic-Tac-Toe. See Lesson 10.1 (page 158) for directions.

Activity: Subtract Groups of 10

In the last lesson, you learned to add multiples of 10. Today, you'll use the same kind of thinking to subtract multiples of 10.

Let's play Cookie Store again. Let's say you have 5 bags of sugar cookies to sell. Place 5 bags of counters on the table.

I'd like to buy 4 bags, please. Pretend to buy 4 of the bags. **How many bags do you have left?** *1.* Have your child write an equation to match: *5 – 4 = 1.*

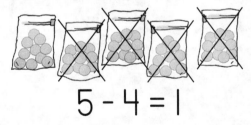

$$5 - 4 = 1$$

Now, let's write a subtraction equation about the cookies instead of the bags.

You started with 5 bags of cookies. How many cookies is that? *50.*

Then, I bought 4 bags. How many cookies is that? *40.* Write 50 – 40 = on a piece of paper.

$$5 - 4 = 1$$
$$50 - 40 =$$

You already know 5 minus 4 is 1. So, 5 groups of 10 minus 4 groups of 10 equals how many groups of 10? *1.*

1 group of 10 is just 10, so the answer is 10. Have your child complete the equation.

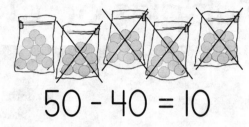

$$50 - 40 = 10$$

Repeat this process with the following equations. Have your child model each problem with bags of counters.

- $4 - 2 = 2; 40 - 20 = 20$

$$4 - 2 = 2$$
$$40 - 20 = 20$$

- $6 - 1 = 5; 60 - 10 = 50$
- $7 - 3 = 4; 70 - 30 = 40$
- $8 - 3 = 5; 80 - 30 = 50$
- $9 - 5 = 4; 90 - 50 = 40$

Workbook: Subtract Multiples of 10 and Review

Have your child complete workbook pages 15.3A and 15.3B. Allow her to use bags of counters to model the problems as needed.

Lesson 15.4
Pairs That Make 100

	Purpose	Materials
Warm-up	• Count five-dollar bills by 5s • Practice memory work • Review identifying pairs that make 10	• Play money
Activities	• Use place-value thinking to find pairs of multiples of 10 that make 100	• Number Cards • Counters
Workbook	• Identify combinations of multiples of 10 that make 100	• Workbook pages 15.4A and 15.4B

Warm-up: Counting, Memory Work, and Review

- Place 8 five-dollar bills on the table. Have your child count by 5s to find the total value. **How many dollars are the bills worth?** *$40.*

- **Name the even numbers in order to 20.** *2, 4, 6, 8, 10, 12, 14, 16, 18, 20.* **Name the odd numbers in order to 19.** *1, 3, 5, 7, 9, 11, 13, 15, 17, 19.*

- Have your child use his "X-ray vision" to identify the hidden number in the following equations with missing addends (as in Lesson 6.2). Secretly write each equation on a piece of paper and then hide the addend indicated.

$$5 + \boxed{5} = 10 \qquad 9 + \boxed{1} = 10 \qquad 7 + \boxed{3} = 10$$

$$\boxed{6} + 4 = 10 \qquad 8 + \boxed{2} = 10$$

> This activity reviews the pairs that make 10 to prepare your child to find pairs of multiples of 10 that make 100 (like 60 and 40).

Activity: Find Pairs That Make 100 on the Part-Total Mat

In the last two lessons, you learned how to add and subtract multiples of 10. Today, you'll learn how to find pairs of these numbers that make 100.

Place 10 bags of counters on the table. **Let's pretend we want to share the cookies today. How many bags of cookies are there?** *10.*

Take 1 bag. **If I take 1 bag of cookies, how many bags do you get?** *9.* Place Number Cards on the Part-Total Mat to match.

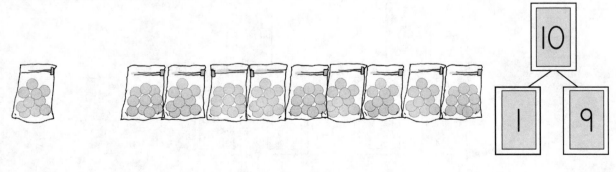

Now, let's think about how many cookies each of us gets. Each bag has 10 cookies in it. How many cookies do I get? *10.* **How many cookies do you get?** *90.* **How many cookies are there in total?** *100.* If your child is not sure, have him count by 10s to check.

Have your child change the Number Cards on the Part-Total Mat to match the number of cookies rather than the number of bags:

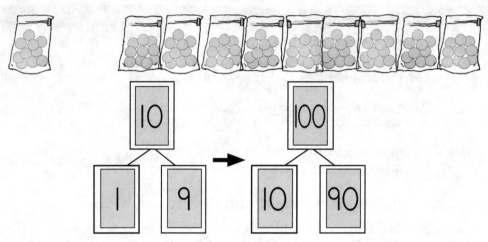

Repeat this process with the following equations. Have your child model each problem with bags of counters.

- **If I take 5 bags of cookies, how many bags do you get?** *5.* **How many cookies do I get?** *50.* **How many cookies do you get?** *50.*

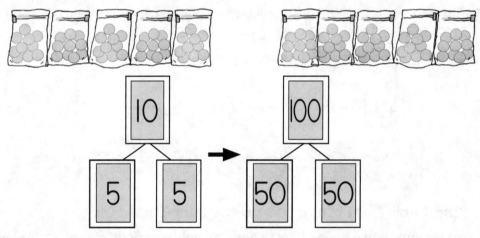

- **If I take 2 bags of cookies, how many bags do you get?** *8.* **How many cookies do I get?** *20.* **How many cookies do you get?** *80.*

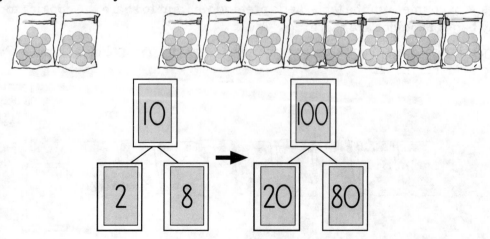

- **If I take 7 bags of cookies, how many bags do you get?** *3.* **How many cookies do I get?** *70.* **How many cookies do you get?** *30.*

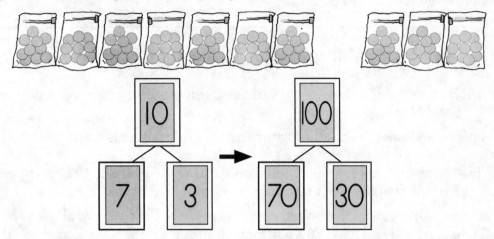

- **If I take 0 bags of cookies, how many bags do you get?** *10.* **How many cookies do I get?** *0.* **How many cookies do you get?** *100.*

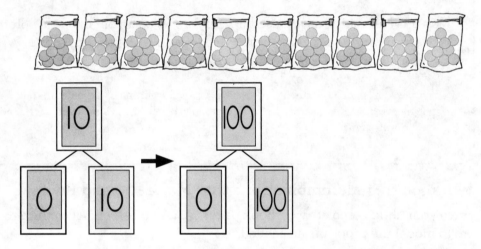

Activity: Multiples of 10 Go Fish

Play one round of Multiples of 10 Go Fish.

Multiples of 10 Go Fish

Materials: 2 sets of Multiples of 10 Number Cards (10, 20, 30, etc. up to 90. You will not need Number Card 100.)

Object of the Game: Collect the most pairs of cards that make 100.

Shuffle the Number Cards together. Deal out 5 cards to yourself and 5 cards to your child. Spread the rest of the cards face down on the table to be the "fishpond."

On your turn, ask for a card that would create a sum of 100 with a card already in your hand. (For example, if you have a 60, ask for a 40.) Your opponent must give you the card if he has it. If he doesn't have the card, he says, "Go fish!" and you take a card from the fishpond. If you get a pair, place it face-up in front of you.

Play until all the cards are used up. Players who run out of cards before the fishpond is used up may take 2 cards from the fishpond to continue playing. Whoever has more pairs at the end of the game is the winner.

> If your child is not sure which card to ask for, have him think of the pairs that make 10. For example, if he has an 80 and isn't sure what to ask for: 80 is 8 tens. 8 and 2 make 10, so you need the card that's the same as 2 tens.

Workbook: Find Combinations that Make 100 and Review

Have your child complete workbook pages 15.4A and 15.4B. Allow him to use bags of counters to model the problems as needed.

Lesson 15.5
Enrichment and Review (Optional)

	Purpose	Materials
Warm-up	• Review counting • Review memory work • Review your child's favorite or most challenging activities from Week 15	• Varies, depending on the activities you choose
Picture Book	• Count 100 pictures by 1s and 10s	• *Let's Count to 100!,* by Masayuki Sebe
Enrichment Activity	• Put 10 groups of 10 together to make 100	• 100 small craft items, such as stickers, pompoms, dried beans, beads, or small paper squares • Paper, preferably construction paper • Tape, optional • Glue

Warm-up: Counting, Memory Work, and Review

- Have your child count to 100 by 1s, 2s, 5s, or 10s. (Choose whichever counting sequence your child needs to practice the most.)

- Quiz your child on the memory work through Week 14. See page 499 for the full list.

- If you have time, repeat one or two of the activities from this week's lessons. Choose activities your child especially enjoyed or found challenging.

Math Picture Book: *Let's Count to 100!*

Read *Let's Count to 100!,* by Masayuki Sebe. Have your child count to check there are really 100 animals on one of the two-page spreads. Also point out how the author organizes the animals: on several of the two-page spreads, the animals are organized into 10 groups of 10. Have her check that there are 10 animals in each group and count the groups by 10s.

Enrichment Activity: 10 Tens Craft Project

Have your child count out 100 small craft items (such as stickers, pompoms, dried beans, beads, or paper squares).

Draw lines on a sheet of paper to divide it into 10 rectangles as shown. Have your child glue 10 craft items into each box. (If the craft items are too large to fit on one sheet of paper, tape together multiple pieces of paper and divide the joined paper into 10 rectangles).

After your child is finished, discuss whether the 100 objects look larger or smaller than she expected.
Children often think of the number 100 as very large, so she may be surprised at how little space 100 objects take up.

Week 15 Answer Key

15.1A

Match. Each bag has 10 cookies.

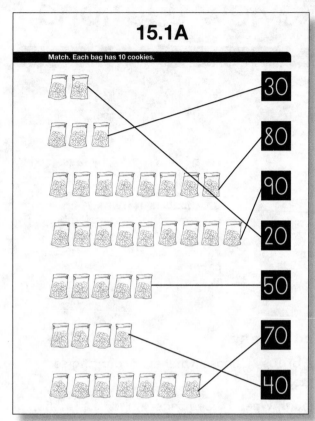

15.1B

Circle the squares. X the shapes that are not squares.

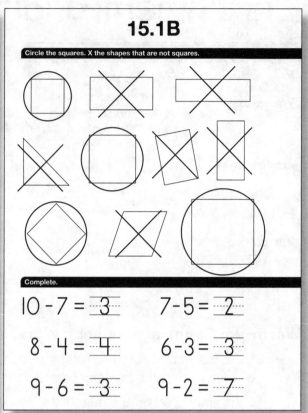

Complete.

$10 - 7 = 3$ $7 - 5 = 2$

$8 - 4 = 4$ $6 - 3 = 3$

$9 - 6 = 3$ $9 - 2 = 7$

15.2A

Complete.

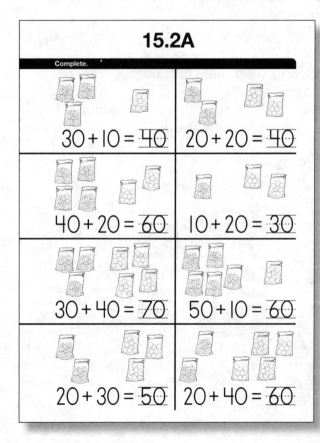

$30 + 10 = 40$ $20 + 20 = 40$

$40 + 20 = 60$ $10 + 20 = 30$

$30 + 40 = 70$ $50 + 10 = 60$

$20 + 30 = 50$ $20 + 40 = 60$

15.2B

Complete.

$9 + 1 = 10$ $5 + 1 = 6$

$4 + 5 = 9$ $2 + 6 = 8$

$8 + 0 = 8$ $3 + 7 = 10$

Match pairs that make 20.

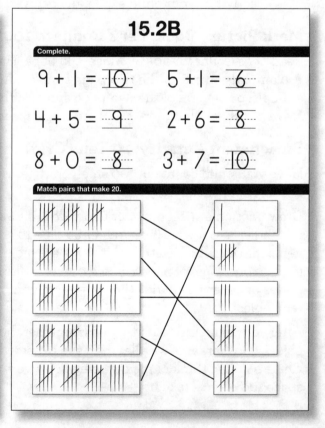

Week 15 Answer Key

15.3A

Complete.

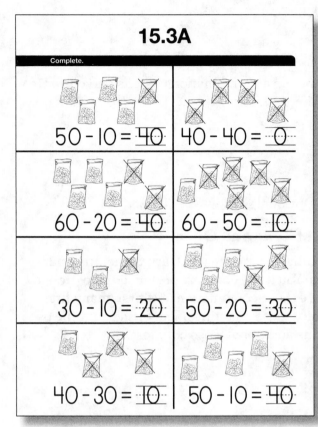

$50 - 10 = 40$ | $40 - 40 = 0$

$60 - 20 = 40$ | $60 - 50 = 10$

$30 - 10 = 20$ | $50 - 20 = 30$

$40 - 30 = 10$ | $50 - 10 = 40$

15.3B

Complete.

$9 - 5 = 4$ $10 - 5 = 5$

$8 - 2 = 6$ $6 - 5 = 1$

$10 - 1 = 9$ $9 - 9 = 0$

Write how many.

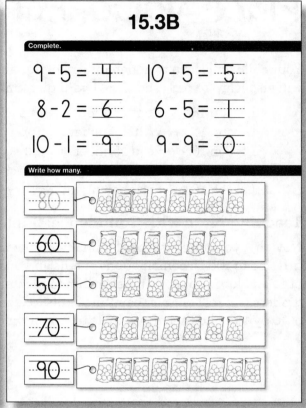

80

60

50

70

90

15.4A

Complete.

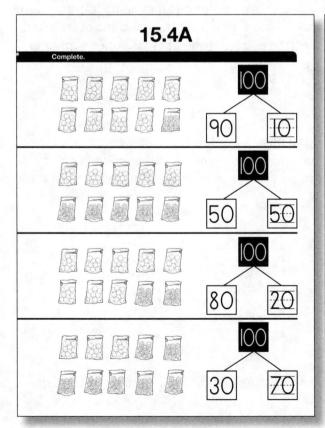

100 → 90, 10

100 → 50, 50

100 → 80, 20

100 → 30, 70

15.4B

Write how many.

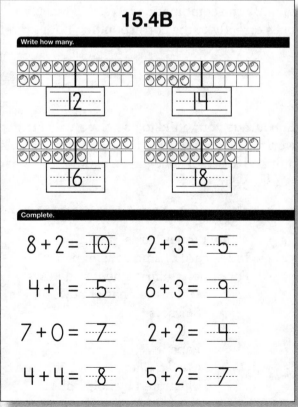

12   14

16   18

Complete.

$8 + 2 = 10$ $2 + 3 = 5$

$4 + 1 = 5$ $6 + 3 = 9$

$7 + 0 = 7$ $2 + 2 = 4$

$4 + 4 = 8$ $5 + 2 = 7$

Week 16
Place Value, Part 2

Overview

Your child will learn to understand two-digit numbers as combinations of tens and ones. He will also learn to read and write two-digit numbers.

Lesson 16.1   Combinations of Tens and Ones
Lesson 16.2   Write Numbers to 100
Lesson 16.3   Read Numbers to 100
Lesson 16.4   Sums of Tens and Ones
Lesson 16.5   Enrichment and Review (Optional)

Teaching Math with Confidence: Sums of Tens and Ones

Now that your child is more familiar with the multiples of 10, he will learn to identify quantities up to 100 as combinations of tens and ones. You'll use counters organized into groups of 10 and loose counters to teach him to recognize these combinations. At first, many first graders will rely on their counting skills to identify these quantities. They will count the bags of 10 by 10s, and then count by 1s to "count on" the additional loose counters.

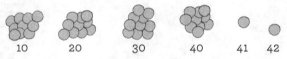

Counting by 10s and 1s to find the total number.

The goal this week is to teach your child to use place-value thinking rather than counting to identify the combinations. You will teach your child to translate the combinations of tens and ones directly to the corresponding number rather than counting the tens and ones separately.

4 tens and 2 make 42.

Encourage your child to use place-value thinking to identify quantities this week, but don't worry if he continues to feel more comfortable counting by 10s and 1s. Place value is a difficult and abstract concept, and your child will continue to deepen his understanding throughout the year.

Extra Materials Needed for Week 16

- 4 blank index cards
- Index card or small slip of paper
- For optional Enrichment and Review Lesson:
    - Old magazines or newspapers
    - Scissors
    - Glue
    - Paper
    - *Chicka Chicka, 1, 2, 3*, written by Bill Martin Jr. and Michael Sampson and illustrated by Lois Ehlert

Lesson 16.1
Combinations of Tens and Ones

	Purpose	Materials
Warm-up	• Count backward from 20 • Practice memory work • Review combinations of "10 and some more"	• 100 Chart (Blackline Master 3), optional • Counters • Double ten-frames • Paper
Activities	• Use place-value thinking to identify combinations of 10s and 1s • Count out combinations of 10s and 1s to match spoken numbers	• Counters
Workbook	• Identify combinations of 10s and 1s	• Workbook pages 16.1A and 16.1B

Warm-up: Counting, Memory Work, and Review

- Have your child count backwards from 30 to 1. Encourage her to try to do this from memory. If she has trouble, have her point to each number on the 100 Chart as she says it. *30, 29, 28, ...*

- Have your child rhythmically say the Tens Chant: *1 ten. Ten! 2 tens. Twenty!* etc. See Lesson 15.1 (page 236) for the full chant.

- Secretly place 19 counters on the double ten-frames and cover the counters with a piece of paper. Reveal the counters for just a few seconds and then have your child tell you how many counters there are. After your child responds, lift the paper and allow her to check her answer.

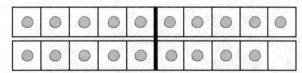

Repeat with 12, 15, 17, 20, and 11 counters. Encourage your child to think about the combinations of "10 and some more" to find the numbers of counters.

> Your child will use similar reasoning to name larger two-digit numbers in this lesson.

Activity: Count Combinations of Tens and Ones

In the last few lessons, you learned a lot about groups of 10. Today, you'll learn how to use combinations of 10s and 1s to quickly tell how many counters there are.

Let's pretend I wanted to buy 4 bags of cookies and 2 individual cookies. Place 4 bags of counters and 2 loose counters on the table.

I'm going to show you two different ways to find how many cookies there are. Both ways work, but one way is faster than the other.

One way is to count by 10s and 1s. Count the bags by 10s, pointing to each bag as you count it: **10, 20, 30, 40.** Point to the 2 extra counters: **41, 42.**

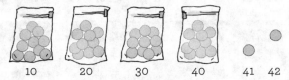

Counting by 10s and 1s to find the total number.

That's a lot faster than counting one-by-one. But there's an even faster way! I know 4 tens make 40. 40 and 2 make 42, so there are 42 cookies.

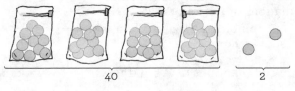

40 and 2 make 42.

If I dumped out all the bags and counted all the cookies one-by-one, how many would there be? *42.*

Asking this "how many" question assesses whether your child understands what she is doing when she counts by 10s and 1s. If she does not confidently know the answer, dump out the bags and have her count all the counters one-by-one to verify that there are 42. Continue to ask her this question as she works with 10s and 1s to ensure she's not just following a rote procedure without understanding.

Show your child the following arrangements of bags of 10 and loose counters. Have your child tell how many counters are in each arrangement. Encourage her to use place-value thinking (the "faster way") but allow her to count by 10s and 1s if she's not sure.

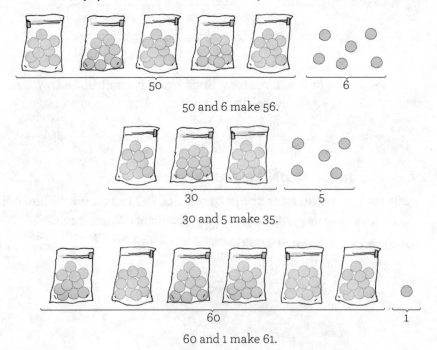

50 and 6 make 56.

30 and 5 make 35.

60 and 1 make 61.

As your child works, emphasize that once you know the name of each part of the quantity, you can put the names together to find the total quantity. For example, thirty and five make thirty-five. This activity does not include written numbers so your child can focus on the logic of the spoken number names.

Activity: Count Out Combinations of Tens and Ones

We can also use this kind of thinking to quickly find the number of cookies we want. I'd like 31 cookies, please. *Child gives you 3 bags of counters and 1 extra counter.*

If your child hesitates, encourage her to listen carefully to the word *thirty-one* and hear the two numbers within it: *thirty* and *one*. These give the clue that she should give you 3 bags of 10 (thirty) and 1 more.

Also pretend to buy 45 cookies, 73 cookies, and 54 cookies. Encourage your child to use place-value thinking find each quantity quickly.

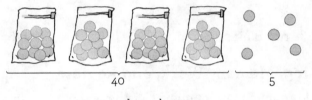

40 and 5 make 45.

See the Week 16 **Teaching Math with Confidence** for more on the importance of developing place-value thinking.

Workbook: Combinations of Tens and Ones and Review

Have your child complete workbook pages 16.1A and 16.1B. After your child completes 16.1A, have her tell how many total counters are in each arrangement. For example, for the top exercise: 30 and 7 make 37.

Your child will learn how to write two-digit numbers in the next lesson. If she already feels confident writing two-digit numbers, allow her to write the total number of cookies next to each arrangement on 16.1A.

Lesson 16.2
Write Numbers to 100

	Purpose	Materials
Warm-up	• Count out a given number of counters and estimate how many groups of 10 it contains • Practice memory work • Review fact families and *sum* and *difference*	• Counters • Part-Total Mat (Blackline Master 4) • Number Cards
Activities	• Understand the meaning of the tens-place and ones-place in written numbers • Write two-digit numbers	• Place-Value Chart (Blackline Master 7) • Number Cards • Counters • Bags of 10 counters assembled in previous lessons
Workbook	• Write two-digit numbers	• Workbook pages 16.2A and 16.2B

Warm-up: Counting, Memory Work, and Review

• Have your child count out 25 counters. (Ask her to count by 1s or 2s if she starts counting by a larger number.) **How many groups of 10 do you think we'll be able to make from these 25 counters?** *Answers will vary.* Help your child organize the counters into piles of 10. You should end up with 2 groups of 10 and 5 extra counters.

Leave these counters out for the first lesson activity.

• Have your child rhythmically say the Tens Chant: *1 ten. Ten! 2 tens. Twenty! etc.* See Lesson 15.1 (page 236) for the full chant.

• Place Number Cards 2, 7, and 9 on the Part-Total Mat. Have your child write the matching fact family.

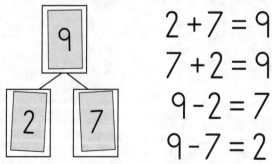

$$2 + 7 = 9$$
$$7 + 2 = 9$$
$$9 - 2 = 7$$
$$9 - 7 = 2$$

What do we call the answer to an addition problem? *The sum.*

What do we call the answer to a subtraction problem? *The difference.*

Activity: Introduce the Place-Value Chart

In the last lesson, you used combinations of tens and ones to quickly find numbers of counters. Today, you'll learn how to write two-digit numbers.

Write your child's name on a piece of paper. **When I write your name, I have to write each letter in the right place. If I write the letters in the wrong places, it doesn't spell your name.** Write the letters of your child's name in an incorrect order to demonstrate.

James   emaJs

Numbers are like words. You have to write the digits in the right order, just like you have to write letters in the right order to spell a word.

Show your child the Place-Value Chart (Blackline Master 7). **We call this chart the Place-Value Chart, because it helps us write each digit in the place that matches its value. That way, the digits will be in the right order.**

tens	ones

> Many first graders still have trouble telling right from left. This can make it difficult for them to read and write two-digit numbers, since the value of each digit depends on which place it is in. Using the Place-Value Chart will help your child keep the tens-place and ones-place straight.

Point out the labels at the top of the chart. **The left side of the chart is the tens-place. It tells how many groups of 10 are in the number. The right side is the ones-place. It tells how many extra ones there are after you make as many groups of 10 as you can.**

Point to the 25 counters your child counted out in the warm-up. **25 has 2 groups of 10 and 5 extra ones. So, to show 25 on the Place-Value Chart, we put a 2 in the tens-place and a 5 in the ones-place.** Place Number Cards 2 and 5 on the Place-Value Chart.

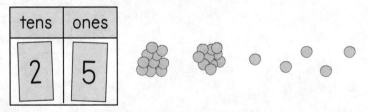

> If you find the Number Cards cumbersome, slip the Place-Value Chart into a plastic page protector and write the numbers with a dry-erase marker instead.

What does the 2 stand for? *The 2 groups of 10.*

What does the 5 stand for? *The 5 extra ones.*

How many digits are in the number 25? *2.*

Here's how to write the number 25 without the Place-Value Chart. Demonstrate how to write the number 25 on a piece of paper.

25

Switch the 2 and 5 on the Place-Value Chart. **This number has a 2 and 5 like 25, but it doesn't say 25 anymore!** Help your child model the number with 5 bags of counters and 2 loose counters. **How many counters is this?** *52.*

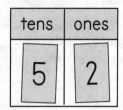 

52 is a lot more than 25! That's why it's so important we write the digits in the correct order.

Activity: Use the Place Value Chart to Write Two-Digit Numbers

Let's pretend that you're preparing some orders at the Cookie Store and want to label how many cookies are in each order.

Place 5 bags and 4 loose counters on the table. **How many cookies are there in this order?** *54.* Have your child place Number Cards on the Place-Value Chart to match. Then, have him write 54 on a slip of paper and place it next to the arrangement.

 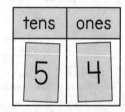

Repeat with the following quantities. Encourage your child to use place-value thinking to find the number of counters in each arrangement, but allow him to count by 10s and 1s if he's not sure.

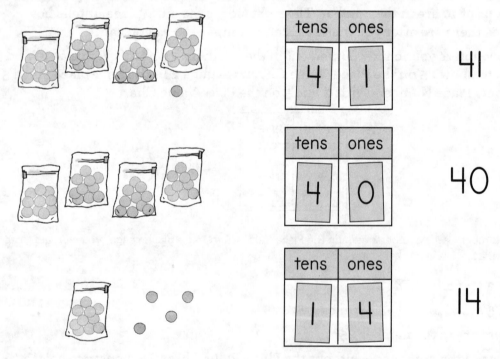

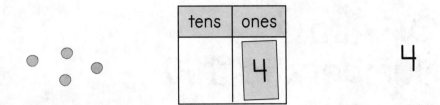

If your child places a 0 in the tens-place for 4, explain that it's not needed. **We only include 0s in numbers if they're needed to show another digit's place. We know that 4 is in the ones-place, so we don't have to put a 0 before it.**

Workbook: Write Two-Digit Numbers and Review

Have your child complete workbook pages 16.2A and 16.2B. If your child has trouble writing the digits directly on 16.2A, have him first model each number with counters and construct the number with Number Cards on the Place-Value Chart. Then, he can copy the digits onto the page.

Lesson 16.3
Read Numbers to 100

	Purpose	Materials
Warm-up	• Count out a given number of counters and estimate how many groups of 10 it contains • Practice memory work • Review take-away subtraction word problems	• Counters • Play money
Activities	• Review the meaning of the tens-place and ones-place • Read two-digit numbers and model them with concrete objects	• Counters • Place-Value Chart • Number Cards
Workbook	• Read two-digit numbers	• Workbook pages 16.3A and 16.3B

Warm-up: Counting, Memory Work, and Review

- Have your child count out 38 counters. (Ask her to count by 1s or 2s if she starts counting by a larger number.) **How many groups of 10 do you think we'll be able to make from these 38 counters?** *Answers will vary.* Help your child organize the counters into piles of 10. You should end up with 3 groups of 10 and 8 extra counters.

Leave these counters out for the first lesson activity.

- Have your child rhythmically say the Tens Chant: *1 ten. Ten! 2 tens. Twenty! etc.* See Lesson 15.1 (page 236) for the full chant.

- Read the following word problems to your child. Have her model each problem with counters or play money, then write and solve an equation to match.

    ✗ **I had 7 crackers. Then I ate 2. How many did I have left?** *5.*

    $$7 - 2 = 5$$

    ✗ **I had $8. Then I spent $4. How much money do I have left?** *$4.*

    $$8 - 4 = 4$$

What do these word problems have in common? *Sample answers: Both are about using things up. You can use subtraction to solve both problems.*

Activity: Review Place Value

In the last lesson, you learned how to use the Place-Value Chart to write two-digit numbers. Today, you'll use the Place-Value Chart to read two-digit numbers.

Have your child place Number Cards on the Place-Value Chart to match the 38 counters she counted out in the warm-up. Then, have her write the number 38 on a piece of paper.

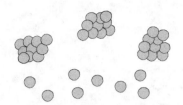 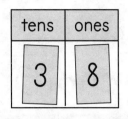

38

Use the following questions to briefly review place value:

- **What number is this?** *38.*
- **How many digits are in the number?** *2.*
- **Point to the 3. What's the name of this place in a number?** *The tens-place.*
- **What does the 3 stand for?** *The 3 groups of 10.*
- **Point to the 8. What's the name of this place in a number?** *The ones-place.*
- **What does the 8 stand for?** *The 8 extra ones.*

Activity: Use the Place-Value Chart to Read Two-Digit Numbers

Cookie Store time! I'm going to use the Place-Value Chart to give you my orders today.

Arrange Number Cards on the Place-Value Chart as shown below. **May I have this number of cookies, please?** *Child gives you 2 bags of counters and 3 loose counters.* **How many cookies are in my order?** *23.*

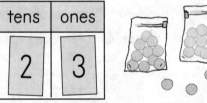

If your child is not sure, prompt her to think about the combination of tens and ones: **How many cookies are in the bags?** *20.* **How many extra cookies are there?** *3.* **So, what do 20 and 3 make?** *23.*

Pretend to pay for the cookies. Then, repeat this process with the following cookie orders. Place each order with cards on the Place-Value Chart. Then, have your child give you the matching number of counters and read the number.

- 73
- 55
- 5
- 64
- 90
- 46
- 8
- 81
- 18

Including both one- and two-digit numbers in this activity reminds your child to pay attention to whether the digit is in the tens-place or ones-place.

Workbook: Read Two-Digit Numbers and Review

Have your child complete workbook pages 16.3A and 16.3B. Encourage her to use place-value thinking to match the numbers and pictures. For example: **35 has a 3 in the tens-place and a 5 in the ones-place. So, you need to find a picture with 3 groups of 10 and 5 extra ones.**

Lesson 16.4
Sums of Tens and Ones

	Purpose	Materials
Warm-up	• Count forward from any number from 1 to 100 • Practice memory work • Review subtraction facts	• 100 Chart (Blackline Master 3) • Subtraction Climb to the Top game board (Workbook page 11.1A) • Playing cards • Counters
Activities	• Write addition equations to match combinations of tens and ones • Identify missing addends in addition equations that describe combinations of tens and ones	• Counters • Number Cards • Part-Total Mat (Blackline Master 4) • Index card or small slip of paper
Workbook	• Identify combinations of tens and ones on the Part-Total Mat and in addition equations	• Workbook pages 16.4A and 16.4B

Warm-up: Counting, Memory Work, and Review

- **Point to 74 on the 100 Chart.** *Child points to 74.* **Count forward to the end of the row. Point to each number as you say it.** *74, 75, 76, 77, 78, 79, 80.*

1	2	3	4	5	6	7	8	9	10
11	12	13	14	15	16	17	18	19	20
21	22	23	24	25	26	27	28	29	30
31	32	33	34	35	36	37	38	39	40
41	42	43	44	45	46	47	48	49	50
51	52	53	54	55	56	57	58	59	60
61	62	63	64	65	66	67	68	69	70
71	72	73	74	75	76	77	78	79	80
81	82	83	84	85	86	87	88	89	90
91	92	93	94	95	96	97	98	99	100

Repeat with 33 and 96.

> Children often have trouble switching decades when counting (for example, going from 39 to 40, or from 79 to 80). This activity gives your child practice with this important aspect of counting. It also reinforces the connection between the spoken counting sequence and the printed numbers.

- Have your child rhythmically say the Tens Chant: *1 ten. Ten! 2 tens. Twenty! etc.* See Lesson 15.1 (page 236) for the full chant.

- Play Subtraction Climb to the Top. See Lesson 11.1 (page 175) for directions.

Activity: Write Addition Equations to Match Combinations of Tens and Ones

You have learned how to think of two-digit numbers as combinations of tens and ones. Today, you'll learn how to write addition equations to match these combinations.

Place 3 bags of counters and 4 loose counters on the table. **How many counters are in the bags?** *30.* **How many loose counters are there?** *4.* **So, how many counters are there in all?** *34.*

Let's put Number Cards on the Part-Total Mat to match the combination of tens and ones.

- **The 3 bags have 30 counters.** Place a 30 on one of the lower boxes on the Part-Total Mat.
- **There are 4 extra ones.** Place a 4 in the other lower box on the Part-Total Mat.
- **There are 34 counters in total.** Write 34 on an index card and place the card in the upper box on the Part-Total Mat.

Also have your child write an equation to match the Part-Total Mat: 30 + 4 = 34.

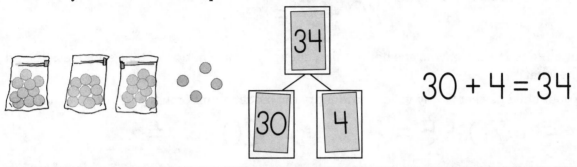

$$30 + 4 = 34$$

> If you find the Number Cards cumbersome, slip the Part-Total Mat into a plastic page protector and write the numbers with dry-erase marker instead.

Repeat this process with 21, 93, and 56 counters.

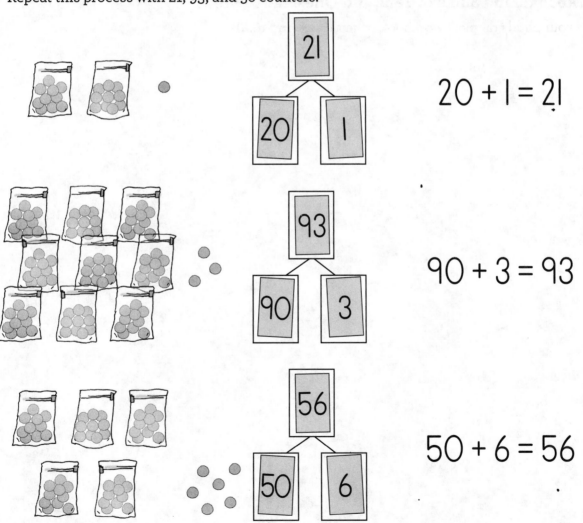

$$20 + 1 = 21$$

$$90 + 3 = 93$$

$$50 + 6 = 56$$

Activity: X-Ray Vision with Sums of Tens and Ones

Let's pretend you have X-ray vision again. I'm going to write an addition equation and hide one of the numbers. See if you can use your X-ray vision to tell me what number I hide.

Secretly write 80 + 7 = 87 on a piece of paper and cover the 87 with an index card or small slip of paper. **What number did I hide?** *87.*

$$80 + 7 = \boxed{87}$$

If your child isn't sure, encourage her to think about the combination of tens and ones: **80 and 7 make what?**

Have your child use her "X-ray vision" to identify the hidden number in the following equations.

$$70 + 5 = \boxed{75} \qquad 20 + 9 = \boxed{29}$$

$$60 + 4 = \boxed{64} \qquad 10 + 7 = \boxed{17}$$

Workbook: Find Sums of Tens and Ones and Review

Have your child complete workbook pages 16.4A and 16.4B.

Lesson 16.5
Enrichment and Review (Optional)

	Purpose	Materials
Warm-up	• Review counting • Review memory work • Review your child's favorite or most challenging activities from Week 16	• Varies, depending on the activities you choose
Picture Book	• Read two-digit numbers	• *Chicka Chicka, 1, 2, 3*, written by Bill Martin Jr. and Michael Sampson and illustrated by Lois Ehlert
Enrichment Activity	• Recognize two-digit numbers in magazines and newspapers	• Old magazines or newspapers • Scissors • Glue • Paper

Warm-up: Counting, Memory Work, and Review

- Have your child count to 100 by 1s, 2s, 5s, or 10s (choose whichever counting sequence your child needs to practice the most)

- Quiz your child on the memory work through Week 16. See page 499 for the full list.

- If you have time, repeat one or two of the activities from this week's lessons. Choose activities your child especially enjoyed or found challenging.

Math Picture Book: *Chicka Chicka, 1, 2, 3*

Read *Chicka Chicka, 1, 2, 3*, written by Bill Martin Jr. and Michael Sampson and illustrated by Lois Ehlert. As you read, have your child help you read the two-digit numbers.

Enrichment Activity: Numbers to 100 Collage

Have your child look for two-digit numbers in old magazines or newspapers. Then, have him cut them out, glue them to a piece of paper, and make a simple collage of the numbers. As he looks for the numbers and cuts them out, encourage him to read the numbers. Talk about what each number means in context. **The pack of gum in the supermarket flyer costs 79¢.** Or, **That basketball team got 86 points!**

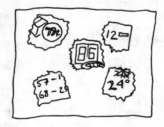

Week 16 Answer Key

16.1A

Complete.

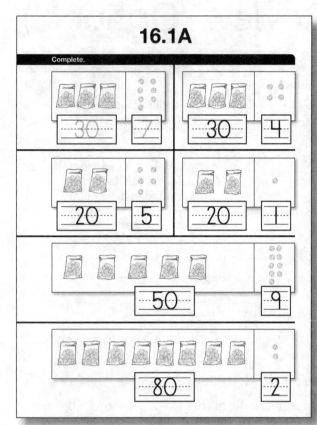

16.1B

Complete.

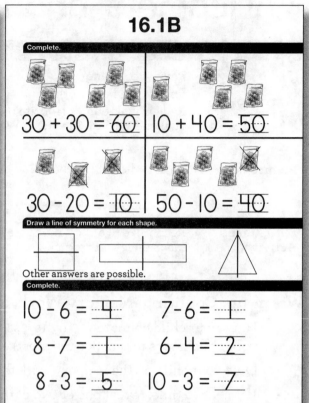

$30 + 30 = 60$ | $10 + 40 = 50$

$30 - 20 = 10$ | $50 - 10 = 40$

Draw a line of symmetry for each shape.

Other answers are possible.

Complete.

$10 - 6 = 4$ $7 - 6 = 1$

$8 - 7 = 1$ $6 - 4 = 2$

$8 - 3 = 5$ $10 - 3 = 7$

16.2A

Write how many.

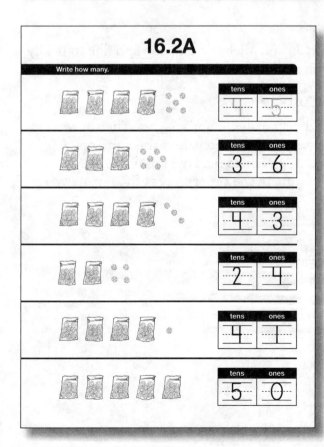

16.2B

Complete.

$7 + 3 = 10$ $5 + 3 = 8$

$4 + 3 = 7$ $2 + 4 = 6$

$6 + 1 = 7$ $3 + 6 = 9$

Match pairs that make 100.

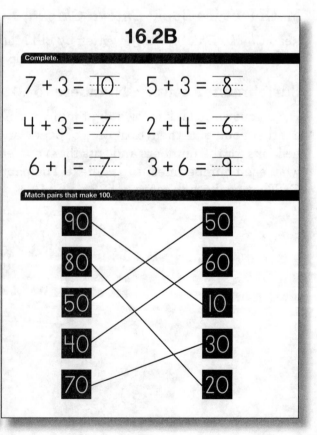

Week 16 Answer Key

16.3A

Match.

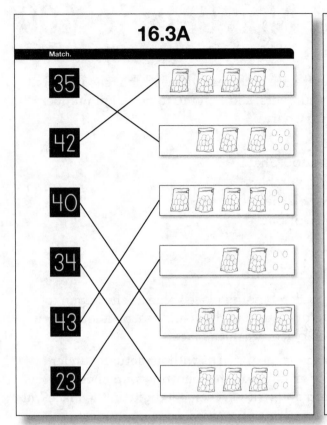

16.3B

Complete.

$10 - 8 = 2$ $9 - 7 = 2$

$9 - 3 = 6$ $4 - 0 = 4$

$8 - 8 = 0$ $7 - 4 = 3$

Complete.

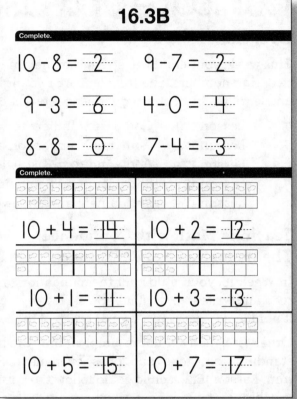

$10 + 4 = 14$ $10 + 2 = 12$

$10 + 1 = 11$ $10 + 3 = 13$

$10 + 5 = 15$ $10 + 7 = 17$

16.4A

Complete.

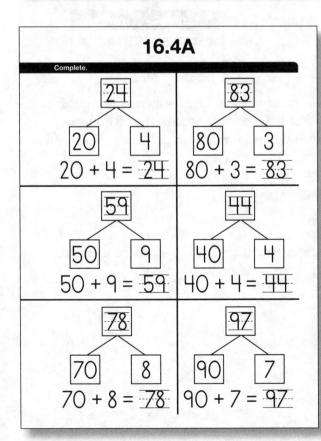

$20 + 4 = 24$ $80 + 3 = 83$

$50 + 9 = 59$ $40 + 4 = 44$

$70 + 8 = 78$ $90 + 7 = 97$

16.4B

Sara made a tally chart of the animals she saw on a nature walk. Use the chart to answer the questions.

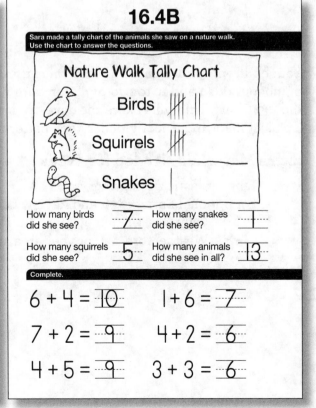

Nature Walk Tally Chart

Birds

Squirrels

Snakes

How many birds did she see?   7

How many snakes did she see?   1

How many squirrels did she see?   5

How many animals did she see in all?   13

Complete.

$6 + 4 = 10$ $1 + 6 = 7$

$7 + 2 = 9$ $4 + 2 = 6$

$4 + 5 = 9$ $3 + 3 = 6$

Week 17
Compare and Use Numbers to 100

Overview

This week, your child will strengthen her understanding of place value as she reasons about two-digit numbers. She will compare two-digit numbers, add 1 and 10 to two-digit numbers, and learn to shift counting sequences on the 100 Chart.

Lesson 17.1   Compare Numbers to 100
Lesson 17.2   Compare Numbers on the 100 Chart
Lesson 17.3   Add 1 and 10 to Two-Digit Numbers
Lesson 17.4   Shift Counting Sequences on the 100 Chart
Lesson 17.5   Enrichment and Review (Optional)

Teaching Math with Confidence:
The Importance of Reasoning about Place Value

In Week 16, your child built the foundation for understanding place value as she began to read and write two-digit numbers. However, children need to think and reason about two-digit numbers to develop a deeper grasp of the tens-place and ones-place.

Otherwise, many children simply mimic the place-value patterns without actually understanding what "tens" and "ones" even mean. For example, in the following worksheet exercise from Lesson 16.2, a child could follow the pattern and write the correct digits in the Place-Value Chart without connecting these digits to the concrete quantities.

Your child will go deeper with place-value thinking this week as she compares two-digit numbers, adds 1 and 10 to two-digit numbers, and practices more sophisticated counting on the 100 Chart. This will ensure she develops a thorough understanding of place value—and isn't just following a poorly-understood pattern.

Extra Materials Needed for Week 17

- Empty plastic zip-top bag
- For optional Enrichment and Review Lesson:
    × *Only One*, written by Marc Harshman and illustrated by Barbara Garrison
    × Weather forecast for your area, either printed or electronic

Lesson 17.1
Compare Numbers to 100

	Purpose	Materials
Warm-up	• Count one-dollar bills by 1s • Practice memory work • Review take-apart subtraction word problems	• Play money • Counters
Activities	• Compare two-digit numbers	• Number Cards • Place-Value Chart (Blackline Master 7) • Counters
Workbook	• Compare two-digit numbers	• Workbook pages 17.1A and 17.1B

Warm-up: Counting, Memory Work, and Review

- Place 9 one-dollar bills on the table. Have your child count by 1s to find the total value. **How many dollars is this?** *$9.*

- **Stomp your left foot. Stomp your right foot.**

- Ask your child the following word problems. Have her model each problem with counters and then write and solve a subtraction equation to match.

    × **A mother rabbit has 8 baby rabbits. Some are brown and some are gray. If 6 are brown, how many are gray?** *2.*

$$8 - 6 = 2$$

    × **If 4 are brown, how many are gray?** *4.*

$$8 - 4 = 4$$

    × **If 0 are brown, how many are gray?** *8.*

$$8 - 0 = 8$$

> If your child has trouble writing the subtraction equations, have her place Number Cards on the Part-Total Mat before writing each equation.

Activity: Compare Two-Digit Numbers

You have learned how to read and write two-digit numbers. Today, you'll learn how to compare them.

Place Number Cards 7 and 3 on the Place-Value Chart to make the number 73. Use the following questions to review the meaning of the digits in the number.

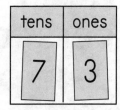

- **How many digits does this number have?** *2.*
- **What are the digits?** *7 and 3.*
- **Point to the 7. What's the name of this place in a number?** *The tens-place.*
- **So, what does the 7 stand for?** *7 groups of 10.* Have your child place 7 bags of counters next to the Place-Value Chart.
- **Point to the 3. What's the name of this place in a number?** *The ones-place.*
- **So, what does the 3 stand for?** *3 extra ones.* Have your child place 3 loose counters next to the Place-Value Chart.
- **What number is this?** *73.*

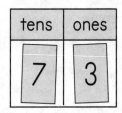

Switch the two cards' positions on the Place-Value Chart to make the number 37. **What number is this now?** *37.* Have your child model 37 with 3 bags of counters and 7 loose counters.

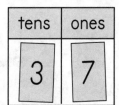

Which number is greater, 73 or 37? *73.* **How do you know?** *Sample answer: 73 has 7 tens, but 37 only has 3 tens.*

Repeat this process with the numbers 46 and 64. **Which number is greater, 46 or 64?** *64.* **How do you know?** *Sample answer: 64 has 6 tens, but 46 only has 4 tens.*

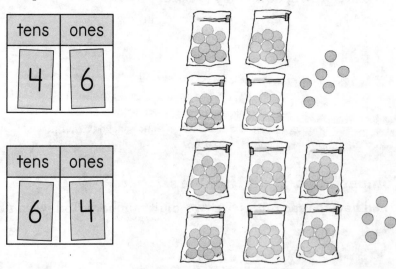

Activity: Play Two-Digit War

Play 2 rounds of Two-Digit War. Have your child say the names of the numbers aloud as she plays so she practices reading the numbers. Keep the Place-Value Chart and counters nearby in case your child needs to model the numbers.

Two-Digit War

Materials: 2 sets of Number Cards (1-9)

Object of the Game: Win the most cards.

Shuffle the Number Cards and deal the cards face down in two piles. Both players flip over the top two cards in their pile and use the digits to make the greatest possible two-digit number. (For example, if you turn over a 9 and 1, you can make the number 19 or 91. Choose number 91, since it is greater.)

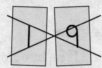

Make the greatest possible two-digit number from your pair of Number Cards.

Whoever has the greater number wins both cards.

If the numbers are equal, leave the cards face-up on the table and have both players make a new two-digit number with the next 2 cards in their piles. Whoever creates the greater number wins all the face-up cards.

Play until the piles run out. Whoever has won more cards wins the game.

Variation: Continue playing until one player has won all the cards.

If your child finds it confusing to decide which number is greater, simply have her put the first card she turns over in the tens-place and the second card she turns over in the ones-place.

Workbook: Compare Two-Digit Numbers and Review

Have your child complete workbook pages 17.1A and 17.1B. Keep the Place-Value Chart and counters nearby in case your child needs to model the numbers before she can tell which is greater.

Lesson 17.2
Compare Numbers on the 100 Chart

	Purpose	Materials
Warm-up	• Count backward from 40 • Practice memory work • Review writing numbers to 100	• 100 Chart (Blackline Master 3), optional
Activities	• Find and identify two-digit numbers on the 100 Chart • Use *greater than* and *less than* to compare two-digit numbers on the 100 Chart	• 100 Chart (Blackline Master 3) • Counters
Workbook	• Identify and write missing numbers on the 100 Chart	• Workbook pages 17.2A and 17.2B

Warm-up: Counting, Memory Work, and Review

- Have your child count backwards from 40 to 25. If he has trouble, have him point to each number on the 100 Chart as he says it.

- **How many sides does a triangle have?** *3.* **A square?** *4.* **A rectangle?** *4.*

- Point to the following numbers on the 100 Chart (one at a time) and have your child identify them: 44, 87, 12, 50, 91, 9.

  Then, ask your child to point to the following numbers on the 100 Chart (one at a time): 1, 6, 16, 38, 25, 76, 99, 80, 100.

  > If your child has trouble, ask him to first imagine what the number looks like and then look for the row where the numbers start the same way. For example, for the number 76, he should look for the row where all the numbers start with a 7.

Activity: Find Two-Digit Numbers on the 100 Chart

In the last lesson, you learned how to compare two-digit numbers. Today, we'll use two-digit numbers to compare ages.

Make a simple chart with the names and ages of 6-8 family members. Include relatives with a wide range of ages.

Name	Age
Sam	6
Gabe	2
Kristen	9
Mom	35
Dad	34
Grandma	62
Grandpa	66
Great-grandma	87

Sample chart

Have your child place counters on the 100 Chart to match each age.

Choose two people on the list. Have your child tell which person is older, and which person is younger. For example: **Who's older, Dad or Great-grandma?** *Great-grandma!*

Repeat with several different pairs of family members.

Activity: Play Guess the Secret Number (1-100)

Play Guess the Secret Number (1-100) several times. Take turns with your child choosing the secret number.

Guess the Secret Number (1-100)

Materials: 100 Chart (Blackline Master 3), counters

Object of the Game: Guess the secret number.

Secretly choose a number between 1 and 100 and write it on a slip of paper.

Place a counter on the 1 and the 100 on the 100 Chart. **My secret number is greater than 1 and less than 100.**

The other player guesses the secret number. If the guess is incorrect, move one counter to the number he guesses, so the secret number is still between the two counters. For example, if the secret number is 74, and your child guesses 40, move the counter from the 1 to the 40 and say: **My secret number is greater than 40.**

Have your child continue guessing. Keep moving the counters so your secret number is between the two counters. Once your child guesses correctly, reveal your written number.

Workbook: Identify Missing Numbers on the 100 Chart and Review

Have your child complete workbook pages 17.2A and 17.2B.

You may need to explain to your child that 17.2A shows only a small portion of the 100 Chart.

Lesson 17.3
Add 1 and 10 to Two-Digit Numbers

	Purpose	Materials
Warm-up	• Count forward from any number from 1 to 100 • Practice memory work • Review addition facts	• 100 Chart (Blackline Master 3) • Counters • Addition Climb to the Top game board (on Workbook page 5.1A) • 2 decks of playing cards
Activities	• Add 1 to two-digit numbers • Add 10 to two-digit numbers	• Number Cards • Place-Value Chart (Blackline Master 7) • Counters • Empty plastic zip-top bag
Workbook	• Add 1 or 10 to two-digit numbers	• Workbook pages 17.3A and 17.3B

Warm-up: Counting, Memory Work, and Review

- **Point to 62 on the 100 Chart.** *Child points to 62.* **Count forward to the end of the row. Point to each number as you say it.** *62, 63, 64, 65, 66, 67, 68 69, 70.*

  Repeat with 27 and 85.

- Have your child rhythmically say the Tens Chant: *1 ten. Ten! 2 tens. Twenty! etc.* See Lesson 15.1 (page 236) for the full chant.

- Play Addition Climb to the Top. See Lesson 5.1 (page 81) for directions.

Activity: Add 1 to Two-Digit Numbers

In the last lesson, you found numbers on the 100 Chart and compared them. Today, you'll learn how to add 1 or 10 to two-digit numbers.

I'd like this number of cookies, please! Place Number Cards 2 and 5 on the Place-Value Chart to make the number 25. Have your child read the number and model it with 2 bags of counters and 5 loose counters.

tens	ones
2	5

These cookies smell delicious! I'll think I'll buy another one. Add 1 counter to the pile. Write 25 + 1 = on a piece of paper. **How many cookies are there now?** *26.* Have your child change the Number Cards to match and write the answer to the equation.

   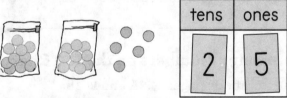

Continue adding 1 counter at a time to the arrangement and writing the corresponding addition equation until there are 29 counters. Have your child change the Number Cards to match the counters each time. Also have her complete the equations.

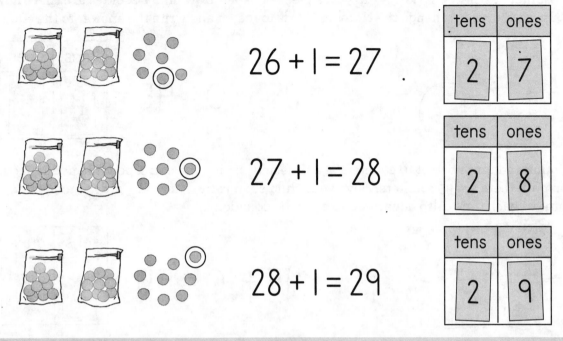

tens	ones
2	7

$$26 + 1 = 27$$

tens	ones
2	8

$$27 + 1 = 28$$

tens	ones
2	9

$$28 + 1 = 29$$

Children often mistakenly think the equals sign means "the answer is coming." As a result, they write related equations in a horizontal row, like this:

$$26 + 1 = 27 + 1 = 28 + 1 = 29$$

Incorrect way to write a series of equations.

But, this way of writing the equations makes it seem like 26 + 1, 27 + 1, 28 +1, and 29 are all equal to each other. Writing each equation separately and in a vertical list (as shown above) teaches your child to use the equals sign correctly.

Write 29 +1 = on a piece of paper and add 1 more counter (for a total of 30). **Now you can fill another bag of 10!** Help your child seal the 10 loose counters in a zip-top bag before she changes the Number Cards and completes the equation.

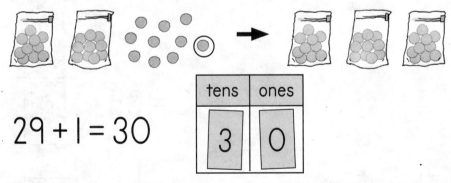

tens	ones
3	0

$$29 + 1 = 30$$

Continue adding 1 counter at a time and writing the corresponding addition equations until there are 35 counters.

How do the digits usually change when you add 1? *Sample answer: The digit in the ones-place goes up by 1.* Point out both the tens-place and ones-place changed when you added 1 to 29.

Making this generalization about adding 1 helps your child begin to reason more abstractly about place value.

Activity: Add 10 to Two-Digit Numbers

I'm really hungry for cookies today! I think I'll add another bag to my order. Add 1 bag of 10 counters to the 35. Write 35 + 10 = on a piece of paper. **How many cookies are there now?** *45.* Have your child change the Number Cards to match and write the answer to the equation.

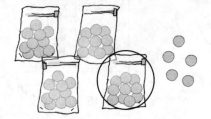

$$35 + 10 = 45$$

tens	ones
4	5

Continue adding 1 bag of 10 counters at a time and writing the corresponding addition equation until there are 95 counters. Have your child change the Number Cards to match the counters each time. Also have her complete the equations.

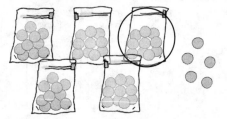

$$45 + 10 = 55$$

tens	ones
5	5

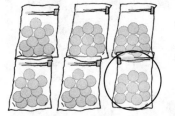

$$55 + 10 = 65$$

tens	ones
6	5

$$65 + 10 = 75$$

tens	ones
7	5

$$75 + 10 = 85$$

tens	ones
8	5

$$85 + 10 = 95$$

tens	ones
9	5

How do the digits change when you add a group of 10? *Sample answer: The digit in the tens-place goes up by 1.*

What do you think would happen if we added another group of 10? *Sample answer: We would have more than 100 counters!* **Then we could bundle up 10 of the groups of 10 to make 100!**

Your child will learn about place value in the hundreds in second grade.

Workbook: Add 1 or 10 to Two-Digit Numbers and Review

Have your child complete workbook pages 17.3A and 17.3B.

Lesson 17.4
Shift Counting Sequences on the 100 Chart

	Purpose	Materials
Warm-up	• Count ten-dollar bills by 10s • Practice memory work • Review comparing two-digit numbers	• Play money • Number Cards
Activities	• Count by 10s starting at a number other than 10 • Learn to shift counting sequences on the 100 Chart (for example, count by 10s and then switch to counting by 5s)	• 100 Chart (Blackline Master 3) • Counters
Workbook	• Complete counting sequences	• Workbook pages 17.4A and 17.4B

Warm-up: Counting, Memory Work, and Review

- Place 7 ten-dollar bills on the table. Have your child count by 10s to find the total value. **How many dollars is this?** *$70.*

- **Name the even numbers in order to 20.** *2, 4, 6, 8, 10, 12, 14, 16, 18, 20.* **Name the odd numbers in order to 19.** *1, 3, 5, 7, 9, 11, 13, 15, 17, 19.*

- Play Two-Digit War. See Lesson 17.1 (page 269) for directions.

Activity: Count by 10s on the 100 Chart Starting at 10

In the last lesson, you learned how to add 1 or 10 to two-digit numbers. Today, we'll explore how counting by 10s is like adding 10 over and over. You'll also learn a new way to count by 10s on the 100 Chart.

Put 1 bag of 10 counters on the table. **How many counters are there?** *10.* Have your child cover the number 10 on the 100 Chart with a counter.

Let's add another group of 10. Add another bag of counters. **How many counters are there now?** *20.* Have your child cover the number 20 on the 100 Chart.

Continue in this way until you have 10 bags and your child has covered all the multiples of 10 up to 100. **Counting by 10s is just like adding 10 over and over.**

Activity: Count by 10s on the 100 Chart Starting at Other Numbers

Let's try starting with a different number and adding 10 over and over. Place 4 counters on the table. **How many counters are there?** *4.* Have your child cover the number 4 on the 100 Chart with a counter.

Let's add another group of 10. Add 1 bag of counters. **How many counters are there now?** *14.* Have your child cover the number 14 on the 100 Chart.

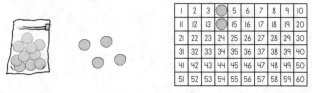

Continue in this way until you reach 94.

What do you notice about the numbers you covered? *Sample answer: They're all in a line!*

Why is the ones-place the same in all the numbers you covered? *The number of ones didn't change.*

Why did the tens-place in the numbers on the 100 Chart increase by 1 each time we added a bag of counters? *Each bag of counters is 1 group of 10, so the tens-place went up by 1.*

Have your child try counting by 10s on the 100 Chart starting at 9. Have him point to each number as he says it, and prompt her as needed: *9, 19, 29, 39, 49, 59, 69, 79, 89, 99.*

Activity: Pretend to be a Counting Robot

Let's pretend you are a counting robot. We'll pretend this is your computer panel. Draw a "computer panel" with 4 small rectangles labeled as shown.

I'm going to press one of the buttons. You're a counting robot, so your job is to count by whatever number I press. Point to the numbers on the 100 Chart as you say them. Stop as soon as I press the Off button. I'll say "beep!" whenever I press a button.

Saying "beep!" whenever you press a button on the "computer panel" gives your child a sound cue as well as a visual cue.

- **Beep!** Press the 10 button. *10, 20, 30, 40, 50, 60, 70.* Press the Off button once your child reaches 70. **Beep!**

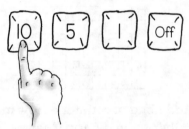

- **Beep!** Press the 5 button. *5, 10, 15, 20, 25, 30, 35, 40, 45, 50, 55.* Press the Off button once your child reaches 55. **Beep!**
- **Beep!** Press the 1 button. *1, 2, 3, 4, 5, 6, 7, 8, 9, 10, 11, 12, 13.* Press the Off button once your child reaches 13. **Beep!**

If your child doesn't enjoy pretending to be a robot, simply tell him what number to count by and when to stop and start.

Now, let's try counting by one number and then switching to counting by a different number on the 100 Chart.

- **Beep!** Press the 10 button. *10, 20, 30, 40, 50.* **Beep!** Press the 5 button. *55, 60, 65, 70, 75, 80.* **Beep!** Press the Off button once your child reaches 80.
- **Beep!** Press the 10 button. *10, 20, 30, 40, 50, 60.* **Beep!** Press the 1 button. *61, 62, 63, 64, 65, 66, 67.* **Beep!** Press the Off button once your child reaches 67.
- **Beep!** Press the 5 button. *5, 10, 15, 20, 25, 30, 35.* **Beep!** Press the 1 button. *36, 37, 38, 39, 40, 41, 42, 43, 44.* **Beep!** Press the Off button once your child reaches 44.
- **Beep!** Press the 1 button. *1, 2, 3, 4, 5, 6, 7, 8.* **Beep!** Press the 10 button. *18, 28, 38, 48, 58, 68, 78, 88, 98.* **Beep!** Press the Off button once your child reaches 98.

Learning how to switch from counting by one number to counting by a different number helps your child better understand the relationships between numbers. It also prepares him to count combinations of coins or paper bills in Unit 9.

Workbook: Complete Counting Sequences and Review

Have your child complete workbook pages 17.4A and 17.4B.

Lesson 17.5
Enrichment and Review (Optional)

	Purpose	Materials
Warm-up	• Review counting • Review memory work • Review your child's favorite or most challenging activities from Week 17	• Varies, depending on the activities you choose
Picture Book	• Preview numbers greater than 100	• *Only One*, written by Marc Harshman and illustrated by Barbara Garrison
Enrichment Activity	• Understand two-digit numbers in the context of temperatures	• Weather forecast for your area, either printed or electronic

Warm-up: Counting, Memory Work, and Review

- Have your child count to 100 by 1s, 2s, 5s, or 10s. (Choose whichever counting sequence your child needs to practice the most.)

- Quiz your child on the memory work through Week 16. See page 499 for the full list.

- If you have time, repeat one or two of the activities from this week's lessons. Choose activities your child especially enjoyed or found challenging.

Math Picture Book: *Only One*

Read *Only One*, written by Marc Harshman and illustrated by Barbara Garrison. This lovely book introduces numbers beyond 100, with collages depicting items at a county fair, such as bees, pumpkins, and quilts. Marvel at these large numbers and let her know she'll learn more about these large numbers in future years of math.

Enrichment Activity: Compare Temperatures

Show your child the temperature forecast for your area for the coming week. Have your child read the temperatures for the highs for the next few days, and discuss whether the weather is expected to become warmer or colder. For example: **The high is 24 today, but it's supposed to be 39 tomorrow. That will feel warmer, but it will still be pretty cold!**

Week 17 Answer Key

17.1A

Circle the greater number in each pair.

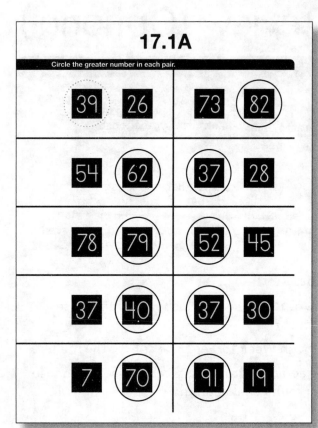

17.1B

Complete.

$30+50 = 80$ $20+40 = 60$

$60+30 = 90$ $40+40 = 80$

$70+20 = 90$ $10+80 = 90$

Color the even numbers on the 100 Chart.

Even Numbers to 20

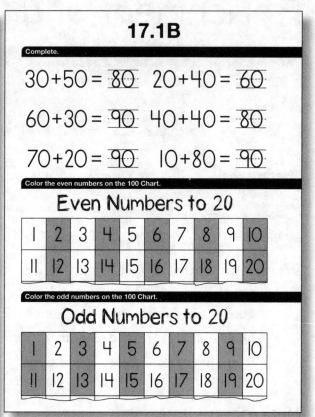

Color the odd numbers on the 100 Chart.

Odd Numbers to 20

17.2A

Complete the missing numbers on the 100 Chart.

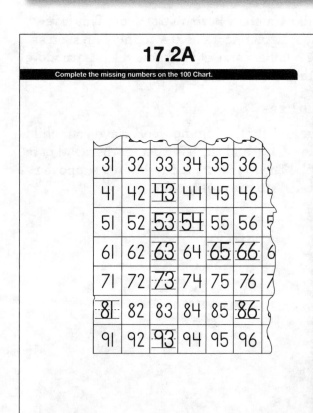

17.2B

Match.

$5 + 5 = 10$ $0 + 9 = 9$

$4 + 6 = 10$ $8 + 1 = 9$

$7 + 1 = 8$ $3 + 5 = 8$

Circle the greater number in each pair.

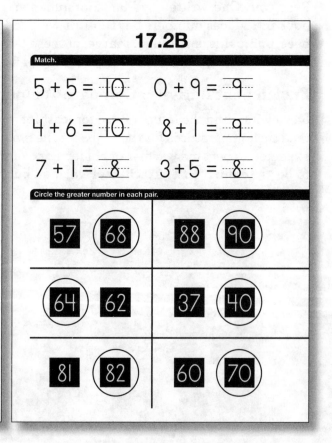

Week 17 Answer Key

17.3A

Complete.

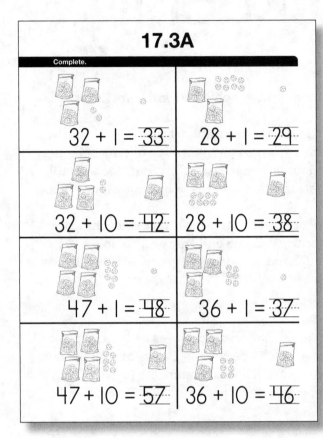

32 + 1 = **33**   28 + 1 = **29**

32 + 10 = **42**   28 + 10 = **38**

47 + 1 = **48**   36 + 1 = **37**

47 + 10 = **57**   36 + 10 = **46**

17.3B

Complete.

10 - 4 = **6**   5 - 5 = **0**

9 - 1 = **8**   9 - 4 = **5**

8 - 5 = **3**   10 - 2 = **8**

Complete the missing numbers on the 100 Chart.

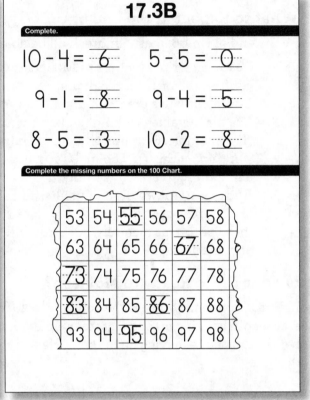

53	54	**55**	56	57	58
63	64	65	66	**67**	68
73	74	75	76	77	78
83	84	85	**86**	87	88
93	94	**95**	96	97	98

17.4A

Complete the number patterns.

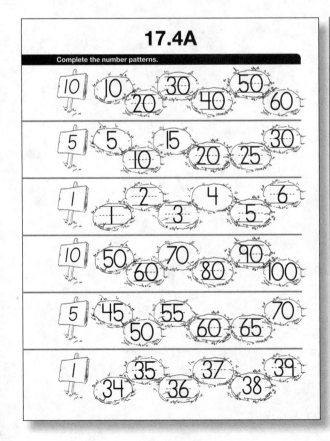

17.4B

Match pairs that make 100.

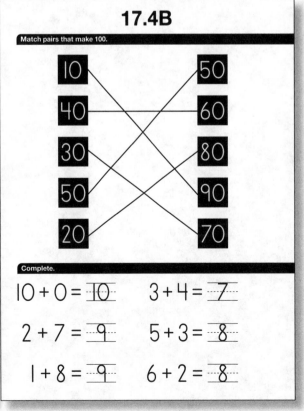

Complete.

10 + 0 = **10**   3 + 4 = **7**

2 + 7 = **9**   5 + 3 = **8**

1 + 8 = **9**   6 + 2 = **8**

Unit 6 Checkpoint

What to Expect at the End of Unit 6

By the end of Unit 6, most children will be able to:

- Read and write numbers to 100 mostly fluently. Many children will sometimes still confuse the order of the digits.
- Confidently use *greater than* or *less than* to compare numbers to 100.
- Use place-value thinking to identify quantities arranged in groups of tens and ones. (For example: 6 groups of 10 and 2 extra counters make 62.) Children who are still working on this may count by 10s and then 1s to identify these quantities instead of using direct place-value thinking.
- Add 1 or 10 to two-digit numbers; add and subtract groups of 10; and identify pairs of multiples of 10 that make 100 (like 70 and 30). Some children will be able to solve these problems mentally, but most will still need to model these problems with hands-on materials.

Is Your Child Ready to Move on?

In Unit 7, your child will use the numbers to 20 for real-life measurements as he learns to measure length with inches and feet. Your child does not need to be completely fluent with the numbers to 100 before moving on to Unit 7. He will continue to review the numbers to 100 throughout the unit.

Unit 7
Length

Overview

In Unit 7, your child will learn how to estimate and measure length in inches and feet (or centimeters and meters, depending on which measurement system your family uses). You'll use pattern blocks (or centimeter squares), rulers, and a homemade measuring rope to help your child grasp the important idea that we use repeated units to measure length.

Week 18	Measure in Inches (or Centimeters)
Week 19	Measure in Feet (or Meters)

What Your Child Will Learn

In this unit your child will learn to:

- Compare lengths directly, indirectly, and with units
- Know the approximate length of an inch and a foot (or a centimeter and a meter)
- Estimate lengths in inches and feet (or centimeters and meters)
- Use a ruler to measure in inches and feet (or centimeters and meters)

Recommended Math Picture Books (Optional)

These picture books are scheduled in the optional Enrichment and Review lessons at the end of each week.

- *Measuring Penny*, by Loreen Leedy. Henry Holt and Company, 1997.
- *How Big Is a Foot?*, by Rolf Myller. Yearling, 1990.

Week 18
Measure in Inches (or Centimeters)

Overview

This week, your child will learn to compare lengths and measure length in inches. He will use pattern blocks and a simplified ruler to understand the fundamental idea that we use repeated units to measure length.

Lesson 18.1   Compare and Measure Paths
Lesson 18.2   Measure with Pattern Blocks
Lesson 18.3   Measure with Pattern Blocks, Part 2
Lesson 18.4   Measure with a Simplified Ruler
Lesson 18.5   Enrichment and Review (Optional)

Teaching Math with Confidence:
What Are the Benefits of Measuring with Pattern Blocks Before Rulers?

During the elementary years, your child will learn to estimate and measure length, weight, and capacity with standard units (such as inches, pounds, and cups or centimeters, kilograms, and liters). In first grade, you will focus on length as you teach your child the fundamental principle of measurement: we use repeated units to measure. For example, if we say a pencil is 7 inches, we mean 7 inch-long sticks equal the length of the pencil.

Children love using measuring tools, so it may be tempting to skip straight to using a ruler. But when children use rulers too soon, they often miss this concept of repeated units. Instead, they develop the mistaken notion that the goal is to count the marks on the ruler rather than the spaces between the marks.

When children use a standard ruler too early, they often mistakenly think measuring means counting the lines—not the spaces between the lines.

To make this abstract concept of repeated units more concrete, your child will first use 1-inch square pattern blocks (or centimeter squares) to measure length. He'll line up pattern blocks next to an item and count the number of blocks to find the length of the item.

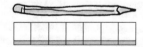

Then, he'll measure with a simplified paper ruler (found on Blackline Master 8). This ruler doesn't have any numbers or extra lines, so your child focuses on counting the spaces on the ruler (and not the marks) as he measures length.

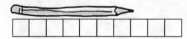

Finally, you and your child will compare and contrast a standard ruler with the simplified ruler. Some first graders will be ready to use the standard ruler to measure at this point. Others may find the numbers and extra lines on the standard ruler confusing and prefer the simplified ruler. Either way, working with pattern blocks and the simplified ruler will help your child understand the important concept of measuring with repeated units. You'll build on this essential idea throughout his elementary math education.

Extra Materials Needed for Week 18

- 5 pieces of yarn with the following lengths: 9 in., 6 in., 5 in., 4 in., and 2 in. (if your family uses U.S. standard units) or 9 cm, 6 cm, 5 cm, 4 cm, and 2 cm (if your family uses metric units)
- Small toy animal, doll, or figurine
- Yarn, string, or embroidery floss
- Tape
- 5 "skinny" household items such as a toothpick, pencil, screwdriver, fork, or comb
- 8 narrow paper strips, about 8 inches long and ¼-inch wide
- Scissors
- Glue, optional
- Construction paper, optional
- 5 writing utensils of varying lengths (pens, pencils, colored pencils, crayons, etc.)
- For optional Enrichment and Review Lesson:
  - × *Measuring Penny*, by Loreen Leedy
  - × Bathroom scale or kitchen scale

You will need yarn, string, or embroidery floss to measure lengths and distances in this unit. Try to use a type of fiber without much stretch so your measurements are as accurate as possible.

You will also need a 1-foot (or 30 cm) ruler this week, so make sure you have one in your Math Kit.

Materials Note for Families That Use the Metric System

If you use the metric system, look for notes at the beginning of each lesson that explain how to modify them. You'll need either centimeter squares (cut out from Blackline Master 8) or plastic centimeter cubes (available from school supply stores or online). Most children find it easier to handle blocks rather than small squares of paper, but either will do the job.

You'll also need the metric versions of the workbook pages for this unit, since the Student Workbook uses inches and feet. You can download these pages at welltrainedmind.com/mwc. Note that this download only includes Side A for each lesson. Your child should still complete Side B in the Student Workbook, as these pages review previously learned material.

Lesson 18.1
Compare and Measure Paths

	Purpose	Materials
Warm-up	• Practice shifting counting sequences on the 100 Chart • Practice memory work • Review subtraction facts	• 100 Chart (Blackline Master 3) • Coins • Subtraction Climb to the Top game board (Workbook page 11.1A) • Playing cards • Counters
Activities	• Compare paths' lengths with yarn • Measure paths' lengths on a grid	• Paper • Small toy animal, doll, or figurine • Yarn, string, or embroidery floss • Tape, optional • *If you use U.S. customary units:* workbook page 18.1A • *If you use the metric system:* metric workbook page 18.1A
Workbook	• Review	• Workbook page 18.1B

Note for Families that Use the Metric System

To modify this lesson for the metric system:

• say "centimeters" instead of "inches" every place it appears in the lesson
• use metric workbook page 18.1A (See the Week 18 Materials Note for download instructions.)

Warm-up: Counting, Memory Work, and Review

• **Let's pretend you're a counting robot again.** Draw a "computer panel" as in Lesson 17.4.

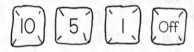

- × **Beep!** Press the 10 button. *10, 20, 30, 40, 50, 60.*
- × **Beep!** Press the 5 button. *65, 70, 75, 80, 85.*
- × **Beep!** Press the 1 button. *86, 87, 88, 89, 90, 91, 92.*
- × **Beep!** Press the Off button once your child reaches 92.

• Show your child a penny, nickel, and dime, and have her tell the name and value of each coin.

• Play Subtraction Climb to the Top. See Lesson 11.1 (page 175) for directions.

Activity: Compare Paths with Yarn

We are starting a new unit on measuring length today. Today, you'll compare and measure the lengths of paths.

Place a sheet of paper on the table. Place a small toy animal, doll, or figurine in the bottom left corner of the paper and draw a small house in the top right corner.

Let's pretend the toy wants to go home. There are lots of different paths it could take.
Draw the following paths on the paper as you describe them:

- **The toy might decide to walk along the edges of the paper.**

- **The toy might wander around and take a curved path.**

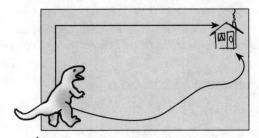

- **Or, the toy might decide to walk straight home.**

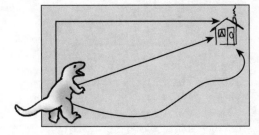

Which path do you think is the shortest? Which path do you think is the longest? *Answers will vary.*

Looking at the paths gives us an idea of which is the longest or the shortest, but it doesn't prove which is longest or shortest. We'll use yarn to compare their lengths so we know for sure.

Place the end of a piece of yarn at the end of one of the paths. Carefully lay the yarn on top of the path until you reach the other end. Cut the yarn at the other end of the path, so the path is entirely covered by the yarn.

If the yarn slides off the path, use a few small pieces of tape to keep it in place.

Repeat for the other two paths.

Now we can compare the pieces of yarn to see which path is the longest and which path is the shortest. Remove the yarn from the paper and align the yarn edges as shown below. Keep track of which piece of yarn corresponds to which path.

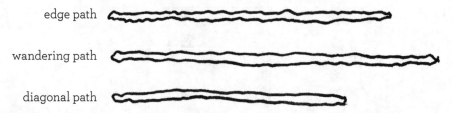

Which path is shortest? Which path is longest? *Answers will vary, depending on how you drew the paths.*

The shortest path between two points is always a straight line, so you should find the diagonal, "straight home" path shortest. You will likely find the "wandering" path is the longest, but it depends on how you drew it.

Activity: Compare and Measure Paths on a Grid

Show your child workbook page 18.1A. The ant, the ladybug, and the snail all want to get to the flower.

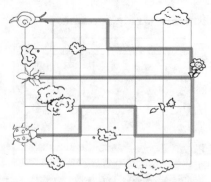

If your family uses the metric system, use metric workbook page 18.1A. See the Week 18 Overview for directions on where to download this workbook page and the other metric-version pages you'll need for Unit 7.

Have your child trace each path with her finger. **Which path do you think is the longest? Which path do you think is the shortest?** *Answers will vary.*

Have your child help you cover each path with yarn (as in the activity above) and then compare the lengths of the yarn. You should find the ladybug's path is the longest, and the ant's path is the shortest.

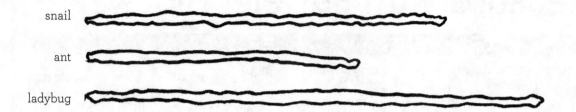

The edge of each box in the grid is one inch long. Let's count to find out how many inches each animal traveled. Show your child how to trace the snail's path and count each inch in the path.

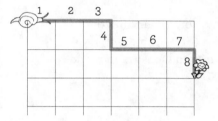

Have your child find the other path's length and answer the questions on the page.

> If your child has trouble keeping track of the path segments, have her use a highlighter to highlight each segment on the path as she counts it.

> Your child will learn more about inches (or centimeters) in the next lesson.

Workbook: Review

Have your child complete workbook page 18.1B. (Your child completed page 18.1A in the lesson activity.)

Lesson 18.2
Measure with Pattern Blocks

	Purpose	Materials
Warm-up	• Count by 10s starting at with a one-digit number • Practice memory work • Review finding pairs that equal 20	• 100 Chart (Blackline Master 3) • Coins • Number Cards

Activities	• Compare objects' lengths indirectly
	• Introduce inches (or centimeters)
	• Use repeated units to measure in inches (or centimeters)
		• *If you use U.S. customary units:*
		  × square pattern blocks
		  × 5 pieces of yarn with the following lengths: 9 inches, 6 inches, 5 inches, 4 inches, 2 inches
		• *If you use metric units:*
		  × centimeter cubes or squares
		  × 5 pieces of yarn with the following lengths: 9 cm, 6 cm, 5 cm, 4 cm, 2 cm
		• Tape
		• Index cards or slips of paper

Workbook	• Use repeated units to measure in inches (or centimeters)	• Workbook pages 18.2A (or metric 18.2A) and 18.2B

Note for Families that Use the Metric System

To modify this lesson for the metric system:

- say "centimeters" instead of "inches" every place it appears in the lesson
- use centimeter blocks or cubes to measure each item instead of square pattern blocks. (See the Week 18 Materials Note for more details.)
- use metric workbook page 18.2A (See the Week 18 Materials Note for download instructions.)

Note for Families that Use the U.S. Customary System

Most square pattern blocks are one inch wide, but they occasionally vary. Use a ruler to check yours before you begin this lesson. If you find that your pattern blocks are not exactly one inch wide, cut out and use the inch squares on Blackline Master 8 instead.

Warm-up: Counting, Memory Work, and Review

- **Count by 10s starting at 4.** Have your child point to each number on the 100 Chart as he says it: *4, 14, 24, 34, 44, 54, 64, 74, 84, 94.*

- Show your child a penny, nickel, and dime, and have him tell the name and value of each coin.

- Play Make 20 Memory. See Lesson 13.4 (page 212) for directions.

Activity: Compare Lengths Indirectly

In the last lesson, you compared the lengths of paths and measured them on a grid. Today, you'll learn more about comparing and measuring length.

In the last lesson, you used yarn to compare the lengths of paths. It was easy to see which piece of yarn was shortest and which piece of yarn was longest when you lined them up. But it's more difficult to compare lengths if they are not lined up.

Tape 5 pieces of yarn of different lengths to the table. (See Materials for their lengths.) Arrange them far away from each other and tilt them so it is difficult to visually compare their lengths.

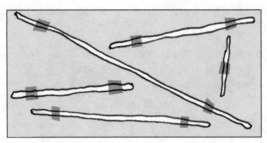

One way to compare the lengths is with our fingers. Show your child how to use your fingers to compare the lengths of two of the pieces of yarn: Hold your fingers apart the same length as one piece. Then, keep your fingers in the same position and compare the distance between your fingers to the length of the other piece of yarn.

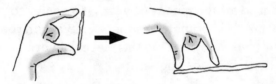

Have your child compare several pairs of yarn lengths in this way.

Using his fingers to compare the lengths helps your child understand the concept of length kinesthetically.

Activity: Introduce Inches (or Centimeters)

We can also compare the yarn's lengths by measuring them. We will use inches to measure the pieces of yarn. Show your child a square pattern block. **This block is one inch across.**

1 inch

Can you find a few things in this room about one inch long? *Possible answers: eraser, paper clip, my pinkie.*

Try to hold your thumb and first finger one inch apart. *Child holds thumb and forefinger about one inch apart.* Place the pattern block between the thumb and finger to check his estimate.

Activity: Measure Lengths with Pattern Blocks

Point to the shortest piece of yarn. **How many inches long do you think this piece of yarn is?** *Answers will vary.* If he's not sure, encourage him to hold this thumb and first finger about an inch apart and see how many times the inch fits along the yarn.

Show your child how to measure the yarn by placing square pattern blocks in a line along it. Make sure there are no gaps or overlaps between the blocks.

How long is this piece of yarn? *2 inches.* Write "2 inches" on an index card or slip of paper and place the card next to the yarn.

Repeat this process with the other pieces of yarn.

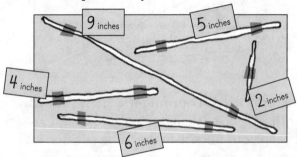

Now that we've measured all the pieces of yarn, it's easier to put them in order from short-est to longest. Have your child point to the pieces of yarn in order from shortest to longest. Then, check your child's answers: un-tape the pieces of yarn and place them in order from shortest to longest with their edges aligned.

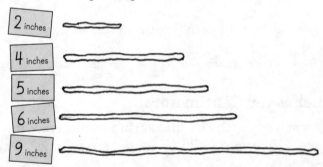

See the Week 18 **Teaching Math with Confidence** for the benefits of measuring with pattern blocks before introducing rulers.

Workbook: Measure Length and Review

Have your child complete workbook pages 18.2A and 18.2B. Explain that each printed square on the page is the same size as a square pattern block. He can place real pattern blocks on top to check.

If you use the metric system, have your child complete metric workbook page 18.2A. Explain that each square on the page is the same size as a centimeter square.

Lesson 18.3
Measure with Pattern Blocks, Part 2

	Purpose	Materials
Warm-up	• Count backward from 50 • Practice memory work • Review take-apart subtraction word problems	• 100 Chart (Blackline Master 3), optional • Coins • Counters

Activities	• Measure length with repeated units
	• Estimate and measure length in inches (or centimeters)
	• Use repeated units to measure and cut a given length
		• 5 "skinny" household items, such as a toothpick, pencil, screwdriver, fork, and comb
		• *If you use U.S. customary units:*
		  × square pattern blocks
		• *If you use metric units:*
		  × centimeter cubes or squares
		• Index cards or small slips of paper
		• 8 narrow paper strips, about 8 inches long (or 10 cm) and ¼-inch (or 0.5 cm) wide
		• Scissors
		• Glue, optional
		• Construction paper, optional

Workbook	• Measure length with repeated units	• Workbook pages 18.3A (or metric 18.3A) and 18.3B

Note for Families that Use the Metric System

To modify this lesson for the metric system:

- say "centimeters" instead of "inches" every place it appears in the lesson
- use centimeter blocks or cubes instead of square pattern blocks
- use metric workbook page 18.3A (See the Week 18 Materials Note for download instructions.)

Warm-up: Counting, Memory Work, and Review

- Have your child count backward from 50 to 35. If she has trouble, have her point to each number on the 100 Chart as she says it.

- Show your child a penny, nickel, and dime, and have her tell the name and value of each coin.

- Read the following word problems to your child. Have her model each problem with counters and then write and solve a subtraction equation to match.

    × **10 children are playing tag. If 5 are boys, how many are girls?** *5.*

$$10 - 5 = 5$$

× **You have 8 lollipops. Some are cherry-flavored, and some are watermelon-flavored. If 7 are cherry-flavored, how many are watermelon-flavored?** *1.*

$$8 - 7 = 1$$

If your child has trouble writing the subtraction equations, have her place Number Cards on the Part-Total Mat before writing each equation.

What do these word problems have in common? *Sample answers: Both are take-apart subtraction problems. Both are about finding part of a total. You can use subtraction to solve both problems.*

Activity: Measure Household Items in Inches (or Centimeters)

In the last lesson, you measured pieces of yarn with square pattern blocks. Show your child a square pattern block. **Do you remember how long the edge of each square pattern block is?** *1 inch.* **Today, you'll use pattern blocks to measure objects in inches.**

Try to hold your thumb and first finger one inch apart. *Child holds thumb and forefinger about one inch apart.* Place the pattern block between the thumb and finger to check his estimate.

Show your child 5 household items of different lengths. (See Materials for suggestions.) **Which is shortest?** *Answers will vary.* **Which is the longest?** *Answers will vary.* Have your child put the items in order from the shortest to the longest.

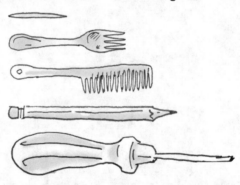

Point to the shortest item. **How many inches long do you think this item is?** *Answers will vary.*

Have your child measure the item by placing square pattern blocks in a line next to the item. Have her record the item's length in inches on an index card and place the card next to it.

Have your child measure the rest of the items with square pattern blocks. Make sure she estimates the length of each object before measuring.

You may find some of the items are not a whole number of inches. Use phrases like "a little more than 6 inches" or "a little less than 4 inches" to describe these lengths. Round these items' lengths to the nearest whole number of inches as you record them.

Activity: Use Pattern Blocks to Measure and Cut Paper Strips

We also measure when we need to cut things to the right size. Let's cut some paper strips to make a picture.

Place a paper strip on the table. **The first paper strip should be 5 inches long.** Line up 5 pattern blocks under the paper strip, starting at the left edge of the strip. Draw a line at the end of the blocks, and cut the strip along this line.

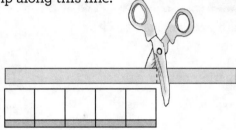

Have your child measure and cut the following sizes of paper strips:

- 1 additional 5-inch strip (for a total of 2)
- 3 6-inch strips
- 2 4-inch strips
- 1 3-inch strip

Show your child how to arrange these strips in the shape of a house as shown. If you have time, she can glue the strips to a piece of construction paper and add more details to the picture.

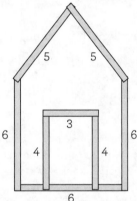

Workbook: Measure in Inches (or Centimeters) and Review

Have your child complete workbook pages 18.3A and 18.3B. Your child will need square pattern blocks to measure the straws on 18.3A.

If you use the metric system, have your child complete metric workbook page 18.3A. Your child will need centimeter squares or cubes to measure the lines.

You may need to show your child how to line up the pattern blocks along the vertical lines.

Lesson 18.4
Measure with a Simplified Ruler

	Purpose	Materials
Warm-up	• Count forward from any number from 1 to 100 • Practice memory work • Review comparing numbers to 100	• 100 Chart (Blackline Master 3) • Coins • Number Cards

Activities	• Use a simplified ruler to measure length in inches (or centimeters)
	• Compare and contrast a simplified ruler with a standard ruler
		• *If you use U.S. customary units:*
		  × Paper ruler (inch version) from Blackline Master 8
		  × Square pattern blocks
		  × Standard 1-foot ruler
		• *If you use metric units:*
		  × Paper ruler (centimeter version) from Blackline Master 8
		  × Centimeter squares or cubes
		  × Standard 30-centimeter ruler
		• 5 writing utensils of varying lengths (pens, pencils, colored pencils, crayons, etc.)

Workbook	• Use a ruler to measure length in inches (or centimeters)	• Workbook pages 18.4A (or metric 18.4A) and 18.4B

Note for Families that Use the Metric System

To modify this lesson for the metric system:

- say "centimeters" instead of "inches" every place it appears in the lesson
- use the centimeter version of the paper ruler from Blackline Master 8
- use centimeter squares or cubes instead of square pattern blocks
- use metric workbook page 18.4A (see the Week 18 Overview for download instructions)

Warm-up: Counting, Memory Work, and Review

- **Point to 35 on the 100 Chart.** *Child points to 35.* **Count forward to the end of the row. Point to each number as you say it.** *35, 36, 37, 38, 39, 40.*

  Repeat with 48 and 77.

- Show your child a penny, nickel, and dime, and have him tell the name and value of each coin.

- Play Two-Digit War. See Lesson 17.1 (page 269) for directions.

Activity: Measure with a Simplified Ruler

In the last two lessons, you used square pattern blocks to measure in inches. It can take a while to line up the pattern blocks, and sometimes they slide out of place. That's why people usually use rulers to measure in inches, not blocks. Today, you'll learn how to use a paper ruler to measure in inches.

Show your child the paper ruler (Blackline Master 8). **Each square on the ruler is 1 inch wide.** Have your child place square pattern blocks on the ruler to verify this.

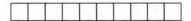

Spread 5 writing utensils of different lengths on the table. Have your child choose one. **How many inches long do you think this is?** *Answers will vary.*

Show your child how to use the paper ruler to measure the writing utensil as shown. **How many inches long is it?** *Answers will vary.*

The pencil is a little longer than 7 inches.

Have your child estimate and measure the length of the rest of the writing utensils.

> You may find some of the writing utensils are not a whole number of inches. Encourage your child to use phrases like "a little more than 6 inches" or "a little less than 4 inches" to describe these lengths.

Activity: Compare the Paper Ruler and a Standard Ruler

Show your child a standard 1-foot ruler. **What's different about the two rulers?** *Possible answers: They are made of different materials. The paper ruler only has a few lines, but the other ruler has a lot of lines. The paper ruler doesn't have any numbers on it, but the other ruler has numbers. The paper ruler is shorter.*

What do the two rulers have in common? *Possible answers: They both have lines. They both have marks every inch.* Hold the rulers next to each other so your child can see the inch marks on the paper ruler line up with the inch marks on the standard ruler.

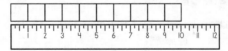

> You may need to offset one of the rulers slightly if the standard ruler does not start measuring at the edge.

We use this kind of ruler just like the paper ruler. Show your child how to use the standard ruler to measure one of the writing utensils. Line up the edge of the ruler with the edge of the utensil and point out how the printed number on the ruler counts the number of inches up to that line.

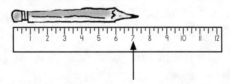

Workbook: Measure in Inches (or Centimeters) and Review

Have your child complete workbook pages 18.4A and 18.4B. Your child may use either the paper ruler or the standard ruler to measure the lines.

> If you use the metric system, have your child complete metric workbook page 18.4A. Your child may use either the paper centimeter ruler or a standard 30-centimeter ruler to measure the lines.

> First graders often find the many lines on a standard ruler confusing. Most children will find it easier to use the paper ruler for the workbook page.

Lesson 18.5
Enrichment and Review (Optional)

	Purpose	Materials
Warm-up	• Review counting • Review memory work • Review your child's favorite or most challenging activities from Week 18	• Varies, depending on the activities you choose
Picture Book	• Understand many different attributes can be measured (such as length, weight, and capacity)	• *Measuring Penny*, by Loreen Leedy
Enrichment Activity	• Explore measuring weight	• 3-5 household items, each weighing less than 5 pounds • Bathroom scale or kitchen scale

Warm-up: Counting, Memory Work, and Review

- Have your child count to 100 by 1s, 2s, 5s, or 10s. (Choose whichever counting sequence your child needs to practice the most.)

- Quiz your child on the memory work through Week 18. See page 499 for the full list.

- If you have time, repeat one or two of the activities from this week's lessons. Choose activities your child especially enjoyed or found challenging.

Math Picture Book: *Measuring Penny*

Read *Measuring Penny,* by Loreen Leedy. After you read, discuss the many ways the girl measures the dog in the book.

Enrichment Activity: Explore Weight

Unit 7 focuses on measuring length. This enrichment activity will give your child experience with another measurable attribute: weight. He will learn more about measuring and comparing weight in later grades.

Have your child choose 3-5 items from around the house. Encourage him to choose items with a range of weights less than 5 pounds. (For example, he might use a box of facial tissues, a hardcover book, and a bag of potatoes.)

Have him put the items in order from lightest to heaviest. Then, have him use a kitchen scale or bathroom scale to weigh the items and check the order.

If you have time, also have your child weigh himself and tell him how much he weighed when he was born.

Week 18 Answer Key

18.1A

The map shows the animals' paths to the flowers.
Use the map to answer the questions.

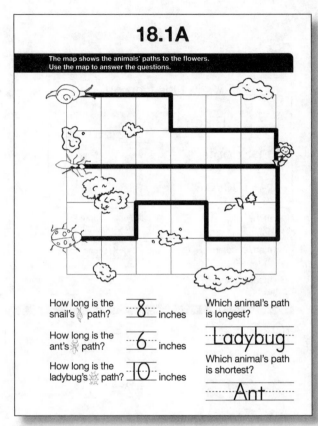

How long is the snail's 🐌 path? __8__ inches

How long is the ant's 🐜 path? __6__ inches

How long is the ladybug's 🐞 path? __10__ inches

Which animal's path is longest?

Ladybug

Which animal's path is shortest?

Ant

18.1B

Complete.

$9 + 1 = $ __10__ $5 + 1 = $ __6__

$4 + 5 = $ __9__ $2 + 6 = $ __8__

$8 + 0 = $ __8__ $3 + 7 = $ __10__

Complete the missing numbers on the 100 chart.

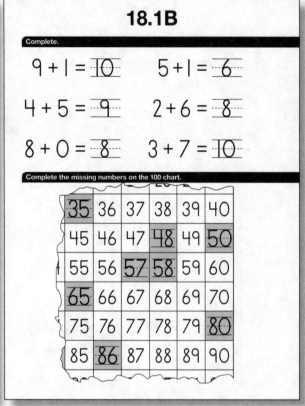

35	36	37	38	39	40
45	46	47	48	49	50
55	56	57	58	59	60
65	66	67	68	69	70
75	76	77	78	79	80
85	86	87	88	89	90

18.2A

Write the length of each ribbon.

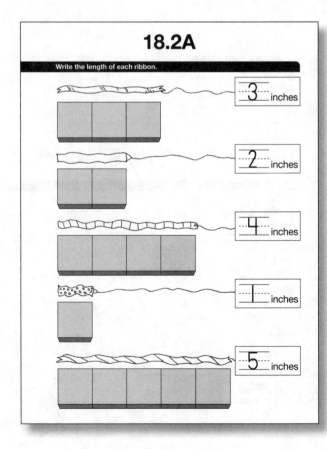

__3__ inches

__2__ inches

__4__ inches

__1__ inches

__5__ inches

18.2B

Complete.

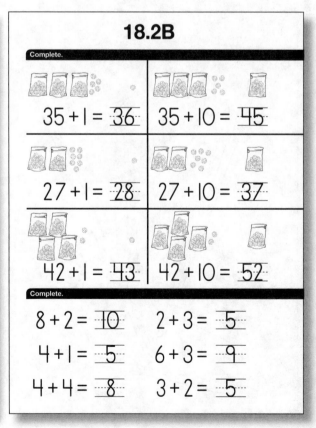

$35 + 1 = $ __36__ $35 + 10 = $ __45__

$27 + 1 = $ __28__ $27 + 10 = $ __37__

$42 + 1 = $ __43__ $42 + 10 = $ __52__

Complete.

$8 + 2 = $ __10__ $2 + 3 = $ __5__

$4 + 1 = $ __5__ $6 + 3 = $ __9__

$4 + 4 = $ __8__ $3 + 2 = $ __5__

Week 18 Answer Key

18.3A

Use square pattern blocks to measure the straws in inches.

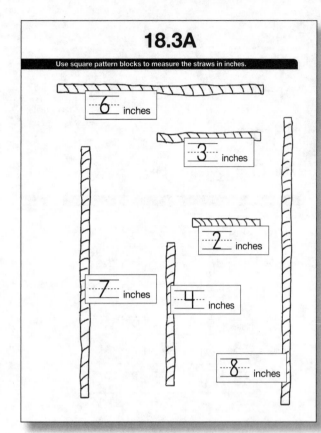

__6__ inches

__3__ inches

__2__ inches

__7__ inches

__4__ inches

__8__ inches

18.3B

Michael made a bar graph of the toys in his family's garage.
Use the bar graph to answer the questions.

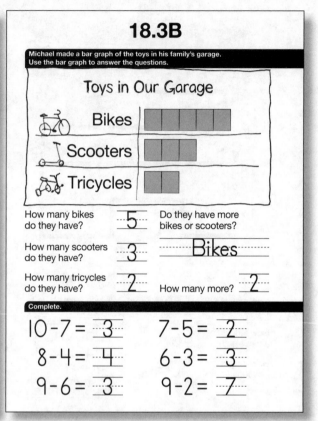

Toys in Our Garage

Bikes

Scooters

Tricycles

How many bikes do they have? __5__

How many scooters do they have? __3__

How many tricycles do they have? __2__

Do they have more bikes or scooters?

__Bikes__

How many more? __2__

Complete.

$10 - 7 = 3$ $7 - 5 = 2$

$8 - 4 = 4$ $6 - 3 = 3$

$9 - 6 = 3$ $9 - 2 = 7$

18.4A

Use a ruler to measure the sticks in inches.

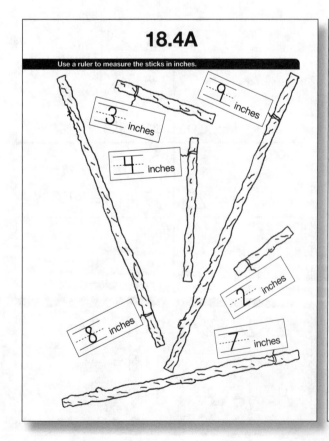

__9__ inches

__3__ inches

__4__ inches

__2__ inches

__8__ inches

__7__ inches

18.4B

Complete.

$7 + 3 = 10$ $5 + 3 = 8$

$4 + 3 = 7$ $2 + 4 = 6$

$6 + 1 = 7$ $3 + 6 = 9$

Write how many.

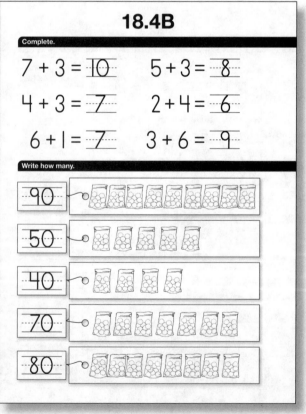

__90__

__50__

__40__

__70__

__80__

Week 19
Measure in Feet (or Meters)

Overview

This week, your child will learn to estimate and measure length in feet (or meters). She will use a one-foot ruler (or meterstick) and a homemade measuring rope to further understand the idea that we use repeated units to measure length.

Lesson 19.1   Shorter Than, Longer Than, or Equal to a Foot (or Meter)
Lesson 19.2   Measure Objects
Lesson 19.3   Measure Distance
Lesson 19.4   Measure in Feet and Inches (or Meters and Centimeters)
Lesson 19.5   Enrichment and Review (Optional)

Teaching Math with Confidence: Developing a Sense of the Magnitude of Units

Last week, your child learned how to estimate and measure in inches (or centimeters). This week, you'll teach your child how to estimate and measure in feet (or meters). Just like last week, you'll use a variety of hands-on activities to help your child develop a concrete sense of the length of these units.

- *Benchmarks:* In Lesson 19.1, you'll find several objects around the house equal to one foot so your child can begin to form a mental picture of the length of one foot.
- *Approximation:* Your child will practice approximating the length of a foot with her hands throughout the week. Each time, you'll use a one-foot ruler to check how accurate her approximation is. This repeated feedback should help your child gradually become more accurate.
- *Estimation:* Your child will also estimate lengths in feet throughout the week. Each time, she'll also measure the length to see how close her estimate was. As with approximation, this feedback will help her refine her estimates over the course of the week.

Developing a sense of the magnitude of units is an important part of learning to measure. With a strong concrete grasp of the size of these units, your child will be well-prepared to solve measurement word problems and find equivalencies in later grades.

Extra Materials Needed for Week 19

- Tape
- Yarn, string, or embroidery floss
- Beanbag, crumpled wad of paper, or soft, unbreakable toy
- Scissors
- Tape measure
- For optional Enrichment and Review Lesson:
    × *How Big Is a Foot?,* by Rolf Myller

Materials Note for Families That Use the Metric System

As in Week 19, you'll also need metric versions of the workbook pages this week. You can download these pages at welltrainedmind.com/mwc. Note that this download only includes Side A for each lesson. Your child should still complete Side B in the Student Workbook, as these pages review previously learned material.

Lesson 19.1
Shorter Than, Longer Than, or Equal to a Foot (or Meter)

	Purpose	Materials
Warm-up	• Practice shifting counting sequences on the 100 Chart • Practice memory work • Review finding combinations of multiples of 10 that make 100 (like 20 and 80)	• 100 Chart (Blackline Master 3) • Number Cards

Activities	• Introduce feet (or meters)
	• Learn that 12 inches equal 1 foot (or that 100 centimeters equal 1 meter)
	• Identify whether objects are shorter than, longer than, or equal to a foot (or meter)
		• *If you use U.S. customary units:*
		  × Paper ruler (inch version) from Blackline Master 8
		  × Standard 1-foot ruler
		  × Square pattern blocks
		• *If you use metric units:*
		  × Paper ruler (centimeter version) from Blackline Master 8
		  × Standard 30-centimeter ruler
		  × Centimeter squares or cubes

Workbook	• Identify whether objects are shorter, longer, or equal to a foot (or meter)	• Workbook pages 19.1A (or metric 19.1A) and 19.1B • 1-foot ruler

Note for Families that Use the Metric System

To modify this lesson for the metric system:

- say "meters" instead of "feet" and "centimeters" instead of "inches" every place they appear in the lesson
- use the paper centimeter ruler from Blackline Master 8
- use a meterstick (or 1-meter long piece of string) in place of the 1-foot ruler
- use metric workbook page 19.1A (see the Week 19 Materials Note for download instructions)

Warm-up: Counting, Memory Work, and Review

- **Let's pretend you're a counting robot again.** Draw a "computer panel" as in Lesson 17.4.

    × **Beep!** Press the 10 button. *10, 20, 30, 40.*
    × **Beep!** Press the 5 button. *45, 50, 55, 60, 65.*
    × **Beep!** Press the 1 button. *66, 67, 68, 69, 70, 71, 72, 73.*
    × **Beep!** Press the Off button once your child reaches 73.

- Have your child rhythmically say the Tens Chant: *1 ten. Ten! 2 tens. Twenty! etc.* See Lesson 15.1 (page 236) for the full chant.
- Play Multiples of 10 Go Fish. See Lesson 15.4 (page 246) for directions.

Activity: Introduce Feet (or Meters)

You have learned how to measure in inches. This week, you will learn to measure in feet.

When we want to know the length of something small, we usually measure with inches. Place a pencil on the table. Have your child measure the length of the pencil with either the paper ruler or a standard ruler. **How many inches long is the pencil?** *Answers will vary.*

Sometimes we need to find the length of something longer, like the length of this table or the length of this room. It would take a lot of inches to measure lengths like these! Instead, we usually use feet. Show your child a 1-foot ruler. **This ruler is one foot long. It's called a foot because it's about the length of an adult's foot.**

If your child is interested, briefly discuss yards and miles (or kilometers). She'll learn more about these units in later grades.

Try to hold your hands about one foot apart. *Child holds hands about one foot apart.* Place the ruler between her hands to check her estimate.

Have your child compare the length of her foot to the ruler. **Why do you think we don't use our own feet to measure length?** *Possible answer: People's feet are different lengths.*

You'll explore the importance of standard units in greater depth in the picture book and enrichment activity in Lesson 19.5.

1 foot is equal to 12 inches. Have your child line up 12 square pattern blocks along the ruler to verify that 1 foot is 12 inches long.

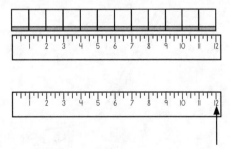

Also point out the 12-inch mark on the end of the ruler.

If you are using a meterstick, show your child how the meter equals 100 centimeters and point out the 100-centimeter mark. You don't need to line up 100 centimeter squares on it, though!

Activity: 1 Foot (or Meter) Scavenger Hunt

Now, we're going to go on a scavenger hunt. This scavenger hunt has 3 parts.

First, find 3 things in the house a lot shorter than a foot. *Sample answers: fork, alarm clock, paperback book.* Have your child compare each object with the 1-foot ruler to check it is shorter than a foot.

Next, find 3 things in the house about a foot long. *Sample answers: piece of paper, height of a box of cereal, heating vent.* Again, have your child compare each object with the 1-foot ruler to verify it is about a foot long.

It's fine if these objects are 1-2 inches longer or shorter than a foot.

Last, find 3 things in the house longer than a foot. *Sample answers: chair, table, hockey stick.* Have your child place the 1-foot ruler against each object to show the object is longer than a foot.

Workbook: Compare Objects to a Foot and Review

Have your child complete workbook pages 19.1A and 19.1B. Have her use a one-foot ruler to check whether each item on 19.1A is shorter than, about equal to, or longer than a foot.

If you use the metric system, have your child complete metric workbook page 19.1A. Have her use the meter-stick to check whether each item on metric 19.1A is shorter than, about equal to, or longer than a meter.

Lesson 19.2
Measure Objects

	Purpose	Materials
Warm-up	• Count by 10s starting at with a one-digit number • Practice memory work • Review adding and subtracting multiples of 10 (like 20 or 60)	• 100 Chart (Blackline Master 3) • Counters

Activities	• Estimate and measure lengths of objects in feet (or meters)	• *If you use U.S. customary units:*
		  × Standard 1-foot ruler
		• *If you use metric units:*
		  × Standard meterstick (or 1-meter long piece of string)

Workbook	• Measure length in feet (or meters)	• Workbook pages 19.2A (or metric 19.2A) and 19.2B

Note for Families that Use the Metric System

To modify this lesson for the metric system:

- say "meters" instead of "feet" and "centimeters" instead of "inches" every place they appear in the lesson
- use a meterstick (or 1-meter long piece of string) in place of the 1-foot ruler
- use metric workbook page 19.2A (see the Week 19 Overview for download instructions)

Warm-up: Counting, Memory Work, and Review

- **Count by 10s starting at 1.** Have your child point to each number on the 100 Chart as he says it: *1, 11, 21, 31, 41, 51, 61, 71, 81, 91.*

- **Name the even numbers in order to 20.** *2, 4, 6, 8, 10, 12, 14, 16, 18, 20.* **Name the odd numbers in order to 19.** *1, 3, 5, 7, 9, 11, 13, 15, 17, 19.*

- Have your child model the following equations with bags of counters and find the answers.

  ×   30 + 20 = 50
  ×   50 + 40 = 90
  ×   80 − 10 = 70
  ×   90 − 80 = 10

Activity: Estimate and Measure Length in Feet (or Meters)

In the last lesson, you learned how long one foot is. Today, you'll learn how to measure objects in feet.

Show your child a 1-foot ruler and point at the table. **How many feet long do you think this table is?** *Answers will vary.* Encourage your child to imagine placing the ruler along the table to find a reasonable estimate (but don't allow him to actually measure it yet).

If you use the metric system, have your child estimate and measure the length of a small room instead of the table.

Show your child how to measure the length of the table with the 1-foot ruler. Align the ruler with one edge of the table. Then, place your finger at the end of the ruler and slide the ruler to the other side of your finger. Have your child help you move the ruler and count how many feet long the table is.

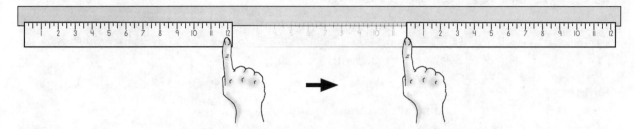

So, how many feet long is the table? *Answers will vary.*

Use phrases like "a little longer" or "a little shorter" to describe the length if it is not a whole number of feet. For example: The table is a little longer than 4 feet.

Activity: Estimate and Measure Length around the House

We're going to measure some things around the house in feet. We'll record our results in a chart. What would you like to measure? *Answers will vary.*

If your child is not sure, suggest several objects about 2-6 feet long, such as the length of the television, height of a doorway, or length of the bathtub.

If you use the metric system, have your child estimate and measure the length of several different-sized rooms in your home.

Go around the house and measure 5-8 objects. Have your child estimate the length of each object before measuring and round each measurement to the nearest number of whole feet. Make a simple chart to record the estimates and measurements. Your finished chart should look something like this:

Object	Estimate	Measurement
Bathtub	3 feet	5 feet
Bed	5 feet	6 feet
Dog bed	3 feet	3 feet
Doorway	6 feet	7 feet
Kitchen table	5 feet	5 feet
Guitar	3 feet	3 feet
Block castle	2 feet	2 feet

Workbook: Measure in Feet (or Meters) and Review

Have your child complete workbook pages 19.2A and 19.2B. Explain that the 1-foot rulers on the page are pictures of rulers and that the printed pictures are not actually 1 foot long.

If you use the metric system, have your child complete metric workbook page 19.2A.

Lesson 19.3
Measure Distance

	Purpose	Materials
Warm-up	• Count backward from 60 • Practice memory work • Review comparing two-digit numbers on the 100 Chart	• 100 Chart (Blackline Master 3) • Counters

Activities	• Repeat a unit to make a measuring tool
	• Estimate and measure distances in feet (or meters)
		• *If you use U.S. customary units:*
		  × Standard 1-foot ruler
		• *If you use metric units:*
		  × Standard meterstick (or 1-meter long piece of string)
		• Tape
		• 20-foot (or 5-meter) piece of yarn
		• Beanbag, crumpled wad of paper, or soft, unbreakable toy

Workbook	• Measure distances in feet (or meters)	• Workbook pages 19.3A (or metric 19.3A) and 19.3B

Note for Families that Use the Metric System

To modify this lesson for the metric system:

• say "meters" instead of "feet" and "centimeters" instead of "inches" every place they appear in the lesson
• use a meterstick (or 1-meter long piece of string) in place of the 1-foot ruler
• use metric workbook page 19.3A (see the Week 19 Overview for download instructions)

You will need a large room with at least 15-20 feet of open space for the activity in this lesson. Or, teach it outside if the weather allows.

This is a longer lesson than usual, but most families find it very memorable and a lot of fun! Divide the lesson over two days if you don't have time to complete it in one session. Or, save time by using a standard measuring tape instead of making the measuring rope.

Warm-up: Counting, Memory Work, and Review

• Have your child count backward from 60 to 45, either by memory or with the 100 Chart.
• Have your child say the days of the week. **How many days are in a week?** 7.
• Play several rounds of Guess the Secret Number with the numbers from 1 to 100. See Lesson 17.2 (page 271) for directions.

Activity: Estimate and Measure Distance

In the last lesson, you learned how to measure objects in feet. Today, you'll learn how to measure distances in feet.

Make a small X with tape on the floor. Make another X with tape about 10 feet (or 3 meters) away. **About how far do you think the Xs are from each other?** *Answers will vary.*

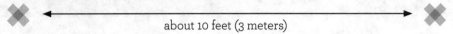

about 10 feet (3 meters)

Let's measure the distance in feet. Help your child measure the distance by placing a ruler end-to-end from one X to the other. Encourage your child to frequently check she is on a straight-line path from one X to the other.

What's the distance between the two Xs? *Answers will vary.*

What made it hard to measure the distance between the Xs with a one-foot ruler? *Possible answers: You have to move the ruler many times. It's hard to measure a straight line.*

Let's make a measuring rope to make it easier to measure in feet. Stretch a long piece of yarn (about 20 feet, or 5 meters) on the floor. Beginning at one end, use a ruler to measure 1-foot (or 1-meter) lengths along the yarn. Fold a piece of tape over the yarn at each 1-foot length.

Use the measuring rope to measure the distance between the Xs. Discuss how much easier it is to use a measuring rope rather than a 1-foot ruler.

> If you use the metric system, make your measuring rope a little longer than 5 meters and mark the increments in meters.

> This measuring rope is essentially a homemade tape measure with one-foot increments. Creating the measuring rope helps your child understand that measuring tools are made by repeating a unit over and over.

Activity: Estimate and Measure Throws

Let's estimate and measure some more distances. Mark a starting spot on the floor with a piece of tape and give your child an object she can safely throw, such as a beanbag, crumpled wad of paper, or soft toy.

> Choose your object based on how much space you have, how vigorously your child throws, and what you have on hand.

Have your child throw the object. **How far do you think you threw it?** *Answers will vary.* Start a simple chart and have your child record her estimate. Then, have her measure the actual distance with the measuring rope and record the distance in the chart.

Have your child throw the object 5-8 times. Your finished chart should look like this:

Estimate	Measurement
6 feet	9 feet
7 feet	8 feet
10 feet	12 feet
11 feet	11 feet
14 feet	15 feet
8 feet	7 feet

Use the following questions to discuss the finished chart. (Note the sample answers are based on the sample chart above. Your child's answers should be based on her chart.)

- **How far was your shortest throw?** *Sample answer: 7 feet.*
- **How far was your longest throw?** *Sample answer: 15 feet.*
- **Which of your estimates was most different from the actual measurement?** *Sample answer: I thought the first throw was 6 feet, but it was actually 9 feet.*
- **Which of your estimates was closest to the actual measurement?** *Sample answer: The 11-foot estimate was exactly right!*

You do not need to keep this measuring rope for future lessons, although your child may enjoy experimenting with it during her play time.

Workbook: Measure Distances in Feet (or Meters) and Review

Have your child complete workbook pages 19.3A and 19.3B. As in Lesson 19.2, explain that the 1-foot rulers on the page are pictures of rulers, and that the printed pictures are not actually 1 foot long.

If you use the metric system, have your child complete metric workbook page 19.3A.

Lesson 19.4
Measure in Feet and Inches (or Meters and Centimeters)

	Purpose	Materials
Warm-up	• Count forward from any number from 1 to 100 • Practice memory work • Review solving word problems	• 100 Chart (Blackline Master 3) optional • Counters

Activities	• Measure height in feet and inches (or meters and centimeters)	• Tape, optional
		• Yarn, string, or embroidery floss
		• Scissors
		• *If you use U.S. customary units:*
		  × Standard 1-foot ruler
		• *If you use metric units:*
		  × Standard meterstick (or 1-meter long piece of string)

Workbook	• Measure height in feet (or meters)	• Workbook pages 19.4A (or metric 19.4A) and 19.4B

Note for Families that Use the Metric System

To modify this lesson for the metric system:

- say "meters" instead of "feet" and "centimeters" instead of "inches" every place they appear in the lesson
- use a meterstick (or 1-meter long piece of string) in place of the 1-foot ruler
- use metric workbook page 19.4A (see the Week 19 Overview for download instructions)

You will need to know your child's length at birth in this lesson. If you don't have this information, either use the earliest height you have recorded for him or skip that portion of the lesson.

You will need a tape measure for this lesson. You can use either a flexible sewing tape measure or a hard-cased metal tape measure. If you use a metal tape measure, supervise your child carefully so he doesn't cut himself on the edges or pinch his fingers.

Warm-up: Counting, Memory Work, and Review

- Have your child count forward from the following numbers. Stop him after he reaches the last number listed in the sample answers.

    - × **Count forward from 36:** *36, 37, 38, 39, 40.*
    - × **Count forward from 78:** *78, 79, 80, 81, 82.*
    - × **Count forward from 59:** *59, 60, 61, 62, 63.*

    Children often have trouble crossing the decade when counting (for example, from the 30s to 40, or from the 70s to 80). This activity gives your child practice with this important skill. If he has trouble, allow him to first point to the numbers on the 100 Chart before reciting them from memory.

- Show your child a penny, nickel, and dime, and have him tell the name and value of each coin.

- Ask your child the following word problems. Have your child model each problem with counters and then write and solve an equation to match.
  - × **You have 5 donuts in one box and 4 donuts in another box. How many donuts do you have?** *9.*

$$5 + 4 = 9$$

  - × **You have 7 donuts. Then, you give 2 of them to a friend. How many donuts do you have now?** *5.*

$$7 - 2 = 5$$

What do these word problems have in common? *Sample answers: Both are about donuts.*

How are these word problems different from each other? *One is about joining two groups of donuts, but the other is about taking away some donuts. You use addition for one and subtraction for the other.*

Activity: Measure Height

You have learned how to measure with feet and with inches. Today, you'll learn how to combine feet and inches in the same measurement.

Use a piece of tape or a light pencil mark to mark your child's height on the wall. Place the end of a piece of yarn at the floor. Hold the yarn along the wall and cut it so it is the same length as your child's height.

Transferring your child's height to a length of yarn makes it easier to measure.

Have your child use a one-foot ruler to measure the yarn. **About how many feet tall are you?** *Answers will vary.*

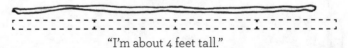

"I'm about 4 feet tall."

Measuring your height in feet isn't very exact. Discuss how close your child's height is to a whole number of feet. For example: **You're actually a few inches shorter than 4 feet.**

We could measure your height in inches to get a more exact measurement. Show your child how to use a tape measure to measure the yarn. **How many inches tall are you?** *Answers will vary.*

"I'm 45 inches tall."

We usually use both feet and inches to measure heights. First, we measure as many whole feet as possible. Then, we measure the rest in inches. Show your child how to use the one-foot ruler to measure the yarn in feet and inches.

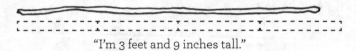

"I'm 3 feet and 9 inches tall."

Tell your child your own height in feet and inches.

Activity: Measure Your Child's Newborn Length in Feet and Inches

Tell your child how long he was when he was born. For example: **You were only 19 inches long when you were born!** Use a tape measure to cut a piece of yarn to match this length.

Have your child use a one-foot ruler to measure this piece of yarn in feet and inches. Help him measure as many whole feet as possible and then measure the rest in inches.

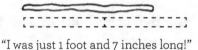

"I was just 1 foot and 7 inches long!"

Compare this piece of yarn with the piece of yarn that matches his current height.

> If you make marks on a door to record your child's height (or have records of your child's height at various ages), show these records to your child and discuss how much he has grown over the years.

Workbook: Measure Height and Review

Have your child complete workbook pages 19.4A and 19.4B. If needed, remind your child that the 1-foot rulers on the page are pictures of rulers, and that the printed pictures are not actually 1 foot long.

> If you use the metric system, have your child complete metric workbook page 19.4A.

Lesson 19.5
Enrichment and Review (Optional)

	Purpose	Materials
Warm-up	• Review counting • Review memory work • Review your child's favorite or most challenging activities from Week 19	• Varies, depending on the activities you choose
Picture Book	• Understand the value of standard units	• *How Big Is a Foot?*, by Rolf Myller
Enrichment Activity	• Explore how different-sized units result in different measurements.	• None

Warm-up: Counting, Memory Work, and Review

- Have your child count to 100 by 1s, 2s, 5s, or 10s. (Choose whichever counting sequence your child needs to practice the most.)

- Quiz your child on the memory work through Week 18. See page 499 for the full list.

- If you have time, repeat one or two of the activities from this week's lessons. Choose activities your child especially enjoyed or found challenging.

Math Picture Book: *How Big Is a Foot?*

Read *How Big Is a Foot?*, by Rolf Myller.

Enrichment Activity: Use Different-Sized Feet to Measure Length

Show your child how to measure the length of the room with your own feet. Walk across the room, placing each foot directly in front of the previous foot, with no gaps. Count how many steps you take.

Have your child use her feet to measure the length of the room as well. Compare your results and discuss why they are different from each other. For example: **The room is as long as 26 of my feet, but 34 of your feet! Why do you think there's such a difference?**

Also, discuss the importance of using a standard unit for measurement. For example: **What do you think would happen if everyone used their own feet to measure instead of a ruler?**

Week 19 Answer Key

19.1A

Use a 1-foot ruler to see whether each object is shorter than a foot, about equal to a foot, or longer than a foot. Check the box that matches.

Object	Shorter than a foot	About equal to a foot	Longer than a foot
The length of this page		✓	
The width of this page	✓		
Your hand	✓		
Your foot	✓		
Your bed			✓
Your pencil	✓		
Your chair			✓

19.1B

Complete.

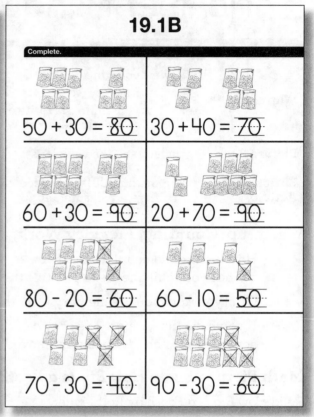

50 + 30 = 80   30 + 40 = 70

60 + 30 = 90   20 + 70 = 90

80 - 20 = 60   60 - 10 = 50

70 - 30 = 40   90 - 30 = 60

19.2A

Write the length of each box. Each ruler is 1 foot long.

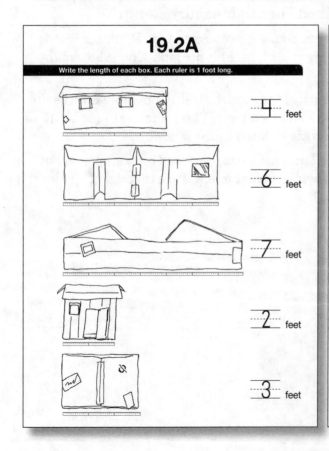

4 feet

6 feet

7 feet

2 feet

3 feet

19.2B

Complete.

5 + 5 = 10   0 + 9 = 9

4 + 6 = 10   8 + 1 = 9

7 + 1 = 8   3 + 5 = 8

Complete.

34
30   4
30 + 4 = 34

87
80   7
80 + 7 = 87

52
50   2
50 + 2 = 52

99
90   9
90 + 9 = 99

Week 19 Answer Key

19.3A

Write the length of each jump. Each ruler is 1 foot long.

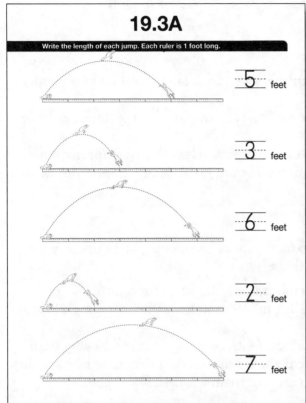

5 feet

3 feet

6 feet

2 feet

7 feet

19.3B

Complete.

$9 - 5 = 4$ $10 - 5 = 5$
$8 - 2 = 6$ $6 - 5 = 1$
$10 - 1 = 9$ $9 - 9 = 0$

Write how many.

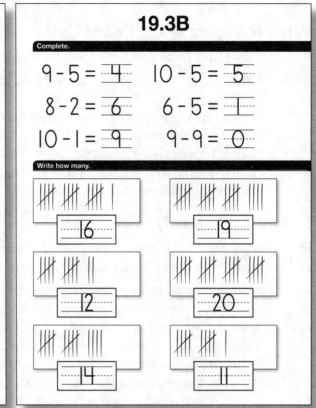

16   19

12   20

14   11

19.4A

Write the height of each robot. Each ruler is 1 foot long.

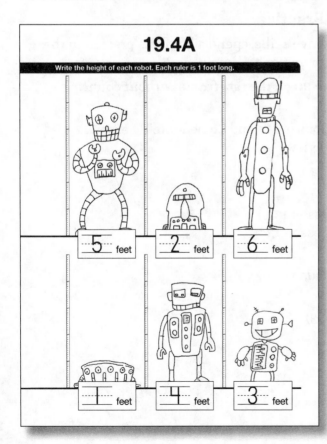

5 feet   2 feet   6 feet

1 feet   4 feet   3 feet

19.4B

Match pairs that make 100.

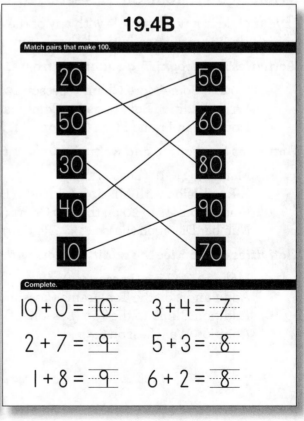

Complete.

$10 + 0 = 10$ $3 + 4 = 7$
$2 + 7 = 9$ $5 + 3 = 8$
$1 + 8 = 9$ $6 + 2 = 8$

Unit 7 Checkpoint

What to Expect at the End of Unit 7

By the end of Unit 7, most children will be able to:

- Approximate the length of an inch (or centimeter) and the length of a foot (or meter) with their hands.
- Accurately measure length in inches (or centimeters) with lined-up pattern blocks or a simplified paper ruler.
- Place a 1-foot ruler (or meterstick) end-to-end to measure length in feet (or meters).
- Estimate lengths in inches or feet (or centimeters or meters). Many first-graders' estimates will still be quite inaccurate.

Is Your Child Ready to Move on?

In Unit 8, your child will learn the addition facts up to 10 + 10. Before moving on to Unit 8, your child should have already mastered the following skills:

- Recognize quantities from 11 to 20 on the ten-frame without counting.
- Read and write numbers to 20 automatically and accurately (it's fine if your child still reverses the digits sometimes).
- Know the answers to most of the addition facts (with sums up to 10) without counting on fingers or counting one by one. It's fine if she is still working to master a few of the facts, but she should know the answers to most of them within a few seconds.

Your child does not need to have fully mastered measuring length before moving on to Unit 8.

What to Do If Your Child Needs More Practice

If your child is having trouble with any of the above skills, spend a few days practicing the corresponding review activities below before moving on to Unit 8.

Activities for recognizing quantities from 11 to 20 on the ten-frame without counting

- "10 and Some More Chant" (Lesson 12.2)
- Write Addition Equations for Combinations of "10 and Some More" (Lesson 12.3)
- Double Ten-Frame Flash (Lesson 16.1, Review)

Activities for reading and writing numbers to 20

- Memory (11-20) (Lesson 12.2)
- X-Ray Vision with Missing Addends (Lesson 12.3)
- Find Numbers to 20 on the 100 Chart (Lesson 13.2)
- Number Dictation (Lesson 13.4, Review)

Activities to practice the addition facts with sums to 10

- Make 10 Go Fish (Lesson 3.3)
- Add 1 and 2 on the Ten-Frame (Lesson 4.3)
- Addition Climb to the Top (Lesson 5.1)
- Addition War (Lesson 6.4)

Unit 8
Addition Facts to 20

Overview

In Unit 2, your child learned the addition facts with sums to 10. In Unit 8, he will build on this knowledge to learn the rest of the single-digit addition facts with sums to 20.

Week 20	+9 Addition Facts
Week 21	+8 Addition Facts
Week 22	+6 and +7 Addition Facts

What Your Child Will Learn

In this unit your child will learn to:

- solve addition facts up to 10 + 10
- solve addition word problems with numbers up to 10 + 10

Recommended Math Picture Books (Optional)

These picture books are scheduled in the optional Enrichment and Review lessons at the end of each week.

- *12 Ways to Get to 11*, written by Eve Merriam and illustrated by Bernie Karlin. Aladdin, 1996.
- *What's New at the Zoo? An Animal Adding Adventure*, written by Suzanne Slade and illustrated by Joan Waites. Sylvan Dell Publishing, 2009.
- *100 Snowmen*, written by Jen Arena and illustrated by Stephen Gilpin. Two Lions Publishing, 2013.

Week 20
+9 Addition Facts

Overview

This week, your child will learn the +9 addition facts. You'll use the double ten-frames to help him visualize the problems and find answers without counting.

Lesson 20.1   Introduce +9 Facts
Lesson 20.2   Practice +9 Facts
Lesson 20.3   Add +9 Facts in Any Order
Lesson 20.4   Word Problems with +9 Facts
Lesson 20.5   Enrichment and Review (Optional)

Teaching Math with Confidence: Why Not Just Memorize the Addition Facts?

Your child will use a "make 10" strategy to learn the +9 addition facts this week. Since the sums for these facts are greater than 10, you will use 2 ten-frames to model the problems.

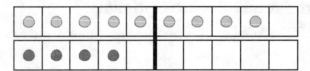

9 + 4 modeled on the ten-frames.

To solve these problems, your child will move 1 counter from the bottom ten-frame to the top ten-frame to make a complete group of 10 on the top ten-frame. Once he moves the counter, he can use his knowledge of place value to "see" the answer: since there are 10 counters on the top ten-frame and 3 counters on the bottom ten-frame, the answer is 13.

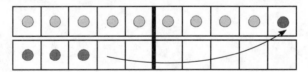

Moving 1 counter makes it easier to see that 9 + 4 equals 13.

Using a strategy approach like this one (rather than rote memorization) has many benefits:

- Learning strategies make the addition facts feel less overwhelming. Instead of memorizing every addition fact individually, all it takes is a few simple strategies to master all of them.
- Focusing on strategies is more efficient. Children learn the facts more quickly–and remember them better–when they use strategies to find the answers rather than memorizing each fact separately.
- Using strategies helps children understand that math is a subject to be understood, not just memorized.

Think of this unit's addition strategies as stepping stones. You don't stand on a stepping stone intending to stay there forever. Instead, you stop briefly to help you get across the river. In the same way, the purpose of math fact strategies is to help your child get to the ultimate destination: mastering all the addition facts! You'll teach your child the rest of the addition facts to 20 in Weeks 21 and 22.

Extra Materials Needed for Week 20

- 3-5 writing utensils of different lengths
- For optional Enrichment and Review Lesson:
    - × *12 Ways to Get to 11*, written by Eve Merriam and illustrated by Bernie Karlin

Lesson 20.1
Introduce +9 Facts

	Purpose	Materials
Warm-up	• Practice shifting counting sequences on the 100 Chart • Practice memory work • Review identifying combinations of tens and ones	• 100 Chart (Blackline Master 3) • Index card or slip of paper
Activities	• Introduce the +9 addition facts	• Counters • Double ten-frames (Blackline Master 1) • Adding 9s Bingo game board (on Workbook page 20.1A) • Playing cards
Workbook	• Practice the +9 addition facts	• Workbook page 20.1B

Warm-up: Counting, Memory Work, and Review

- **Let's pretend you're a counting robot again.** Draw a "computer panel" as in Lesson 17.4.

    [10] [5] [1] [Off]

    × **Beep!** Press the 5 button. *5, 10, 15, 20, 25, 30, 35.*
    × **Beep!** Press the 10 button. *45, 55, 65, 75, 85.*
    × **Beep!** Press the 5 button. *90, 95, 100.*
    × **Beep!** Press the Off button once your child reaches 100.

1	2	3	4	5	6	7	8	9	10
11	12	13	14	15	16	17	18	19	20
21	22	23	24	25	26	27	28	29	30
31	32	33	34	35	36	37	38	39	40
41	42	43	44	45	46	47	48	49	50
51	52	53	54	55	56	57	58	59	60
61	62	63	64	65	66	67	68	69	70
71	72	73	74	75	76	77	78	79	80
81	82	83	84	85	86	87	88	89	90
91	92	93	94	95	96	97	98	99	100

- **How many inches equal 1 foot?** *12.*

- Have your child use her "X-ray vision" to identify the hidden number in the following equations.

$$80 + 5 = \boxed{85} \qquad 30 + 9 = \boxed{39} \qquad 60 + \boxed{1} = 61$$

$$\boxed{40} + 8 = 48 \qquad \boxed{70} + 2 = 72$$

Activity: Introduce +9 Addition Facts

You have already learned the addition facts with sums to 10. In this new unit, you'll learn the rest of the single-digit addition facts. Today, you'll learn to solve addition problems with 9 as an addend.

Write "9 + 7 =" on a piece of paper. Place 9 counters of one color on the top ten-frame and 7 counters of another color on the bottom ten-frame.

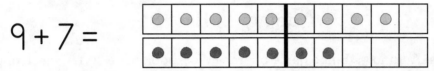

It's easier to see the answer if I move 1 counter to make a 10. Move 1 counter as shown.

How many counters are on the top ten-frame now? *10.* **How many counters are on the bottom ten-frame now?** *6.* **So, how many counters are there in all?** *16.*

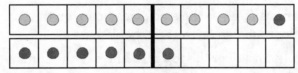

Moving 1 counter to make a 10 makes it a lot easier to find the answer. Instead of adding 9 plus 7, I can just add 10 and 6. Have your child complete the written addition problem: 9 + 7 = 16.

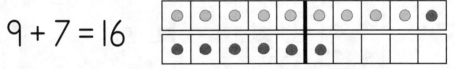

Repeat with the other +9 addition facts listed below. Have your child physically move a counter from the bottom ten-frame to the top ten-frame each time to complete the row of 10 and make the problem easier to solve.

- 9 + 2 = *11*
- 9 + 8 = *17*
- 9 + 4 = *13*
- 9 + 3 = *12*
- 9 + 5 = *14*
- 9 + 9 = *18*
- 9 + 6 = *15*

Remind your child to use the combinations of "10 and some more" (and not counting) as she finds the total number of counters on the ten-frames.

If your child can immediately find the answers mentally, don't require her to use the ten-frame and counters.

Activity: Play Adding 9s Bingo

We're going to play a game called Adding 9s Bingo to practice the +9 addition facts. Play one round of Adding 9s Bingo.

This game is like traditional Bingo with your child as the "caller."

Adding 9s Bingo

Materials: Adding 9s Bingo game boards (Workbook page 20.1A); deck of playing cards, with 10s and face cards removed (36 cards total); counters

B	I	N	G	O
13	14	17	16	12
16	11	15	12	17
18	15	FREE	11	10
11	18	12	14	13
14	10	13	17	15

Object of the Game: Be the first player to fill in an entire column, row, or diagonal.

Shuffle the cards and place the stack face down on the table. Have each player choose which game board to use on the workbook page.

Have your child turn over the top card and say the sum of the card plus 9. For example, if the card is a 7, your child says, *"9 + 7 equals 16."* Then, each of you uses a counter to cover a square containing that sum on your game board.

B	I	N	G	O
13	14	17	⊙	12
16	11	15	12	17
18	15	FREE	11	10
11	18	12	14	13
14	10	13	17	15

B	I	N	G	O
10	13	11	16	17
15	11	16	10	14
13	14	FREE	12	15
17	18	13	14	12
⊙	12	15	13	18

Continue until one of you wins by filling an entire column, row, or diagonal.

Encourage your child to use the ten-frame and counters to model the problems as needed. Don't be concerned if she needs to model every problem, since this lesson is her first experience with adding beyond 10.

Workbook: Practice +9 Facts

Have your child complete workbook page 20.1B.

 Save the Adding 9 Bingo game boards (workbook page 20.1A) so you can play again.

Lesson 20.2
Practice +9 Facts

	Purpose	Materials
Warm-up	• Count backward from 70 • Practice memory work • Review measuring in inches with a ruler	• 100 Chart (Blackline Master 3), optional • 3-5 writing utensils of different lengths • Paper ruler (Blackline Master 8) or 1-foot ruler
Activities	• Practice visualizing moving a counter to solve +9 addition facts	• Counters • Double ten-frames (Blackline Master 1) • Adding 9s Bingo game board (on Workbook page 20.1A) • Playing cards
Workbook	• Practice the +9 addition facts	• Workbook pages 20.2A and 20.2B

Warm-up: Counting, Memory Work, and Review

- Have your child count backward from 70 to 55, either by memory or with the 100 Chart.

- **How many inches equal 1 foot?** *12.*

- Have your child estimate and measure the length of several different writing utensils. He can use either the paper ruler or a standard ruler.

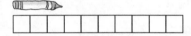

Activity: Visualize +9 Facts

In the last lesson, you solved addition problems with 9s. Today, you'll practice the +9 addition facts some more.

Put 9 counters of one color on the top ten-frame and 5 counters of another color on the bottom ten-frame. **What addition problem do the counters show?** *9 + 5.*

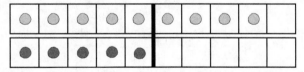

Have your child move 1 counter from the bottom ten-frame to the top ten-frame as shown.

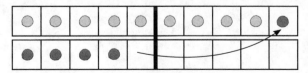

So, what's 9 + 5? *14.*

Put 9 counters on the top ten-frame and 2 counters on the bottom ten-frame. **This time try to** *imagine* **moving a counter to the top ten-frame instead of moving it with your hands. What's 9 + 2?** *11*.

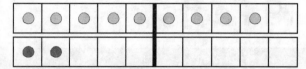

This activity helps your child learn to visualize the ten-frame so he can eventually find the sums mentally. If your child has trouble imagining moving the counter, allow him to physically move it.

Repeat this process with the following +9 addition facts. Encourage your child to imagine moving 1 counter from the bottom row of the ten-frame to the top ten-frame each time.

- 9 + 4 = *13*
- 9 + 7 = *16*
- 9 + 3 = *12*
- 9 + 8 = *17*
- 9 + 9 = *18*
- 9 + 6 = *15*

If your child immediately knows the answers without counters, simply practice the +9 facts quickly without counters and move on to Adding 9s Bingo.

Activity: Play Adding 9s Bingo

Play Adding 9s Bingo. See Lesson 20.1 (page 322) for directions.

Keep the ten-frame and counters available to model the addition problems as you play. Encourage your child to visualize moving a counter from the bottom ten-frame to the top ten-frame rather than actually moving it.

Workbook: Practice +9 Facts and Review

Have your child complete workbook pages 20.2A and 20.2B. Keep the ten-frame and counters available for your child to use if needed.

Lesson 20.3
Add +9 Facts in Any Order

	Purpose	Materials
Warm-up	• Count by 10s starting at a number other than 0 • Practice memory work • Review combinations of "10 and some more"	• 100 Chart (Blackline Master 3), optional • Counters • Double ten-frames (Blackline Master 1) • Paper
Activities	• Revisit the idea that you can add numbers in any order without changing the sum • Revisit the idea that it's usually easier to begin with the greater number when adding • Practice +9 addition facts	• Counters • Double ten-frames (Blackline Master 1) • Adding 9s Bingo game board (on Workbook page 20.1A) • Playing cards
Workbook	• Practice +9 addition facts	• Workbook pages 20.3A and 20.3B

Warm-up: Counting, Memory Work, and Review

• **Count by 10s starting at 2.** *2, 12, 22, 32, 42, 52, 62, 72, 82, 92.* Have your child point to the numbers on the 100 Chart only if needed.

• **How many inches equal 1 foot?** *12.*

• Secretly place 16 counters on the double ten-frames and cover the counters with a piece of paper. Reveal the counters for just a few seconds and then have your child tell you how many there are. After your child responds, lift the paper and allow her to check her answer.

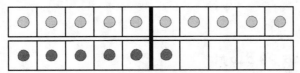

Repeat with 19, 14, 20, 18, and 13 counters. Encourage your child to think about the combinations of "10 and some more" to find each quantity.

Activity: Review Adding in Any Order

In the last lesson, you solved addition problems with 9 as an addend. Today, you'll practice these +9 addition facts some more.

You have already learned we can add numbers in any order and still get the same sum. Write 9 + 5 = and 5 + 9 = on a piece of paper.

$$9 + 5 = \qquad\qquad 5 + 9 =$$

Model both problems with counters on the ten-frames and discuss how the ten-frames show that the answers to both problems are the same: **I can move a counter from the bottom ten-frame to the top ten-frame, or I can move a counter from the top ten-frame to the bottom ten-frame. Either way, the sum is 14.**

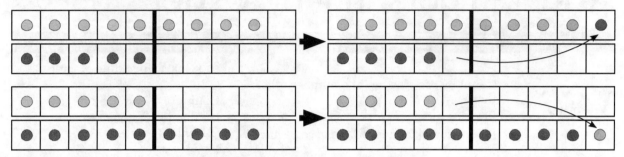

Activity: Review Starting with the Greater Number

Write 7 + 9 = on a piece of paper. **Adding in your head is usually easier when you start with the greater addend and then add on the lesser addend, no matter what order the addends are written in.**

To find the answer, I think "What's 9 + 7?" Have your child find the answer, either mentally or with counters on the ten-frame and complete the written equation.

$$7 + 9 = 16$$

Repeat with the following problems. Have your child begin with the greater number in each problem to find the answer.

- 4 + 9 = *13*
- 8 + 9 = *17*
- 5 + 9 = *14*
- 9 + 9 = *18*
- 6 + 9 = *15*
- 2 + 9 = *11*
- 3 + 9 = *12*

Activity: Play Adding 9s Bingo

Play Adding 9s Bingo. See Lesson 20.1 (page 322) for directions. Keep 9 counters on the ten-frame visible as you play. Ask your child to visualize the second number in the problem before constructing it with counters. (Or, even better, instead of constructing it with counters.) This will help her continue to progress towards finding the answers mentally.

Workbook: Practice +9 Facts and Review

Have your child complete workbook pages 20.3A and 20.3B. Keep the ten-frame and counters available for your child to use if needed.

Lesson 20.4
Word Problems with +9 Facts

	Purpose	Materials
Warm-up	• Count ten-dollar bills by 10s • Practice memory work • Review approximating the length of a foot and an inch	• Play money • Counters • 1-foot ruler • Square pattern block
Activities	• Write equations to match addition word problems and solve the equations • Practice +9 addition facts	• Counters • Double ten-frames (Blackline Master 1) • Adding 9s Bingo game board (on Workbook page 20.1A) • Playing cards
Workbook	• Solve addition word problems • Practice +9 addition facts	• Workbook pages 20.4A and 20.4B

Your child has already learned how to model word problems with hands-on materials or drawings. He has also learned how to write equations to match word problems with sums up to 10. In this lesson, he'll build on those skills as he solves word problems with larger numbers.

Warm-up: Counting, Memory Work, and Review

• Place 9 ten-dollar bills on the table. Have your child count by 10s to find the total value. **How many dollars is this?** *$90.*

• **How many inches equal 1 foot?** *12.*

• Ask your child to hold his hands 1 foot apart. Place a ruler between his hands to show him how well he approximated the length.

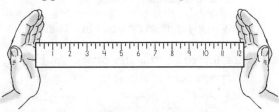

Then, ask your child to hold his hands 1 inch apart. Place a square pattern block between his hands to show him how accurately he approximated an inch.

Activity: Solve Addition Word Problems

You have been working on learning the +9 addition facts. Today, you'll use the +9 facts to solve addition word problems. But watch out: there may be a subtraction problem mixed in, too!

When children expect word problems to all use the same operation, they're often tempted to mindlessly add or subtract the numbers. Telling your child in advance that the word problems could include both addition and subtraction nudges him to pay closer attention.

Read the following word problems to your child. Have your child model each problem with counters on the ten-frame and then write and solve an equation to match.

- **You found 9 round pinecones and 5 long pinecones. How many pinecones did you find?** *14.*

$9 + 5 = 14$

- **You made 9 snowballs. 4 of the snowballs melted. How many snowballs did you have left?** *5.*

$9 - 4 = 5$

- **You see 9 birds in the morning and 7 birds in the afternoon. How many birds did you see?** *16.*

$9 + 7 = 16$

Activity: Introduce Written Word Problems

Show your child workbook page 20.4A. **There are word problems on your workbook page for the first time today. We'll solve the first problem together, and then you can solve the rest on your own when you do the workbook page.**

Children often find it challenging to switch from solving oral word problems to written word problems. Working through the first problem together helps ease this transition.

There are three main steps for solving word problems. The first step is to read the problem slowly and carefully. Have your child read aloud the first problem (or read it aloud to him).

You have 9 donuts in one box.
You have 3 donuts in the other box.
How many donuts do you have in all?

The next step is to write an equation to match the problem. Have your child write an equation to match the problem in the space provided on the worksheet.

$9 \oplus 3 =$

If your child is not sure whether to write a plus sign or minus sign in the circle, point out the picture on the worksheet. **Are we joining two groups together or separating two groups?** *Joining.* **So, since we're joining two groups, this is an addition problem.**

The final step is to complete the equation and write the answer in the sentence.

$9 \oplus 3 = 12$

I have __12__ donuts in all.

Seeing the answer in sentence form encourages your child to think about whether the answer makes sense. For example, if your child got 6 for an answer, seeing it in the sentence might prompt him to consider whether it's possible for the total number of donuts to be less than the number of donuts in one of the boxes.

Activity: Play Adding 9s Bingo

Play Adding 9s Bingo. See Lesson 20.1 (page 322) for directions.

Keep the ten-frame and counters available as you play. If your child has trouble remembering the answer to an addition fact, encourage him to visualize both numbers on the ten-frame (rather than constructing them with counters). If this is too challenging, allow him to put counters on the ten-frame to find the answer.

Workbook: Solve Word Problems and Review

Have your child complete workbook pages 20.4A and 20.4B. Help your child read the problems as needed and encourage him to follow the steps you practiced in the lesson.

Try to keep the focus on the math--not the reading--as your child solves word problems. Read the problems aloud if needed, and make sure he fully understands each problem before trying to solve it.

Lesson 20.5
Enrichment and Review (Optional)

	Purpose	Materials
Warm-up	• Count to 100 by 1s, 2s, 5s, or 10s • Review memory work • Review your child's favorite or most challenging activities from Week 20	• Varies, depending on the activities you choose
Picture Book	• Understand that numbers can be split into parts in many ways • See examples of ways to split the number 11	• *12 Ways to Get to 11*, written by Eve Merriam and illustrated by Bernie Karlin
Enrichment Activity	• Split a number many ways	• Counters

Warm-up: Counting, Memory Work, and Review

- Have your child count to 100 by 1s, 2s, 5s, or 10s. (Choose whichever counting sequence your child needs to practice the most.)

- Quiz your child on the memory work through Week 20. See page 499 for the full list.

- If you have time, repeat one or two of the activities from this week's lessons. Choose activities your child especially enjoyed or found challenging.

Math Picture Book: *12 Ways to Get to 11*

Read *12 Ways to Get to 11*, written by Eve Merriam and illustrated by Bernie Karlin. As you read, discuss how each illustration shows the number 11. For example: 9 pinecones and 2 acorns equal 11.

Enrichment Activity: Split a Number Many Ways

Have your child choose a number between from 12 to 20 and find several different ways to split it. Have him record each way in a chart and model it with counters or household objects.

For example, if your child picks the number 17, he might create the following chart:

Ways to Split 17				
1	5	10	8	6
16	12	7	9	11

For an extra challenge, your child can try to find all possible ways to split the number. (To find the total number of ways possible to split a number, add 1 to the number.) For example, there are 18 ways to split 17:

Ways to Split 17																	
0	1	2	3	4	5	6	7	8	9	10	11	12	13	14	15	16	17
17	16	15	14	13	12	11	10	9	8	7	6	5	4	3	2	1	0

Week 20 Answer Key

20.1A

See *Instructor Guide* for directions on how to play.
Save this game board for future lessons.

Adding 9s Bingo
Game Boards

B	I	N	G	O
13	14	17	16	12
16	11	15	12	17
18	15	FREE	11	10
11	18	12	14	13
14	10	13	17	15

B	I	N	G	O
10	13	11	16	17
15	11	16	10	14
13	14	FREE	12	15
17	18	13	14	12
16	12	15	13	18

20.1B

Complete.

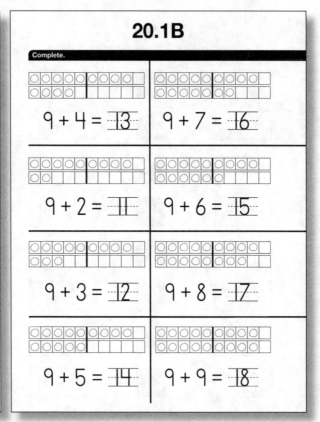

$9 + 4 = 13$ $9 + 7 = 16$

$9 + 2 = 11$ $9 + 6 = 15$

$9 + 3 = 12$ $9 + 8 = 17$

$9 + 5 = 14$ $9 + 9 = 18$

20.2A

Complete.

$9 + 5 = 14$ $9 + 3 = 12$

$9 + 8 = 17$ $9 + 4 = 13$

$9 + 7 = 16$ $9 + 2 = 11$

$9 + 6 = 15$ $9 + 9 = 18$

Use the key to color the flowers.

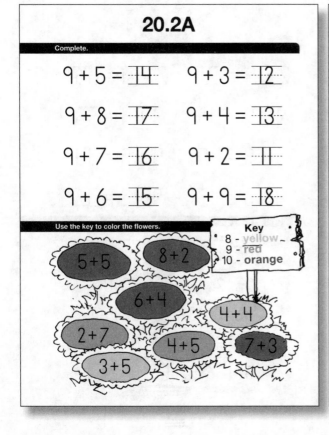

Key
8 - yellow
9 - red
10 - orange

5+5   8+2   6+4   4+4   2+7   4+5   7+3   3+5

20.2B

Match.

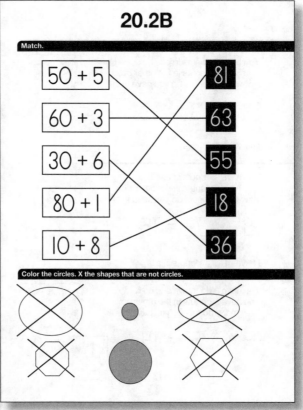

$50 + 5$ 81

$60 + 3$ 63

$30 + 6$ 55

$80 + 1$ 18

$10 + 8$ 36

Color the circles. X the shapes that are not circles.

Week 20 Answer Key

20.3A

Match.

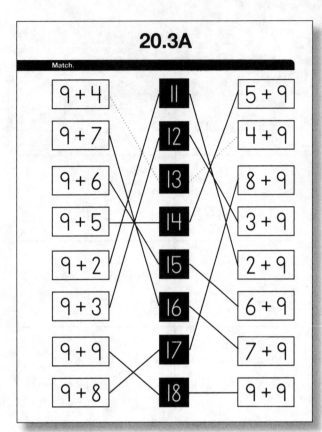

9 + 4   11   5 + 9
9 + 7   12   4 + 9
9 + 6   13   8 + 9
9 + 5   14   3 + 9
9 + 2   15   2 + 9
9 + 3   16   6 + 9
9 + 9   17   7 + 9
9 + 8   18   9 + 9

20.3B

Circle the greater number in each pair.

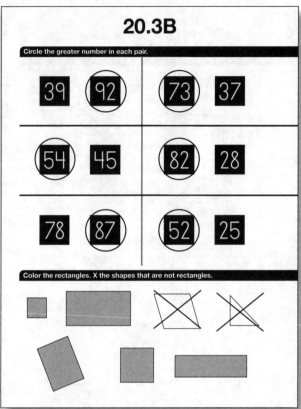

39   (92)   (73)   37

(54)   45   (82)   28

78   (87)   (52)   25

Color the rectangles. X the shapes that are not rectangles.

20.4A

Complete the equations and sentences to match the word problems.

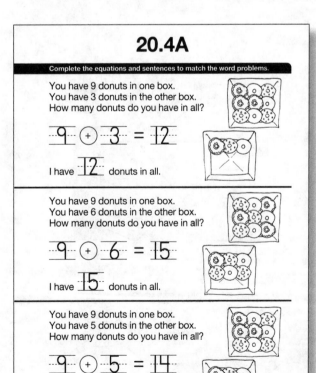

You have 9 donuts in one box.
You have 3 donuts in the other box.
How many donuts do you have in all?

$9 + 3 = 12$

I have 12 donuts in all.

You have 9 donuts in one box.
You have 6 donuts in the other box.
How many donuts do you have in all?

$9 + 6 = 15$

I have 15 donuts in all.

You have 9 donuts in one box.
You have 5 donuts in the other box.
How many donuts do you have in all?

$9 + 5 = 14$

I have 14 donuts in all.

20.4B

Complete.

$2 + 9 = 11$ $7 + 9 = 16$

$9 + 9 = 18$ $9 + 4 = 13$

$6 + 9 = 15$ $5 + 9 = 14$

$9 + 8 = 17$ $9 + 3 = 12$

Complete the missing numbers on the 100 Chart.

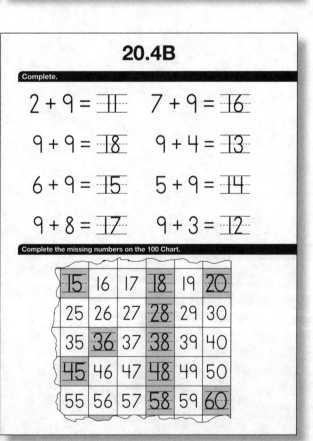

15	16	17	18	19	20
25	26	27	28	29	30
35	36	37	38	39	40
45	46	47	48	49	50
55	56	57	58	59	60

Week 21
+8 Addition Facts

Overview

This week, your child will learn +8 addition facts. She'll use a "make 10" strategy similar to the one she used with the +9 facts in Week 20.

Lesson 21.1   Introduce +8 Facts
Lesson 21.2   Practice +8 Facts
Lesson 21.3   Word Problems with +8 Facts
Lesson 21.4   Review Adding 10 and 0
Lesson 21.5   Enrichment and Review (Optional)

Teaching Math with Confidence:
Using the "Make 10" Strategy for the +8 Facts

This week, your child will again use a "make 10" strategy as she learns the +8 addition facts. Like last week, you'll begin by modeling the +8 facts on the double ten-frames.

Then, your child will move 2 counters from the bottom ten-frame to the top ten-frame to make a complete group of 10 on the top ten-frame. She'll again use her knowledge of place value to "see" the answer: there are 10 counters on the top and 2 counters on the bottom, so the answer is 12.

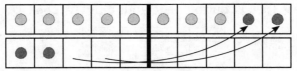

Moving 2 counters makes it easier to see 8 + 4 equals 12.

Extra Materials Needed for Week 21

- For optional Enrichment and Review Lesson:
    × *What's New at the Zoo? An Animal Adding Adventure,* written by Suzanne Slade and illustrated by Joan Waites
    × 20 items from your child's favorite collection, such as stuffed animals, rocks, toy cars, ponies, toy trains, or plastic figurines

Lesson 21.1
Introduce +8 Facts

	Purpose	Materials
Warm-up	• Practice shifting counting sequences on the 100 Chart • Practice memory work • Review pairs that equal 20	• 100 Chart (Blackline Master 3) • Number Cards
Activities	• Introduce the +8 addition facts	• Counters • Double ten-frames (Blackline Master 1) • Adding 8s Crash game board (on Workbook page 21.1A) • Playing cards
Workbook	• Practice the +8 addition facts	• Workbook page 21.1B

Warm-up: Counting, Memory Work, and Review

• **Let's pretend you're a counting robot again.** Draw a "computer panel" as in Lesson 17.4.

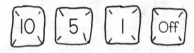

× **Beep!** Press the 5 button. *5, 10, 15, 20, 25.*
× **Beep!** Press the 10 button. *35, 45, 55, 65, 75.*
× **Beep!** Press the 1 button. *76, 77, 78, 79, 80, 81, 82, 83.*
× **Beep!** Press the Off button once your child reaches 83.

1	2	3	4	5	6	7	8	9	10
11	12	13	14	15	16	17	18	19	20
21	22	23	24	25	26	27	28	29	30
31	32	33	34	35	36	37	38	39	40
41	42	43	44	45	46	47	48	49	50
51	52	53	54	55	56	57	58	59	60
61	62	63	64	65	66	67	68	69	70
71	72	73	74	75	76	77	78	79	80
81	82	83	84	85	86	87	88	89	90
91	92	93	94	95	96	97	98	99	100

• **Raise your right hand. Raise your left hand.**

• Shuffle Number Cards 11-20. Show your child one card at a time. Have him name the number that goes with the number on the card to make 20. For example, if you show him 18: *18 and 2 make 20.*

Activity: Introduce +8 Addition Facts

In the last few lessons, you learned the +9 addition facts. You made the problems easier by making a 10. Today, you'll learn to make a 10 to solve the +8 addition facts.

Write "8 + 5 =" on a piece of paper. Place 8 counters of one color on the top ten-frame and 5 counters of another color on the bottom ten-frame.

When you added 9, you moved 1 counter to make a 10. But when you add 8, you move 2 counters to make a 10. Move 2 counters as shown.

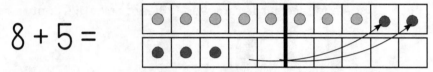

How many counters are on the top ten-frame? *10.* **How many counters are on the bottom ten-frame?** *3.* **So, how many counters are there in all?** *13.*

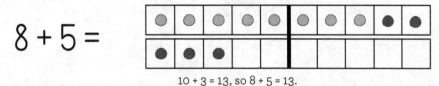

10 + 3 = 13, so 8 + 5 = 13.

Moving 2 counters to make a 10 helps find the answer. Instead of adding 8 plus 5, you can just add 10 plus 3. Have your child complete the written addition problem: 8 + 5 = 13.

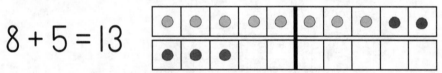

Repeat with the other +8 addition facts listed below. Have your child physically move 2 counters from the bottom ten-frame to the top ten-frame each time to complete the row of 10 and make each problem easier to solve.

- 8 + 3 = *11*
- 8 + 7 = *15*
- 8 + 4 = *12*
- 8 + 8 = *16*
- 8 + 6 = *14*

Remind your child to use the combinations of "10 and some more" (and not counting) as she finds the total number of counters on the ten-frames.

If your child can immediately find the answers mentally, don't require her to use the ten-frame and counters.

Activity: Play Adding 8s Crash

We're going to play a game called Adding 8s Crash to practice the +8 addition facts. Play one round of Adding 8s Crash. Allow your child to use the ten-frame and counters as needed.

Adding 8s Crash

Materials: Adding 8s Crash game board (Workbook page 21.1A); deck of playing cards with aces, 2s, 10s and face cards removed (28 cards total); 5 counters of two different colors each.

Object of the Game: Place 5 counters on the game board.

Shuffle the cards and place the stack face down on the table. Give 5 counters of one color to one player and 5 counters of a different color to the other player.

On your turn, flip over the top card. Add 8 to the number on the card and place one of your counters on a matching square. For example, if you flip over a 7, place your counter on a square with a 15, since 8 + 7 = 15.

If the other player already has a counter on the square with your sum, you may "crash" into their counter, remove it, and place your own counter on the number. Continue until one player places all 5 counters on the board.

Crashing into your opponent isn't required—you can put your counter in an empty box instead—but it makes the game more competitive and fun.

Workbook: Practice +8 Facts

Have your child complete workbook page 21.1B.

 Save the Adding 8s Crash game board (workbook page 21.1A) so you can play again.

Lesson 21.2
Practice +8 Facts

	Purpose	Materials
Warm-up	• Count backward from 80 • Practice memory work • Review money combinations	• 100 Chart (Blackline Master 3), optional • Play money
Activities	• Practice visualizing moving counters to solve +8 addition facts	• Counters • Double ten-frames (Blackline Master 1) • Adding 8s Crash game board (on Workbook page 21.1A) • Playing cards
Workbook	• Practice the +8 addition facts	• Workbook pages 21.2A and 21.2B

Warm-up: Counting, Memory Work, and Review

- Have your child count backward from 80 to 65, either by memory or with the 100 Chart.

- **How many sides does a triangle have?** *3.* **A square?** *4.* **A rectangle?** *4.*

- Have your child tell the value of the following play money combinations.

  × 2 one-dollar bills *($2)*
  × 2 five-dollar bills *($10)*
  × 2 ten-dollar bills *($20)*
  × 1 ten-dollar bill and 3 one-dollar bills *($13)*
  × 1 ten-dollar bill and 7 one-dollar bills *($17)*
  × 1 ten-dollar bill and 1 five-dollar bill *($15)*
  × 1 ten-dollar bill, 1 five-dollar bill, and 3 one-dollar bills *($18)*

Activity: Visualize +8 Facts

In the last lesson, you solved addition problems with 8s. Today, you'll practice the +8 addition facts some more.

Put 8 counters of one color on the top ten-frame and 4 counters of another color on the bottom ten-frame. **What addition problem do the counters show?** *8 + 4.*

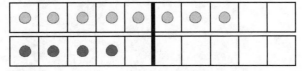

Have your child move 2 counters from the bottom ten-frame to the top ten-frame as shown.

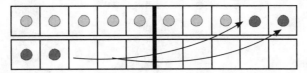

So, what's 8 + 4? *12.*

Put 8 counters on the top ten-frame and 3 counters on the bottom ten-frame. **This time try to imagine moving a counter to the top ten-frame instead of moving it with your hands. What's 8 + 3?** *11.*

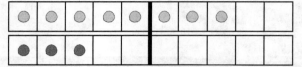

> This activity helps your child learn to visualize the ten-frame so he can find the sums mentally. If your child has trouble imagining moving the counters, allow him to physically move them instead.

Repeat this process with the following +8 addition facts. Encourage your child to imagine moving 2 counters from the bottom row of the ten-frame to the top ten-frame each time.

- 8 + 7 = *15*
- 8 + 5 = *13*
- 8 + 8 = *16*
- 8 + 6 = *14*

> If your child immediately knows the answers without counters, simply practice the +8 facts quickly without counters and move on to Adding 8s Crash.

Activity: Play Adding 8s Crash

Play Adding 8s Crash. See Lesson 21.1 (page 336) for directions.

Keep the ten-frame and counters available to model the addition problems as you play. Ask your child to imagine moving 2 counters from the bottom ten-frame to the top ten-frame rather than actually moving them.

Workbook: Practice +8 Facts and Review

Have your child complete workbook pages 21.2A and 21.2B. Keep the ten-frame and counters available for your child to use as he completes the addition problems on 21.2A.

Lesson 21.3
Word Problems with +8 Facts

	Purpose	Materials
Warm-up	• Count nickels by 5s • Practice memory work • Review identifying numbers on the 100 Chart	• Coins • 100 Chart (Blackline Master 3) • Counters
Activities	• Write equations to match addition word problems and solve the equations • Practice +8 addition facts	• Counters • Double ten-frames (Blackline Master 1) • Adding 8s Crash game board (on Workbook page 21.1A) • Playing cards
Workbook	• Solve addition word problems • Practice +8 addition facts	• Workbook pages 21.3A and 21.3B

Warm-up: Counting, Memory Work, and Review

• Place 11 nickels on the table. Have your child count by 5s to find the total value. **How many cents is this?** *55¢*.

• Have your child say the months. **How many months are in a year?** *12*.

• Have your child cover the following numbers on the 100 Chart with counters: 76, 36, 43, 67, 27, 28, 24, 25, 49, 33, 39, 58, 54, 65. The final arrangement of counters should look like a heart.

Activity: Solve +8 Addition Word Problems

You have been working on learning the +8 addition facts. Today, you'll use the +8 facts to solve addition word problems. But watch out: there may be a subtraction problem mixed in, too!

Read the following word problems to your child. Have her model each problem with counters on the ten-frame and then write and solve an equation to match.

• **You have 8 square crackers. Then you get 5 round crackers. How many crackers do you have now?** *13*.

$8 + 5 = 13$

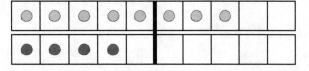

• **You have 8 almonds. Then you get 4 pistachios. How many nuts do you have now?** *12*.

$8 + 4 = 12$

- **You have 8 strawberries. Then you eat 6 of the strawberries. How many strawberries do you have now?** *2.*

$$8 - 6 = 2$$

Activity: Practice Written Word Problems

Show your child workbook page 21.3A. **Let's practice the 3 steps for solving word problems.**

The first step is to read the problem slowly and carefully. Have your child read aloud the first problem (or read it aloud to her).

> You have 8 blue balloons.
> You have 3 yellow balloons.
> How many balloons do you have?

The second step is to write an equation to match the problem. Have your child write an equation to match the problem in the space provided on the worksheet.

$$8 \oplus 3 = $$

> If your child is not sure whether to write a plus sign or minus sign in the circle, point out the picture on the worksheet. **Are we joining two groups together or separating two groups?** *Joining.* **So, since we're joining two groups, this is an addition problem.**

The third step is to complete the equation and write the answer in the sentence.

$$8 \oplus 3 = 11$$

I have 11 balloons.

Activity: Play Adding 8s Crash

Play Adding 8s Crash. See Lesson 21.1 (page 336) for directions. Keep 8 counters on the ten-frame visible as you play. Ask your child to visualize the second number in the problem before constructing it with counters. (Or, instead of constructing it with counters.) This will help her continue to learn to visualize the answers.

Workbook: Solve Word Problems and Review

Have your child complete workbook pages 21.3A and 21.3B. Help your child read the problems as needed and encourage her to follow the steps she practiced in the lesson.

Lesson 21.4
Review Adding 10 and 0

	Purpose	Materials
Warm-up	• Count by 10s starting with a one-digit number • Practice memory work • Review tallies and combinations of "10 and some more"	• 100 Chart (Blackline Master 3), optional • Tally Cards
Activities	• Review adding 10 to a single-digit number • Review adding 0	• Counters • Double ten-frames (Blackline Master 1) • Adding 8s Crash game board (on Workbook page 21.1A) • Playing cards
Workbook	• Practice adding 0 or 10 to a single-digit number • Practice the +8 addition facts	• Workbook pages 21.4A and 21.4B

Warm-up: Counting, Memory Work, and Review

- **Count by 10s starting at 8.** *8, 18, 28, 38, 48, 58, 68, 78, 88, 98.* Have your child point to the numbers on the 100 Chart only if needed.

- Have your child rhythmically say the "10 and Some More" Chant: **10 and 1. Eleven! 10 and 2. Twelve!** etc. See Lesson 12.2 (page 193) for the full chant.

- Show your child the following pairs of Tally Cards. Have him identify the total number of tallies on both cards.

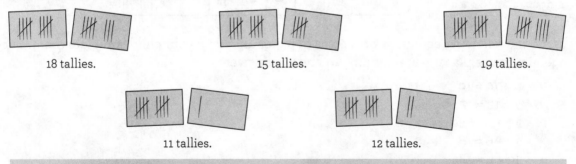

18 tallies.   15 tallies.   19 tallies.

11 tallies.   12 tallies.

Encourage your child to use the combinations of "10 and some more" to find the total tallies.

Activity: Review Adding 0

You have been learning the +8 addition facts. Today, we'll review adding 0 and adding 10 to numbers. Then, we'll practice the +8 addition facts some more.

Write 8 + 0 = on a piece of paper. Have your child complete the written equation and read it aloud: *8 plus 0 equals 8.*

$$8 + 0 = 8$$

Have your child model the equation with counters on the ten-frame if he hesitates or isn't sure.

Why doesn't the 8 change when we add 0 to it? *Possible answer: Adding 0 means you don't add anything else to the 8.*

Write the following equations on a piece of paper and have your child complete them.

- 9 + 0 = *9*
- 0 + 10 = *10*
- 27 + 0 = *27*
- 0 + 45 = *45*
- 99 + 0 = *99*
- 100 + 0 = *100*

Activity: Review Adding 10

Write 10 + 8 = on a piece of paper. Have your child complete the written equation and read it aloud: *10 plus 8 equals 18.*

$$10 + 8 = 18$$

Model the equation with counters on the ten-frame if your child hesitates or isn't sure.

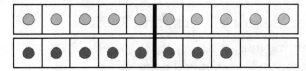

Point out that place-value thinking makes this problem easy: **1 group of 10 and 8 more make 18.**

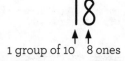

1 group of 10   8 ones

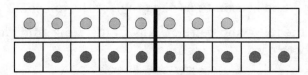

Write the following equations on a piece of paper and have your child complete them. Encourage him to use place-value thinking to find the answers.

- 9 + 10 = *19*
- 7 + 10 = *17*
- 10 + 10 = *20*
- 10 + 6 = *16*
- 10 + 4 = *14*
- 1 + 10 = *11*

Activity: Play Adding 8s Crash

Play Adding 8s Crash. See Lesson 21.1 (page 336) for directions. Keep the ten-frame and counters available as you play. If your child has trouble remembering the answer to an addition fact, encourage him to visualize both numbers on the ten-frame. If this is too challenging, allow him to put counters on the ten-frame to find the answer.

Workbook: Review Adding 10 and 0 and Review

Have your child complete workbook pages 21.4A and 21.4B.

Lesson 21.5
Enrichment and Review (Optional)

	Purpose	Materials
Warm-up	• Count to 100 by 1s, 2s, 5s, or 10s • Review memory work • Review your child's favorite or most challenging activities from Week 21	• Varies, depending on the activities you choose
Picture Book	• Understand the connection between illustrations and printed addition equations	• *What's New at the Zoo? An Animal Adding Adventure*, written by Suzanne Slade and illustrated by Joan Waites
Enrichment Activity	• Write equations about a favorite collection	• 20 items from your child's favorite collection, such as stuffed animals, rocks, toy cars, ponies, toy trains, or plastic figurines

Warm-up: Counting, Memory Work, and Review

- Have your child count to 100 by 1s, 2s, 5s, or 10s. (Choose whichever counting sequence your child needs to practice the most.)

- Quiz your child on the memory work through Week 20. See page 499 for the full list.

- If you have time, repeat one or two of the activities from this week's lessons. Choose activities your child especially enjoyed or found challenging.

Math Picture Book: *What's New at the Zoo? An Animal Adding Adventure*

Read *What's New at the Zoo? An Animal Adding Adventure*, written by Suzanne Slade and illustrated by Joan Waites. As you read, discuss how the animal illustrations match the printed equations and have your child find the answers to the equations.

Enrichment Activity: Write Equations about a Collection

Have your child choose about 20 objects from one of her favorite collections. (See Materials for examples.) Have her sort the objects into some smaller groups and then write equations about the smaller groups. Help as needed with writing the equations.

For example, if she has a collection of stuffed animals, she might write equations like the following:

- 10 water animals + 6 land animals = 16 animals
- 5 puppies + 2 kittens = 7 baby animals
- 2 cows + 4 horses + 1 pig = 7 farm animals

Or, if she has a collection of toy trains, she might write equations such as:

- 4 blue trains + 7 green trains = 11 trains
- 12 steam trains + 3 electric trains = 15 trains
- 4 coal cars + 9 freight cars = 13 train cars

Week 21 Answer Key

21.1A

See *Instructor Guide* for directions on how to play.
Save this game board for future lessons.

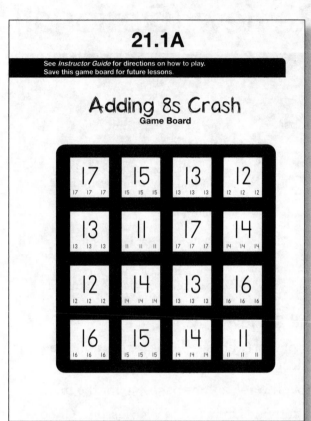

Adding 8s Crash
Game Board

21.1B

Complete.

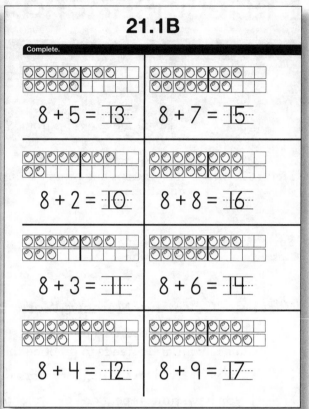

$8 + 5 = 13$ $8 + 7 = 15$

$8 + 2 = 10$ $8 + 8 = 16$

$8 + 3 = 11$ $8 + 6 = 14$

$8 + 4 = 12$ $8 + 9 = 17$

21.2A

Match.

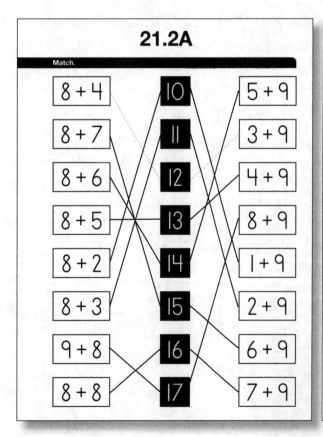

21.2B

X the shape that doesn't belong in each row.

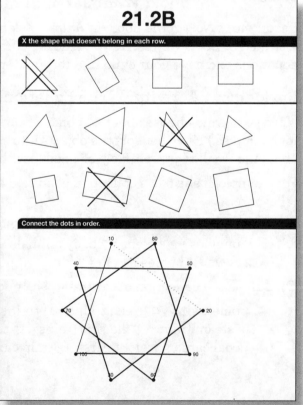

Connect the dots in order.

Week 21 Answer Key

21.3A

Complete the equations and sentences to match the word problems.

You have 8 blue balloons.
You have 3 yellow balloons.
How many balloons do you have?

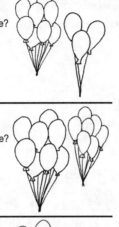

$8 \oplus 3 = 11$

I have 11 balloons.

You have 8 red balloons.
You have 7 yellow balloons.
How many balloons do you have?

$8 \oplus 7 = 15$

I have 15 balloons.

You have 8 green balloons.
You have 6 yellow balloons.
How many balloons do you have?

$8 \oplus 6 = 14$

I have 14 balloons.

21.3B

Complete.

$3 + 8 = 11$ $8 + 8 = 16$
$9 + 8 = 17$ $8 + 4 = 12$
$6 + 8 = 14$ $5 + 8 = 13$
$8 + 7 = 15$ $2 + 8 = 10$

Complete.

$33 + 1 = 34$ $33 + 10 = 43$

$48 + 1 = 49$ $48 + 10 = 58$

$25 + 1 = 26$ $25 + 10 = 35$

21.4A

Complete.

$10 + 1 = 11$ $10 + 9 = 19$
$10 + 8 = 18$ $0 + 8 = 8$
$7 + 0 = 7$ $7 + 10 = 17$
$10 + 3 = 13$ $2 + 10 = 12$

Color the addition facts that equal the number in the star.

★ 14	★ 15	★ 16
10 + 4	9 + 6	8 + 8
8 + 6	10 + 6	6 + 9
4 + 8	8 + 7	7 + 9
9 + 5	9 + 5	10 + 6

21.4B

Maria made a tally chart of how many times she did her chores.
Use the chart to answer the questions.

How many times did she set the table? 5

How many times did she make her bed? 7

How many times did she feed the dog? 10

Did she make her bed or set the table more times?

$\underline{\text{Make her bed}}$

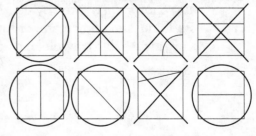

Circle the squares that are split in half. X the squares that are not split in half.

Week 22
+6 and +7 Addition Facts

Overview

This week, your child will learn the rest of the addition facts up to 10+10. You'll use a strategy called "look at the leftovers" to help her master these final addition facts.

Lesson 21.1   Introduce +6 and +7 Facts
Lesson 21.2   Practice +6 and +7 Facts
Lesson 21.3   Word Problems with +6 and +7 Facts
Lesson 21.4   Practice Addition Facts to 20
Lesson 21.5   Enrichment and Review (Optional)

Teaching Math with Confidence:
"Look at the Leftovers" Strategy for the +6 and +7 Facts

Your child has already learned several of the +6 and +7 facts in previous weeks. This week, he'll learn the last few. The goal is for him to know all the single-digit addition facts by the end of this week.

In Weeks 20 and 21, you taught your child to "make 10" to find answers to the +9 and +8 facts. You'll teach your child to make a 10 in a different way to find the answers to the +6 and +7 facts. Instead of moving counters, he'll learn to combine 5s to create a 10 and then look at the "leftovers" to find the answer.

For example, to solve 7 + 6, your child will look for a group of 5 in each addend and combine the 5s to make 10. Then, he'll add on the "leftover" counters. In this case, there are 3 additional counters, so 7 + 6 equals 10 + 3, or 13.

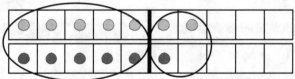

7 + 6 can be thought of as 2 groups of 5, plus 3 "leftover" counters. So, 7 + 6 equals 10 + 3, or 13.

Some children prefer to solve the +6 and +7 addition problems by moving counters to make a 10. Either way is fine. The main goal is for your child to develop mastery with the addition facts, no matter which mental strategy he uses.

Extra Materials Needed for Week 22

- 2 decks of playing cards
- For optional Enrichment and Review Lesson:
    × *100 Snowmen*, written by Jen Arena and illustrated by Stephen Gilpin
    × Pudding, shaving cream, or fingerpaint
    × Large washable tray, clean counter, or finger painting paper

Lesson 22.1
Introduce +6 and +7 Facts

	Purpose	Materials
Warm-up	• Practice shifting counting sequences on the 100 Chart • Practice memory work • Review finding coin combinations	• 100 Chart (Blackline Master 3) • Coins
Activities	• Introduce the +6 and +7 addition facts	• Counters • Double ten-frames (Blackline Master 1) • Addition Tic-Tac-Toe game board (on Workbook page 22.1A) • Playing cards
Workbook	• Practice the +6 and +7 addition facts	• Workbook page 22.1B

Warm-up: Counting, Memory Work, and Review

- **Let's pretend you're a counting robot again.** Draw a "computer panel" as in Lesson 17.4.

- × **Beep!** Press the 10 button. *10, 20, 30, 40.*
- × **Beep!** Press the 5 button. *45, 50, 55, 60, 65.*
- × **Beep!** Press the 1 button. *66, 67, 68, 69, 70, 71, 72, 73, 74.*
- × **Beep!** Press the Off button once your child reaches 74.

1	2	3	4	5	6	7	8	9	10
11	12	13	14	15	16	17	18	19	20
21	22	23	24	25	26	27	28	29	30
31	32	33	34	35	36	37	38	39	40
41	42	43	44	45	46	47	48	49	50
51	52	53	54	55	56	57	58	59	60
61	62	63	64	65	66	67	68	69	70
71	72	73	74	75	76	77	78	79	80
81	82	83	84	85	86	87	88	89	90
91	92	93	94	95	96	97	98	99	100

- **How many cents equal 1 dollar?** *100.*
- Show your child the following coin combinations and have her tell the value of each combination.

    - × 1 dime and 2 pennies *(12¢)*
    - × 2 dimes *(20¢)*
    - × 1 dime and 6 pennies *(16¢)*
    - × 1 dime, 1 nickel, and 1 penny *(16¢)*
    - × 6 dimes *(60¢)*
    - × 6 nickels *(30¢)*
    - × 6 pennies *(6¢)*

Activity: Introduce +6 and +7 Addition Facts

You have learned how to solve the +9 and +8 addition facts by making a 10. There are just 6 addition facts left to learn for you to know all of the addition facts!

Today, you'll learn a strategy called "look at the leftovers" to solve the +6 and + 7 addition facts.

Some children prefer to solve +6 and +7 problems by moving counters to make a 10, as in Weeks 20 and 21. That's fine! As long as your child has an efficient and reliable approach for solving these addition problems, she can use whichever approach makes the most sense to her.

Write "7 + 6 =" on a piece of paper. Place 7 counters of one color on the top ten-frame and 6 counters of another color on the bottom ten-frame. Point out the group of 5 in each ten-frame. **How many counters are in the 2 groups of 5?** *10.*

Point out the "leftover counters," as shown below. **There are 2 counters leftover in the top row and 1 counter leftover in the bottom row. How many counters is this?** *3.*

So, instead of adding 7 plus 6, you can just add 10 plus 3. Have your child complete the written addition problem: *7 + 6 = 13.*

How is this strategy different from the strategy you used to solve the +8 and +9 addition facts? *Sample answer: We don't move any counters.* **How are the strategies similar?** *Sample answer: We make a 10, just in a different way.*

Repeat with the other +6 and +7 addition facts listed below. Encourage your child to "look at the leftovers" each time to find the answer.

- 6 + 5 = *11*
- 6 + 6 = *12*
- 7 + 7 = *14*
- 7 + 5 = *12*
- 7 + 4 = *11*

For 7 + 4, have your child imagine taking 1 counter from the 7 and adding it to the row of 4 to make a 5.

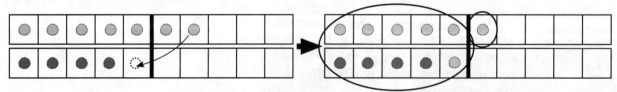

How to visualize 7 + 4.

Activity: Play Addition Tic-Tac-Toe

We're going to play a game called Addition Tic-Tac-Toe to practice the +6 and +7 addition facts. This game is just like Subtraction Tic-Tac-Toe, but with different numbers. Play one round of Addition Tic-Tac-Toe. Allow your child to use the ten-frame and counters as needed.

Addition Tic-Tac-Toe

Materials: Addition Tic-Tac-Toe game board (Workbook page 22.1A); 5s, 6s, and 7s from a deck of playing cards (12 cards total); 5 counters of 2 different colors

Object of the Game: Be the first player to fill three boxes in a row, either horizontally, vertically, or diagonally.

Shuffle the cards and place the stack face down on the table. On your turn, flip over the top card. Choose whether to add either 6 or 7 to the card and place one of your counters on the box that matches the sum. For example, if you draw a 5, you can add 5 plus 6 and place a counter on a box with a 11. Or, you can add 5 plus 7 and place a counter on a box with a 12.

One possible play if you draw a 5. Since 5 + 6 = 11, you can cover an 11.

Another possible play if you draw a 5. Since 5 + 7 = 12, you can cover a 12.

If you draw a card and no open square matches either possible sum, pick another card. Play then passes to the other player. Continue until one player has completed an entire row, column, or diagonal.

Workbook: Practice +6 and +7 Facts

Have your child complete workbook page 22.1B.

 Save the Addition Tic-Tac-Toe game board (workbook page 22.1A) so you can play again.

Lesson 22.2
Practice +6 and +7 Facts

	Purpose	Materials
Warm-up	• Count backward from 90 • Practice memory work • Review symmetry	• 100 Chart (Blackline Master 3), optional • Pattern blocks • Paper, optional
Activities	• Practice the +6 and +7 addition facts	• Counters • Double ten-frames (Blackline Master 1) • Addition Tic-Tac-Toe game board (on Workbook page 22.1A) • Playing cards
Workbook	• Practice the +6 and +7 addition facts	• Workbook pages 22.2A and 22.2B

Warm-up: Counting, Memory Work, and Review

- Have your child count backward from 90 to 75, either by memory or with the 100 Chart.
- **How many cents equal 1 dollar?** *100.*
- Have your child create a symmetric design with pattern blocks.

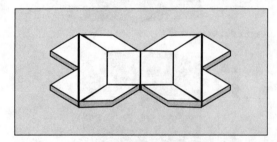

Your child can make the design as simple or complex as he likes.

Activity: Practice +6 and +7 Facts

In the last lesson, you solved addition problems with 6s and 7s. Today, you'll practice these facts some more.

Put 6 counters of one color on the top ten-frame and 5 counters of another color on the bottom ten-frame. **What addition problem do the counters show?** *6 + 5.*

Point out the group of 5 in each ten-frame and the "leftover" counter, as shown below.

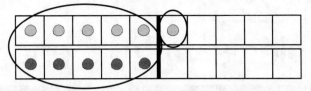

2 groups of 5 make 10 counters. Then, there's 1 leftover counter. So, what's 6 + 5? *11*.

Repeat this process with the rest of the +6 and +7 facts. Model each problem on the ten-frame and encourage your child to "look at the leftovers" to find the answers.

- 7 + 6 = *13*
- 6 + 6 = *12*
- 7 + 7 = *14*
- 7 + 5 = *12*
- 7 + 4 = *11*

Activity: Play Addition Tic-Tac-Toe

Play Addition Tic-Tac-Toe. See Lesson 22.1 (page 349) for directions. Keep the ten-frame and counters available to model the addition problems as you play.

Workbook: Practice +6 and +7 Facts and Review

Have your child complete workbook pages 22.2A and 22.2B. Keep the ten-frame and counters available.

Lesson 22.3
Word Problems with +6 and +7 Facts

	Purpose	Materials
Warm-up	• Count five-dollar bills by 5s • Practice memory work • Review odd and even numbers	• Play money • Number Cards
Activities	• Write equations to match addition word problems and solve the equations • Practice +6 and +7 addition facts	• Counters • Double ten-frames (Blackline Master 1) • Addition Tic-Tac-Toe game board (on Workbook page 22.1A) • Playing cards
Workbook	• Solve addition word problems • Practice +6 and +7 addition facts	• Workbook pages 22.3A and 22.3B

Warm-up: Counting, Memory Work, and Review

• Place 13 five-dollar bills on the table. Have your child count by 5s to find the total value. **How many dollars is this?** *$65.*

• **How many cents equal 1 dollar?** *100.*

• **Name the even numbers in order to 20.** *2, 4, 6, 8, 10, 12, 14, 16, 18, 20.* **Name the odd numbers in order to 19.** *1, 3, 5, 7, 9, 11, 13, 15, 17, 19.* Shuffle number cards 1-20. Show your child one card at a time and have her tell whether the number is even or odd.

Activity: Solve +6 and +7 Addition Word Problems

You have been working on learning the +6 and +7 addition facts. Today, you'll use these facts to solve word problems. Most will be addition but watch out for the subtraction problem!

Read the following word problems to your child. Have her model each problem with counters on the ten-frame and then write and solve an equation to match.

• **You build a tower with 6 square blocks and 5 triangle blocks. How many blocks do you use?** *11.*

$$6 + 5 = 11$$

• **You build a tower with 6 square blocks. Then, you decorate the top with 7 triangle blocks. How many blocks do you use?** *13.*

$$6 + 7 = 13$$

- **You build a tower with 7 blocks. 5 of the blocks are squares, and the rest are triangles. How many blocks are triangles?** *2.*

$7 - 5 = 2$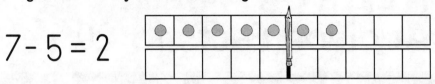

Your child can use a pencil to split the counters into groups.

Activity: Practice Written Word Problems

Show your child workbook page 22.3A. **Let's practice the steps for solving word problems.**

The first step in solving a word problem is to read the problem slowly and carefully. Have your child read aloud the first problem (or read it aloud to her).

> You have 6 red apples.
> You have 5 green apples.
> How many apples do you have?

The next step is to write an equation to match the problem. Have your child write an equation to match the problem in the space provided on the worksheet.

$$6 \oplus 5 = \underline{\quad}$$

If your child is not sure whether to write a plus sign or minus sign in the circle, point out the picture on the worksheet. **Are we joining two groups together or separating two groups?** *Joining.* **So, since we're joining two groups, this is an addition problem.**

The final step is to complete the equation and write the answer in the sentence.

$$6 \oplus 5 = 11$$

I have ___11___ apples.

Activity: Play Addition Tic-Tac-Toe

Play Addition Tic-Tac-Toe. See Lesson 22.1 (page 349) for directions. Keep the ten-frame and counters available to model the addition problems as you play.

Workbook: Solve Word Problems and Review

Have your child complete workbook pages 22.3A and 22.3B.

Lesson 22.4
Practice Addition Facts to 20

	Purpose	Materials
Warm-up	• Count dimes by 10s • Practice memory work • Review identifying numbers on the 100 Chart	• Coins • 100 Chart (Blackline Master 3) • Counters
Activities	• Practice addition facts to 20 • Informally assess your child's progress with the addition facts to 20	• 2 decks of playing cards
Workbook	• Practice addition facts to 20	• Workbook pages 22.4A and 22.4B

Warm-up: Counting, Memory Work, and Review

- Place 10 dimes on the table. Have your child count by 10s to find the total value. **How many cents is this?** *100¢.*

- **How many cents equal 1 dollar?** *100.*

- Have your child cover the following numbers on the 100 Chart with small counters: 64, 65, 66, 67, 14, 17, 49, 53, 42, 58. The final arrangement of counters should look like a smiley face.

Activity: Play Addition War (5-10)

Let's play a new version of Addition War to practice the more difficult addition facts. Play two rounds of Addition War. Have your child use the ten-frame if he's unsure of any answers.

Addition War (5-10)

Materials: 5s, 6s, 7s, 8s, 9s and 10s from 2 decks of cards (48 cards total)

Object of the Game: Win the most cards.

Shuffle the cards together and deal out all the cards into 2 face-down piles.

To play, flip over the top 2 cards in your pile. Find the sum of the 2 cards. For example, if you flip over a 7 and a 9, say, "7 plus 9 equals 16." Then, the other player turns over two cards and announces their sum. Whoever's sum is greater wins all 4 cards. If the sums are equal, play again. The player whose sum is greater wins all 8 cards.

Play until both players use up all the cards they were dealt. The player with more cards wins the game.

This game informally assesses how well your child knows the addition facts to 20.

Workbook: Practice Addition Facts and Review

Have your child complete workbook pages 22.4A and 22.4B.

Lesson 22.5
Enrichment and Review (Optional)

	Purpose	Materials
Warm-up	• Count to 100 by 1s, 2s, 5s, or 10s • Review memory work • Review your child's favorite or most challenging activities from Week 22	• Varies, depending on the activities you choose
Picture Book	• Understand addition equations in context	• *100 Snowmen*, written by Jen Arena and illustrated by Stephen Gilpin
Enrichment Activity	• Practice the addition facts in a fun and kinesthetic way	• Pudding, shaving cream, or fingerpaint • Large washable tray, clean counter, or large sheet of paper

Warm-up: Counting, Memory Work, and Review

- Have your child count to 100 by 1s, 2s, 5s, or 10s. (Choose whichever counting sequence your child needs to practice the most.)

- Quiz your child on the memory work through Week 22. See page 499 for the full list.

- If you have time, repeat one or two of the activities from this week's lessons. Choose activities your child especially enjoyed or found challenging.

Math Picture Book: *100 Snowmen*

Read *100 Snowmen*, written by Jen Arena and illustrated by Stephen Gilpin. As you read, discuss how the addition equations match the illustrations.

Enrichment Activity: Messy Math Facts

Spread pudding on a tray, shaving cream on a counter, or finger paint on a large sheet of paper. Choose 8-10 of the addition facts your child finds most challenging. Have him use his finger to write each addition fact (with its answer) in the goo.

Week 22 Answer Key

22.1A

See *Instructor Guide* for directions on how to play.
Save this game board for future lessons.

Addition Tic-Tac-Toe
Game Board

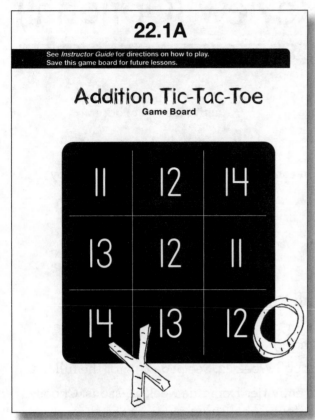

22.1B

Complete.

$6 + 5 = 11$ $7 + 7 = 14$

$7 + 6 = 13$ $5 + 7 = 12$

$7 + 5 = 12$ $6 + 6 = 12$

$7 + 4 = 11$ $6 + 7 = 13$

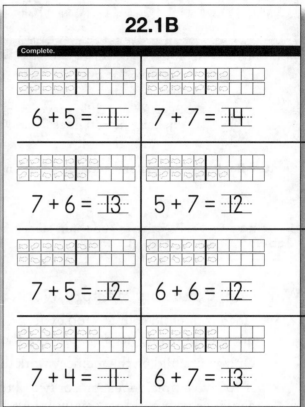

22.2A

Complete.

$5 + 6 = 11$ $6 + 7 = 13$

$7 + 7 = 14$ $6 + 6 = 12$

$5 + 7 = 12$ $6 + 5 = 11$

$7 + 6 = 13$ $4 + 7 = 11$

Match.

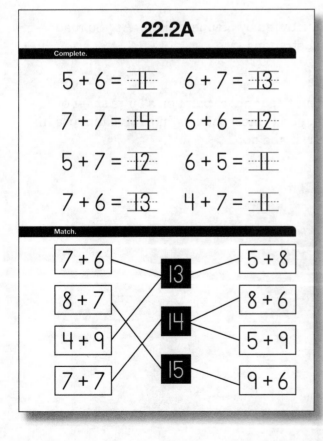

22.2B

Circle the squares that are split into fourths.
X the squares that are not split into fourths.

Circle the greater number in each pair.

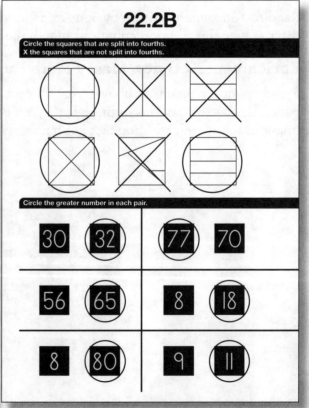

Week 22 Answer Key

22.3A

Complete the equations and sentences to match the word problems.

You have 6 red apples.
You have 5 green apples.
How many apples do you have?

6 (+) 5 = 11

I have 11 apples.

You have 6 red apples.
You have 6 green apples.
How many apples do you have?

6 (+) 6 = 12

I have 12 apples.

You have 7 red apples.
You have 4 green apples.
How many apples do you have?

7 (+) 4 = 11

I have 11 apples.

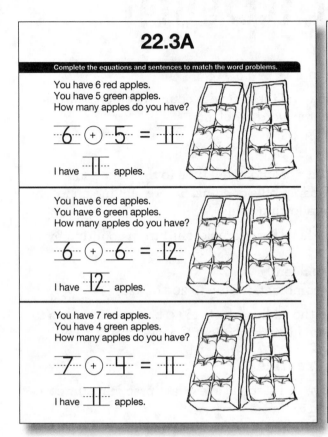

22.3B

Complete.

$$5 + 6 = 11 \qquad 6 + 7 = 13$$

$$7 + 7 = 14 \qquad 6 + 6 = 12$$

$$5 + 7 = 12 \qquad 6 + 5 = 11$$

$$7 + 6 = 13 \qquad 4 + 7 = 11$$

Match pairs that make 100.

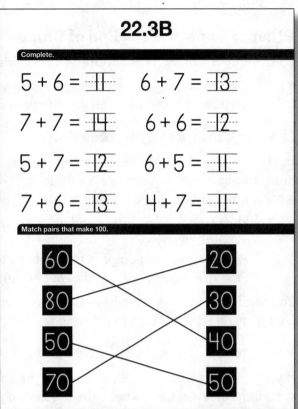

60	20
80	30
50	40
70	50

22.4A

Color the addition facts that equal the number in the star.

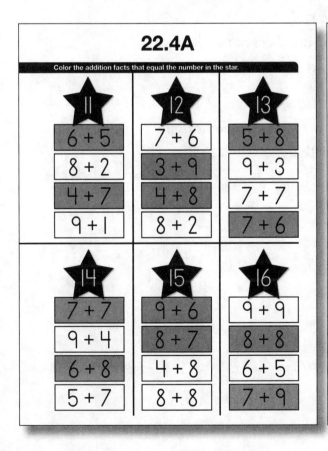

★ 11
| 6 + 5 |
| 8 + 2 |
| 4 + 7 |
| 9 + 1 |

★ 12
| 7 + 6 |
| 3 + 9 |
| 4 + 8 |
| 8 + 2 |

★ 13
| 5 + 8 |
| 9 + 3 |
| 7 + 7 |
| 7 + 6 |

★ 14
| 7 + 7 |
| 9 + 4 |
| 6 + 8 |
| 5 + 7 |

★ 15
| 9 + 6 |
| 8 + 7 |
| 4 + 8 |
| 8 + 8 |

★ 16
| 9 + 9 |
| 8 + 8 |
| 6 + 5 |
| 7 + 9 |

22.4B

Match.

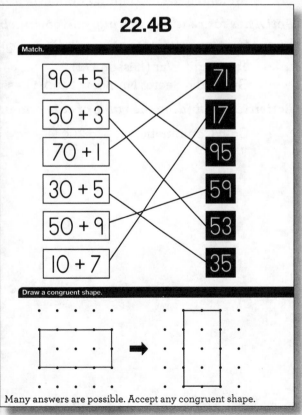

90 + 5	71
50 + 3	17
70 + 1	95
30 + 5	59
50 + 9	53
10 + 7	35

Draw a congruent shape.

Many answers are possible. Accept any congruent shape.

Unit 8 Checkpoint

What to Expect at the End of Unit 8

By the end of Unit 8, most children will be able to:

- Find most single-digit sums mentally and find the rest with counters on ten-frames.
- Write and solve addition equations to match word problems.

Is Your Child Ready to Move on?

In Unit 9, your child will learn to read the date on a calendar, tell time to the hour and half hour, and count more complex combinations of paper bills or coins. Before moving on to Unit 9, your child should have already mastered the following skills:

- Shift from one counting sequence to another. (For example, shift from counting by 10s to counting by 5s.)
- Read, write, and compare numbers to 100 fluently.
- Find the value of coin and paper money combinations (up to 20¢ or $20).

Your child does not need to have fully mastered the addition facts to 20 before moving on to Unit 9, as he will continue to practice the addition facts throughout the new unit.

What to Do If Your Child Needs More Practice

If your child is having trouble with any of the above skills, spend a few days practicing the corresponding review activities below before moving on to Unit 9.

Activities for shifting counting sequences

- Pretend to be a Counting Robot (Lesson 17.4)

Activities for reading, writing, and comparing numbers to 100

- Find Two-Digit Numbers on the 100 Chart (Lesson 17.2)
- Two-Digit War (Lesson 17.1)
- Guess the Secret Number (1-100) (Lesson 17.2)

Activities for finding the value of coin and paper money combinations

- Coin Combinations up to 20¢ (Review activity, Lesson 22.1)

Unit 9
Time and Money

Overview

In Unit 9, your child will learn to read the date on a calendar and tell time to the hour and half hour on a clock with hands. She will also learn to count more complex combinations of paper bills or coins, and she'll solve word problems involving money.

Week 23   Calendars and Clocks
Week 24   Paper Bills
Week 25   Coins

What Your Child Will Learn

In this unit your child will learn to:

- Identify the date and day of the week on a monthly calendar
- Tell time to the hour and half hour on a clock with hands
- Know common time equivalents
- Count combinations of ten-dollar, five-dollar, and one-dollar bills
- Count combinations of dimes, nickels, and pennies
- Count quarters by 25s
- Solve word problems involving money

Recommended Math Picture Books (Optional)

These picture books are scheduled in the optional Enrichment and Review lessons at the end of each week.

- *Game Time!*, written by Stuart J. Murphy and illustrated by Cynthia Jaber. Great Source, 2000.
- *A Chair for My Mother*, by Vera B. Williams. Greenwillow Books, 2007.
- *The Penny Pot*, written by Stuart J. Murphy and illustrated by Lynne Cravath. Scholastic, 1998.

Week 23
Calendars and Clocks

Overview

This week, your child will learn to read the date on a monthly calendar and tell time on a clock with hands to the hour and half hour.

Lesson 23.1	Read the Date on a Calendar
Lesson 23.2	Hours, Minutes, and Seconds
Lesson 23.3	Tell Time to the Hour
Lesson 23.4	Tell Time to the Half Hour
Lesson 23.5	Enrichment and Review (Optional)

Teaching Math with Confidence:
The Benefits of Learning to Read Clocks with Hands

This week, your child will learn to tell time to the hour and half hour on clocks with hands. Most children are much more familiar with digital clocks than analog clocks, and many families no longer even own clocks with hands. So, why spend time teaching children the difficult skill of reading time on an analog clock?

Learning to tell time on clocks with hands gives children a concrete understanding of what hours and minutes mean. The sweep of the two hands gives them a physical experience of the passing of time (as opposed to the mysteriously-changing numbers on digital clocks). Children also develop a better understanding of the relationship between hours and minutes as they compare the hour hand's slower speed with the minute hand's faster speed.

You'll focus on these key properties of clocks with hands as you teach your child to tell time to the hour and half hour this week. Your child will learn how to tell time more precisely in second grade.

Extra Materials Needed for Week 23

- 3-5 eating utensils of different lengths (such as forks or spoons)
- Printed 12-month calendar
- Digital clock
- Clock with hands
- For optional Enrichment and Review Lesson:
    × *Game Time!*, written by Stuart J. Murphy and illustrated by Cynthia Jaber
    × Materials for creating an obstacle course
    × Stopwatch, phone with a stopwatch app, or clock with a second hand

If you don't have a paper monthly calendar, find one online and print it out to use this week.

You will need a clock with hands to teach your child to tell time this week. Your clock should have:

- Clear, easy-to-read numbers (No Roman numerals!)
- Tick marks along the edge for each minute
- Hands your child can easily move

If your family's clocks don't meet these criteria, you may want to buy an inexpensive plastic teaching clock (sometimes called a "Judy clock") to make these lessons easier to teach.

Lesson 23.1
Read the Date on a Calendar

	Purpose	Materials
Warm-up	• Count forward from any number between 1 and 100 • Practice memory work • Review measuring in inches with a ruler	• 100 Chart (Blackline Master 3), optional • 3-5 eating utensils of different lengths (such as forks or spoons) • Paper ruler (Blackline Master 8) or 1-foot ruler
Activities	• Read the date and day of the week on a calendar • Use ordinal numbers to read dates on a calendar (such as *sixth* or *fourteenth*)	• Printed 12-month calendar (January-December)
Workbook	• Identify missing dates and the day of the week on a monthly calendar	• Workbook pages 23.1A and 23.1B

If your child can already read the date and day of the week on a calendar, make this a short review lesson or combine it with lesson 23.2.

Warm-up: Counting, Memory Work, and Review

- Have your child count forward from the following numbers. Stop her after she reaches the last number listed in the sample answers.

    × **Count forward from 77:** *77, 78, 79, 80, 81.*
    × **Count forward from 57:** *57, 58, 59, 60, 61.*
    × **Count forward from 96:** *96, 97, 98, 99, 100.*

    If your child has trouble, have her first point to the numbers on the 100 Chart before reciting them from memory.

- Have your child say the months. **How many months are in a year?** *12.* Have your child say the days of the week. **How many days are in a week?** *7.*

- Have your child estimate and measure the length of several eating utensils. She can use either the paper ruler or a standard ruler.

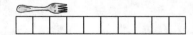

Activity: Read the Date on the Calendar

This week, you'll learn about time. Today, you'll learn how to read the date and day of the week on the calendar.

Show your child a paper monthly calendar. Flip through the pages from January to December and read the name of each month together. Also tell your child the current month and show her the corresponding page on the calendar. (For example: **The month right now is March.**)

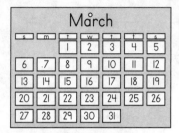

Each row on the calendar is one week. Point out the current week on the calendar.

Point to the current day on the calendar and tell your child the date. For example: **Today is March 7th.**

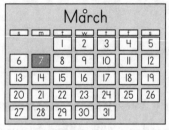

Point to yesterday's date and tomorrow's date and read them to your child. For example: **Yesterday was March 6th. Tomorrow is March 8th.**

Each column on the calendar shows a different day of the week. Point to the days of the week at the top of the calendar and read them with your child.

Point to the current date and show your child how to find the current day of the week on the calendar. For example: **Today is in the Monday column of the calendar. So, today is a Monday.**

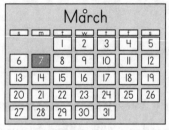

Point to a few dates in the current month and ask your child to identify them. (If you have appointments or events written on the calendar, use these.) For example: **What date is this? What day of the week is it?** Sample answer: *March 18th. It's a Friday.*

What date is your birthday? *Answers will vary.* Help your child find the month with her birthday. Have her find the date of her birthday and identify the day of the week.

Activity: Practice Reading Ordinal Numbers on the Calendar

We use numbers like *one, two,* and *three* to count and tell how many. But we use numbers like *first, second,* and *third* to name numbers on the calendar.

The usual counting numbers (like one, two, and three) are called *cardinal* numbers. The numbers we use to describe order or position (like first, second, or third) are called *ordinal* numbers. Your child does not need to know these terms, as they are used here simply for clarity.

Read the current month's dates to your child, in order from the first day of the month to the last day of the month. For example: **March first, March second, March third...**

Have your child join you as much as she can. Point out most of the dates are simply the usual counting number with a "th" at the end (such as sixth or fourteenth). Also point out that 21st through 25th follow the same pattern as the 1st through 5th (twenty-*first,* twenty-*second,* etc.)

Workbook: Identify Missing Dates and Review

Have your child complete workbook pages 23.1A and 23.1B. If needed, help your child read the questions on page 23.1A.

Lesson 23.2
Hours, Minutes, and Seconds

	Purpose	Materials
Warm-up	• Count backward from 100 • Practice memory work • Review reading the date on a calendar	• 100 Chart (Blackline Master 3), optional • Printed 12-month calendar (January-December)
Activities	• Learn real-life approximations for the length of an hour, minute, or second • Learn to read written times	• None
Workbook	• Trace important time equivalents • Read written "o'clock" times	• Workbook pages 23.2A and 23.2B

Warm-up: Counting, Memory Work, and Review

- Have your child count backward from 100 to 85, either by memory or with the 100 Chart.
- **How many inches equal 1 foot?** *12*.
- Point to the current date on the calendar. Have your child read the date and identify the day of the week. Also point to a few other dates on the calendar and have your child read them and identify the days of the week.

> Make sure your child uses ordinal numbers (like *sixth* or *seventeenth*) to read the dates rather than simply reading the written numerals,

Activity: Introduce Hours, Minutes, and Seconds

In the last lesson, you learned how to read the date on a calendar. Today, you'll learn about hours, minutes, and seconds, and you'll learn how to read written times.

Each day is divided into 24 hours. Tell your child several one-hour activities your family does. For example:

- **It takes about an hour to bake brownies.**
- **Church lasts about an hour.**
- **Watching two shows takes about an hour.**
- **A soccer game lasts about an hour.**

Each hour is divided into 60 minutes. Tell your child several one-minute activities that your family does. For example:

- **It takes about a minute to make toast.**
- **Putting away the silverware from the dishwasher takes about a minute.**
- **Tying your shoes takes about a minute.**

Each minute is divided into 60 seconds. Seconds are very short! It takes about a second to say the word *Mississippi*. Say *Mississippi*. *Mississippi*. **That took you about 1 second.**

> Your child will memorize these equivalents during the Memory Work portion of Week 24. For now, simply help your child develop a rough sense of the length of each unit of time.

Activity: Make a Time Chart

At the top of a piece of paper, write *My Day*. **Let's write down the times of some of the important events in your day today.**

> This activity makes learning to tell time more meaningful and helps your child see the purpose of clocks and written times.

Make a simple chart showing 5-8 events in your child's day, along with their times. Include the approximate time your child wakes up, eats meals, and goes to bed, as well as a few other events of the day.

Include some "o'clock" times without minutes (such as 9:00 or 11:00) and some times with minutes (such as 1:30 or 7:15). Read each time to your child as you write it.

My Day	
7:00	Wake up
8:45	School lessons
10:30	Go to library story hour
12:00	Eat lunch
1:00	Rest
3:00	Eat a snack
3:15	Play outside

Sample chart. Adjust the times and events to fit your own family.

Activity: Read Written Times

Write 9:00 on a piece of paper. **Written times have 3 parts: the hours, the minutes, and the colon that separates them. Can you point to the 2 dots in the middle of this time?** *Child points to the colon in 9:00.* **These two dots are called a colon. They separate the hours and minutes so we can read them more easily.**

The number on the left side of the colon tells the hour. Point to the 9 in 9:00. **What hour does this say?** *9.*

The number on the right side of the colon tells how many minutes past the hour. Point to the 00 in 9:00. *When there are 0 minutes past the hour, we say o'clock. So, this time is 9 o'clock.*

> Your child does not need to remember the two dots are called a colon. Naming the colon simply makes it easier to discuss, and drawing attention to it helps your child distinguish between the hours and minutes.

Write 10:00, 8:00, 4:00 and 6:00 on a piece of paper and have your child read each time.

10:00   4:00
8:00   6:00

Have your child read the times on your My Day chart.

Workbook: Read Written Times and Review

Have your child complete workbook pages 23.2A and 23.2B.

Lesson 23.3
Tell Time to the Hour

	Purpose	Materials
Warm-up	• Count nickels by 5s • Practice memory work • Review +9 addition facts	• Coins • Adding 9s Bingo game board (on Workbook page 20.1A) • Playing cards • Counters
Activities	• Learn to tell time on a digital clock • Learn to tell time to the hour on a clock with hands	• Digital clock • Clock with hands
Workbook	• Tell time to the hour on a clock with hands	• Workbook pages 23.3A and 23.3B

Warm-up: Counting, Memory Work, and Review

- Place a handful of nickels on the table. Have your child count by 5s to find the total value.

- Have your child rhythmically say the Tens Chant: **1 ten. Ten! 2 tens. Twenty!** etc. See Lesson 15.1 (page 236) for the full chant.

- Play Adding 9s Bingo. See Lesson 20.1 (page 322) for directions.

Activity: Tell the Time on a Digital Clock

Clocks tell us what time it is. How many different clocks do you think we have in our home? *Answers will vary.* Walk around the house and count how many different clocks you have. Make sure to include clocks on watches, microwaves, and other electronic equipment.

There are two main kinds of clocks: digital clocks and clocks with hands. We can use either kind of clock to tell the time. Today, you'll learn how to read the time to the hour on both kinds of clocks.

Show your child a digital clock. **Digital clocks show all 3 parts of a written time: the hours, the minutes, and the colon.**

Have your child point to the hour, minutes, and colon on the digital clock. Read the current time to your child. For example: **Right now, it's 9:47. That means 47 minutes have passed since 9 o'clock.**

hour   colon   minutes

Set the digital clock to 4:00, 10:00, 3:00, 5:00, 8:00, and 12:00 and have your child read each time.

Activity: Tell the Time on a Clock with Hands

Show your child a clock with hands. Spin the hands forward (and let your child move the hands, too) so that she sees how the hands move. **The two hands spin around in a circle and point to the time.**

Point to the shorter hand. **The shorter hand is called the hour hand. It tells us what hour it is.**

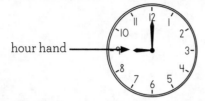

Point to the longer hand. **The longer hand is called the minute hand. It tells us how many minutes past the hour the time is.**

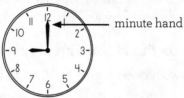

If your clock has a second hand, explain this hand measures the number of seconds that pass. Tell your child to ignore this hand when reading the time on the clock.

The numbers around the edge of the clock tell the hour. Have your child point to the numbers and read them, from 1 to 12. **The numbers on clocks are always arranged like this. The 12 is always at the top, and the 6 is always at the bottom.**

Set the clock to 8:00. Have your child identify the hour hand and minute hand.

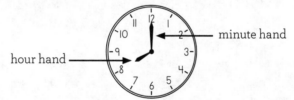

To what number is the hour hand pointing? *8.* **Since the hour hand is pointing to the 8, the hour is 8.**

Every hour begins with the minute hand pointing to the 12 at the top of the clock. So, this clock is set to 8 o'clock.

As the hour passes, the minute hand moves around the clock to show how many minutes have passed since the start of the hour. Have your child slowly spin the minute hand forward and notice how both hands move. **The hour hand moves closer and closer to 9 as the hour passes.**

Point out that the hour hand moves from 8 to 9 as the minute hand moves forward.

Children often find it difficult to identify the hour when the hour hand is between two numbers (as in the clock above). Moving the hands and paying attention to how the hour hand moves prepares your child to learn to tell time to the half hour in Lesson 23.4.

Have your child continue moving the minute hand forward until the clock is set to 9:00. **Once the minute hand goes all the way around the clock, an hour has passed. What time does the clock show now?** *9 o'clock.*

Have your child turn the clock's hands forward another hour and identify the time. Have her continue moving the clock forward by an hour at a time until you reach 8:00 again.

Workbook: Tell Time to the Hour and Review

Have your child complete workbook pages 23.3A and 23.3B.

Lesson 23.4
Tell Time to the Half Hour

	Purpose	Materials
Warm-up	• Count ten-dollar bills by 10s • Practice memory work • Review reading the date on a calendar	• Play money • Printed 12-month calendar (January–December)
Activities	• Tell time to the half hour on a clock with hands	• Clock with hands
Workbook	• Tell time to the half hour on a clock with hands	• Workbook pages 23.4A and 23.4B

Warm-up: Counting, Memory Work, and Review

- Place 10 ten-dollar bills on the table. Have your child count by 10s to find the total value. **How many dollars is this?** *$100.*

- **How many cents equal 1 dollar?** *100.*

- Point to the current date on the calendar. Have your child read the date and identify the day of the week. Also point to a few other dates on the calendar and have your child read them and identify the days of the week.

Activity: Practice Reading a Clock with Hands to the Hour

In the last lesson, you learned how to tell time to the hour on a clock with hands. Today, you'll learn to tell time to the half hour.

Set a clock with hands to 7:00 and have your child identify the hour hand and minute hand.

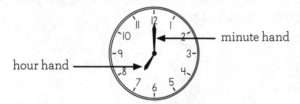

To what number is the hour hand pointing? *7.* **To what number is the minute hand pointing?** *12.* **So, what time does this clock show?** *7 o'clock.* Have your child write 7:00 on a piece of paper.

7:00

Set the clock to 11:00. **What time does this clock show?** *11 o'clock.* Have your child write 11:00 on a piece of paper.

Repeat with 1:00, 5:00, 6:00, 10:00, and 12:00. Each time, have your child name the time and write it on a piece of paper.

Activity: Tell Time to the Half Hour on a Clock with Hands

Set a clock with hands to 2:00. **What time does this clock show?** *2 o'clock.*

The minute hand tells us how many minutes past the hour the time is. But the tricky part about reading the minute hand is that the numbers for the minutes aren't printed on the clock!

Your child will learn to tell time to the half hour in this lesson. He does not need to learn to tell time to the minute. This brief introduction to how the minute hand moves will help him understand why the minute hand points to the 6 on the clock face at 30 minutes past the hour.

Move the minute hand to the first tick mark past 12 (so the time reads 2:01). **As each minute passes, the minute hand moves to the next tick mark. The minute hand is 1 tick mark past 2:00, so the clock now shows 2:01.**

Have your child move the minute hand forward to the next tick mark. **What time does the clock show now?** *2:02.*

Have your child continue to move the minute hand forward one minute at a time and identify the time until he reaches 2:15.

Turn the minute hand to the 6 (so the time reads 2:30). **Can you figure out what time the clock says now?** *2:30.* Suggest he count the tick marks up to the printed 6 if he's not sure. Have your child write 2:30 on a piece of paper.

2:30

When the minute hand points to the 6, the time is 30 minutes past the hour. Another way to remember it is to notice the minute hand is halfway through the hour. A half hour is 30 minutes, so the time is 30 minutes past the hour.

Point out the hour hand on the clock. **Where is the hour hand now?** *Between the 2 and the 3.*

We know it's 2:30 and not 3:30, because the hour hand hasn't gotten to the 3 yet. Have your child slowly spin the minute hand forward to 3:00. **The hour hand moves closer and closer to 3 as the hour passes. Once the hour passes, the minute hand returns to the top of the clock again.**

Set the clock to 4:30. **What time does this clock show?** *4:30.* If your child says 5:30, remind him the hour hand hasn't reached the 5 yet. Have your child write 4:30 on a piece of paper.

4:30

Repeat with 5:30, 8:30, 10:30, 12:30, and 3:30. Each time, have your child name the time and write it on a piece of paper.

Your child is not expected to fully master telling time to the half hour during this lesson. He will practice it more in the warm-ups and workbook pages during the next several weeks.

Workbook: Tell Time to the Half Hour and Review

Have your child complete workbook pages 23.4A and 23.4B.

Lesson 23.5
Enrichment and Review (Optional)

	Purpose	Materials
Warm-up	• Count to 100 by 1s, 2s, 5s, or 10s • Review memory work • Review your child's favorite or most challenging activities from Week 23	• Varies, depending on the activities you choose
Picture Book	• Understand units of time in the context of soccer	• *Game Time!*, written by Stuart J. Murphy and illustrated by Cynthia Jaber
Enrichment Activity	• Estimate and measure time in seconds	• Materials for creating an obstacle course • Stopwatch, phone with a stopwatch app, or clock with a second hand

Warm-up: Counting, Memory Work, and Review

- Have your child count to 100 by 1s, 2s, 5s, or 10s. (Choose whichever counting sequence your child needs to practice the most.)

- Quiz your child on the memory work through Week 22. See page 499 for the full list.

- If you have time, repeat one or two of the activities from this week's lessons. Choose activities your child especially enjoyed or found challenging.

Math Picture Book: *Game Time!*

Read *Game Time!*, written by Stuart J. Murphy and illustrated by Cynthia Jaber. As you read, discuss the different units of time included in the book. If your child participates in a sport, talk about how long your child's practices and games take.

Enrichment Activity: Measuring Seconds with an Obstacle Course

Have your child create a simple obstacle course, either inside or outside. Ask her to predict how long it will take to for her to complete the course. Then, use a stopwatch to time how long it takes for her to run the obstacle course, and compare the actual time to the predicted time.

Have your child run the course several times. Write down how long each run takes, and discuss whether each run is faster or slower than the previous one.

Week 23 Answer Key

23.1A

Complete the missing dates.

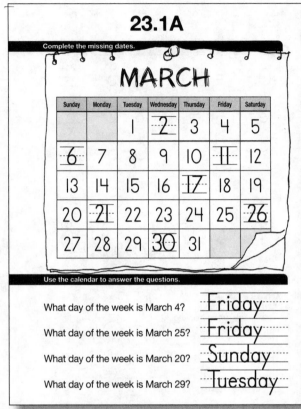

MARCH

Sunday	Monday	Tuesday	Wednesday	Thursday	Friday	Saturday
		1	2	3	4	5
6	7	8	9	10	11	12
13	14	15	16	17	18	19
20	21	22	23	24	25	26
27	28	29	30	31		

Use the calendar to answer the questions.

What day of the week is March 4? Friday

What day of the week is March 25? Friday

What day of the week is March 20? Sunday

What day of the week is March 29? Tuesday

23.1B

Complete.

$9 + 4 = 13$ $6 + 8 = 14$

$8 + 7 = 15$ $5 + 7 = 12$

$7 + 10 = 17$ $8 + 8 = 16$

$4 + 9 = 13$ $4 + 5 = 9$

Trace.

1 foot = 12 inches

Draw a line of symmetry for each shape.

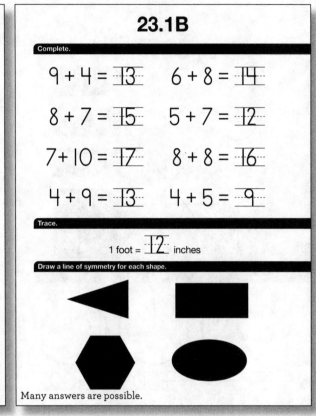

Many answers are possible.

23.2A

Trace.

1 year = 12 months

1 week = 7 days

1 day = 24 hours

1 hour = 60 minutes

1 minute = 60 seconds

Match.

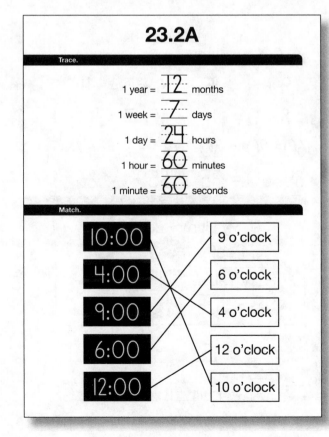

10:00	9 o'clock
4:00	6 o'clock
9:00	4 o'clock
6:00	12 o'clock
12:00	10 o'clock

23.2B

Complete.

$9 + 5 = 14$ $6 + 6 = 12$

$8 + 4 = 12$ $9 + 7 = 16$

$30 + 40 = 70$ $30 + 4 = 34$

$45 + 10 = 55$ $45 + 1 = 46$

Complete the number patterns.

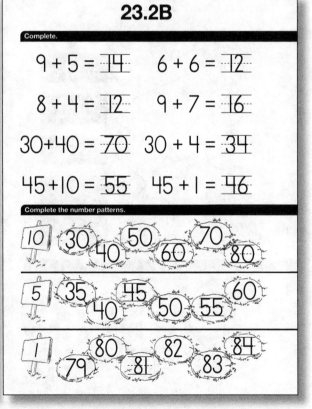

10, 30, 40, 50, 60, 70, 80

5, 35, 40, 45, 50, 55, 60

1, 79, 80, 81, 82, 83, 84

Week 23 Answer Key

23.3A

Match.

Write the time.

7:00   4:00   11:00

23.3B

Complete.

$10 - 7 = 3$ $9 - 5 = 4$
$8 - 4 = 4$ $8 - 2 = 6$
$9 - 6 = 3$ $10 - 5 = 5$
$7 - 3 = 4$ $6 - 5 = 1$

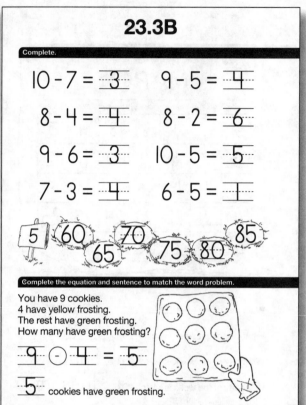

5 60 65 70 75 80 85

Complete the equation and sentence to match the word problem.

You have 9 cookies.
4 have yellow frosting.
The rest have green frosting.
How many have green frosting?

$9 - 4 = 5$

5 cookies have green frosting.

23.4A

Match.

12:30
1:30
5:30
7:30
9:30

Write the time.

2:30   11:30   5:30

23.4B

Complete.

$9 + 6 = 15$ $6 + 5 = 11$
$8 + 3 = 11$ $7 + 7 = 14$
$60 + 20 = 80$ $60 + 2 = 62$
$85 + 10 = 95$ $85 + 1 = 86$

Emma made a bar graph of the books she checked out from the library. Use the bar graph to answer the questions.

My Library Books
Poetry
Fairy Tales
Science

How many fairy tale books did she check out? 5

How many science books did she check out? 3

Did she check out more science or fairy tale books? Fairy Tale

How many more? 2

Week 24
Paper Bills

Overview

This week, your child will count combinations of ten-dollar, five-dollar, and one-dollar bills. He'll also compare groups of paper bills and solve word problems involving money.

Lesson 24.1   Count Paper Bills
Lesson 24.2   Compare Money
Lesson 24.3   Count Out Paper Bills
Lesson 24.4   Money Word Problems
Lesson 24.5   Enrichment and Review (Optional)

Teaching Math with Confidence: Counting Out Money

In kindergarten, your child learned how to count out a given number of counters. For example, when you asked him to count out 30 counters, he learned how to keep the target number in his memory and stop after each number to consider whether he had reached 30 yet.

Counting out money is similar, but with a significant wrinkle. Not only does your child need to keep the target number in mind, but he also has to consider which type of bill to use to get as close as possible to the target number without going over.

For example, say you've asked your child to count out $68. So far, he's counted out 6 ten-dollar bills. At this point, he has to decide what kind of bill to use next. Should he use a ten-dollar bill, a five-dollar bill, or a one-dollar bill?

Which bill should I add next to reach $68 as quickly as possible?

To make this decision, your child has to consider all 3 possibilities and calculate their effects.

- A ten-dollar bill is too much, because $10 more than $60 is $70.
- A one-dollar bill could work, but it would take 8 of them to reach $68.
- A five-dollar bill is the best choice, because $5 more than $60 is $65. Then, he'll need just 3 one-dollar bills to reach $68.

Besides the practical value of learning to count out money, thinking through these possibilities also builds your child's understanding of place value and two-digit numbers. It may take him some trial-and-error to count out the correct number of bills. With practice and guidance, he'll begin to develop efficient strategies for counting out bills and strengthen his number sense at the same time.

Extra Materials Needed for Week 24

- Clock with hands
- 5 small toys or household items for a pretend store
- For optional Enrichment and Review Lesson:
    × *A Chair for My Mother,* by Vera B. Williams
    × Toy catalog or access to a website with items your child would like to buy

Lesson 24.1
Count Paper Bills

	Purpose	Materials
Warm-up	• Practice shifting counting sequences on the 100 Chart • Practice memory work • Review telling time to the hour or half hour	• 100 Chart (Blackline Master 3) • Clock with hands
Activities	• Sort, order, and count combinations of ten-dollar, five-dollar, and one-dollar bills	• Play money
Workbook	• Count combinations of ten-dollar, five-dollar, and one-dollar bills	• Workbook pages 24.1A and 24.1B

Warm-up: Counting, Memory Work, and Review

- **Let's pretend you're a counting robot again.** Draw a "computer panel" as in Lesson 17.4.

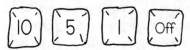

- × **Beep!** Press the 10 button. *10, 20, 30, 40, 50.*
- × **Beep!** Press the 5 button. *55, 60, 65.*
- × **Beep!** Press the 1 button. *66, 67, 68, 69, 70, 71.*
- × **Beep!** Press the Off button once your child reaches 71.

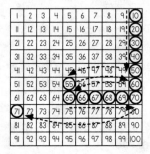

- **This week, you will learn a Time Chant to memorize important information about time.** Demonstrate the following chant for your child. Say each line rhythmically and encourage your child to join in as much as she can. Encourage your child to stomp, march, or tap the table as she chants to emphasize the rhythm.

Time Chant

1 year equals 12 months.
1 week equals 7 days.
1 day equals 24 hours.
1 hour equals 60 minutes.
1 minute equals 60 seconds.

- Set a clock with hands to the following times and have your child read the times: 4:00, 4:30, 9:00, 9:30, 11:00, 11:30.

Activity: Sort, Order, and Count Paper Bills

In Unit 6, you learned how to use place-value thinking to identify combinations of tens and ones. Place 3 ten-dollar bills and 2 one-dollar bills on the table.

Let's pretend you earned this money. You could use place-value thinking to find how much money there is. Have your child use place-value thinking to find the value: *3 tens and 2 more make 32.*

Place-value thinking is a good approach when there are only a few paper bills. But if we have more than a few bills, we usually count each bill to find how much the money is worth. Today, you'll learn how to organize and count paper bills.

Let's pretend you work at a store, and I'm the customer. When clerks at a store count the money the customers give them, they usually follow 3 steps: sort, order, and count. Pretend to buy something and give your child 5 ten-dollar bills, 3 five-dollar bills, and 6 one-dollar bills, all mixed together.

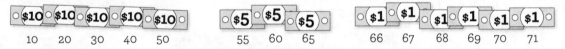

The first step is to sort the money. Have your child sort the bills by type.

The second step is to put the piles in order from the bills with the greatest value to the bills with the least value. Help your child order the piles as shown.

The last step is to count. We start by counting the bills with the greatest value. Demonstrate how to count the bills. Point to each bill as you count it. Begin with the ten-dollar bills, move next to the five-dollar bills, and finish with the one-dollar bills: **10, 20, 30, 40, 50, 55, 60, 65, 66, 67, 68, 69, 70, 71.**

$10 $10 $10 $10 $10	$5 $5 $5	$1 $1 $1 $1 $1 $1
10 20 30 40 50	55 60 65	66 67 68 69 70 71

Your child may notice that the numbers she says as she counts the money are the same as the numbers she counted on the 100 Chart in the warm-up. If she doesn't, point out that counting money is like "robot counting," since you shift from one counting sequence to another as you count each type of bill.

If your child has trouble counting the money, have her move a counter on the 100 Chart to match the value of each bill as she counts. For example, for the above combination of bills, she would move the counter as follows:

1	2	3	4	5	6	7	8	9	⑩
11	12	13	14	15	16	17	18	19	⑳
21	22	23	24	25	26	27	28	29	㉚
31	32	33	34	35	36	37	38	39	㊵
41	42	43	44	45	46	47	48	49	㊿
51	52	53	54	㊱	56	57	58	59	60
61	62	63	64	65	66	67	68	69	70
71	72	73	74	75	76	77	78	79	80
81	82	83	84	85	86	87	88	89	90
91	92	93	94	95	96	97	98	99	100

Allow her to use the counter on the 100 Chart with the next activity as well, if needed.

Activity: Practice Sorting, Ordering, and Counting Paper Bills

Have your child sort, order, and count the following combinations of paper bills. Mix up the bills before giving them to your child to count.

- 7 ten-dollar bills, 2 five-dollar bills, and 3 one-dollar bills *(10, 20, 30, 40, 50, 60, 70, 75, 80, 81, 82, 83. $83.)*
- 2 ten-dollar bills, 6 five-dollar bills, and 4 one-dollar bills *(10, 20, 25, 30, 35, 40, 45, 50, 51, 52, 53, 54. $54.)*
- 6 ten-dollar bills, 5 five-dollar bills, and 9 one-dollar bills *(10, 20, 30, 40, 50, 60, 65, 70, 75, 80, 85, 86, 87, 88, 89, 90, 91, 92, 93, 94. $94.)*

Workbook: Count Paper Bills and Review

Have your child complete workbook pages 24.1A and 24.1B. Encourage your child to touch each printed bill as she counts it, and remind her to count the bills with the largest value first.

Lesson 24.2
Compare Money

	Purpose	Materials
Warm-up	• Count by 10s starting at a number other than 0 • Practice memory work • Review +6 and +7 addition facts	• 100 Chart (Blackline Master 3), optional • Addition Tic-Tac-Toe game board (on Workbook page 22.1A) • Playing cards • Counters
Activities	• Count combinations of ten-dollar, five-dollar, and one-dollar bills • Compare quantities of money	• Play money • Die
Workbook	• Compare quantities of money	• Workbook pages 24.2A and 24.2B

Warm-up: Counting, Memory Work, and Review

- **Count by 10s starting at 5.** *5, 15, 25, 35, 45, 55, 65, 75, 85, 95.* Have your child point to the numbers on the 100 Chart only if needed.

- Have your child rhythmically recite the Time Chant. See Lesson 24.1 (page 376) for the full chant.

- Play Addition Tic-Tac-Toe. See Lesson 22.1 (page 349) for directions.

Activity: Compare Money

In the last lesson, you learned how to organize and count paper bills. Today, you'll compare piles of paper bills to see which is worth more.

Make 2 piles of paper bills on the table. Put 2 ten-dollar bills, 5 five-dollar bills, and 9 one-dollar bills in one pile. Put 6 ten-dollar bills, 1 five-dollar bill, and 2 one-dollar bills in the other pile. **Which pile do you think is worth more?** *Answers will vary.*

Have your child sort, order, and count the money. He should find the first pile has $54 and the second pile has $67. **Which pile is worth more?** *The one with $67.* **Is that what you expected?** *Answers will vary.* Point out the pile with $67 is worth more than the other pile even though it has fewer bills.

Activity: Play Money War

Play one round of Money War to practice comparing money.

Money War

Materials: Play money (ten-dollar, five-dollar, and one-dollar bills); die

Object of the Game: Win 3 rounds.

In each round, both players take turns rolling the die 3 times.

- For your first roll, take as many ten-dollar bills as dots on the die. (For example, if you roll a 3, take 3 ten-dollar bills.)
- For your second roll, take as many five-dollar bills as dots on the die.
- For your third roll, take as many one-dollar bills as dots on the die.

Count the money you have collected. The player with more money wins the round. Play until one player has won 3 rounds.

Workbook: Compare Money and Review

Have your child complete workbook pages 24.2A and 24.2B.

Lesson 24.3
Count Out Paper Bills

	Purpose	Materials
Warm-up	• Count forward from any number between 1 and 100 • Practice memory work • Review telling time to the hour and half hour	• 100 Chart (Blackline Master 3), optional • Clock with hands
Activities	• Find different combinations of bills with the same value • Count out a given number of dollars	• Play money • 5 index cards or small slips of paper • 5 small toys or household items for a pretend store
Workbook	• Count combinations of ten-dollar, five-dollar, and one-dollar bills	• Workbook pages 24.3A and 24.3B

Warm-up: Counting, Memory Work, and Review

• Have your child count forward from the following numbers. Stop her after she reaches the last number listed in the sample answers.

  × **Count forward from 39:** *39, 40, 41, 42, 43.*
  × **Count forward from 88:** *88, 89, 90, 91, 92.*
  × **Count forward from 96:** *96, 97, 98, 99, 100.*

> If your child has trouble, have her first point to the numbers on the 100 Chart before reciting them from memory.

• Rhythmically say the Time Chant. Have your child join as much as possible. See Lesson 24.1 (page 376) for the full chant.

• Set a clock with hands to the following times and have your child read the times: 3:00, 7:30, 12:00, 12:30, 1:00.

Activity: Find Multiple Ways to Pay $37

In the last two lessons, you learned how to organize and count paper bills. Mix up 4 ten-dollar bills, 3 five-dollar bills, and 8 one-dollar bills on the table. Have your child sort, order, and count the money. **How much is this money worth?** *$63.*

Today, we'll set up a pretend store so you can pretend to buy some things and count out the correct number of dollars. Set up a pretend store by laying five small toys in a row. Write $37, $76, $95, $68, and $19 on 5 index cards and place an index card in front of each item.

Let's pretend you wanted to buy the $37 toy. You could use many different combinations of bills.

Have your child find several different combinations that equal $37. Leave each on the table.

Possible ways to make $37.

See the Week 24 **Teaching Math with Confidence** for more on the complexities of counting out money.

After your child has found 3-4 combinations, ask: **Which combination uses the least number of bills? Which uses the greatest number of bills?** *Answers will vary.*

You could use any of these combinations to buy the toy. But clerks at stores appreciate it if we use as few bills as possible, so they don't have so many bills to count. Show your child the combination with the fewest bills: 3 tens, 1 five, and 2 ones.

If your child is interested, discuss the opposite question as well: **What combination of bills uses the greatest number of bills to make $37?** *37 one-dollar bills.*

Activity: Pretend Store with Paper Bills

Give your child play money to use to pretend to buy the items at the pretend store. Ask her to use as few bills as possible as he pays for each item. For example, for the $76 item, she should use 7 ten-dollar bills, 1 five-dollar bill, and 1 one-dollar bill.

Encourage your child to use as few bills as possible to pay for the items at the pretend store.

If your child gives you more bills than needed, help her trade the lower-value bills for a higher-value bill. For example, if she gives you 2 five-dollar bills, help her trade them for 1 ten-dollar bill.

Workbook: Count Paper Bills and Review

Have your child complete workbook pages 24.3A and 24.3B. Encourage your child to touch each printed bill as she counts it, and remind her to count the bills with the largest value first.

Lesson 24.4
Money Word Problems

	Purpose	Materials
Warm-up	• Count backward from any number between 1 and 100 • Practice memory work • Review subtracting from 10	• 100 Chart (Blackline Master 3), optional • Number Cards
Activities	• Solve word problems involving money • Review adding and subtracting multiples of 10 • Review adding 1 or 10 to a two-digit number	• Play money
Workbook	• Solve word problems involving money	• Workbook pages 24.4A and 24.4B • Play money, optional

Warm-up: Counting, Memory Work, and Review

- Have your child count backward from the following numbers. Stop him after he reaches the last number listed in the sample answers.

  - ✕ **Count backward from 38:** *38, 37, 36, 35, 34.*
  - ✕ **Count backward from 60:** *60, 59, 58, 57, 56.*
  - ✕ **Count backward from 32:** *32, 31, 30, 29, 28.*

  > If your child has trouble, have him first point to the numbers on the 100 Chart before reciting them from memory.

- Have your child rhythmically recite the Time Chant. See Lesson 24.1 (page 376) for the full chant.

- Play Subtract from 10 Memory. See Lesson 9.3 (page 147) for directions.

  > If your child can easily subtract from 10, play Subtraction Tic-Tac-Toe or Subtraction Climb to the Top instead.

Activity: Solve Money Word Problems

You have been learning to count and compare money. Today, you'll solve money word problems. Read the following word problems to your child. Have him model each problem with play money and then write and solve an equation to match.

> Your child learned how to solve mental math problems like these in Unit 6. But, don't be concerned if he struggles to find the answers at first, since children often find it challenging to apply their skills to a new context (in this case, money rather than bags of cookies). If your child has trouble, remind him of the work he did in Unit 6 and reassure him that he can think about the ten-dollar bills the same way he thought about the bags of 10 counters.

- **You have $50. Then, you spend $20 on a toy. How much money do you have now?** *$30.*

$$50 - 20 = 30$$

- **You have $20. Then, you earn $20 more. How much money do you have now?** *$40.*

$$20 + 20 = 40$$

- **You have $45. Then, you earn $10 more. How much money do you have now?** *$55.*

$$45 + 10 = 55$$

- **You have $55. Then, you earn $1 more. How much money do you have now?** *$56.*

$$55 + 1 = 56$$

Activity: Practice Written Word Problems

Show your child workbook page 24.4A. **Let's practice the steps for solving word problems.**

The first step is to read the problem slowly and carefully. Have your child read aloud the first problem (or read it to him). Discuss how the illustration matches the words.

You have $40.
Then, you earn $20 more.
How much do you have now?

The next step is to write an equation to match the problem. Have your child write an equation to match the problem in the space provided on the worksheet.

$$40 \oplus 20 = \underline{\hspace{2cm}}$$

The final step is to complete the equation and write the answer in the sentence.

$$40 \oplus 20 = 60$$

I have $ 60 .

Workbook: Solve Money Word Problems and Review

Have your child complete workbook pages 24.4A and 24.4B. Allow your child to model the problems with play money as needed.

Lesson 24.5
Enrichment and Review (Optional)

	Purpose	Materials
Warm-up	• Count to 100 by 1s, 2s, 5s, or 10s • Review memory work • Review your child's favorite or most challenging activities from Week 24	• Varies, depending on the activities you choose
Picture Book	• Understand small amounts of money can be saved to make larger purchases	• *A Chair for My Mother,* by Vera B. Williams
Enrichment Activity	• Practice counting out paper bills for a purchase	• Toy catalog or access to a website with items your child would like to buy • Play money

Warm-up: Counting, Memory Work, and Review

- Have your child count to 100 by 1s, 2s, 5s, or 10s. (Choose whichever counting sequence your child needs to practice the most.)

- Quiz your child on the memory work through Week 24. See page 499 for the full list.

- If you have time, repeat one or two of the activities from this week's lessons. Choose activities your child especially enjoyed or found challenging.

Math Picture Book: *A Chair for My Mother*

Read *A Chair for My Mother,* by Vera B. Williams. After you read, discuss the importance of saving and your child's experiences with saving money.

Enrichment Activity: Shopping Spree

Give your child 10 ten-dollar play bills. Have him choose items he would like to buy from a toy catalog or website and pretend to pay for each item with the play money.

Help your child trade 1 ten-dollar bill for 10 one-dollar bills if he needs smaller bills for the purchases. If any of the prices involve cents, round them to the nearest dollar.

Have him continue to choose items until he has spent all the money.

Week 24 Answer Key

24.1A

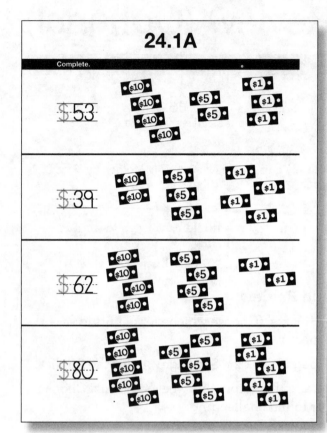

Complete.

$53

$39

$62

$80

24.1B

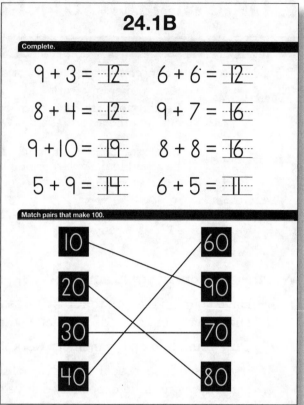

Complete.

$9 + 3 = 12$ $6 + 6 = 12$

$8 + 4 = 12$ $9 + 7 = 16$

$9 + 10 = 19$ $8 + 8 = 16$

$5 + 9 = 14$ $6 + 5 = 11$

Match pairs that make 100.

24.2A

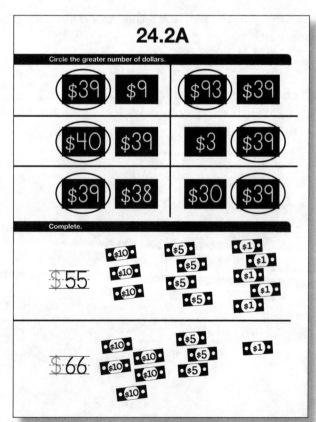

Circle the greater number of dollars.

($39) $9   ($93) $39

($40) $39 $3 ($39)

($39) $38 $30 ($39)

Complete.

$55

$66

24.2B

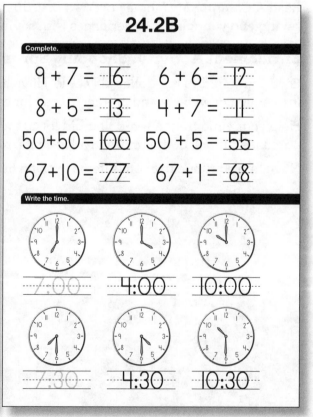

Complete.

$9 + 7 = 16$ $6 + 6 = 12$

$8 + 5 = 13$ $4 + 7 = 11$

$50 + 50 = 100$ $50 + 5 = 55$

$67 + 10 = 77$ $67 + 1 = 68$

Write the time.

7:00   4:00   10:00

7:30   4:30   10:30

Week 24 Answer Key

24.3A

Match.

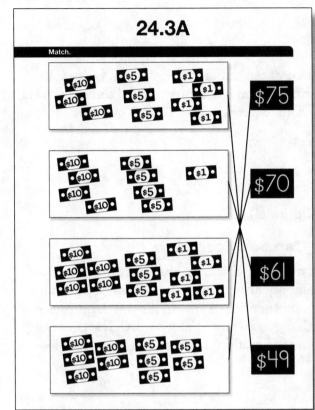

24.3B

Complete.

$$10 - 6 = 4 \qquad 10 - 9 = 1$$
$$8 - 7 = 1 \qquad 9 - 3 = 6$$
$$8 - 3 = 5 \qquad 8 - 4 = 4$$
$$9 - 2 = 7 \qquad 7 - 6 = 1$$

Complete or trace.

1 year = 12 months

1 week = 7 days

1 day = 24 hours

1 hour = 60 minutes

1 minute = 60 seconds

24.4A

Complete the equations and sentences to match the word problems.

You have $40.
Then, you earn $20 more.
How much do you have now?

$$40 + 20 = 60$$

I have $60.

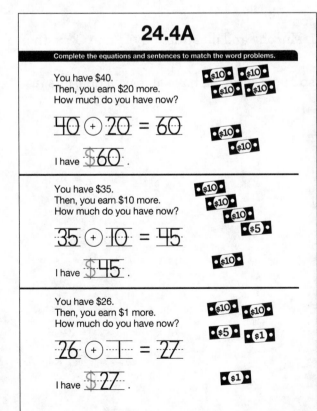

You have $35.
Then, you earn $10 more.
How much do you have now?

$$35 + 10 = 45$$

I have $45.

You have $26.
Then, you earn $1 more.
How much do you have now?

$$26 + 1 = 27$$

I have $27.

24.4B

Complete.

$$9 + 2 = 11 \qquad 6 + 8 = 14$$
$$8 + 8 = 16 \qquad 6 + 7 = 13$$
$$30 + 50 = 80 \qquad 30 + 5 = 35$$
$$79 + 10 = 89 \qquad 79 + 1 = 80$$

Write the time.

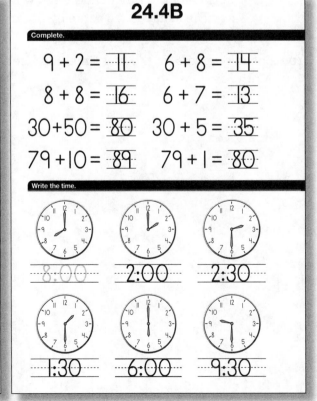

8:00   2:00   2:30

1:30   6:00   9:30

Week 25
Coins

Overview

Last week, your child learned to count combinations of ten-dollar, five-dollar, and one-dollar bills. This week, your child will use similar reasoning to count combinations of dimes, nickels, and pennies. You'll also introduce her to quarters and teach her how to count quarters by 25s.

Lesson 25.1   Count Coins
Lesson 25.2   Race to 100¢
Lesson 25.3   Quarters
Lesson 25.4   Coin Word Problems
Lesson 25.5   Enrichment and Review (Optional)

Teaching Math with Confidence: Looks Can Be Deceiving

As your child counts and compares quantities of money in this unit, she's gaining hands-on experience with a fundamental principle of mathematical reasoning: looks can be deceiving! Just because one pile of money looks larger than another doesn't mean it's worth more. For example, a pile of 58 pennies looks much larger than 3 quarters—but it's worth less. Learning to count and measure (rather than trusting a visual estimation) is an important part of learning to think mathematically.

Extra Materials Needed for Week 25

- Printed 12-month calendar (January-December)
- Clock with hands
- For optional Enrichment and Review Lesson:
  - × *The Penny Pot*, written by Stuart J. Murphy and illustrated by Lynne Cravath
  - × Coins to spend

You'll need quarters for the first time this week, so make sure you have at least 4 quarters in your Math Kit.

Lesson 25.1
Count Coins

	Purpose	Materials
Warm-up	• Practice shifting counting sequences on the 100 Chart • Practice memory work • Review subtraction facts	• 100 Chart (Blackline Master 3) • Subtraction Tic-Tac-Toe game board (on Workbook page 10.1A) • Playing cards • Counters
Activities	• Sort, order, and count coin combinations	• Coins • 100 Chart (Blackline Master 3) • Counter
Workbook	• Count coin combinations	• Workbook pages 25.1A and 25.1B

Warm-up: Counting, Memory Work, and Review

- **Let's pretend you're a counting robot again.** Draw a "computer panel" as in Lesson 17.4.

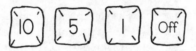

- × **Beep!** Press the 10 button. *10, 20, 30.*
- × **Beep!** Press the 5 button. *35, 40, 45.*
- × **Beep!** Press the 1 button. *46, 47, 48, 49.*
- × **Beep!** Press the Off button once your child reaches 49.

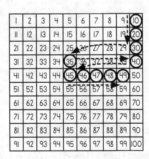

- Have your child rhythmically recite the Time Chant. See Lesson 24.1 (page 376) for the full chant.
- Play Subtraction Tic-Tac-Toe. See Lesson 10.1 (page 158) for directions.

Activity: Count Coin Combinations

Last week, you learned how to organize and count paper bills. This week, we'll focus on coins. Today, you'll learn how to organize and count coin combinations, just like you learned how to organize and count paper bills.

Mix up 3 dimes, 3 nickels, and 4 pennies on the table.

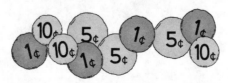

We follow the same 3 steps when we count coins as when we count paper bills: sort, order, and count. First, put each type of coin in its own pile. Have your child sort the coins by type.

Next, put the piles in order from the coins with the greatest value to the coins with the least value. Help your child put the piles in order as shown.

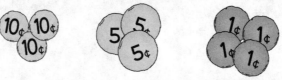

Last, count the coins. Start by counting the coins with the greatest value. Have your child count the coins: *10, 20, 30, 35, 40, 45, 46, 47, 48, 49. 49¢.*

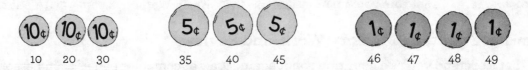

Your child may notice that the numbers she says as she counts the money are the same as the numbers she counted on the 100 Chart in the warm-up. If she doesn't, point out that counting money is like "robot counting," since you shift from one counting sequence to another.

If your child has trouble shifting from one counting sequence to another, have her move a counter on the 100 Chart to match the value of each coin as she counts. For the above coin combination, she would move the counter as follows:

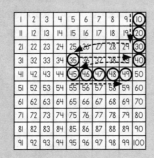

Have your child sort, order, and count the following coin combinations. Mix up the coins before giving them to your child.

- 6 dimes, 2 nickels, and 3 pennies (*10, 20, 30, 40, 50, 60, 65, 70, 71, 72, 73. 73¢*)
- 5 dimes, 5 nickels, and 5 pennies (*10, 20, 30, 40, 50, 55, 60, 65, 70, 75, 76, 77, 78, 79, 80. 80¢*)
- 1 dime, 6 nickels, and 1 penny (*10, 15, 20, 25, 30, 35, 40, 41. 41¢*)

Workbook: Count Coins and Review

Have your child complete workbook pages 25.1A and 25.1B. If your child has trouble counting the coins on the page, have her place a real coin on top of each printed coin first. Also allow her to use the 100 Chart as needed.

Lesson 25.2
Race to 100¢

	Purpose	Materials
Warm-up	• Count by 10s starting at a number other than 0 • Practice memory work • Review take-away subtraction word problems	• 100 Chart (Blackline Master 3), optional • Play money
Activities	• Practice counting coin combinations	• Coins • 100 Chart (Blackline Master 3) • Counter • Playing cards
Workbook	• Count coin combinations	• Workbook pages 25.2A and 25.2B

Warm-up: Counting, Memory Work, and Review

- **Count by 10s starting at 2.** *2, 12, 22, 32, 42, 52, 62, 72, 82, 92.* Have your child point to the numbers on the 100 Chart only if needed.

- **Name the even numbers in order to 20.** *2, 4, 6, 8, 10, 12, 14, 16, 18, 20.* **Name the odd numbers in order to 19.** *1, 3, 5, 7, 9, 11, 13, 15, 17, 19.*

- Read the following word problems to your child. Have him model each problem with counters or play money and then write and solve an equation to match.

    × **You have 8 cookies. Then you eat 7. How many do you have left?** *1.*

    $$8 - 7 = 1$$

    × **You have $9. Then you spend $5. How much money do you have left?** *$4.*

    $$9 - 5 = 4$$

    What do these word problems have in common? *Sample answers: Both are about using things up. You can use subtraction to solve both problems.*

Activity: Count Coin Combinations

In the last lesson, you learned how to organize and count coins. Today, you'll practice counting coins some more.

Show your child each of the following coin combinations. Mix up the coins in each combination, and ask your child to sort, order, and count the money. If needed, have him use the 100 Chart to track his counting (as in Lesson 25.1).

- 5 dimes, 8 nickels, 10 pennies *(10, 20, 30, 40, 50, 55, 60, 65, 70, 75, 80, 85, 90, 91, 92, 93, 94, 95, 96, 97, 98, 99, 100. 100¢)*
- 9 dimes, 2 nickels *(10, 20, 30, 40, 50, 60, 70, 80, 90, 95, 100. 100¢.)*
- 4 dimes, 11 nickels, 5 pennies *(10, 20, 30, 40, 45, 50, 55, 60, 65, 70, 75, 80, 85, 90, 95, 96, 97, 98, 99, 100. 100¢)*

What do all of these coin combinations have in common? *All of them equal 100¢.* **Some of the combinations have a lot of coins, and some of them have only a few coins. But they all are worth the same amount.**

See the Week 25 **Teaching Math with Confidence** for more on this fundamental math principle.

Activity: Play Race to 100¢

Play one round of Race to 100¢.

Race to 100¢

Materials: Aces, 5s, and 10s from a deck of cards (12 cards total); coins

Object of the Game: Be the first player to collect 100 cents.

Shuffle the cards and place them in a face-down pile. Make a simple scorecard to record the score.

Sam	
Mom	

On your turn flip over a card. Take a coin whose value matches the number on the card (take a penny if you draw an ace, a nickel if you draw a 5, or a dime if you draw a 10). Count the value of your coins and write the new value on a piece of paper.

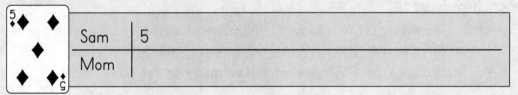

Sam	5
Mom	

If you have a combination of coins worth 10¢ (2 nickels, 1 nickel and 5 pennies, or 10 pennies), trade them for a dime.

Take turns flipping over a card, taking the corresponding coin, and counting and recording the value of the coins. Continue until one player reaches 100 cents.

Sam	5 15 16 26 36 41 42 52 57 67 68 78 88 98 103
Mom	5 6 16 17 22 23 24 29 39 44 45 50 60 65

Most first-graders will need to count their entire pile of coins after each turn (rather than mentally adding the new coin to the previous total). Your child will learn mental addition with two-digit numbers in Unit 11.

Workbook: Count Coins and Review

Have your child complete workbook pages 25.2A and 25.2B. If your child has trouble counting the coins on the page, have him place a real coin on top of each printed coin first. Also allow him to use the 100 Chart as needed.

Lesson 25.3
Quarters

	Purpose	Materials
Warm-up	• Count backward from any number between 1 and 100 • Practice memory work • Review telling time on a clock with hands	• 100 Chart (Blackline Master 3), optional • Clock with hands
Activities	• Learn quarters are worth 25¢ • Learn to count quarters by 25s	• Coins
Workbook	• Count coin combinations	• Workbook pages 25.3A and 25.3B

Warm-up: Counting, Memory Work, and Review

- Have your child count backward from the following numbers. Stop her after she reaches the last number listed in the sample answers.

    × **Count backward from 81:** *81, 80, 79, 78, 77.*
    × **Count backward from 53:** *53, 52, 51, 50, 49.*
    × **Count backward from 90:** *90, 89, 88, 87, 86.*

    > If your child has trouble, have her first point to the numbers on the 100 Chart and then try to recite them from memory.

- **Wink your left eye. Wink your right eye.**

- Set a clock with hands to the following times and have your child read the times: 5:00, 5:30, 8:00, 9:30, 11:30.

Activity: Introduce Quarters

In the last two lessons, you learned how to organize and count dimes, nickels, and pennies. Today, you'll learn about another type of coin: the quarter.

Show your child a quarter. **This coin is a quarter. It's worth 25 cents. What do you notice about how the quarter looks?** *Sample answers: it's silver; it's round; it's larger than a dime, nickel, or penny.* Read the writing on the coin to your child and point out the word "quarter."

A quarter is worth 25 cents. How many pennies make 25 cents? *25.* Count out 25 pennies with your child and place them next to the quarter.

How many nickels make 25¢? *5.* If your child isn't sure, have her count nickels by 5s until she reaches 25. Place 5 nickels next to the quarter.

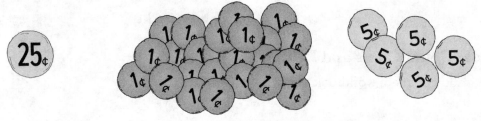

How many dimes make 25¢? *Sample answer: That's not possible with only dimes!* Allow your child to experiment with dimes to discover it's not possible to make 25¢ from dimes alone. Place 2 dimes and 1 nickel next to the quarter. **2 dimes and 1 nickel make 25¢.**

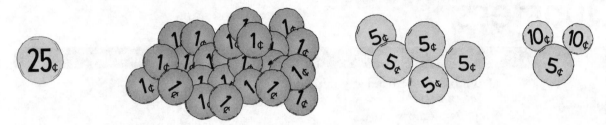

These piles have different numbers of coins in them, but they all are worth the same amount: 25 cents.

These are only a few of the possible ways to make 25¢. If your child is interested, allow her to experiment with the coins to find some more.

Activity: Count Quarters by 25s

Since each quarter is worth 25 cents, we count quarters by 25s.

Place 4 quarters on a piece of paper. **1 quarter is worth 25 cents.** Write 25¢ below the first quarter.

25¢

25 plus 25 equals 50. So, 2 quarters are worth 50 cents. Write 50¢ below the second quarter.

50 plus 25 equals 75. So, 3 quarters are worth 75 cents. Write 75¢ below the third quarter.

75 plus 25 equals 100. So, 4 quarters are worth 100 cents. Write 100¢ below the fourth quarter.

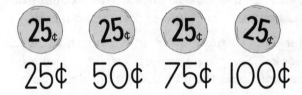

25¢ 50¢ 75¢ 100¢

Have your child practice counting the quarters by 25s: 25, 50, 75, 100.

Leave the quarters and paper out for your child to refer to as she completes workbook page 25.3A.

This lesson teaches your child to count by 25s by rote, since she has not yet learned how to add two-digit numbers.

Workbook: Count Coins and Review

Have your child complete workbook pages 25.3A and 25.3B.

Lesson 25.4
Coin Word Problems

	Purpose	Materials
Warm-up	• Count by 25s • Practice memory work • Review subtraction facts	• Subtraction Climb to the Top game board (Workbook page 11.1A) • Playing cards • Counters
Activities	• Solve word problems involving coins • Review adding and subtracting multiples of 10 • Review adding 1 or 10 to a two-digit number	• Coins
Workbook	• Solve word problems involving coins	• Workbook pages 25.4A and 25.4B

Warm-up: Counting, Memory Work, and Review

- Demonstrate how to count by 25s to 100: **25, 50, 75, 100.** Then, have your child try it on his own.

- Have your child rhythmically recite the Time Chant. See Lesson 24.1 (page 376) for the full chant.

- Play Subtraction Climb to the Top. See Lesson 11.1 (page 175) for directions.

Activity: Solve Coin Word Problems

You have been learning to count coins. Today, you'll solve word problems about coins.
Read the following word problems to your child. Have him model each problem with coins and then write and solve an equation to match.

- **You have 70¢. Then, you earn 30¢. How much money do you have now?** *100¢, or $1.*

$$70 + 30 = 100$$

- **You have 50¢. Then, you spend 40¢. How much money do you have now?** *10¢.*

$$50 - 40 = 10$$

- **You have 79¢. Then, you earn 10¢ more. How much money do you have now?** *89¢.*

$$79 + 10 = 89$$

- **You have 79¢. Then, you earn 1¢ more. How much money do you have now?** *80¢.*

$$79 + 1 = 80$$

These word problems give your child practice with the adding and subtracting skills he learned in Unit 6. He will build on these skills with more mental math in Unit 11.

Activity: Practice Written Word Problems

Show your child workbook page 25.4A. **Let's practice the steps for solving word problems.**

What's the first step? *Read the problem slowly and carefully.* Have your child read the first problem aloud (or read it aloud to him). Discuss how the illustration matches the words.

You have 90¢.
Then, you spend 50¢.
How much do you have now?

What's the next step? *Write an equation to match the problem.* Have your child write an equation to match the problem in the space provided on the worksheet.

$$90 - 50 = \underline{}$$

What's the final step? *Complete the equation and write the answer in the sentence.*

$$90 - 50 = 40$$

I have 40 ¢.

Workbook: Coin Word Problems and Review

Have your child complete workbook pages 25.4A and 25.4B. Allow your child to act out the problems with play money as needed.

Lesson 25.5
Enrichment and Review (Optional)

	Purpose	Materials
Warm-up	• Count to 100 by 1s, 2s, 5s, or 10s • Review memory work • Review your child's favorite or most challenging activities from Week 25	• Varies, depending on the activities you choose
Picture Book	• Appreciate how coins are used in real life	• *The Penny Pot,* written by Stuart J. Murphy and illustrated by Lynne Cravath
Enrichment Activity	• Use coins in real life	• Coins to spend

Warm-up: Counting, Memory Work, and Review

- Have your child count to 100 by 1s, 2s, 5s, or 10s. (Choose whichever counting sequence your child needs to practice the most.)

- Quiz your child on the memory work through Week 24. See page 499 for the full list.

- If you have time, repeat one or two of the activities from this week's lessons. Choose activities your child especially enjoyed or found challenging.

Math Picture Book: *The Penny Pot*

Read *The Penny Pot,* written by Stuart J. Murphy and illustrated by Lynne Cravath. As you read, use real pennies to model the number of pennies in the penny pot.

Enrichment Activity: Use Coins at the Store

Take a field trip to a store and allow your child to buy a small item that costs less than a dollar. Help her count out the correct coins to pay for the item.

Week 25 Answer Key

25.1A

Complete.

10 10 10 10 5¢ 1¢ 1¢ 1¢ → 48¢

10 10 5¢ 5¢ 5¢ 1¢ 1¢ → 37¢

5¢ 5¢ 5¢ 5¢ 5¢ 1¢ → 26¢

5¢ 5¢ 5¢ 5¢ 1¢ 1¢ 1¢ → 24¢

10¢ 10¢ 10¢ 10¢ 10¢ 10¢ 5¢ 5¢ 5¢ 5¢ 5¢ 1¢ 1¢ 1¢ → 88¢

10¢ 10¢ 10¢ 10¢ 10¢ 5¢ 1¢ 1¢ 1¢ 1¢ 1¢ 1¢ → 61¢

25.1B

Complete.

9 + 9 = 18	6 + 7 = 13
8 + 7 = 15	3 + 7 = 10
1 + 10 = 11	5 + 8 = 13
2 + 9 = 11	3 + 5 = 8

Write the time.

8:30   11:00   12:30

12:00   4:00   4:30

25.2A

Complete.

10¢ 10¢ 10¢ 10¢ 10¢ 10¢ 5¢ 5¢ 5¢ 5¢ 5¢ 5¢ 1¢ 1¢ → 92¢

10¢ 10¢ 10¢ 10¢ 10¢ 10¢ 10¢ 5¢ 5¢ 5¢ 5¢ 1¢ 1¢ 1¢ → 93¢

10¢ 10¢ 10¢ 10¢ 5¢ 5¢ 5¢ 5¢ 5¢ 1¢ 1¢ → 68¢

10¢ 10¢ 10¢ 10¢ 10¢ 5¢ 5¢ 1¢ 1¢ 1¢ 1¢ 1¢ 1¢ → 66¢

25.2B

Complete.

9 − 7 = 2	10 − 5 = 5
9 − 3 = 6	8 − 7 = 1
10 − 7 = 3	8 − 4 = 4
7 − 5 = 2	9 − 5 = 4

Complete.

1 foot = 12 inches

Complete the equation and sentence to match the word problem.

There are 8 flowers.
3 are red. The rest are yellow.
How many flowers are yellow?

8 − 3 = 5

5 flowers are yellow.

Week 25 Answer Key

25.3A

Complete.

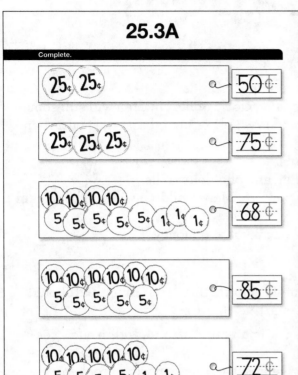

25.3B

Complete.

$10 - 6 = 4$ $7 - 3 = 4$

$8 - 6 = 2$ $9 - 1 = 8$

$8 - 5 = 3$ $9 - 8 = 1$

$10 - 2 = 8$ $7 - 4 = 3$

Write the time.

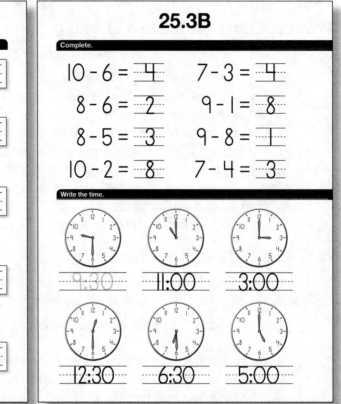

9:30   11:00   3:00

12:30   6:30   5:00

25.4A

Complete the equations and sentences to match the word problems.

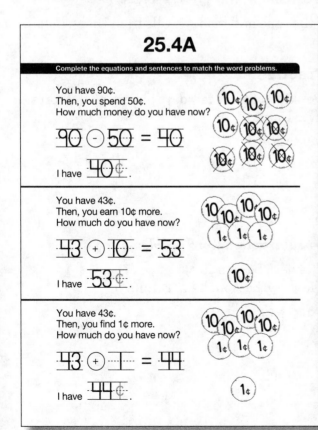

You have 90¢.
Then, you spend 50¢.
How much money do you have now?

$90 - 50 = 40$

I have 40¢.

You have 43¢.
Then, you earn 10¢ more.
How much do you have now?

$43 + 10 = 53$

I have 53¢.

You have 43¢.
Then, you find 1¢ more.
How much do you have now?

$43 + 1 = 44$

I have 44¢.

25.4B

Complete.

$9 + 8 = 17$ $6 + 9 = 15$

$8 + 6 = 14$ $4 + 7 = 11$

$60 + 20 = 80$ $60 + 2 = 62$

$29 + 10 = 39$ $29 + 1 = 30$

Use a ruler to measure the ribbons in inches.

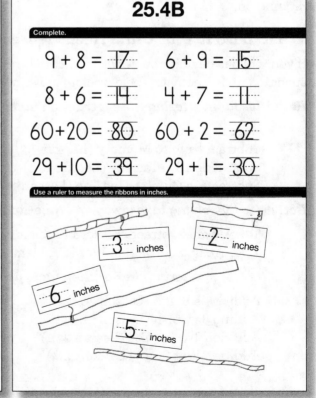

3 inches   2 inches

6 inches

5 inches

Unit 9 Checkpoint

What to Expect at the End of Unit 9

By the end of Unit 9, most children will be able to:

- Identify the date and day of the week on a monthly calendar.
- Tell time to the hour and half hour on an analog clock. Some children will still sometimes have trouble remembering which hand is which, or identifying the hour when the hour hand is between two numbers.
- Know most of the common time equivalents.
- Count combinations of ten-dollar, five-dollar, and one-dollar bills.
- Count combination of dimes, nickels, and pennies. Many children will still be working on counting quarters by 25s.
- Solve addition and subtraction word problems involving money.

Is Your Child Ready to Move on?

In Unit 10, your child will begin to learn the rest of the subtraction facts. Your child should have already mastered the following skills before starting Unit 10:

- Know the answers to the subtraction facts with numbers up to 10, within a few seconds.
- Write equations to match take-away and take-apart subtraction word problems.
- Know the answers to most of the addition facts (up to 10 + 10) without counting on fingers or counting one-by-one. It's fine if she is still working to master a few of the facts, but she should know the answers to most of them within a few seconds.

Your child does not need to have mastered all of the time and money skills from Unit 9 before moving on.

What to Do If Your Child Needs More Practice

If your child is having trouble with any of the above skills, spend a few days practicing the corresponding review activities below before moving on to Unit 10.

Activities for mastering the subtraction facts up to 10

- Race to 0 (Lesson 9.2)
- Subtract from 10 Memory (Lesson 9.3)
- Subtraction Tic-Tac-Toe (Lesson 10.1)
- Subtraction Climb to the Top (Lesson 11.1)

Activities for solving take-away and take-apart subtraction word problems

- Take-Away Subtraction Word Problems (Review, Lesson 16.3)
- Take-Apart Subtraction Word Problems (Review, Lessons 12.2, 17.1, 18.3)

Activities for mastering the addition facts up to 10 + 10

- Adding 9s Bingo (Lesson 20.1)
- Adding 8s Crash (Lesson 21.1)
- Addition Tic-Tac-Toe (Lesson 22.1)
- Addition War (5-10) (Lesson 22.4)

Unit 10
Subtraction Facts in the Teens

Overview

In Unit 10, you will introduce your child to the rest of the subtraction facts, up to 18 – 9. He will build on the strategies he learned in Unit 4, when he learned the subtraction facts up to 10. He will also solve more take-away and take-apart subtraction word problems, and he will learn how to use subtraction in comparison situations.

Many first graders are not developmentally ready to fully master these more-challenging subtraction facts. Don't be concerned if your child uses the ten-frames and counters to find answers throughout these lessons, since this unit is meant as an introduction to the subtraction facts in the teens. Working on these facts now in first grade will make full mastery much easier in second grade.

Week 26	–2, –3, –4, and –5 Facts
Week 27	–8 and –9 Facts
Week 28	–6 and –7 Facts

What Your Child Will Learn

In this unit your child will learn to:

- solve subtraction facts up to 18 – 9
- use the relationship between addition and subtraction to solve subtraction problems
- solve subtraction word problems, including take-away, take-apart, and comparison problems

Recommended Math Picture Books (Optional)

These picture books are scheduled in the optional Enrichment and Review lessons at the end of each week.

- *Ready, Set, Hop!*, written by Stuart J. Murphy and illustrated by Jon Buller. Harper-Collins, 1996.
- *Math for All Seasons: Mind-Stretching Math Riddles*, written by Greg Tang and illustrated by Harry Briggs. Scholastic Paperbacks, 2005.
- *Counting on Frank*, by Rod Clement. Gareth Stevens Publishing, 1991.

Week 26
-2, -3, -4, and -5 Facts

Overview

This week, your child will learn how to subtract 2, 3, 4, or 5 from numbers greater than 10. You'll teach him to subtract counters from the ten-frame in two steps to find the answers to these subtraction facts.

Lesson 26.1   Introduce -2, -3, -4, and -5 Facts
Lesson 26.2   Practice -2, -3, -4, and -5 Facts
Lesson 26.3   Word Problems
Lesson 26.4   Review Fact Families
Lesson 26.5   Enrichment and Review (Optional)

Teaching Math with Confidence: Using a Two-Step Take-Away Strategy

In Week 10, you taught your child to subtract 3 or 4 from the numbers up to 10. He imagined removing counters from the ten-frame, and he used the dark line in the middle of the ten-frame as a visual anchor.

$$7 - 3 = 4$$

This week, your child will learn to subtract 2, 3, 4, and 5 from numbers greater than 10. You'll teach him to use a similar two-step take-away strategy. This approach works well for these facts since he can use the break between ten-frames to help visualize the problems. For example, to solve 12 – 3, you'll arrange 12 counters on the ten-frames.

Then, your child will remove 3 counters in two steps. First, he'll take away the 2 counters on the bottom ten-frame. Then, he'll remove 1 more counter to see that the answer is 9.

$$12 - 3 = 9$$

Extra Materials Needed for Week 26

- For optional Enrichment and Review Lesson:
    - × *Ready, Set, Hop!*, written by Stuart J. Murphy and illustrated by Jon Buller
    - × Tape

Lesson 26.1
Introduce -2, -3, -4, and -5 Facts

	Purpose	Materials
Warm-up	• Count by 25s • Practice memory work • Review addition facts	• Coins
Activities	• Introduce the -2, -3, -4, and -5 facts	• Double ten-frames (Blackline Master 1) • Counters • Subtraction Roll and Cover game boards (workbook page 26.1A) • Die
Workbook	• Practice the -2, -3, -4, and -5 facts	• Workbook page 26.1B

Warm-up: Counting, Memory Work, and Review

- Have your child count by 25s to 100: 25, 50, 75, 100.

- Show your child a penny, nickel, dime, and quarter, and have her tell the name and value of each coin.

- Do a brief oral review of the following addition facts. Ask your child each addition fact and have her give the answer as quickly as possible.

    ×   9 + 2 = *11*
    ×   5 + 9 = *14*
    ×   8 + 4 = *12*
    ×   6 + 5 = *11*
    ×   3 + 9 = *12*
    ×   5 + 8 = *13*
    ×   7 + 4 = *11*
    ×   3 + 8 = *11*
    ×   5 + 7 = *12*
    ×   4 + 9 = *13*

> Reviewing these addition facts prepares your child to find answers to the related subtraction facts in the lesson.

Activity: Introduce -2, -3, -4, and -5 Subtraction Facts

You have already learned many of the subtraction facts. In this unit, you'll learn how to find answers to the rest of the subtraction facts. These facts are especially tricky, so it's okay if you don't learn them all by heart in first grade. We'll work on them more in second grade, and the work you do this year will make it easier to learn them all next year!

This week, you'll work on problems where you subtract 2, 3, 4, or 5 from numbers greater than 10.

Write 14 – 5 = on a piece of paper and place 14 counters on the ten-frame. **Let's take away 5 counters. I'll do it in 2 steps. First, I take away the 4 counters on the bottom ten-frame.** Take away the 4 counters on the bottom ten-frame.

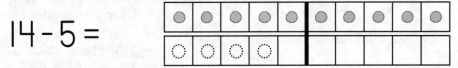

How many more counters do I need to take away? *1*. Remove 1 more counter. **How many counters are left?** *9*. Have your child complete the written equation and read it aloud: *14 minus 5 equals 9.*

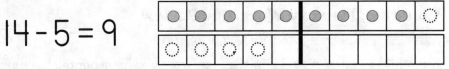

Have your child use similar reasoning to complete the following subtraction equations. Encourage your child to remove the counters in 2 steps rather than counting one-by-one to find the answers.

- 11– 2 = *9*
- 12 – 4 = *8*
- 11 – 5 = *6*
- 12 – 3 = *9*
- 13 – 5 = *8*
- 11 – 4 = *7*
- 12 – 5 = *7*
- 11 – 3 = *8*
- 13 – 4 = *9*

Activity: Play Subtraction Roll and Cover

We're going to play a game called Subtraction Roll and Cover to practice these subtraction facts. Play one round of Subtraction Roll and Cover. Allow your child to use the tenframe and counters as needed.

Subtraction Roll and Cover

Materials: Subtraction Roll and Cover game boards (Workbook page 26.1A); counters; 1 die

Object of the Game: Be the first player to cover all the spaces on your game board.

Have each player choose a game board. On your turn, roll the die. Use the number you roll to create a subtraction problem with a number in a star and a number in a circle, so the circled number minus the number on the die equals the starred number. Cover both the circled number and starred number with counters.

$$\boxed{12} - \boxed{\because} = \star 9$$

For example, if you roll a 3, you could cover a circled 12 from the left side of the board and a starred 9 from the right side since 12 – 3 = 9. Or, you could choose to cover a circled 11 and a starred 8 since 11 – 3 = 8.

1s are wild. If you roll a 1, you may cover any one circled number and one starred number.

Take turns until one player covers all the spaces on her game board.

This game appears simple, but you increase your chance of winning if you are strategic about where you put your counters. As you and your child play the game over the course of the week, discuss the strategies that you find for placing your counters. For example: **I can only cover 14 if I roll a 5 or 6. So, I'm going to use this 5 that I rolled to cover a 14. Or, 11 is the only number I can cover if I roll a 2, so I'm going to save my 11 for when I roll a 2.**

Workbook: Practice Subtraction Facts and Review

Have your child complete workbook page 26.1B. Encourage your child to imagine removing counters from the printed ten-frames in 2 steps. If that is too challenging for her, have her model each problem with real counters on the double ten-frames instead.

 Save this workbook page with your math materials so you can play Subtraction Roll and Cover again.

Lesson 26.2
Practice -2, -3, -4, and -5 Facts

	Purpose	Materials
Warm-up	• Count combinations of paper bills • Practice memory work • Review reading the date on a calendar	• Play money • Coins • Printed 12-month calendar (January-December)
Activities	• Practice the -2, -3, -4, and -5 facts	• Double ten-frames (Blackline Master 1) • Counters • Subtraction Roll and Cover game boards (workbook page 26.1A) • Die
Workbook	• Practice the -2, -3, -4, and -5 facts	• Workbook pages 26.2A and 26.2B

Warm-up: Counting, Memory Work, and Review

- Mix up 3 ten-dollar bills, 5 five-dollar bills, and 6 one-dollar bills on the table. Have your child sort, order, and count the money. **How many dollars is this?** *$61.*

- Show your child a penny, nickel, dime, and quarter, and have him tell the name and value of each coin.

- Point to the current date on the calendar. Have your child read the date and identify the day of the week. Also point to a few other dates on the calendar and have your child read them and identify the days of the week.

Activity: Visualize -2, -3, -4, and -5 Facts

In the last lesson, you subtracted 2, 3, 4, or 5 from numbers greater than 10. Today, you'll practice visualizing these facts so you can "see" the answers in your head.

Put 13 counters on the ten-frame and cover the ten-frame with a piece of paper. Write 13 – 5 = on a piece of paper.

$$13 - 5 =$$

Imagine taking away 5 of the counters. How many would be left? *8.* Encourage your child to visualize removing the counters in 2 steps: first the 3 counters on the bottom ten-frame, then the 2 counters on the top ten-frame.

$$13 - 5 =$$

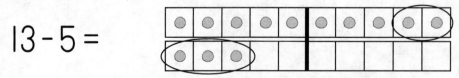

Encourage your child to imagine removing the counters in 2 steps.

Once your child has visualized removing the counters, have him physically remove the 5 counters to check his answer. Then, have him complete the written equation and read it: *13 minus 5 equals 8.*

Repeat with the following subtraction facts. For each, encourage your child to visualize removing the counters in 2 steps before physically removing them.

- 11 – 4 = *7*
- 12 – 5 = *7*
- 11 – 3 = *8*
- 13 – 4 = *9*
- 11– 2 = *9*
- 12 – 4 = *8*
- 11 – 5 = *6*
- 12 – 3 = *9*
- 14 – 5 = *9*

This activity helps your child learn to visualize the subtraction problems so he can transition to finding the answers mentally.

Activity: Play Subtraction Roll and Cover

Play one round of Subtraction Roll and Cover. See Lesson 26.1 (page 405) for directions.

Keep the ten-frame and counters available as you play. Encourage your child to visualize removing the counters before physically taking them away.

Workbook: Practice Subtraction Facts and Review

Have your child complete workbook pages 26.2A and 26.2B. Encourage your child to imagine removing counters from the printed ten-frames in 2 steps. If that is too challenging for him, have him model the problems with real counters on the double ten-frames instead.

If your child feels overwhelmed by the number of problems on workbook page 26.2A, reassure him that there is a pattern to the problems that will help him solve them. After your child finishes, discuss these patterns. For example: **What do you notice about the answers in each set of problems?** *They go down by 1.* **Why do you think that happens?** *Sample answer: We take away 1 more each time.*

Lesson 26.3
Word Problems

	Purpose	Materials
Warm-up	• Count quarters by 25s • Practice memory work • Review the -2, -3, -4, and -5 facts	• Coins • Counters • Subtraction Roll and Cover game boards (workbook page 26.1A) • Die • Double ten-frames (Blackline Master 1)
Activities	• Solve word problems	• Double ten-frames (Blackline Master 1) • Counters
Workbook	• Solve word problems • Practice the -2, -3, -4, and -5 facts	• Workbook pages 26.3A and 26.3B

Warm-up: Counting, Memory Work, and Review

- Place 4 quarters on the table and have your child count them by 25s. **How many cents is this?** *100¢.*

- Show your child a penny, nickel, dime, and quarter, and have her tell the name and value of each coin.

- Play one round of Subtraction Roll and Cover. See Lesson 26.1 (page 405) for directions. Keep the ten-frame and counters available as you play.

Activity: Solve Subtraction Word Problems

You have been working on subtracting 2, 3, 4, or 5 from numbers greater than 10. Today, you'll use these facts to solve word problems. Most will be subtraction, but there may be an addition problem, too!

Ask your child the following word problems. Have your child model each problem with counters on the ten-frame and then write and solve an equation to match.

- **You have 12 pieces of candy. Then you eat 3 pieces. How many pieces do you have left?** *9.*

$$12 - 3 = 9$$

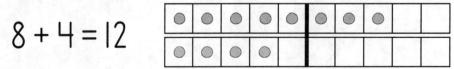

- **You have 8 pieces of caramel candy and 4 pieces of chocolate candy. How many pieces of candy do you have?** *12.*

$$8 + 4 = 12$$

- **You have 13 pieces of candy. 5 are grape and the rest are strawberry. How many are strawberry?** *8.*

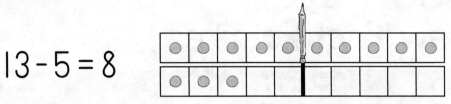

Place a pencil after the first 5 counters to show you are separating the 13 counters into 2 groups.

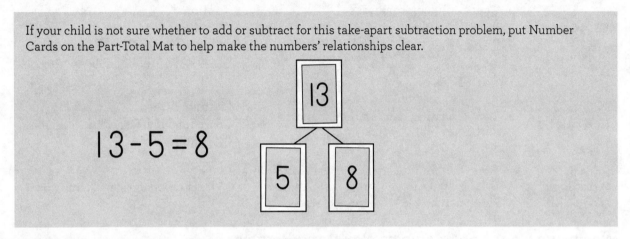

If your child is not sure whether to add or subtract for this take-apart subtraction problem, put Number Cards on the Part-Total Mat to help make the numbers' relationships clear.

Workbook: Solve Word Problems and Review

Have your child complete workbook pages 26.3A and 26.3B. Allow your child to use counters and ten-frames as needed to solve the subtraction problems on 26.3B.

Lesson 26.4
Review Fact Families

	Purpose	Materials
Warm-up	• Count coin combinations • Practice memory work • Review the -2, -3, -4, and -5 facts	• Coins • 100 Chart (Blackline Master 3), optional • Counters • Subtraction Roll and Cover game boards (workbook page 26.1A) • Die
Activities	• Review writing fact families to match the Part-Total Mat	• Number Cards • Part-Total Mat (Blackline Master 4) • Counters
Workbook	• Write fact families to match the Part-Total Mat • Practice the -2, -3, -4, and -5 facts	• Workbook pages 26.4A and 26.4B

Warm-up: Counting, Memory Work, and Review

- Mix up 4 dimes, 3 nickels, and 2 pennies on the table. Have your child sort, order, and count the coins. **How many cents is this?** *57¢.*

- Have your child rhythmically say the Tens Chant: *1 ten. Ten! 2 tens. Twenty! etc.* See Lesson 15.1 (page 236) for the full chant.

- Play one round of Subtraction Roll and Cover. See Lesson 26.1 (page 405) for directions. Keep the ten-frame and counters available as you play.

Activity: Review Fact Families

You have been learning to subtract 2, 3, 4, or 5 from numbers in the teens. Today, we'll review how addition and subtraction are related so you can use what you know about addition to help solve subtraction problems next week.

In Week 27, you will teach your child to use missing addend equations to find answers to the -9 and -8 subtraction facts. Reviewing fact families in this lesson prepares your child to use addition to solve these subtraction problems.

Place Number Cards 9, 3, and 12 on the Part-Total Mat as shown. **Let's write a fact family for these numbers. First, use the numbers on the Part-Total Mat to write 2 addition equations.** *Child writes 9 + 3 = 12 and 3 + 9 = 12.*

$$9 + 3 = 12$$
$$3 + 9 = 12$$

Model the equations by joining a group of 9 counters and a group of 3 counters. **We can add numbers in any order. It doesn't matter whether we start with 9 and add 3, or whether we start with 3 and add 9. Either way, we end up with 12.**

Use the numbers on the Part-Total Mat to write 2 subtraction equations. *Child writes 12 – 9 = 3 and 12 – 3 = 9.* You may need to remind your child that subtraction equations begin with the total from the Part-Total Mat.

$$9 + 3 = 12$$
$$3 + 9 = 12$$
$$12 - 9 = 3$$
$$12 - 3 = 9$$

Model the equations by separating the 12 counters into a group of 9 and a group of 3. **If we subtract 9 from 12, we get 3. If we subtract 3 from 12, we get 9.**

Repeat this process with Number Cards 8, 5, and 13. Place them on the Part-Total Mat as shown, and guide your child to write the four equations in the fact family for these numbers. Also model the equation with counters so your child understands concretely how the parts and total relate to each other.

$$8 + 5 = 13$$
$$5 + 8 = 13$$
$$13 - 8 = 5$$
$$13 - 5 = 8$$

Workbook: Find Fact Families and Review

Have your child complete workbook pages 26.4A and 26.4B. Allow your child to use counters and ten-frames as needed to solve the subtraction problems on 26.4B.

Lesson 26.5
Enrichment and Review (Optional)

	Purpose	Materials
Warm-up	• Count to 100 by 1s, 2s, 5s, and 10s • Review memory work • Review your child's favorite or most challenging activities from Week 26	• Varies, depending on the activities you choose
Picture Book	• Understand addition and subtraction in the context of frogs' hops	• *Ready, Set, Hop!*, written by Stuart J. Murphy and illustrated by Jon Buller
Enrichment Activity	• Solve subtraction problems to catch a "fly" on the number path	• Number Cards 1-15 • Tape • Counter

Warm-up: Counting, Memory Work, and Review

- Have your child count to 100 by 1s, 2s, 5s, or 10s. (Choose whichever counting sequence your child needs to practice the most.)

- Quiz your child on the memory work through Week 26. See page 499 for the full list.

- If you have time, repeat one or two of the activities from this week's lessons. Choose activities your child especially enjoyed or found challenging.

Math Picture Book: *Ready, Set, Hop!*

Read *Ready, Set, Hop!*, written by Stuart J. Murphy and illustrated by Jon Buller. As you read, discuss how the equations match the frogs' hops.

If you read *How Big Is a Foot?* in Week 19, discuss the similarity between the two books. Just as the characters in that book measure the same length with different-sized feet, the two frogs in this book cover the same distance with hops of different lengths.

Enrichment Activity: Catch the Fly on the Number Path

Arrange Number Cards 1-15 in order on the floor. Tape the cards down so child can hop from one card to the other.

Pretend your child is a frog who wants to catch a fly, and pretend a counter is the fly. Have your child stand on one of the numbers from 11 to 15 and place the counter on a number that is 2-5 spaces away.

Ask your child to figure out how many hops he needs to take to "catch" the fly. (For example, if your child is on 12 and the fly is on 9, he needs to take 3 hops to catch the fly.) Have him hop accordingly to check his prediction.

Child

Repeat the game as long as your child is interested, and adjust the difficulty level to best meet your child's needs. Make sure to include some of the subtraction facts your child studied this week. (For example, to practice 13 – 4, have your child stand on 13 and place the counter 4 hops away on 9.)

Week 26 Answer Key

26.1A

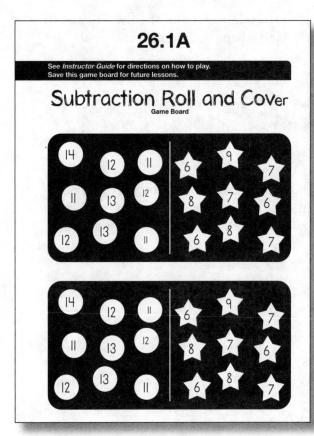

See *Instructor Guide* for directions on how to play.
Save this game board for future lessons.

Subtraction Roll and Cover
Game Board

26.1B

Complete.

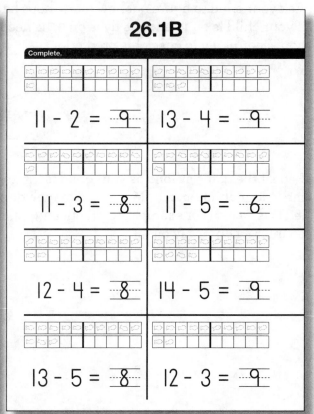

$11 - 2 = 9$ $13 - 4 = 9$

$11 - 3 = 8$ $11 - 5 = 6$

$12 - 4 = 8$ $14 - 5 = 9$

$13 - 5 = 8$ $12 - 3 = 9$

26.2A

Complete. Use the ten-frames to help.

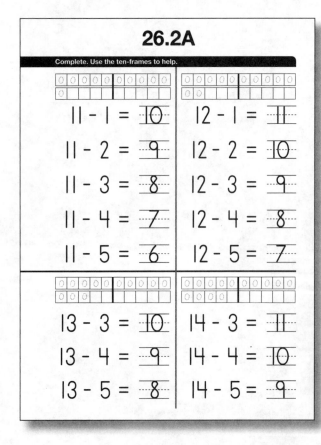

$11 - 1 = 10$ $12 - 1 = 11$

$11 - 2 = 9$ $12 - 2 = 10$

$11 - 3 = 8$ $12 - 3 = 9$

$11 - 4 = 7$ $12 - 4 = 8$

$11 - 5 = 6$ $12 - 5 = 7$

$13 - 3 = 10$ $14 - 3 = 11$

$13 - 4 = 9$ $14 - 4 = 10$

$13 - 5 = 8$ $14 - 5 = 9$

26.2B

Ethan made a bar graph of what he ate for lunch.
Use the bar graph to answer the questions.

My Lunch

Cheese sandwich

Peanut butter sandwich

Ham sandwich

How many times did he have a cheese sandwich?   5

How many times did he have a peanut butter sandwich?   6

How many times did he have a ham sandwich?   3

How many more times did he have peanut butter than ham?   3

How many more times did he have peanut butter than cheese?   1

How many more times did he have cheese than ham?   2

Week 26 Answer Key

26.3A

Complete the equations and sentences to match the word problems.

You have 13 stickers.
You use 5 stickers.
How many stickers are left?

13 ⊖ 5 = 8

There are 8 stickers left.

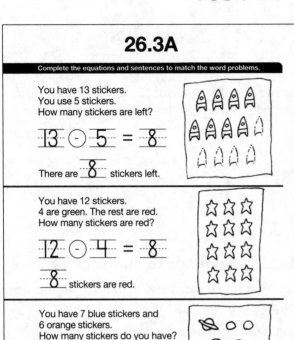

You have 12 stickers.
4 are green. The rest are red.
How many stickers are red?

12 ⊖ 4 = 8

8 stickers are red.

You have 7 blue stickers and
6 orange stickers.
How many stickers do you have?

7 ⊕ 6 = 13

I have 13 stickers.

26.3B

Complete.

$$13 - 4 = 9 \qquad 12 - 3 = 9$$
$$11 - 3 = 8 \qquad 14 - 5 = 9$$
$$12 - 5 = 7 \qquad 11 - 5 = 6$$
$$11 - 4 = 7 \qquad 12 - 4 = 8$$
$$13 - 5 = 8 \qquad 11 - 2 = 9$$

Write the time.

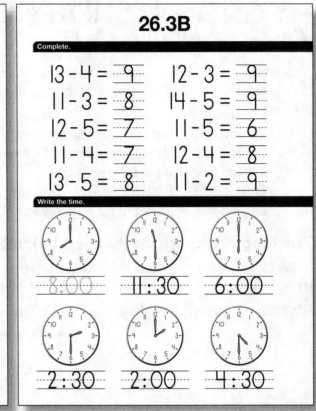

8:00   11:30   6:00

2:30   2:00   4:30

26.4A

Complete the fact families to match the Part-Total Diagrams.

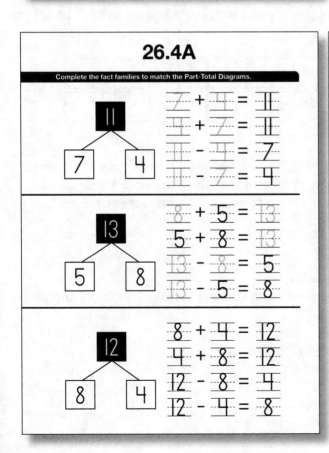

11
7   4

$$7 + 4 = 11$$
$$4 + 7 = 11$$
$$11 - 4 = 7$$
$$11 - 7 = 4$$

13
5   8

$$8 + 5 = 13$$
$$5 + 8 = 13$$
$$13 - 8 = 5$$
$$13 - 5 = 8$$

12
8   4

$$8 + 4 = 12$$
$$4 + 8 = 12$$
$$12 - 8 = 4$$
$$12 - 4 = 8$$

26.4B

Complete.

$$11 - 4 = 7 \qquad 12 - 3 = 9$$
$$11 - 2 = 9 \qquad 13 - 5 = 8$$
$$11 - 5 = 6 \qquad 14 - 5 = 9$$
$$12 - 4 = 8 \qquad 13 - 4 = 9$$
$$12 - 5 = 7 \qquad 11 - 3 = 8$$

Match the pairs that make 100.

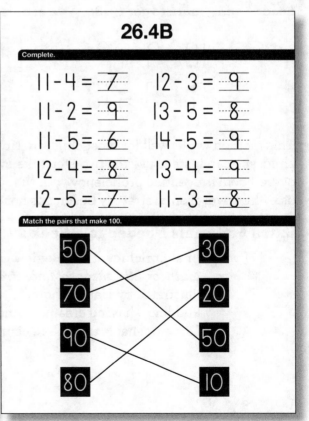

50   30
70   20
90   50
80   10

Week 27
-8 and -9 Subtraction Facts

Overview

This week, your child will learn how to use related addition facts to subtract 8 or 9 from numbers greater than 10. She'll also learn how to use subtraction to compare quantities in word problems.

Lesson 27.1	Introduce -9 Facts
Lesson 27.2	Use Subtraction to Compare
Lesson 27.3	Introduce -8 Facts
Lesson 27.4	Practice -9 and -8 Facts
Lesson 27.5	Enrichment and Review (Optional)

Teaching Math with Confidence: Using Missing Addends to Subtract 8 and 9

In Week 11, you taught your child to use missing addend equations to solve subtraction problems. This week, your child will use a similar strategy as she learns the -9 and -8 facts.

For example, your child will solve 13 – 9 by thinking "9 plus what equals 13?"

$$13 - 9 = ?$$
$$9 + ? = 13$$

You'll show her how to add in two steps to find the answer: **First, I add 1 to make 10. Then, I need to add 3 more to get 13. So, 9 + 4 equals 13.**

$$13 - 9 = ?$$
$$9 + 4 = 13$$

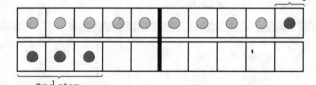

This method works well for most children. However, if you find that it doesn't "click" for your child, she can instead use the two-step take-away approach that she learned in Week 26. The overall goal is eventual proficiency with the subtraction facts, and it's fine for your child to use whichever mental strategy best helps her achieve this.

Extra Materials Needed for Week 27

- For optional Enrichment and Review Lesson:
    - × *Math for All Seasons: Mind-Stretching Math Riddles,* written by Greg Tang and illustrated by Harry Briggs
    - × Pudding, shaving cream, or finger paint
    - × Large washable tray, clean counter, or finger-paint paper

Lesson 27.1
Introduce –9 Facts

	Purpose	Materials
Warm-up	• Count combinations of paper bills • Practice memory work • Review +9 facts	• Play money
Activities	• Introduce –9 facts	• Counters • Double ten-frames (Blackline Master 1) • Number Cards • Part-Total Mat • Subtraction Bingo game boards (on workbook page 27.1A)
Workbook	• Practice –9 facts	• Workbook page 27.1B

Warm-up: Counting, Memory Work, and Review

- Mix up 6 ten-dollar bills, 2 five-dollar bills, and 3 one-dollar bills on the table. Have your child sort, order, and count the money. **How many dollars is this?** *$73.*

- Have your child rhythmically recite the Time Chant. See Lesson 24.1 (page 376) for the full chant.

- Do a brief oral review of the following addition facts. Ask your child each addition fact and have her give the answer as quickly as possible.

  - × 9 + 2 = *11*
  - × 5 + 9 = *14*
  - × 8 + 9 = *17*
  - × 6 + 9 = *15*
  - × 9 + 9 = *18*
  - × 3 + 9 = *12*
  - × 9 + 7 = *16*
  - × 4 + 9 = *13*

  Reviewing the +9 facts prepares your child to use them to help find answers to the –9 facts.

Activity: Introduce –9 Subtraction Facts

Last week, you learned how to subtract 2, 3, 4, or 5 from numbers in the teens. Today, you'll learn how to subtract 9 from numbers in the teens.

Write 13 – 9 = on a piece of paper. **You *could* put 13 counters on the ten-frames and try to imagine taking 9 counters away. But it can be hard to visualize taking away so many counters. It's usually easier to solve –9 problems with missing addends.**

Have your child help you place Number Cards on the Part-Total Mat to match the problem.

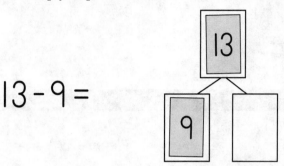

$13 - 9 =$

Now we can think of this as a missing addend problem: 9 plus what equals 13? Write 9 +
____ = 13 below 13 − 9 = on the piece of paper. Also put 9 counters on the ten-frame.

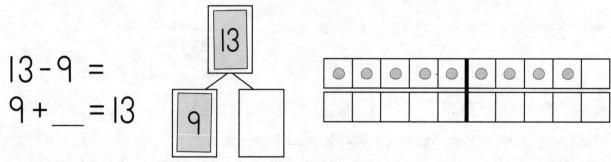

$13 - 9 =$
$9 + \_\_ = 13$

**Let's figure out how many more counters we need to reach 13. We'll do it in 2 steps. First, I
add 1 counter to make 10. Add 1 counter to the top ten-frame.**

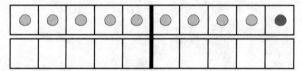

How many more counters do I need to add to make 13? *3.* Add 3 more counters.

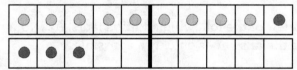

So, 9 plus what equals 13? *4.* Have your child place Number Card 4 on the Part-Total Mat and
complete the missing addend problem: 9 + _4_ = 13.

Since 9 plus 4 equals 13, 13 minus 9 equals 4. Have your child complete the written subtraction problem: 13 − 9 = 4.

$13 - 9 = 4$
$9 + \underline{4} = 13$

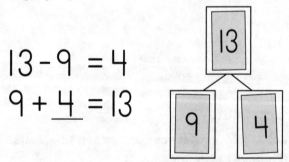

Repeat this process with the following –9 subtraction facts. For each, have your child place Number Cards on the Part-Total Mat and write a missing addend problem to match. Encourage your child to use counters on the ten-frame as needed to find the answers.

- 11 – 9 = *2*
- 15 – 9 = *6*
- 12 – 9 = *3*
- 14 – 9 = *5*
- 16 – 9 = *7*
- 18 – 9 = *9*
- 17 – 9 = *8*

If you find that this method doesn't "click" for your child, she can instead use the two-step take-away approach that she learned in Week 26. For example, to solve 13 – 9, she can first take away the 3 counters on the bottom ten-frame. Then, she can remove 6 more counters to see that the answer is 4.

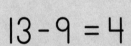 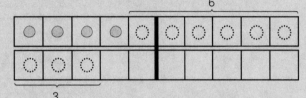

The overall goal is eventual proficiency with the subtraction facts, so it's fine for your child to use whichever mental strategy best helps her accomplish this. See the Week 27 **Teaching Math with Confidence** for more of these strategies.

Activity: Play Subtraction Bingo (-9)

We're going to play Subtraction Bingo to practice the -9 subtraction facts. Play one round of Subtraction Bingo (-9). Keep the ten-frame and counters available for your child to use to find the answers and encourage her to think of the subtraction problems as missing addend problems.

This game is like traditional Bingo with your child as the "caller."

Subtraction Bingo

Materials: Subtraction Bingo game boards (Workbook page 27.1A); 2 copies each of Number Cards 11-18 (16 cards total); counters

B	I	N	G	O
4	5	7	3	6
6	2	8	4	9
9	7	FREE	8	2
3	5	6	5	7
8	4	2	9	3

Object of the Game: Be the first player to fill in an entire column, row, or diagonal.

Shuffle the cards and place the stack face down on the table. Have each player choose which game board to use on the workbook page.

Have your child turn over the top card and subtract 9 from the number on the card. For example, if the card is a 14, your child says, "14 minus 9 equals 5." Then, each of you uses a counter to cover a square containing that number on your game board.

B	I	N	G	O
4	5	7	3	6
6	2	8	4	9
9	7	FREE	8	2
3	5	6	⬤	7
8	4	2	9	3

B	I	N	G	O
5	3	8	7	3
8	2	7	4	6
4	6	FREE	9	⬤
7	9	3	8	2
2	4	6	5	9

Continue until one of you wins by filling an entire column, row, or diagonal.

Workbook: Practice -9 Facts and Review

Have your child complete workbook page 27.1B. Encourage your child to use the printed ten-frames to complete the missing addend equations. Then, she should use each missing addend equation to solve the corresponding subtraction equation.

 Save this workbook page with your math materials so you can play Subtraction Bingo again.

Lesson 27.2
Use Subtraction to Compare

	Purpose	Materials
Warm-up	• Count quarters by 25s • Practice memory work • Review identifying numbers on the 100 Chart	• Coins • 100 Chart (Blackline Master 1) • Counters
Activities	• Practice –9 facts • Use subtraction to compare quantities	• Counters • Number Cards • Subtraction Bingo game boards (on Workbook page 27.1A)
Workbook	• Solve comparison word problems with subtraction	• Workbook pages 27.2A and 27.2B

Warm-up: Counting, Memory Work, and Review

- Place 3 quarters on the table and have your child count them by 25s. **How many cents is this?** *75¢*.

- Show your child a penny, nickel, dime, and quarter, and have her tell the name and value of each coin.

- Have your child cover the following numbers on the 100 Chart with counters: 10, 40, 70, 19, 67, 28, 97, 88, 27, 37, 38, 39, 49, 58, 68, 69, 79. The final arrangement of counters should look like a lightning bolt.

Activity: Use Subtraction to Compare

Today, you'll learn how to use subtraction to compare two amounts. You'll also practice the –9 facts.

First graders often find the Part-Total Mat confusing for comparison problems, so you'll instead model these problems directly with counters. Lining up counters makes the relationships between the numbers clear, and it also provides a foundation for using addition and subtraction to answer a wider variety of comparison questions in second grade.

Let's pretend I have 9 jelly beans and you have 12. Take 9 counters, and give your child 12 counters. **Who has more?** *I do!*

Line up the counters in 2 rows as shown. Make sure each counter in the top row lines up with a counter in the bottom row. **How many more jelly beans do you have than me?** *3*. **How do you know? Sample answer:** *My row is 3 counters longer than yours.*

When we line up the counters like this, it's easy to see how many more you have. But when we compare amounts in real life, we often don't have real objects to line up, or we have so many that it would take a long time. Instead, we use subtraction to find the answer.

Here's how we write a subtraction equation to match this problem. Write 12 – 9 = 3 on a piece of paper.

$$12 - 9 = 3$$

Discuss the relationship between the counters and equation with these questions:

- **Which counters match the 12 in the equation?** *My 12 jelly beans.*
- **Which counters match the 9?** *Your 9 jelly beans.*
- **Which counters match the 3?** *The 3 jelly beans that I have that are more than what you have.*

What do we call the answer to a subtraction problem? *The difference.* **It's called that because the answer to a subtraction problem tells how *different* the numbers are from each other. In this case, 12 is 3 more than 9. The difference between them is 3.**

$$12 - 9 = 3$$
difference   3 ← difference

This time, let's pretend I have 15 jelly beans and you have 9. Take 15 counters, and give your child 9 counters. Line up the counters in 2 rows as shown. **Who has more?** *You do!* **How many more?** *6.*

Let's write a subtraction equation that shows the difference between our numbers of jelly beans. To find how many more I have, I start the equation with the greater number. Then, I subtract the lesser number. Write 15 – 9 = on a piece of paper, and have your child complete the equation. Discuss how the numbers in the equation match the counters.

$$15 - 9 = 6$$

Finally, let's pretend I have 10 jelly beans, and you have 10. Take 10 counters, and give your child 10 counters. Line up the counters in 2 rows as shown. **Who has more?** *Neither of us!* **We have equal numbers of jelly beans.**

Let's write a subtraction equation that shows the difference between our numbers of jelly beans. Write 10 – 10 = on a piece of paper, and have your child complete the equation. **The numbers are equal, so the difference between them is 0.**

$$10 - 10 = 0$$

Activity: Play Subtraction Bingo (–9)

Play Subtraction Bingo (–9). See Lesson 27.1 (page 420) for directions. Keep the ten-frame and counters available as you play, and encourage your child to think of the subtraction problems as missing addend problems.

Workbook: Comparison Word Problems and Review

Have your child complete workbook pages 27.2A and 27.2B. Allow your child to use counters and ten-frames as needed to solve the subtraction problems on 27.2B.

Lesson 27.3
Introduce -8 Facts ·

	Purpose	Materials
Warm-up	• Count coin combinations • Practice memory work • Review +8 facts	• Coins
Activities	• Introduce –8 subtraction facts	• Counters • Double ten-frames (Blackline Master 1) • Number Cards • Part-Total Mat • Subtraction Bingo game boards (on Workbook page 27.1A)
Workbook	• Practice –8 subtraction facts	• Workbook pages 27.3A and 27.3B

Warm-up: Counting, Memory Work, and Review

- Mix up 3 dimes, 4 nickels and 1 penny on the table. Have your child sort, order, and count the coins. **How many cents is this?** *51¢.*

- **How many cents equal 1 dollar?** *100.*

- Do a brief oral review of the following addition facts. Ask your child each addition fact and have her give the answer as quickly as possible.

  - ×   8 + 8 = *16*
  - ×   5 + 8 = *13*
  - ×   6 + 8 = *14*
  - ×   9 + 8 = *17*
  - ×   3 + 8 = *11*
  - ×   8 + 7 = *15*
  - ×   4 + 8 = *12*

Reviewing the +8 facts prepares your child to use them to help find answers to the –8 facts.

Activity: Introduce -8 Subtraction Facts

You have been learning the –9 subtraction facts. Today, you'll learn the –8 facts. You'll use the same strategy you used to subtract 9.

Write 14 – 8 = on a piece of paper. Have your child help you place Number Cards on the Part-Total Mat to match the problem.

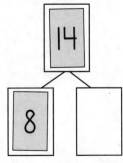

Now we can think of this as a missing addend problem: 8 plus what equals 14? Write 8 + ___ = 14 below 14 – 8 = on the piece of paper. Also put 8 counters on the ten-frame.

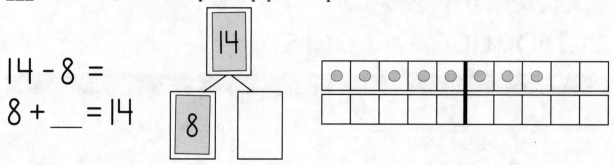

$$14 - 8 =$$
$$8 + \underline{} = 14$$

Let's figure out how many more counters we need to reach 14. We'll do it in 2 steps. First, I add 2 counters to make 10. Add 2 counters to the top ten-frame.

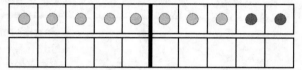

How many more counters do I need to add to make 14? *4.* Add 4 more counters.

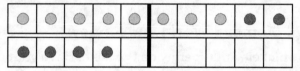

So, 8 plus what equals 14? *6.* Have your child place Number Card 4 on the Part-Total Mat and complete the missing addend problem: 8 + _6_ = 14.

Since 8 plus 6 equals 14, 14 minus 8 equals 6. Have your child complete the written subtraction problem: 14 – 8 = 6.

$$14 - 8 = 6$$
$$8 + \underline{6} = 14$$

Repeat this process with the following –8 subtraction facts. For each, have your child place Number Cards on the Part-Total Mat and write a missing addend problem to match. Encourage your child to use counters on the ten-frame as needed to find the answers.

- 11 – 8 = *3*
- 15 – 8 = *7*
- 12 – 8 = *4*
- 13 – 8 = *5*
- 16 – 8 = *8*
- 17 – 8 = *9*

As in Lesson 27.1, your child can use the two-step take-away approach that she learned in Week 26 if this missing addend approach doesn't "click" for her. For example, to solve 14 – 8, she can first take away the 4 counters on the bottom ten-frame. Then, she can remove 4 more counters to see that the answer is 6.

$$14 - 8 = 6$$

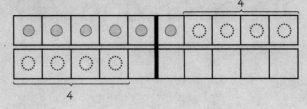

Activity: Play Subtraction Bingo (–8)

We're going to play Subtraction Bingo again. This time, we'll use it to practice the –8 subtraction facts. Play one round of Subtraction Bingo (–8). Keep the ten-frame and counters available for your child to use to find the answers, and encourage her to think of the problems as missing addend problems.

Subtraction Bingo (–8)

Materials: Subtraction Bingo game boards (Workbook page 27.1A); 2 copies each of Number Cards 10-17 (16 cards total); counters

B	I	N	G	O
4	5	7	3	6
6	2	8	4	9
9	7	FREE	8	2
3	5	6	5	7
8	4	2	9	3

Object of the Game: Be the first player to fill in an entire column, row, or diagonal.

Shuffle the cards and place the stack face down on the table. Have each player choose which game board to use on the workbook page.

Have your child turn over the top card and subtract 8 from the number on the card. For example, if the card is a 12, your child says, "12 minus 8 equals 4." Then, each of you uses a counter to cover a square containing that number on your game board.

B	I	N	G	O
●	5	7	3	6
6	2	8	4	9
9	7	FREE	8	2
3	5	6	5	7
8	4	2	9	3

B	I	N	G	O
5	3	8	7	3
8	2	7	4	6
●	6	FREE	9	5
7	9	3	8	2
2	4	6	5	9

Continue until one of you wins by filling an entire column, row, or diagonal.

Workbook: Practice –8 Subtraction Facts and Review

Have your child complete workbook page 27.3A and 27.3B. Encourage your child to use the printed ten-frames to complete the missing addend equations. Then, she should use each missing addend equation to solve the corresponding subtraction equation.

Allow your child to use counters and ten-frames as needed to solve the subtraction problems on 27.3B.

Lesson 27.4
Practice -8 and -9 Facts

	Purpose	Materials
Warm-up	• Count backward from any number up to 100 • Practice memory work • Review shapes	• Shape Cards (Blackline Master 5), cut apart on the dotted lines
Activities	• Practice -8 and -9 facts	• Counters • Number Cards • Subtraction Bingo game boards (on Workbook page 27.1A)
Workbook	• Practice -8 and -9 facts	• Workbook pages 27.4A and 27.4B

Warm-up: Counting, Memory Work, and Review

• Have your child count backward from the following numbers. Stop him after he reaches the last number listed in the sample answers.

   × **Count backward from 44:** *44, 43, 42, 41, 40.*
   × **Count backward from 82:** *82, 81, 80, 79, 78.*
   × **Count backward from 30:** *30, 29, 28, 27, 26.*

• **How many inches equal 1 foot?** *12.*

• Spread the Shape Cards on the table. Have your child find all of the circles, triangles, and rectangles.

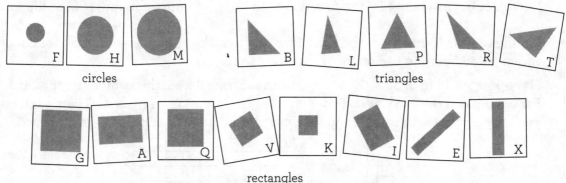

circles   triangles

rectangles

Then have your child find the squares within the group of rectangles.

squares

Activity: Play Subtraction Bingo (-8)

Today, you'll practice both the -8 and -9 facts more with Subtraction Bingo.

Playing both versions of Subtraction Bingo gives your child extra practice with both sets of these difficult subtraction facts. It also highlights the similar strategies your child can use for both sets of facts.

Play Subtraction Bingo (-8). See Lesson 27.3 (page 425) for directions. Keep the ten-frame and counters available as you play, and encourage your child to think of the subtraction problems as missing addend problems.

Activity: Play Subtraction Bingo (-9)

Play Subtraction Bingo (-9). See Lesson 27.1 (page 420) for directions. Keep the ten-frame and counters available as you play, and encourage your child to think of the subtraction problems as missing addend problems.

Don't be concerned if your child often needs the ten-frames and counters to find the answers to these problems. This unit is meant only as an introduction to these challenging subtraction facts, and your child is not expected to achieve full mastery until second grade.

Workbook: Practice -8 and -9 Subtraction Facts and Review

Have your child complete workbook pages 27.4A and 27.4B. Allow him to use counters on the ten-frame as needed.

Lesson 27.5
Enrichment and Review (Optional)

	Purpose	Materials
Warm-up	• Count to 100 by 1s, 2s, 5s, and 10s • Review memory work • Review your child's favorite or most challenging activities from Week 27	• Varies, depending on the activities you choose
Picture Book	• Use addition and subtraction to solve visual number riddles	• *Math for All Seasons: Mind-Stretching Math Riddles*, written by Greg Tang and illustrated by Harry Briggs
Enrichment Activity	• Practice the subtraction facts in a fun and kinesthetic way	• Pudding, shaving cream, or finger paint • Large washable tray, clean counter, or finger-paint paper

Warm-up: Counting, Memory Work, and Review

- Have your child count to 100 by 1s, 2s, 5s, or 10s. (Choose whichever counting sequence your child needs to practice the most.)

- Quiz your child on the memory work through Week 26. See page 499 for the full list.

- If you have time, repeat one or two of the activities from this week's lessons. Choose activities your child especially enjoyed or found challenging.

Math Picture Book: *Math for All Seasons: Mind-Stretching Math Riddles*

Read *Math for All Seasons: Mind-Stretching Math Riddles*, written by Greg Tang and illustrated by Harry Briggs. As you read the riddles to your child, encourage him to use addition or subtraction to find the answers rather than counting one-by-one. (You'll find the author's suggestions for "clever ways" to find the answers at the back of the book.) This book is somewhat long, so you may want to read it over several sessions.

Enrichment Activity: Messy Math Facts

Spread pudding on a tray, shaving cream on a counter, or finger paint on a large sheet of finger-painting paper. Choose 8-10 of the subtraction facts your child finds most challenging. Have her use her finger to write each subtraction fact (with its answer) in the goo.

Week 27 Answer Key

27.1A

See *Instructor Guide* for directions on how to play.
Save these game boards for future lessons.

Subtraction Bingo
Game Boards

B	I	N	G	O
4	5	7	3	6
6	2	8	4	9
9	7	FREE	8	2
3	5	6	5	7
8	4	2	9	3

B	I	N	G	O
5	3	8	7	3
8	2	7	4	6
4	6	FREE	9	5
7	9	3	8	2
2	4	6	5	9

27.1B

Complete.

$9 + 2 = 11$ $9 + 6 = 15$
$11 - 9 = 2$ $15 - 9 = 6$

$9 + 7 = 16$ $9 + 3 = 12$
$16 - 9 = 7$ $12 - 9 = 3$

$9 + 4 = 13$ $9 + 9 = 18$
$13 - 9 = 4$ $18 - 9 = 9$

27.2A

Complete the equations and sentences to match the word problems.

You have 13 green jelly beans.
You have 9 yellow jelly beans.
How many more are green?

$13 \bigcirc 9 = 4$

There are 4 more green jelly beans than yellow.

You have 9 orange jelly beans.
You have 14 purple jelly beans.
How many more are purple?

$14 \bigcirc 9 = 5$

There are 5 more purple jelly beans than orange.

You have 12 red jelly beans.
You have 9 pink jelly beans.
How many more are red?

$12 \bigcirc 9 = 3$

There are 3 more red jelly beans than pink.

27.2B

Complete.

$12 - 9 = 3$ $15 - 9 = 6$

$14 - 9 = 5$ $11 - 9 = 2$

$18 - 9 = 9$ $13 - 9 = 4$

$17 - 9 = 8$ $16 - 9 = 7$

Match.

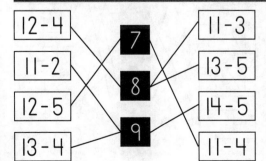

Week 27 Answer Key

27.3A

Complete.

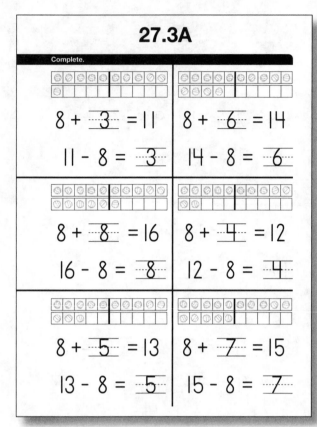

$8 + \underline{3} = 11$ $8 + \underline{6} = 14$

$11 - 8 = \underline{3}$ $14 - 8 = \underline{6}$

$8 + \underline{8} = 16$ $8 + \underline{4} = 12$

$16 - 8 = \underline{8}$ $12 - 8 = \underline{4}$

$8 + \underline{5} = 13$ $8 + \underline{7} = 15$

$13 - 8 = \underline{5}$ $15 - 8 = \underline{7}$

27.3B

Match.

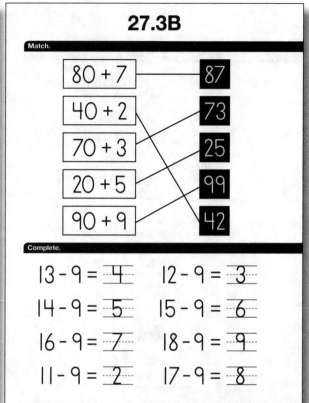

Complete.

$13 - 9 = \underline{4}$ $12 - 9 = \underline{3}$

$14 - 9 = \underline{5}$ $15 - 9 = \underline{6}$

$16 - 9 = \underline{7}$ $18 - 9 = \underline{9}$

$11 - 9 = \underline{2}$ $17 - 9 = \underline{8}$

27.4A

Match.

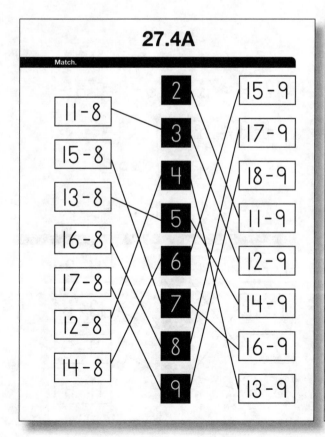

27.4B

Write the time.

8:30   1:00   2:30

4:30   9:00   12:00

Complete the equation and sentence to match the word problem.

You have 37¢.
Then, you earn 10¢ more.
How much do you have now?

$37 + 10 = 47$

I have 47¢

Week 28
–6 and –7 Subtraction Facts

Overview

This week, your child will learn to subtract 6 or 7 from numbers greater than 10. He will also practice solving take-away, take-apart, and comparison subtraction word problems.

Lesson 28.1   Introduce –6 and –7 Facts
Lesson 28.2   Practice –6 and –7 Facts
Lesson 28.3   Use Subtraction to Compare
Lesson 28.4   Word Problems
Lesson 28.5   Enrichment and Review (Optional)

Teaching Math with Confidence: Gradual Subtraction Fact Mastery

First graders often find the subtraction facts in the teens much more difficult than the addition facts, especially the tricky –6 and –7 facts that your child will work on this week. Some first graders are ready to master these challenging subtraction facts, but others won't be developmentally ready until they are a little older.

Consider this unit an *introduction* to the subtraction facts in the teens, and don't worry if your child doesn't fully master them. It's fine if he needs to use counters on the ten-frame as he finds the answers. Even if your child doesn't become fully fluent with the subtraction facts in this unit, the strategies and practice will prepare him to master the subtraction facts thoroughly in second grade.

Extra Materials Needed for Week 28

- Small bag
- For optional Enrichment and Review Lesson:
    × *Counting on Frank*, by Rod Clement

Lesson 28.1
Introduce -6 and -7 Facts

	Purpose	Materials
Warm-up	• Count combinations of paper bills • Practice memory work • Review +6 and +7 facts	• Play money
Activities	• Introduce -6 and -7 facts	• Counters • Double ten-frames (Blackline Master 1) • Connect the Boxes game board (on workbook page 28.1A)
Workbook	• Practice -6 and -7 facts	• Workbook page 28.1B

Warm-up: Counting, Memory Work, and Review

- Mix up 2 ten-dollar bills, 7 five-dollar bills, and 9 one-dollar bills on the table. Have your child sort, order, and count the money. **How many dollars is this?** *$64.*

- Have your child rhythmically recite the Time Chant. See Lesson 24.1 (page 376) for the full chant.

> There is no new memory work this week (or in the rest of the book), so your child has enough time to thoroughly memorize all of it before the end of the year.

- Do a brief oral review of the following addition facts. Ask your child each addition fact and have her give the answer as quickly as possible.

  - ✗ 5 + 6 = *11*
  - ✗ 6 + 8 = *14*
  - ✗ 7 + 5 = *12*
  - ✗ 9 + 7 = *16*
  - ✗ 7 + 7 = *14*
  - ✗ 6 + 6 = *12*
  - ✗ 7 + 8 = *15*
  - ✗ 7 + 6 = *13*
  - ✗ 4 + 7 = *11*

> Reviewing these addition facts prepares your child to use them to help find answers to the related subtraction facts.

Activity: Introduce -6 and -7 Facts

You have already learned how to solve most of the subtraction facts. This week, you'll learn how to solve the last few. Remember, these facts are especially tricky, so it's okay if you don't learn them all by heart in first grade. We'll work on them more in second grade, and the work you do this year will make it easier to learn them all next year!

Write "13 – 6 =" on a piece of paper, and place 13 counters on the ten-frame.

$$13 - 6 =$$

Some children like to imagine taking away counters for subtraction facts like this one, and some prefer to think of them as missing addend problems. We'll talk about both ways and then you can decide which way works better for you.

First, let's try the take-away method. Let's take away 6 counters in 2 steps. First, I take away all the counters on the bottom ten-frame. Take away the 3 counters on the bottom ten-frame.

$$13 - 6 =$$

How many more counters do I need to take away? *3.* Remove 3 more counters. **How many counters are left?** *7.* Have your child complete the written equation and read it aloud: **13 minus 6 equals 7.**

$$13 - 6 =$$

Now, let's try using a missing addend equation to solve the same problem. Write "13 – 6 =" on a piece of paper again. **What missing addend equation matches this subtraction problem?** *6 plus what equals 13.* Write 6 + ___ = 13, and put 6 counters on the ten-frame.

$$13 - 6 =$$
$$6 + \_\_ = 13$$

How many more counters do we need to add to reach 13? *7.* Encourage your child to think about how many counters it takes to fill in the top ten-frame (4) and then how many more are needed on the bottom ten-frame to reach 13 (3).

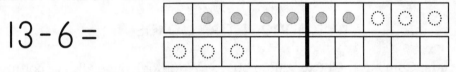

Have your child complete the missing addend problem and subtraction problem.

$$13 - 6 = 7$$
$$6 + \underline{7} = 13$$

Which strategy do you like better: taking away the counters or thinking of a missing addend problem? *Answers will vary.*

There's no right answer to this question. Different strategies "click" better for different children. Whichever way your child prefers is perfectly fine. See the Week 28 **Teaching Math with Confidence** for more on math fact strategies.

Have your child use whichever strategy she prefers to find the answers to the rest of the –6 and –7 subtraction facts.

- 11 – 6 = 5
- 12 – 7 = 5
- 14 – 6 = 8
- 16 – 7 = 9
- 15 – 6 = 9
- 14 – 7 = 7
- 12 – 6 = 6
- 15 – 7 = 8
- 11 – 5 = 6
- 13 – 7 = 6
- 11 – 7 = 4

Activity: Play Connect the Boxes

We're going to play a game called Connect the Boxes to practice the –6 and –7 subtraction facts. Play one round of Connect the Boxes. Keep the ten-frame and counters available for your child to use to find the answers as needed.

Connect the Boxes

Materials: Connect the Boxes game board (Workbook page 28.1A); counters of two different colors

7	11–6	16–7	4	13–7
12–7	8	6	14–6	9
5	15–6	7	15–7	8
6	6	13–6	5	11–7
13–7	14–7	8	9	12–6

Object of the Game: Place more counters in a continuous line of boxes than the other player.

On your turn, choose one subtraction problem on the board and find its answer. Use two counters to cover the box with the subtraction problem and a box with its answer. For example, if you choose 14 – 6, cover a box containing 14 – 6 and a box with an 8.

 Take turns covering pairs of boxes until there are no more pairs to cover. (You will have one number left uncovered.) Count how many boxes in a row each player has covered, either horizontally, vertically, or diagonally. Whoever has the longer unbroken line of counters wins the game.

Workbook: Practice –6 and –7 Facts and Review

Have your child complete workbook page 28.1B. Encourage your child to use the printed ten-frames to help find the answers (either with a missing addend strategy or two-step take-way approach). Or, if the printed ten-frames are confusing, she can model each problem with real counters on the double ten-frames instead.

 Save this workbook page with your math materials so you can play Connect the Boxes again.

Lesson 28.2
Practice -6 and -7 Facts

	Purpose	Materials
Warm-up	• Count quarters by 25s • Practice memory work • Review telling time to the hour and half hour	• Coins • Clock with hands
Activities	• Practice visualizing answers to -6 and -7 facts	• Counters • Double ten-frames (Blackline Master 1) • Connect the Boxes game board (on workbook page 28.1A)
Workbook	• Practice -6 and -7 facts	• Workbook pages 28.2A and 28.2B

Warm-up: Counting, Memory Work, and Review

- Place 4 quarters on the table and have your child count them by 25s. **How many cents is this?** *100¢.*

- **How many sides does a triangle have?** *3.* **A square?** *4.* **A rectangle?** *4.*

- Set a clock with hands to the following times and have your child read the times: *5:00, 9:30, 11:00, 1:30, 6:00.*

Activity: Practice -6 and -7 Facts

In the last lesson, you learned the -6 and -7 facts. Today, you'll practice visualizing these subtraction facts so you can "see" the answers in your head.

Write 14 – 6 = on a piece of paper.

$$14 - 6 =$$

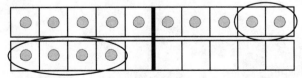

In the last lesson, which strategy did you like better for solving problems like this: taking away the counters or thinking of a missing addend problem? *Answers will vary.*

- If your child prefers the take-away strategy, put 14 counters on the ten-frame and cover the ten-frame with a piece of paper. **Imagine taking away 6 of the counters. How many would be left?** *8.* Encourage your child to visualize removing the counters in 2 steps: first the 4 counters on the bottom ten-frame, then 2 of the counters on the top ten-frame. Then, have him complete the written equation.

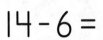 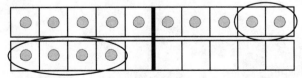

Encourage your child to imagine removing the counters in 2 steps.

- If your child prefers the missing addend strategy, ask: **What missing addend equation matches this subtraction problem?** *6 plus what equals 14.* Write 6 + ____ = 14 on the paper and put 6 counters on the ten-frame. Encourage your child to think about how many counters it takes to fill in the top ten-frame (4) and then how many more are needed on the bottom ten-frame (4). Have him complete the missing addend problem and subtraction problem.

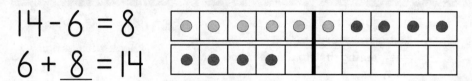

$$14 - 6 = 8$$
$$6 + \underline{8} = 14$$

> This activity helps your child learn to visualize the subtraction problems so he can transition to finding the answers mentally.

Have your child find the answers to the following –6 and –7 facts. Allow him to use whichever strategy works best for him, and encourage him to visualize moving the counters before physically moving them.

- 14 – 7 = *7*
- 12 – 6 = *6*
- 15 – 7 = *8*
- 11 – 5 = *6*
- 13 – 7 = *6*
- 11 – 7 = *4*
- 11 – 6 = *5*
- 12 – 7 = *5*
- 13 – 6 = *7*
- 16 – 7 = *9*
- 15 – 6 = *9*

Activity: Play Connect the Boxes

Play one round of Connect the Boxes. See Lesson 28.1 (page 434) for directions.

Keep the ten-frame and counters available as you play. If your child has trouble remembering the answer to a subtraction fact, encourage him to visualize moving the counters before physically moving them.

Workbook: Practice –6 and –7 Facts and Review

Have your child complete workbook pages 28.2A and 28.2B. Allow your child to use counters and the ten-frames as needed.

Lesson 28.3
Use Subtraction to Compare

	Purpose	Materials
Warm-up	• Count coin combinations • Practice memory work • Review -6 and -7 facts	• Coins • Connect the Boxes game board (on workbook page 28.1A) • Counters
Activities	• Use subtraction to compare tally marks	• Small bag • Counters
Workbook	• Practice -6 and -7 facts	• Workbook pages 28.3A and 28.3B

Warm-up: Counting, Memory Work, and Review

- Mix up 6 dimes, 2 nickels and 4 pennies on the table. Have your child sort, order, and count the coins. **How many cents is this?** *74¢.*

- Have your child say the days of the week. **How many days are in a week?** *7.*

- Play one round of Connect the Boxes. See Lesson 28.1 (page 434) for directions.

Activity: Write Subtraction Equations to Compare Tallies

In Week 27, you learned how to use subtraction to compare numbers of jelly beans. Today, you'll use subtraction to compare tallies.

First, we need to make a tally chart! Place 3 counters of one color and 6 counters of another counter in a small paper or cloth bag. Draw a simple chart like the one below on a piece of paper. Use your counters' colors to label each row.

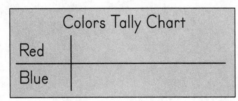

To make the chart, take one counter out of the bag and make a tally to show which color you got. Then, put the counter back in and take out another counter. Keep going until you have 12 tallies for one of the colors.

Which color do you think you will draw more times? *Answers will vary.*

Your child will likely draw the color with more counters more than the color with fewer counters. For example, if you have 6 blue counters and 3 red counters in the bag, she will probably draw blue more times than red. However, sometimes improbable things happen!

Have your child pull a counter out of the bag and then mark a tally to match. For example, if she takes a blue counter, have her make a tally in the Blue row on the chart.

Then, have your child place the counter back in the bag and draw a new counter. Have her continue until one row has 12 tallies. Remind her to mark every fifth tally horizontally across the previous 4 tallies.

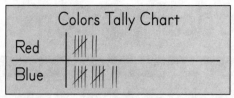

Write a subtraction equation that shows the difference between the number of times you drew each color. Start the equation with the greater number. Then, subtract the lesser number. Help your child to write a subtraction equation that shows the difference between the two quantities of tallies. For example, for the above tally chart, your child would write $12 - 7 = 5$.

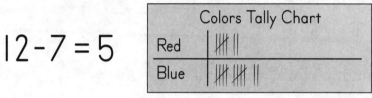

"I picked blue 5 times more than red!"

If you have time, repeat the activity and have your child again write an equation showing the difference between the number of times she drew each color.

Workbook: Use Subtraction to Compare Tallies and Review

Have your child complete workbook pages 28.3A and 28.3B. Allow your child to use counters and the ten-frames as needed.

Lesson 28.4
Word Problems

	Purpose	Materials
Warm-up	• Count by 10s starting at a number other than 0 • Practice memory work • Review –6 and –7 facts	• 100 Chart (Blackline Master 3), optional • Connect the Boxes game board (on workbook page 28.1A) • Counters
Activities	• Solve different types of subtraction word problems	• Counters
Workbook	• Solve different types of subtraction word problems	• Workbook pages 28.4A and 28.4B

Warm-up: Counting, Memory Work, and Review

- **Count by 10s starting at 9.** *9, 19, 29, 39, 49, 59, 69, 79, 89, 99.* Have your child point to the numbers on the 100 Chart only if needed.

- **Name the even numbers in order to 20.** *2, 4, 6, 8, 10, 12, 14, 16, 18, 20.* **Name the odd numbers in order to 19.** *1, 3, 5, 7, 9, 11, 13, 15, 17, 19.*

- Play one round of Connect the Boxes. See Lesson 28.1 (page 434) for directions.

Activity: Solve Subtraction Word Problems

You have learned how to use subtraction in take-away situations, take-apart situations, and comparison situations. Today, you'll solve all three kinds of word problems. Most will be subtraction, but there may be an addition problem, too!

Ask your child the following word problems. Have your child model each problem with counters (as shown) then write and solve an equation to match.

- **You plant 13 tomato seeds. 9 seeds sprout, and the rest don't. How many seeds don't sprout?** *4.*

$$13 - 9 = 4$$

If your child has trouble with any of the problems, put Number Cards on the Part-Total Mat to help make the number relationships clear.

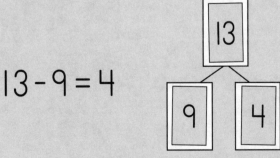

$$13 - 9 = 4$$

13 minus 9 is 4. So, 4 of the seeds don't sprout.

- You plant 10 pumpkin seeds and 7 zucchini seeds. How many seeds do you plant in all? *17.*

$$10 + 7 = 17$$

- You plant 15 pea seeds, but the squirrels eat 8 of them. How many seeds are left? *7.*

$$15 - 8 = 7$$

- You plant 8 marigolds and 14 zinnias. How many more zinnias do you plant than marigolds? *6.*

$$14 - 8 = 6$$

Workbook: Practice Subtraction Facts and Review

Have your child complete workbook pages 28.4A and 28.4B. Allow your child to use counters and the ten-frames as needed.

Lesson 28.5
Enrichment and Review (Optional)

	Purpose	Materials
Warm-up	• Count to 100 by 1s, 2s, 5s, or 10s • Review memory work • Review your child's favorite or most challenging activities from Week 28	• Varies, depending on the activities you choose
Picture Book	• Understand real-life estimates	• *Counting on Frank,* by Rod Clement
Enrichment Activity	• Use subtraction to find differences in ages	• Index cards

Warm-up: Counting, Memory Work, and Review

- Have your child count to 100 by 1s, 2s, 5s, or 10s. (Choose whichever counting sequence your child needs to practice the most.)

- Quiz your child on the memory work through Week 28. See page 499 for the full list.

- If you have time, repeat one or two of the activities from this week's lessons. Choose activities your child especially enjoyed or found challenging.

Math Picture Book: *Counting on Frank*

Read *Counting on Frank,* by Rod Clement. After you read, discuss a few of the estimation questions listed in the back of the book.

Enrichment Activity: Find Differences in Ages

With your child, choose 5-8 family members or friends who are 18 years old or younger. Write each name and age on an index card. Include your child as well.

Have your child choose two of the cards. Show him how to use subtraction to find the difference between the two ages. For example: **You're 6, and Cousin Kayla is 9. 9 minus 6 equals 3, so she is 3 years older than you.**

Have your child choose several different pairs of cards and use subtraction to find the difference between each pair of ages.

Week 28 Answer Key

28.1A

See *Instructor Guide* for directions on how to play.
Save this game board for future lessons.

Connect the Boxes
Game Board

7	11 – 6	16 – 7	4	13 – 7
12 – 7	8	6	14 – 6	9
5	15 – 6	7	15 – 7	8
6	6	13 – 6	5	11 – 7
13 – 7	14 – 7	8	9	12 – 6

28.1B

Complete. Use the ten-frames to help.

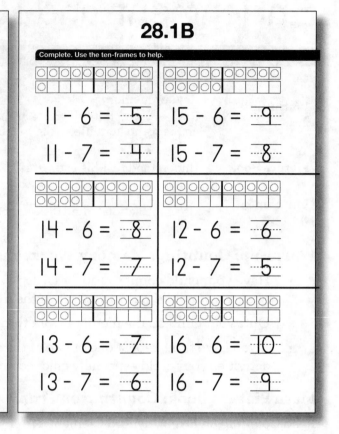

$11 - 6 = 5$ $15 - 6 = 9$

$11 - 7 = 4$ $15 - 7 = 8$

$14 - 6 = 8$ $12 - 6 = 6$

$14 - 7 = 7$ $12 - 7 = 5$

$13 - 6 = 7$ $16 - 6 = 10$

$13 - 7 = 6$ $16 - 7 = 9$

28.2A

Complete the fact family to match.

12

7   5

$7 + 5 = 12$
$5 + 7 = 12$
$12 - 7 = 5$
$12 - 5 = 7$

Color the addition facts that equal the number in the star.

★ 7
13 – 6
15 – 8
12 – 9
11 – 4
14 – 7

★ 8
13 – 4
16 – 8
14 – 6
11 – 6
15 – 7

★ 9
15 – 6
12 – 8
16 – 7
18 – 9
13 – 7

28.2B

Match pairs that make 20.

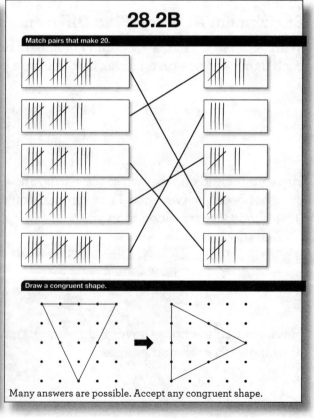

Draw a congruent shape.

Many answers are possible. Accept any congruent shape.

Week 28 Answer Key

28.3A

Tommy made a tally chart of the animals he saw on a nature walk. Use the chart to complete the equations and sentences.

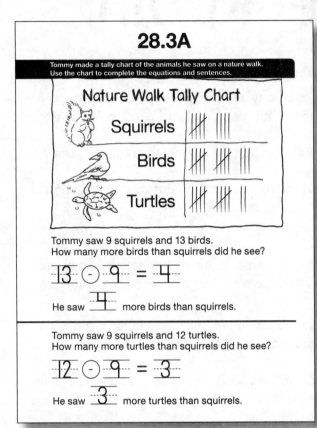

Tommy saw 9 squirrels and 13 birds.
How many more birds than squirrels did he see?

$$13 \ominus 9 = 4$$

He saw __4__ more birds than squirrels.

Tommy saw 9 squirrels and 12 turtles.
How many more turtles than squirrels did he see?

$$12 \ominus 9 = 3$$

He saw __3__ more turtles than squirrels.

28.3B

Match.

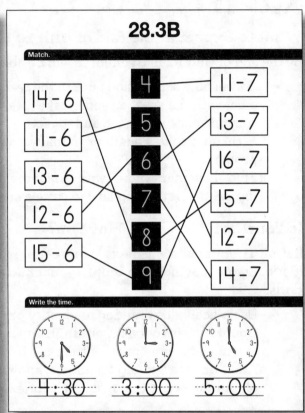

Write the time.

__4:30__   __3:00__   __5:00__

28.4A

Complete the equations and sentences to match the word problems.

You have 12 brown eggs.
You have 7 white eggs.
How many more are brown?

$$12 \ominus 7 = 5$$

There are __5__ more brown eggs than white.

You have 6 brown eggs.
You have 13 white eggs.
How many more are white?

$$13 \ominus 6 = 7$$

There are __7__ more white eggs than brown.

You have 8 brown eggs.
You have 9 white eggs.
How many eggs do you have?

$$8 \oplus 9 = 17$$

You have __17__ eggs.

28.4B

Complete.

$$14 - 6 = 8 \qquad 11 - 7 = 4$$
$$13 - 7 = 6 \qquad 16 - 7 = 9$$
$$13 - 6 = 7 \qquad 11 - 5 = 6$$
$$14 - 7 = 7 \qquad 12 - 7 = 5$$
$$15 - 7 = 8 \qquad 15 - 6 = 9$$
$$11 - 6 = 5 \qquad 12 - 6 = 6$$

Use the key to color the sand pails.

Key
- 6 - green
- 7 - blue
- 8 - yellow

Unit 10 Checkpoint

What to Expect at the End of Unit 10

By the end of Unit 10, most children will be able to:

- Solve some subtraction facts in the teens mentally. Most children will be fairly proficient with the -2, -3, -4, and -5 take-away facts, but many will still need more time to fully master the -6, -7, -8 and -9 facts.
- Write and solve equations to match take-away and take-apart subtraction word problems.
- Find "how many more" with concrete manipulatives. Many children will still be working on understanding how to write a subtraction equation to match.

Is Your Child Ready to Move on?

In Unit 11, your child will develop more sophisticated mental math skills with the numbers to 100. Before moving on to Unit 11, your child should have already mastered the following skills:

- Use place-value thinking to identify quantities arranged in groups of tens and ones.
- Count forward or backward from any number on the 100 Chart, and count by 10s starting at a number other than 0.
- Add 1 or 10 to two-digit numbers, add and subtract multiples of 10, and identify pairs of multiples of 10 that make 100 (for example, 70 and 30).

What to Do If Your Child Needs More Practice

If your child is having trouble with any of the above skills, spend a few days practicing the corresponding review activities below before moving on to Unit 11.

Activities for developing place-value thinking

- Use the Place-Value Chart to Read Two-Digit Numbers (Lesson 16.3)
- X-Ray Vision with Sums of Tens and Ones (Lesson 16.4)

Activities for counting by 1s or 10s on the 100 Chart

- Count by 10s on the 100 Chart (Lesson 17.4)
- Pretend to be a Counting Robot (Lesson 17.4)

Activities for adding 1 or 10 to two-digit numbers, adding multiples of 10, and identifying pairs that make 100

- Add 1 to Two-Digit Numbers (Lesson 17.3)
- Add 10 to Two-Digit Numbers (Lesson 17.3)
- Add Groups of 10 (Lesson 15.2)
- Subtract Groups of 10 (Lesson 15.3)
- Multiples of 10 Go Fish (Lesson 15.4)

Unit 11
Mental Math with Two-Digit Numbers

Overview

Your child will synthesize what she has learned about addition, subtraction, and the numbers to 100 as she learns to mentally add and subtract numbers to 100. This practice will deepen her understanding of place value and prepare her to perform written calculations with these numbers in second grade.

In Week 32, you and your child will review what she has learned this year and celebrate completing the book!

Week 29	Mental Math with Numbers to 25
Week 30	Mental Addition with Numbers to 100
Week 31	Mental Subtraction with Numbers to 100
Week 32	Review and Celebrate

What Your Child Will Learn

In this unit your child will learn to:

- Add a one-digit number to a two-digit number
- Add a multiple of 10 to a two-digit number
- Find missing addends in problems with a multiple of 10 for a sum (like 38 + ___ = 40)
- Subtract a one-digit number from a multiple of 10
- Subtract a multiple of 10 from a two-digit number

Recommended Math Picture Books (Optional)

These picture books are scheduled in the optional Enrichment and Review lessons at the end of each week.

- *Pigs Will Be Pigs: Fun with Math and Money,* written by Amy Axelrod and illustrated by Sharon McGinley-Nally. Aladdin, 1997.
- *What's Faster Than a Speeding Cheetah?,* by Robert E. Wells. INDPB, 1997.
- *One Hundred Hungry Ants,* written by Elinor J. Pinczes and illustrated by Bonnie MacKain. Houghton Mifflin, 1993.

Week 29
Mental Math with Numbers to 25

Overview

Your child will learn several essential mental math strategies as she adds and subtracts numbers to 25. She'll learn how to complete a 10 as she adds single-digit numbers to numbers in the teens, and she'll learn how to break apart a 10 to subtract numbers from 20. She'll apply these strategies to larger numbers in Weeks 30 and 31.

Teaching Math with Confidence: What's the Point of Mental Math?

In this unit, your child will learn mental math strategies for adding and subtracting numbers to 100. As she adds and subtracts, she'll strengthen her understanding of place value, develop deeper number sense with the numbers to 100, and learn more about the properties of addition and subtraction.

When you're calculating a tip or comparing prices at the grocery store, it's often helpful to be able to quickly perform calculations in your head without having to pull out a piece of paper or calculator. But, for first graders, this kind of real-life problem-solving is mostly a side benefit of mental math practice and not the main purpose. The main goal is to give your child a strong, conceptual understanding of place value so that she's well-prepared to understand and master written procedures for adding and subtracting in second grade.

This week, you'll begin with the numbers to 25. These smaller numbers are easier to model with counters and are less overwhelming for first graders, so they serve as a helpful starting point for learning several core mental math strategies. In Weeks 30 and 31, your child will use similar strategies to tackle mental addition and subtraction with larger numbers.

Extra Materials Needed for Week 29

- For optional Enrichment and Review Lesson:
  × *Pigs Will Be Pigs: Fun with Math and Money*, written by Amy Axelrod and illustrated by Sharon McGinley-Nally
  × Play food, optional

You will also need the bags of counters you assembled during Week 15. If you have dumped these out, assemble 10 bags with 10 counters each before you begin this week's lessons.

Lesson 29.1
Add Numbers in the Teens

	Purpose	Materials
Warm-up	• Count to 120 • Practice memory work • Review missing addends to 20	• 150 Chart (Blackline Master 9)
Activities	• Add small numbers to numbers in the teens • Add a series of small numbers, with a sum less than or equal to 20	• Double ten-frames (Blackline Master 1), optional • Counters • Playing cards
Workbook	• Add small numbers to numbers in the teens	• Workbook pages 29.1A and 29.1B

Warm-up: Counting, Memory Work, and Review

- Show your child the 150 Chart. **This chart shows numbers beyond 100.** Demonstrate how to count aloud from 90 to 120, pointing to each number on the 150 Chart as you say it: **90, 91, 92...** Have your child join you as much as she can.

  > During the counting activities in Unit 11, you will teach your child to count by 1s, 2s, 5s, and 10s to 150. Most children pick up the patterns quickly, but your child does not need to fully memorize these counting sequences. She will work on them more in second grade.

- Have your child say the months. **How many months are in a year?** *12.*

- Have your child use her "X-ray vision" to identify the hidden number in the following equations.

$$14 + 6 = 20 \qquad 19 + 1 = 20 \qquad 12 + 8 = 20$$

$$18 + 2 = 20 \qquad 13 + 7 = 20$$

  > If your child has trouble, model the equations with counters on the double ten-frames and encourage her to think about the pairs that make 10. For example: **4 plus what equals 10?** *6.* **So, 14 plus what equals 20?** *6.*

Activity: Add Single-Digit Numbers to Numbers in the Teens

You've already learned how to do some adding and subtracting with the numbers to 100. In this unit, you'll learn more about how to add and subtract with the numbers to 100. Today, you'll learn how to add small numbers to numbers in the teens.

Let's pretend you are collecting shells at the beach. In the morning, you find 3 shells. Then, you find 4 more in the afternoon. Write 3 + 4 = on a piece of paper. Model the equation with 3 counters of one color and 4 counters of another color on the double ten-frames.

$$3 + 4 =$$

How many shells do you have then? *7.* Have your child complete the written equation: *3 + 4 = 7.*

$$3 + 4 = 7$$

The next day, you collect shells again. This time, you find 13 shells in the morning and 4 in the afternoon. Write 13 + 4 = on a piece of paper. Have your child model the equation with counters of two colors on the double ten-frames.

$$13 + 4 =$$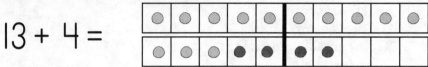

How many seashells do you find that day? *17.* Have your child complete the written equation: *13 + 4 = 17.*

$$13 + 4 = 17$$

Discuss the relationship between the two problems with the following questions.

- **How are these addition problems the same?** *Sample answers: Both are about collecting seashells. Both involve adding 3 ones plus 4 ones.*
- **How are these addition problems different from each other?** *Sample answer: The first problem doesn't have any tens, but the second problem does.*
- **How does knowing 3 + 4 help you figure out 13 + 4?** *Sample answer: I know 3 + 4 is 7, so I can just add 10 to 7 to find the answer to 13 + 4.*

> Many first-graders will have trouble articulating the relationship between the two problems even if they understand it. If your child has trouble describing the relationship in words, encourage her to point to the counters on the ten-frames to demonstrate the similarities and differences.

Have your child find the answers to the following pairs of addition problems. For each problem, encourage your child to use the answer to the first problem to help solve the second problem. Model the problems with counters on the ten-frame as needed.

$$3 + 2 = 5 \qquad 6 + 3 = 9 \qquad 4 + 4 = 8$$
$$13 + 2 = 15 \qquad 16 + 3 = 19 \qquad 14 + 4 = 18$$

Activity: Play Make 20

Play one round of Make 20 to practice adding one-digit numbers.

> This game gives your child practice at adding a series of small numbers. In the next lesson, you will revisit the idea that numbers can be added in any order and teach your child how to use pairs that make 10 to make adding a series of small numbers easier.

Make 20

Materials: Aces, 2s, 3s, 4s, 5s, and 6s from a deck of playing cards (24 cards total)

Object of the Game: Win the most cards by making rows of cards whose sum is 20.

Shuffle the cards and deal 4 cards to both players. Place the rest of the deck in a face-down pile.

To play, take turns laying a card face-up on the table in a row. After you play a card, name the sum of all the cards in the row and pick up a new card to replenish your hand.

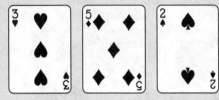

The sum is 10.

Taking turns adding cards to the row until the sum of the cards in the row equals 20. The player whose card makes a sum of 20 captures all of the cards.

The goal of the game is to create rows of cards whose sum is 20.
If you play the card that makes the row equal to 20, take all the cards in the row.

You must add a card to the row as long as your card will not make the row's sum greater than 20. If all of your cards would create a sum greater than 20, you may start a new row instead.

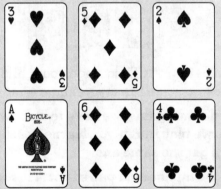

If there are multiple rows of cards, you may add your card to either row.

The game ends when the face-down pile is gone, and no one can play any more cards. The player who has won more cards wins the game.

Workbook: Add in the Teens and Review

Have your child complete workbook pages 29.1A and 29.1B. Encourage your child to use the first problem in each pair to help find the answer to the second problem. For example: 2 plus 4 equals 6, so 12 plus 4 must equal 16.

Lesson 29.2
Add Numbers in Pairs

	Purpose	Materials
Warm-up	• Count to 150 • Practice memory work • Review adding a series of small numbers	• 150 Chart (Blackline Master 9) • Playing cards
Activities	• Use pairs that make 10 to make it easier to add a series of small numbers	• Number Cards
Workbook	• Use pairs that make 10 to make it easier to add a series of numbers	• Workbook pages 29.2A and 29.2B

Warm-up: Counting, Memory Work, and Review

- Demonstrate how to count aloud from 120 to 150, pointing to each number on the 150 Chart as you say it: **120, 121, 122...** Have your child join you as much as he can.

- Have your child rhythmically recite the Time Chant. See Lesson 24.1 (page 376) for the full chant.

- Play Make 20. See Lesson 29.1 (page 449) for directions.

Activity: Add Numbers in Pairs

In the last lesson, you learned how to add numbers in the teens. Today, you'll learn a strategy that makes it easier to add several small numbers.

Let's pretend we played this row of cards in the Make 20 game. Place Number Cards in a row as shown.

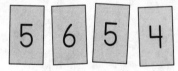

What is the sum of this row of cards? *20.* Encourage your child to add the cards in order from left to right. For example: *5 + 6 equals 11. 11 + 5 equals 16. 16 + 4 = 20.*

When we play the cards in order in a game, we have to start with the first number and then add each new number as we play it. But you learned earlier in the year we can add numbers in any order and still get the same answer.

Sometimes, it's easier to add the numbers in pairs first. This works especially well if any of the pairs equal 10. Are there any pairs of cards in this row that make 10? *5 and 5, 4 and 6.* Rearrange the cards so the numbers in each pair are next to each other.

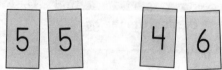

5 plus 5 equals 10, and 4 plus 6 equals 10. So, I can just add 10 plus 10 to find the total of all the cards is 20.

Place Number Cards in a row as shown. **Can you find any pairs of cards that make 10?** *8 and 2.*

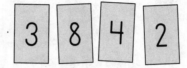

Rearrange the cards so the 8 and 2 are next to each other.

8 plus 2 equals what? *10.* **4 plus 3 equals what?** *7.* **So, what is the sum of all the cards?** *17, since 10 + 7 = 17.*

Workbook: Add Numbers in Pairs and Review

Have your child complete workbook pages 29.2A and 29.2B. Encourage your child to look for pairs that make 10 within each row to make the adding easier.

Lesson 29.3
Complete a 10 to Add

	Purpose	Materials
Warm-up	• Count quarters by 25s • Practice memory work • Review –2, –3, –4 and –5 facts	• Coins • Counters • Subtraction Roll and Cover game boards (workbook page 26.1A) • Die
Activities	• Understand you can complete a group of 10 to add numbers • Add one-digit numbers to numbers in the teens (with a sum greater than 20)	• Counters • Double ten-frames (Blackline Master 1)
Workbook	• Add one-digit numbers to numbers in the teens	• Workbook pages 29.3A and 29.3B

Warm-up: Counting, Memory Work, and Review

• Place 4 quarters on the table and have your child count them by 25s. **How many cents is this?** *100¢.*

• Show your child a penny, nickel, dime, and quarter, and have her tell the name and value of each coin.

• Play one round of Subtraction Roll and Cover. See Lesson 26.1 (page 405) for directions. Keep the ten-frame and counters available as you play.

Activity: Complete a 10 to Add

In the last lesson, you learned how to look for pairs that make 10 to make adding easier. Today, you'll learn how to complete a group of 10 to add single-digit numbers to numbers in the teens.

Let's pretend you are collecting shells at the beach again. In the morning, you find 17 shells. Then, you find 4 more in the afternoon. Write 17 + 4 = on a piece of paper.

Place 17 counters of one color on the double ten-frames. Place 4 counters of another color next to the ten-frames.

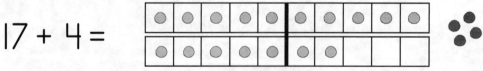

17 + 4 modeled with counters

First, let's move the counters to complete a group of 10 on the ten-frame. It's just like when you made a 10 to solve the +9 and +8 addition facts. Move 3 counters as shown.

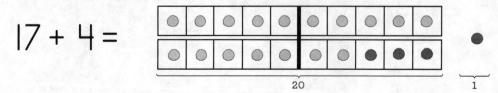

How many counters are on the two ten-frames? *20.* **How many counters are leftover?** *1.* **So, how many counters are there in all?** *21.*

Moving the counters to complete the group of 10 makes it easier to find the answer. Instead of adding 17 + 4, you can just add 20 plus 1. Have your child complete the written addition problem: 17 + 4 = 21.

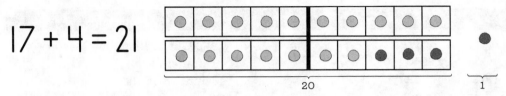

Repeat with the following addition problems. Have your child move counters to complete a group of 10 as she finds the answer to each problem.

- 19 + 5 = *24*

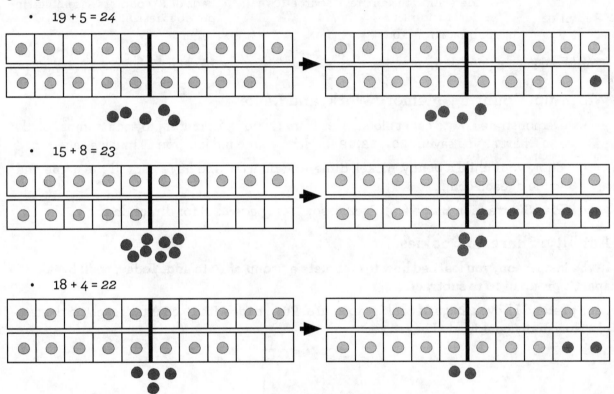

- 15 + 8 = *23*

- 18 + 4 = *22*

- 5 + 16 = *21*. (For this one, remind your child it's often easier to start with the larger number when adding.)

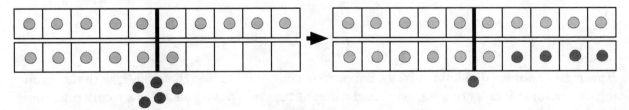

Workbook: Complete a 10 to Add and Review

Have your child complete workbook pages 29.3A and 29.3B.

All of the addition problems on workbook page 29.3A are illustrated with ten-frames. However, only the problems at the top of the page show the counters already moved to complete a group of 10. For the problems at the bottom of the page, your child must visualize moving the counters to compete the 10. If your child finds this difficult, allow her to use real counters on ten-frames to solve the problems.

Lesson 29.4
Break Apart a 10 to Subtract

	Purpose	Materials
Warm-up	• Count by 2s to 150 • Practice memory work • Review -9 facts	• 150 Chart (Blackline Master 9) • Counters • Number Cards • Subtraction Bingo game boards (on Workbook page 27.1A)
Activities	• Understand you can break apart a 10 in order to subtract • Subtract from 20	• Bags of 10 counters assembled in previous lessons • Paper
Workbook	• Subtract from 20	• Workbook pages 29.4A and 29.4B

Warm-up: Counting, Memory Work, and Review

- Demonstrate how to count aloud by 2s from 120 to 150, pointing to each number on the 150 Chart as you say it: **120, 122, 124...** Have your child join you as much as she can.

- Show your child a penny, nickel, dime, and quarter, and have her tell the name and value of each coin.

- Play Subtraction Bingo (-9). See Lesson 27.1 (page 420) for directions.

Activity: Share 20 Cookies

In the last lesson, you learned how to complete a group of 10 to add. Today, we'll break apart a group of 10 to subtract.

Let's pretend I have 2 bags of cookies to share. Put 2 bags with 10 counters each on the table. **How many cookies do I have?** *20.*

I'll give you 3 cookies. Dump out one bag of counters and give your child 3.

How many cookies do I have left? *17.* Encourage your child to find the answer without counting one-by-one. If he's not sure, ask: **I had a bag of 10, and I gave you 3. How many must be left from the bag I opened?** *7.* **There are 10 in the closed bag. So, what's 10 plus 7?** *17.*

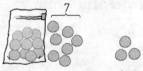

There must be 7 loose counters since you took 3 away from a bag of 10.

Have your child help you write an equation to match the situation: 20 − 3 = 17.

Replace the counters in the bag. Screen both bags with a piece of paper. **I'll give you 12 cookies this time.** Dump out 1 bag behind the screen. Give your child 1 bag of counters and 2 loose counters.

Screening the counters prompts your child to use reasoning (rather than counting) to find the number left.

How many cookies do I have left? *8.* **How do you know?** *Sample answer: 2 and 8 make 10.* **You gave me 2 counters from the bag of 10, so there must be 8 left.** Remove the screen and have your child verify his answer.

Have your child write an equation to match the situation: 20 – 12 = 8.

Activity: Subtract from 20

Have your child solve the following subtraction problems. Have him model each problem with 2 bags of counters (as above), and encourage him to use reasoning rather than counting to find the answers.

- 20 – 5 = *15*
- 20 – 1 = *19*
- 20 – 11 = *9*
- 20 – 6 = *14*
- 20 – 15 = *5*

If needed, screen the counters to encourage your child to find the answers without counting one-by-one.

Workbook: Subtract from 20 and Review

Have your child complete workbook pages 29.4A and 29.4B.

Lesson 29.5
Enrichment and Review (Optional)

	Purpose	Materials
Warm-up	• Count to 100 by 1s, 2s, 5s, or 10s • Review memory work • Review your child's favorite or most challenging activities from Week 29	• Varies, depending on the activities you choose
Picture Book	• Identify combinations of dollars and cents in the context of going to a restaurant	• *Pigs Will Be Pigs: Fun with Math and Money*, written by Amy Axelrod and illustrated by Sharon McGinley-Nally • Play money.
Enrichment Activity	• Use mental math to calculate the cost of 4 or 5 items at a pretend restaurant	• Play money • Play food, optional

Warm-up: Counting, Memory Work, and Review

- Have your child count to 100 by 1s, 2s, 5s, or 10s. (Choose whichever counting sequence your child needs to practice the most.)

- Quiz your child on the memory work through Week 26. See page 499 for the full list.

- If you have time, repeat one or two of the activities from this week's lessons. Choose activities your child especially enjoyed or found challenging.

Math Picture Book: *Pigs Will Be Pigs: Fun with Math and Money*

Read *Pigs Will Be Pigs: Fun with Math and Money*, written by Amy Axelrod and illustrated by Sharon McGinley-Nally. As you read, use play money to model the money the pigs find in their house, and keep a running count of how much money they have found.

Enrichment Activity: Play Restaurant

Help your child write a menu for a pretend restaurant. Include about 8 different food items. Set the prices from $1 to $6, and make all the prices whole numbers of dollars.

Menu	
Juice	$2
Hamburger	$6
Cookie	$1
Fries	$3
Hot dog	$4
Salad	$5

Pretend to be a customer at the restaurant, and have your child pretend to be the waiter.

Order several items from the menu. Have your child use addition to calculate the bill, and use play money to pay your bill.

Week 29 Answer Key

29.1A

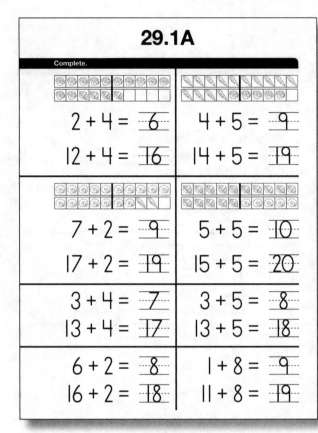

Complete.

$2 + 4 = 6$ $4 + 5 = 9$

$12 + 4 = 16$ $14 + 5 = 19$

$7 + 2 = 9$ $5 + 5 = 10$

$17 + 2 = 19$ $15 + 5 = 20$

$3 + 4 = 7$ $3 + 5 = 8$

$13 + 4 = 17$ $13 + 5 = 18$

$6 + 2 = 8$ $1 + 8 = 9$

$16 + 2 = 18$ $11 + 8 = 19$

29.1B

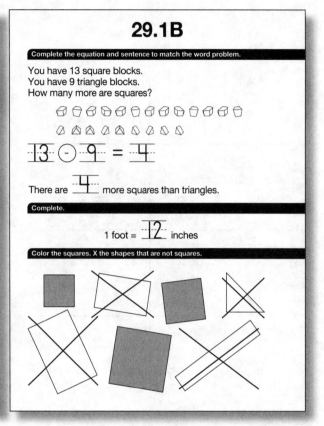

Complete the equation and sentence to match the word problem.

You have 13 square blocks.
You have 9 triangle blocks.
How many more are squares?

$13 - 9 = 4$

There are __4__ more squares than triangles.

Complete.

1 foot = __12__ inches

Color the squares. X the shapes that are not squares.

29.2A

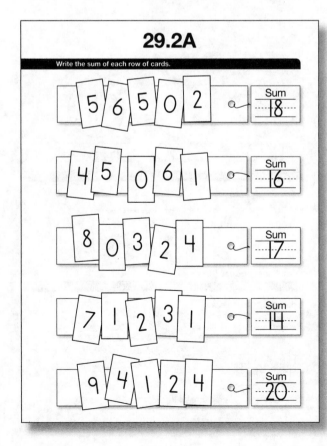

Write the sum of each row of cards.

5 6 5 0 2   Sum 18

4 5 0 6 1   Sum 16

8 0 3 2 4   Sum 17

7 1 2 3 1   Sum 14

9 4 1 2 4   Sum 20

29.2B

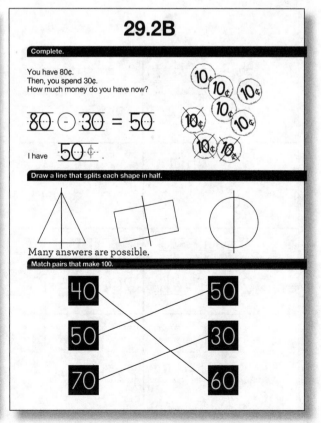

Complete.

You have 80¢.
Then, you spend 30¢.
How much money do you have now?

$80 - 30 = 50$

I have __50__ ¢

Draw a line that splits each shape in half.

Many answers are possible.

Match pairs that make 100.

40   50

50   30

70   60

Week 29 Answer Key

29.3A

Complete.

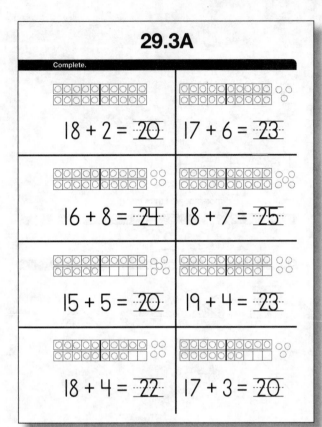

$18 + 2 = 20$ $17 + 6 = 23$

$16 + 8 = 24$ $18 + 7 = 25$

$15 + 5 = 20$ $19 + 4 = 23$

$18 + 4 = 22$ $17 + 3 = 20$

29.3B

Cassie made a tally chart of the weather each day.
Use the chart to complete the equations and sentences.

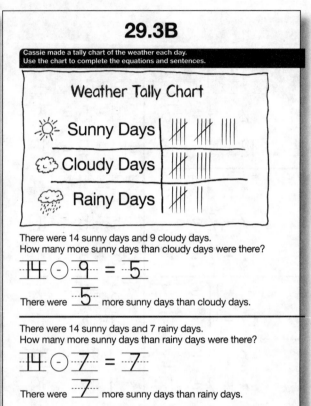

There were 14 sunny days and 9 cloudy days.
How many more sunny days than cloudy days were there?

$14 - 9 = 5$

There were __5__ more sunny days than cloudy days.

There were 14 sunny days and 7 rainy days.
How many more sunny days than rainy days were there?

$14 - 7 = 7$

There were __7__ more sunny days than rainy days.

29.4A

Complete.

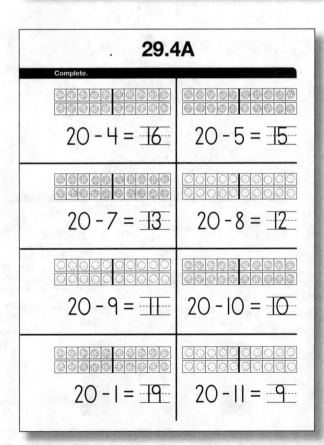

$20 - 4 = 16$ $20 - 5 = 15$

$20 - 7 = 13$ $20 - 8 = 12$

$20 - 9 = 11$ $20 - 10 = 10$

$20 - 1 = 19$ $20 - 11 = 9$

29.4B

Write the time.

1:30   2:00   6:00

Draw lines that split each cake into fourths.

Many answers are possible.

Complete the equation and sentence to match the word problem.

You have 13 crackers.
You eat 6 crackers.
How many crackers are left?

$13 - 6 = 7$

There are __7__ crackers left.

Week 30
Mental Addition with Numbers to 100

Overview

Your child will first learn how to complete missing addend problems with multiples of 10 (such as 68 + __ = 70). Then, she'll build on this skill as she learns two different strategies to add one-digit numbers to two-digit numbers (such as 68 + 4).

Lesson 30.1   Missing Addends with Multiples of 10
Lesson 30.2   Use Place Value to Add Ones or Tens
Lesson 30.3   Complete a 10 to Add One-Digit Numbers to Two-Digit Numbers
Lesson 30.4   Use Related Addition Facts to Add One-Digit Numbers to
             Two-Digit Numbers
Lesson 30.5   Enrichment and Review (Optional)

Teaching Math with Confidence:
How Mental Math Prepares Your Child for Written Addition

This week, you'll teach your child mental addition with the numbers to 100. You'll teach him several different techniques, but you'll emphasize the same underlying concept throughout: we can trade 10 ones for 1 ten.

These mental math strategies lay the foundation for the traditional written addition algorithm that your child will learn in second grade: add the ones, trade 10 ones for 1 ten ("carry the 1"), and then add the tens.

$$\begin{array}{r} 1 \\ 47 \\ +\ 38 \\ \hline 85 \end{array}$$

By developing a firm grasp of trading now, your child will be well-prepared to understand and master the written addition calculations next year in second grade.

Extra Materials Needed for Week 30

- For optional Enrichment and Review Lesson:
    × *What's Faster Than a Speeding Cheetah?*, by Robert E. Wells
    × Car speedometer

Lesson 30.1
Missing Addends with Multiples of 10

	Purpose	Materials
Warm-up	• Count quarters by 25s • Practice memory work • Review –8 facts	• Coins • Counters • Number Cards • Subtraction Bingo game boards (Workbook page 27.1A)
Activities	• Solve missing addend problems in which the sum is a multiple of 10 (such as 38 + ___ = 40)	• Play money
Workbook	• Solve missing addend problems in which the sum is a multiple of 10	• Workbook pages 30.1A and 30.1B

Warm-up: Counting, Memory Work, and Review

- Place 2 quarters on the table and have your child count them by 25s. **How many cents is this?** *50¢.*

- Have your child rhythmically say the Tens Chant: 1 ten. Ten! 2 tens. Twenty! etc. See Lesson 15.1 (page 236) for the full chant.

- Play Subtraction Bingo (–8). See Lesson 27.3 (page 425) for directions.

Activity: How Much More Money Do I Need?

You have learned how to solve lots of missing addend problems this year. Today, you'll learn how to solve missing addend problems in which the sum is a multiple of 10.

Have your child choose a toy to use in the lesson and bring it to the table. **Let's pretend you want to buy this toy, and it costs $40. But, you only have $38.** Write $40 on an index card and give your child $38 in play money.

What missing addend equation matches this problem? *38 plus what equals 40.* Write 38 + ___ = 40 on a piece of paper.

$$38 + \underline{} = 40$$

How much more money do you need? *$2.* If your child isn't sure, prompt her to think about the pairs that make 10: **8 and what make 10?** *2.* **So, if you have 3 tens and 8 ones, how many more ones do you need to make another ten?** *2.*

Give your child the extra $2. **Sometimes we trade smaller bills for larger bills so we don't have to carry around so many bills.** Help your child trade her five-dollar bill and 5 one-dollar bills for a ten-dollar bill. Have her count the bills to verify she now has $40.

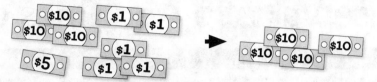

Trading the smaller bills for a ten-dollar bill foreshadows trading (also known as regrouping or carrying) when solving written addition problems, so make sure not so skip this step. See the Week 30 **Teaching Math with Confidence** for more about the importance of this concept.

Have your child complete the missing addend equation: 38 + _2_ = 40.

Activity: Use Money to Solve Missing Addend Problems

Have your child model the following problems with play money and solve them. Help her trade her smaller bills for a ten-dollar bill after she completes each problem.

- 75 + _5_ = 80
- 59 + _1_ = 60
- 26 + _4_ = 30
- 67 + _3_ = 70

Workbook: Solve Missing Addend Problems and Review

Have your child complete workbook pages 30.1A and 30.1B. If your child has trouble with the missing addend problems on 30.1A, have her use play money to model each problem.

Lesson 30.2
Use Place Value to Add Ones or Tens

	Purpose	Materials
Warm-up	• Count by 5s to 150 • Practice memory work • Review place-value vocabulary	• 150 Chart (Blackline Master 9) • Number Cards • Place-Value Chart (Blackline Master 7)
Activities	• Use place-value thinking to add ones or tens to two-digit numbers • Compare and contrast adding ones versus adding tens	• Play money
Workbook	• Add ones or tens to two-digit numbers	• Workbook pages 30.2A and 30.2B

In this lesson, your child will build on his understanding of place value to add ones or tens to two-digit numbers without regrouping or trading. You'll explore addition problems that require regrouping in Lessons 30.3 and 30.4.

Warm-up: Counting, Memory Work, and Review

• Demonstrate how to count by 5s to 150, pointing to each number on the 150 Chart as you say it. Then, have your child try it on his own: *5, 10, 15…*

• Have your child rhythmically recite the Time Chant. See Lesson 24.1 (page 376) for the full chant.

• Place Number Cards on the Place-Value Chart as shown.

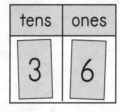

Use the following questions to briefly review place value:

   × **What number is this?** *36.*
   × **How many digits are in the number?** *2.*
   × Point to the 3. **What's the name of this place in a number?** *The tens-place.*
   × Point to the 6. **What's the name of this place in a number?** *The ones-place.*

Activity: Use Place-Value Thinking to Add Ones or Tens

In Unit 6, you learned how to use place-value thinking to add 1 or 10 to two-digit numbers. Write 26 + 1 = and 26 + 10 = on a piece of paper and have your child solve both problems.

$$26 + 1 = 27$$
$$26 + 10 = 36$$

Today, you'll use place-value thinking to add groups of ones or groups of tens to two-digit numbers.

Let's pretend you have $36. Have your child count out $36 in play money.

Then, you find 2 more one-dollar bills. Give your child 2 one-dollar bills. **What addition problem matches this story?** *36 + 2 =* . Have your child write the equation on a piece of paper. Encourage him to use place-value thinking to find the total: *3 tens and 8 ones equal 38.*

$$36 + 2 = 38$$

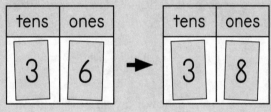

If your child has trouble using place-value thinking to solve the problem, make the number 36 with Number Cards on the Place-Value Chart. **You got 2 more one-dollar bills. So, you got 2 more ones.** Change the Number Cards so that they show 38.

tens	ones		tens	ones
3	6	→	3	8

Let's pretend you have $36 again. Remove the 2 extra one-dollar bills.

This time, let's pretend you found 2 more ten-dollar bills instead of one-dollar bills. Give your child 2 ten-dollar bills. **What addition problem matches this new story?** *36 + 20 =* . Have your child write the equation on a piece of paper. Encourage him to use place-value thinking to find the total.

$$36 + 20 = 56$$

If your child has trouble using place-value thinking to solve the problem, make the number 36 with Number Cards on the Place-Value Chart. **You got 2 more ten-dollar bills. So, you got 2 more tens.** Change the Number Cards so that they show 56.

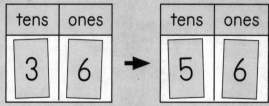

Activity: Compare and Contrast Adding Ones or Tens

Look at the two equations from the previous activity and discuss the relationship between them with your child.

$$36 + 2 = 38$$
$$36 + 20 = 56$$

- **How are these addition problems the same?** *Sample answers: Both are about finding money. Both start with 36 and involve adding 2 of something.*
- **How are these addition problems different from each other?** *Sample answer: In the first problem, you add 2 ones. In the second problem, you add 2 tens.*

Comparing and contrasting the two problems emphasizes how important it is to pay attention to place value when adding.

Have your child find the answers to the following pairs of addition problems. Have your child model each problem with play money, and encourage him to use place-value thinking to find the sum. As he solves them, discuss the relationship between the problems in each pair.

$$23 + 2 = 25 \qquad 55 + 3 = 58 \qquad 34 + 4 = 38$$
$$23 + 20 = 43 \qquad 55 + 30 = 85 \qquad 34 + 40 = 74$$

Workbook: Use Place Value to Add Ones or Tens and Review

Have your child complete workbook pages 30.2A and 30.2B.

If your child has trouble with the addition problems on 30.2A, have him model each problem with play money to make it more concrete.

Lesson 30.3
Complete a 10 to Add One-Digit Numbers to Two-Digit Numbers

	Purpose	Materials
Warm-up	• Count by 5s to 150 • Practice memory work • Review –6 and –7 facts	• 150 Chart (Blackline Master 9) • Counters • Connect the Boxes game board (on Workbook page 28.1A)
Activities	• Add a one-digit number to a two-digit number by completing a 10 • Regroup 10 ones as 1 ten	• Bags of 10 counters assembled in previous lessons • Counters • Double ten-frames (Blackline Master 1) • Empty plastic zip-top bag
Workbook	• Add a one-digit number to a two-digit number	• Workbook pages 30.3A and 30.3B

Warm-up: Counting, Memory Work, and Review

- Have your child count by 5s to 150. Have her point to each number on the 150 Chart as she says it.

- Have your child say the days of the week. **How many days are in a week?** 7.

- Play one round of Connect the Boxes. See Lesson 28.1 (page 434) for directions.

Activity: Complete a 10 to Add a One-Digit Number to a Two-Digit Number

In Week 29, you learned how to complete a group of 10 to add single-digit numbers to numbers in the teens. We pretended that you collected shells at the beach.

Let's pretend you find 18 shells in the morning and 3 more in the afternoon. Write 18 + 3 = on a piece of paper. Place 18 counters of one color on the double ten-frames. Place 3 counters of another color next to the ten-frames.

18 + 3 =

Have your child move 2 loose counters to complete the group of 10 on the ten-frame (as shown below). **How many shells did you find?** *21.* Have her complete the written equation.

18 + 3 = 21

Today, you'll learn how to complete a 10 to add a one-digit number to a larger two-digit number.

Let's pretend you collect seashells again. One day, you collect 49 shells. Have your child set out 4 bags of counters and 9 loose counters. Have her arrange the loose counters on the ten-frame.

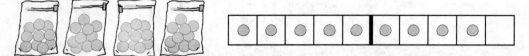

Then, you find 2 more shells. Place 2 counters next to the ten-frame.

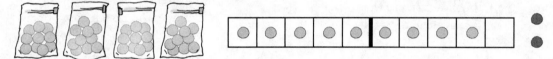

What addition problem matches this story? *49 + 2 = .* Have your child write the equation on a piece of paper.

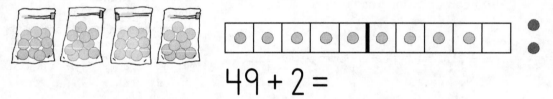

Have your child move 1 loose counter to complete the group of 10 on the ten-frame (as shown below).

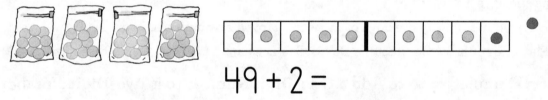

Then, help your child seal the 10 loose counters on the ten-frame in a zip-top bag.

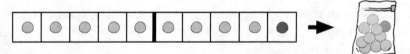

So, how many shells did you find? *51.* Have her complete the written equation.

$$49 + 2 = 51$$

Placing the group of 10 counters in a zip-top bag reinforces the important idea that 10 ones equal 1 ten and previews regrouping in written addition problems.

Activity: Practice Completing a 10 to Add

Have your child find the answers to the following addition problems. Have your child model each problem with bags of counters, and help her seal each group of 10 loose counters in a zip-top bag. Also encourage her to use place-value thinking as she finds the answers.

- 49 + 5 = *54*
- 28 + 3 = *31*
- 36 + 8 = *44*
- 75 + 7 = *82*

Workbook: Add One-Digit Numbers to Two-Digit Numbers and Review

Have your child complete workbook pages 30.3A and 30.3B. Allow your child to use real counters to model the problems if needed.

Lesson 30.4
Use Related Addition Facts to Add One-Digit Numbers to Two-Digit Numbers

	Purpose	Materials
Warm-up	• Count coin combinations • Practice memory work • Review addition facts	• Coins • Playing cards
Activities	• Learn how to use the addition facts to add 1-digit numbers to 2-digit numbers • Regroup 10 ones as 1 ten	• Bags of 10 counters assembled in previous lessons • Empty plastic zip-top bag
Workbook	• Practice adding 1-digit numbers to 2-digit numbers	• Workbook pages 30.4A and 30.4B

Warm-up: Counting, Memory Work, and Review

- Mix up 6 dimes, 5 nickels, and 6 pennies on the table. Have your child sort, order, and count the coins. **How many cents is this?** *91¢.*

- **How many inches equal 1 foot?** *12.*

- Play Addition War (5-10). See Lesson 22.4 (page 354) for directions.

Activity: Use Related Addition Facts to Add One-Digit Numbers to Two-Digit Numbers

In the last lesson, you learned how to complete a 10 to add one-digit numbers to two-digit numbers. Today, you'll learn how to use the addition facts that you already know to help figure out more difficult problems.

> Lessons 30.3 and 30. 4 introduce two different strategies for mentally adding a one-digit number to a two-digit number. If your child prefers the "complete a 10" strategy introduced in Lesson 30.2, it's fine for him to use it to solve these problems.

Write 8 + 6 = on a piece of paper. **What's 8 plus 6?** *14.* Have your child complete the written equation: 8 + 6 = 14.

$$8 + 6 = 14$$

Write 28 + 6 = below the previous equation. Place 2 bags and 8 loose counters on the table, and have your child add 6 counters to the pile.

$$8 + 6 = 14$$
$$28 + 6 =$$

8 plus 6 is 14, so that means there must be 14 loose counters. Help your child seal 10 of the loose counters in a zip-top bag.

How many groups of 10 are there? *3.* **How many loose counters?** *4.* **So, what does 28 + 6 equal?** *34.* Have your child complete the written equation: 28 + 6 = 34.

$$8 + 6 = 14$$
$$28 + 6 = 34$$

How does knowing 8 + 6 help you figure out 28 + 6? *Sample answer: I know 8 + 6 is 14, so I can just add 2 more tens to 14 to find the answer to 28 + 6.*

Have your child solve the following pairs of addition problems. Encourage him to use the first problem to help solve the second in each pair. Model the problems with counters as needed, and discuss how the problems in each pair are related.

$$7 + 4 = 11 \qquad 6 + 6 = 12$$
$$27 + 4 = 31 \qquad 46 + 6 = 52$$

$$5 + 6 = 11 \qquad 9 + 7 = 16$$
$$75 + 6 = 81 \qquad 59 + 7 = 66$$

Some children will be able to solve these problems mentally while others will need to model them with counters. Either way is fine. What's most important is that your child begins to grasp how knowing the addition facts helps solve problems with two-digit numbers.

Workbook: Add One-Digit Numbers to Two-Digit Numbers and Review

Have your child complete workbook pages 30.4A and 30.4B.

Lesson 30.5
Enrichment and Review (Optional)

	Purpose	Materials
Warm-up	• Count to 100 by 1s, 2s, 5s, or 10s • Review memory work • Review your child's favorite or most challenging activities from Week 30	• Varies, depending on the activities you choose
Picture Book	• Understand how numbers are used to express speed	• *What's Faster Than a Speeding Cheetah?*, by Robert E. Wells
Enrichment Activity	• Explore two-digit numbers in the context of speed	• Car speedometer

Warm-up: Counting, Memory Work, and Review

- Have your child count to 100 by 1s, 2s, 5s, or 10s. (Choose whichever counting sequence your child needs to practice the most.)

- Quiz your child on the memory work through Week 26. See page 499 for the full list.

- If you have time, repeat one or two of the activities from this week's lessons. Choose activities your child especially enjoyed or found challenging.

Math Picture Book: *What's Faster Than a Speeding Cheetah?*

Read *What's Faster Than a Speeding Cheetah?*, by Robert E. Wells. After you read, look at the speed chart at the end of the book and discuss the relationship between speed, time, and distance: **The slower you go, the longer it takes to cover a certain distance.**

Enrichment Activity: Explore Speed

Look at a car speedometer with your child. Discuss the numbers on the dial and explain how the pointer shows the car's speed.

As you drive, have him watch how the pointer's position changes as the car goes faster and slower. Point out a few speed limit signs, and compare the speed limits on different roads. For example: **The speed limit in our neighborhood is 25 miles per hour, but the speed limit on the highway is 70 miles per hour. Which is faster?**

Week 30 Answer Key

30.1A

Complete.

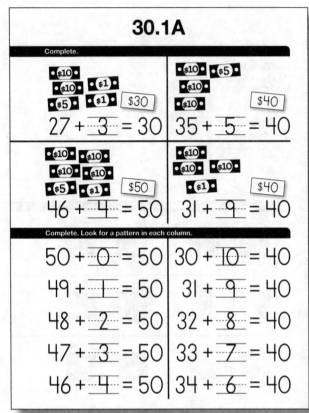

$27 + 3 = 30$ $35 + 5 = 40$

$46 + 4 = 50$ $31 + 9 = 40$

Complete. Look for a pattern in each column.

$50 + 0 = 50$ $30 + 10 = 40$

$49 + 1 = 50$ $31 + 9 = 40$

$48 + 2 = 50$ $32 + 8 = 40$

$47 + 3 = 50$ $33 + 7 = 40$

$46 + 4 = 50$ $34 + 6 = 40$

30.1B

Complete the equation and sentence to match the word problem.

You put 7 green beads and
6 white beads on a string.
How many beads are on the string?

$7 + 6 = 13$

I have 13 beads.

Match the congruent shapes.

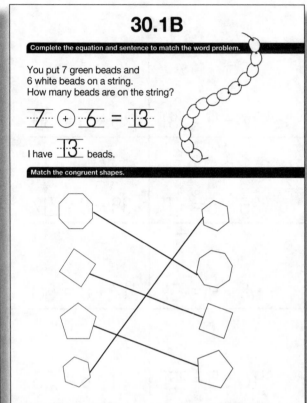

30.2A

Complete.

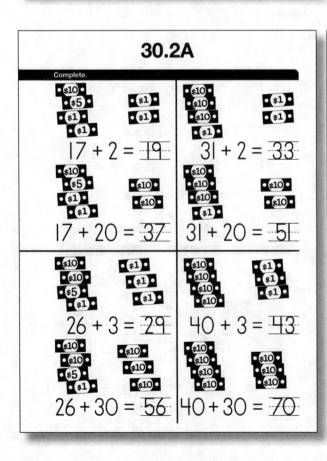

$17 + 2 = 19$ $31 + 2 = 33$

$17 + 20 = 37$ $31 + 20 = 51$

$26 + 3 = 29$ $40 + 3 = 43$

$26 + 30 = 56$ $40 + 30 = 70$

30.2B

Draw a line of symmetry for each shape.

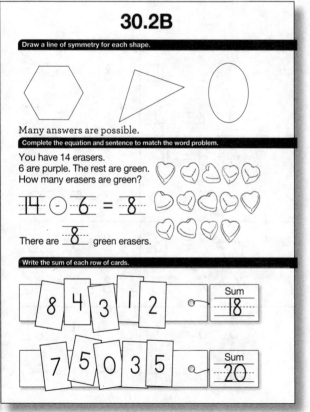

Many answers are possible.

Complete the equation and sentence to match the word problem.

You have 14 erasers.
6 are purple. The rest are green.
How many erasers are green?

$14 - 6 = 8$

There are 8 green erasers.

Write the sum of each row of cards.

8 4 3 1 2   Sum 18

7 5 0 3 5   Sum 20

Week 30 Answer Key

30.3A

Complete.

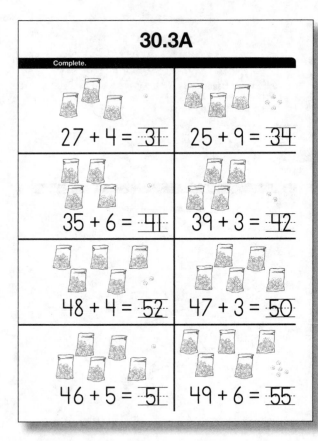

27 + 4 = 31   25 + 9 = 34

35 + 6 = 41   39 + 3 = 42

48 + 4 = 52   47 + 3 = 50

46 + 5 = 51   49 + 6 = 55

30.3B

Complete the equation and sentence to match the word problem.

You have 15 square blocks.
You have 9 triangle blocks.
How many more are squares?

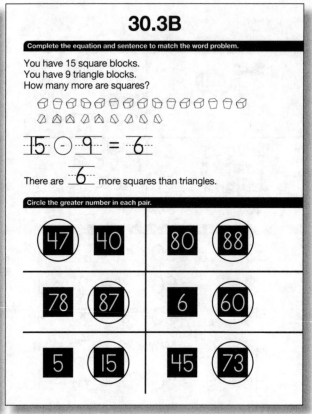

15 ⊖ 9 = 6

There are __6__ more squares than triangles.

Circle the greater number in each pair.

(47)   40   80   (88)

78   (87)   6   (60)

5   (15)   45   (73)

30.4A

Complete.

9 + 2 = 11   8 + 4 = 12

19 + 2 = 21   28 + 4 = 32

5 + 5 = 10   7 + 5 = 12

45 + 5 = 50   57 + 5 = 62

6 + 7 = 13   8 + 8 = 16

76 + 7 = 83   38 + 8 = 46

3 + 8 = 11   9 + 1 = 10

63 + 8 = 71   99 + 1 = 100

30.4B

Complete.

1 year = 12 months

1 week = 7 days

1 day = 24 hours

1 hour = 60 minutes

1 minute = 60 seconds

Complete the fact family to match.

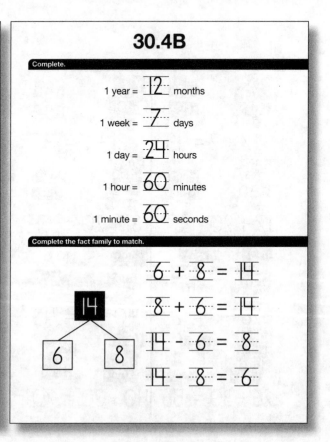

14

6   8

6 + 8 = 14

8 + 6 = 14

14 − 6 = 8

14 − 8 = 6

Week 31
Mental Subtraction with Numbers to 100

Overview

Your child will continue to use place-value reasoning as she subtracts 1-digit numbers from multiples of 10 and explores subtraction patterns.

Lesson 31.1   Use Place Value to Subtract Ones or Tens
Lesson 31.2   Break Apart a 10 to Subtract from Multiples of 10
Lesson 31.3   Explore a Subtraction Pattern
Lesson 31.4   Explore Another Subtraction Pattern
Lesson 31.5   Enrichment and Review (Optional)

Teaching Math with Confidence:
How Mental Math Prepares Your Child for Written Subtraction

This week, you'll teach your child mental subtraction with the numbers to 100. Like last week, you'll emphasize trading tens and ones. Rather than putting together 10 ones to make 1 ten, you'll break apart 1 ten into 10 ones in order to subtract.

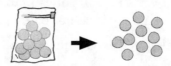

The mental math strategies that your child learns this week lay the foundation for the traditional written subtraction algorithm. Your child will learn this process in second grade: trade 1 ten for 10 ones ("borrow" the 1), subtract the ones, and then subtract the tens.

$$\begin{array}{r} \overset{5\ \ 12}{\cancel{6}\cancel{2}} \\ -48 \\ \hline 14 \end{array}$$

By learning to break apart 1 ten into 10 ones this year, your child will be ready to understand and master this written subtraction algorithm next year.

Extra Materials Needed for Week 31

- For optional Enrichment and Review Lesson:
    × *One Hundred Hungry Ants*, written by Elinor J. Pinczes and illustrated by Bonnie MacKain
    × Large piece of posterboard (or 9 sheets of paper and tape)
    × Beanbag, crumpled wad of paper, or soft, unbreakable toy

Lesson 31.1
Use Place Value to Subtract Ones or Tens

	Purpose	Materials
Warm-up	• Count by 10s to 150 • Practice memory work • Review –2, –3, –4 and –5 facts	• 150 Chart (Blackline Master 9) • Counters • Subtraction Roll and Cover game boards (workbook page 26.1A) • Die
Activities	• Use place-value thinking to subtract ones or tens from two-digit numbers • Compare and contrast subtracting ones versus tens	• Play money
Workbook	• Subtract ones or tens from two-digit numbers	• Workbook pages 31.1A and 31.1B

Warm-up: Counting, Memory Work, and Review

- Demonstrate how to count by 10s to 150, pointing to each number on the 150 Chart as you say it. Then, have your child try it on her own.

- Have your child rhythmically recite the Time Chant. See Lesson 24.1 (page 376) for the full chant.

- Play one round of Subtraction Roll and Cover. See Lesson 26.1 (page 405) for directions.

Activity: Use Place-Value Thinking to Subtract Ones or Tens

Last week, you learned how to add groups of ones or tens to two-digit numbers. Today, you'll use the same kind of thinking to subtract ones or tens from two-digit numbers.

Let's pretend you have $54. Have your child count out $54 in play money.

Then, you spend 3 one-dollar bills. Take away 3 of your child's one-dollar bills. **What subtraction problem matches this story?** *54 – 3 =* . Have your child write the equation on a piece of paper. Encourage her to use place-value thinking as she looks at the play money to find the answer: *5 tens and 1 one equal 51.*

$$54 - 3 = 51$$

Let's pretend you have $54 again. Give your child the 3 one-dollar bills back.

This time, let's pretend you spent 3 ten-dollar bills instead of one-dollar bills. Take away 3 of your child's ten-dollar bills. **What subtraction problem matches this story?** *54 – 30 = .* Have your child write the equation on a piece of paper. Encourage her to use place-value thinking as she looks at the play money to find the answer: *2 tens and 4 ones equal 24.*

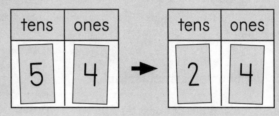

$$54 - 30 = 24$$

If your child has trouble using place-value thinking to solve the problem, make the number 54 with Number Cards on the Place-Value Chart. **You spent 3 ten-dollar bills. So, you need to subtract 3 tens.** Change the Number Cards so that they show 24.

tens	ones		tens	ones
5	4	→	2	4

Look at the two subtraction equations and discuss the relationship between the two problems.

- **How are these subtraction problems the same?** *Sample answers: Both are about spending money. Both start with $54 and then spending 3 bills.*
- **How are these subtraction problems different from each other?** *Sample answer: In the first problem, you subtract 3 ones. In the second problem, you subtract 3 tens.*

Activity: Use Place Value to Subtract Ones or Tens

Have your child find the answers to the following pairs of subtraction problem. Have your child model each problem with play money, and encourage her to use place-value thinking to find answers.

$$23 - 2 = 21 \qquad 58 - 3 = 55 \qquad 64 - 4 = 60$$
$$23 - 20 = 3 \qquad 58 - 30 = 28 \qquad 64 - 40 = 24$$

Workbook: Subtract Ones or Tens and Review

Have your child complete workbook pages 31.1A and 31.1B.

Lesson 31.2
Break Apart a 10 to Subtract from Multiples of 10

	Purpose	Materials
Warm-up	• Count by 10s to 150 • Practice memory work • Review -9 facts	• 150 Chart (Blackline Master 9) • Counters • Number Cards • Subtraction Bingo game boards (on Workbook page 27.1A)
Activities	• Subtract 1-digit numbers from multiples of 10 • Understand you can break apart a 10 in order to subtract	• Bags of 10 counters assembled in previous lessons
Workbook	• Subtract 1-digit numbers from multiples of 10	• Workbook pages 31.2A and 31.2B

Warm-up: Counting, Memory Work, and Review

- Have your child count by 10s to 150. Have him point to each number on the 150 Chart as he says it.

- **Stand on your right leg. Stand on your left leg.**

- Play Subtraction Bingo (-9). See Lesson 27.1 (page 420) for directions.

Activity: Share Bags of Cookies

In Week 29, you learned how to subtract from 20. Write 20 – 4 = on a piece of paper. Place 2 bags of counters on the table.

$$20 - 4 =$$

Let's pretend you have 20 cookies and want to share 4 with me. How many will you have left? *16.* Encourage him to use reasoning rather than counting to find the answer.

Have your child dump out one bag of counters and give you 4 of the counters. Also have him complete the written equation: 20 – 4 = 16.

$$20 - 4 = 16$$

Today, you'll learn how to subtract from larger multiples of 10, like 50, 60, or 90.

This time, let's pretend you have 8 bags of cookies to share. Place 8 bags of counters on the table. **How many cookies do you have?** *80.*

Could I have 4 cookies please? Have your child dump out one bag of counters and give you 4.

How many cookies do you have left? *76.* **How do you know?** *Sample answer: You got 4, so there must be 6 left from the bag I opened. 6 plus the 70 counters in the closed bags equals 76.*

Have your child help you write an equation to match the situation: 80 – 4 = 76.

Activity: Subtract from Multiples of 10

Have your child solve the following subtraction problems. Have him model each problem with bags of counters (as above), and encourage him to use reasoning rather than counting to find the answers.

- 80 – 5 = *75*
- 80 – 2 = *78*
- 50 – 3 = *47*
- 60 – 4 = *56*
- 100 – 5 = *95*

If your child is ready for more of a challenge, screen the counters with a piece of paper (as in Lesson 29.4), and encourage him to find the answers mentally.

Workbook: Subtract from Multiples of 10 and Review

Have your child complete workbook pages 31.2A and 31.2B.

Lesson 31.3
Explore a Subtraction Pattern

	Purpose	Materials
Warm-up	• Count combinations of paper bills • Practice memory work • Review –8 facts	• Paper money • Counters • Number Cards • Subtraction Bingo game boards (on Workbook page 27.1A)
Activities	• Subtract 1-digit numbers from multiples of 10	• Bags of 10 counters assembled in previous lessons
Workbook	• Subtract 1-digit numbers from multiples of 10	• Workbook pages 31.3A and 31.3B

Warm-up: Counting, Memory Work, and Review

- Mix up 3 ten-dollar bills, 6 five-dollar bills, and 2 one-dollar bills on the table. Have your child sort, order, and count the money. **How many dollars is this?** *$62.*

- **How many sides does a triangle have?** *3.* **A square?** *4.* **A rectangle?** *4.*

- Play Subtraction Bingo (–8). See Lesson 27.3 (page 425) for directions.

Activity: Explore a Subtraction Pattern

In the last lesson, you learned how to subtract from multiples of 10. Today, you'll practice subtracting from multiples of 10 as we explore a subtraction pattern.

Write 10 – 3 = on a piece of paper. **Let's pretend you have 10 cookies and want to share 3 with me. How many will you have left?** *7.* Give your child 1 bag of counters, and have her give you 3 of the counters. Also have her complete the written equation: 10 – 3 = 7.

$$10 - 3 = 7$$

Write 20 – 3 = on a piece of paper, and give your child 2 bags of counters. **What if you have 20 cookies and share 3 with me? How many will you have left?** *17.*

$$10 - 3 = 7$$
$$20 - 3 = 17$$

Repeat with 30 – 3, 40 – 3, and so on up to 100 – 3.

$$10 - 3 = 7$$
$$20 - 3 = 17$$
$$30 - 3 = 27$$
$$40 - 3 = 37$$
$$50 - 3 = 47$$
$$60 - 3 = 57$$
$$70 - 3 = 67$$
$$80 - 3 = 77$$
$$90 - 3 = 87$$
$$100 - 3 = 97$$

Once your child grasps the pattern to the answers, she does not need to model every problem with counters. Instead, discuss the pattern and have her complete the sequence of equations. Then, pick one of the problems in the sequence and ask her to use counters to show why the answer is correct.

Look at the list of equations and discuss the pattern.

- **How are these subtraction problems the same?** *Sample answers: All of them involve subtracting 3. All of the answers have a 7 in the ones-place. The first number in every problem is a multiple of 10.*
- **How are these subtraction problems different from each other?** *Sample answers: The first number in the problems are different. The number in the answers' tens-places are different.*
- **What patterns do you notice in the list of equations?** *Sample answers: The first number in the equation goes up by 10 each time. The answers go up by 10 each time. The tens-place in the answer is always 1 less than the tens-place in the first number in the equation.*

If your child doesn't mention it, point out that the tens-place in each answer is one less than the tens-place in the starting number for that equation.

$$50 - 3 = 47$$

The tens-place in the answer is always 1 less than the tens-place in the minuend.

Your child may not be able to articulate why this relationship always holds, but pointing it out emphasizes that a group of 10 is split apart in order to subtract. This previews the written algorithm for subtraction your child will learn in second grade.

Workbook: Complete a Subtraction Pattern and Review

Have your child complete workbook pages 31.3A and 31.3B. Allow her to model the problems with counters as needed.

If your child balks at the number of equations on workbook page 31.3A, reassure her that the problems follow a pattern and that she can use the pattern to quickly complete the page.

Lesson 31.4
Explore Another Subtraction Pattern

	Purpose	Materials
Warm-up	• Count backward from 120 to 90 • Practice memory work • Review -6 and -7 facts	• 150 Chart (Blackline Master 9) • Counters • Connect the Boxes game board (on Workbook page 28.1A)
Activities	• Subtract 1-digit numbers from multiples of 10	• Bags of 10 counters assembled in previous lessons
Workbook	• Subtract 1-digit numbers from multiples of 10	• Workbook pages 31.4A and 31.4B

Warm-up: Counting, Memory Work, and Review

- Have your child count backward from 120 to 90, pointing to each number on the 150 Chart as he says it. *120, 119, 118...*

- **Name the even numbers in order to 20.** *2, 4, 6, 8, 10, 12, 14, 16, 18, 20.* **Name the odd numbers in order to 19.** *1, 3, 5, 7, 9, 11, 13, 15, 17, 19.*

- Play one round of Connect the Boxes. See Lesson 28.1 (page 434) for directions.

Activity: Explore Another Subtraction Pattern

In the last lesson, you explored a subtraction pattern. Today, we'll explore a different subtraction pattern.

Write 50 – 1 = on a piece of paper. **Let's pretend you have 50 cookies and want to share 1 with me.** Give your child 5 bags of counters, and have him dump out 1 bag and give you 1 counter. **How many do you have left?** *49.* Also have him complete the written equation: 50 – 1 = 49.

$$50 - 1 = 49$$

Write 50 – 2 = on a piece of paper, and give your child the counter back. **What if you share 2 with me? How many will you have left?** *48.*

$$50 - 2 = 48$$

Repeat with 50 – 3, 50 – 4, and so on up to 50 – 9.

$$50 - 1 = 49$$
$$50 - 2 = 48$$
$$50 - 3 = 47$$
$$50 - 4 = 46$$
$$50 - 5 = 45$$
$$50 - 6 = 44$$
$$50 - 7 = 43$$
$$50 - 8 = 42$$
$$50 - 9 = 41$$

Once your child grasps the pattern to the answers, he does not need to act out the rest of the problems with counters.

Look at the list of equations and discuss the pattern.

- **How are these subtraction problems the same?** *Sample answers: All of them start with 50. All of the answers have a 4 in the tens-place.*
- **How are these subtraction problems different from each other?** *Sample answer: We subtract a different number each time.*
- **What patterns do you notice in the list of equations?** *Sample answers: The number being subtracted goes up by 1 as you go down the list. The answers go down by 1 as you go down the list.*

Add 50 – 10 to the list of equations. **What if you share 10 cookies with me? How many will you have left?** *40.* Have your child give you 1 bag of counters.

$$50 - 10 = 40$$

Add 50 – 11 to the list of equations. **Can I have 11 cookies please?** Give your child a moment to realize he should give you 1 bag of counters and 1 loose counter. (He will need to dump out a bag of counters in order to do this.) **How many do you have left?** *39.*

$$50 - 11 = 39$$

Workbook: Complete a Subtraction Pattern and Review

Have your child complete workbook pages 31.4A and 31.4B. Allow him to model the problems with counters as needed.

If the number of equations on workbook page 31.4A makes your child anxious, reassure him that the problems follow a pattern and that he can use the pattern to quickly complete the page.

Lesson 31.5
Enrichment and Review (Optional)

	Purpose	Materials
Warm-up	• Count to 100 by 1s, 2s, 5s, or 10s • Review memory work • Review your child's favorite or most challenging activities from Week 31	• Varies, depending on the activities you choose
Picture Book	• Introduce several different ways to split 100 into equal groups	• *One Hundred Hungry Ants*, written by Elinor J. Pinczes and illustrated by Bonnie MacKain
Enrichment Activity	• Use mental math to calculate scores in a carnival game	• Large piece of posterboard (or 9 sheets of paper and tape) • Beanbag, crumpled wad of paper, or soft, unbreakable toy

Warm-up: Counting, Memory Work, and Review

- Have your child count to 100 by 1s, 2s, 5s, or 10s. (Choose whichever counting sequence your child needs to practice the most.)

- Quiz your child on the memory work through Week 26. See page 499 for the full list.

- If you have time, repeat one or two of the activities from this week's lessons. Choose activities your child especially enjoyed or found challenging.

Math Picture Book: *One Hundred Hungry Ants*

Read *One Hundred Hungry Ants*, written by Elinor J. Pinczes and illustrated by Bonnie MacKain

Enrichment Activity: Make a Carnival Game

Help your child divide a sheet of poster board into 9 rectangles. Have her label each rectangle as shown.

10	5	25
1	10	5
25	1	10

If you don't have posterboard on hand, you can tape 9 sheets of paper into a grid instead.

Use the board to play a simple carnival-style game. Take turns standing about 10 feet away from the board, and throw a beanbag, crumpled wad of paper, or soft toy onto the board. Look to see what number is on the square the beanbag landed on, and add this number to your score.

Have each player throw the beanbag 4 times. Whoever has the higher score after 4 throws wins.

Week 31 Answer Key

31.1A

Complete.

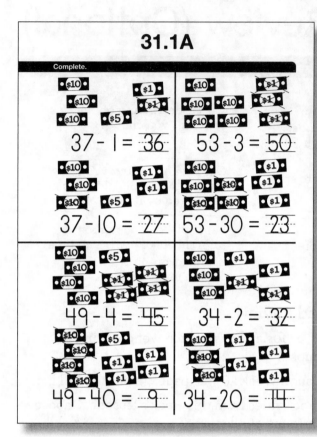

$37 - 1 = 36$

$53 - 3 = 50$

$37 - 10 = 27$

$53 - 30 = 23$

$49 - 4 = 45$

$34 - 2 = 32$

$49 - 40 = 9$

$34 - 20 = 14$

31.1B

Complete the equation and sentence to match the word problem.

You put 6 beads on a string.
Then, you put 8 more beads on the string.
How many beads did you put on the string?

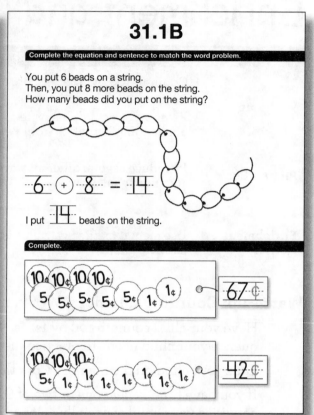

$6 + 8 = 14$

I put 14 beads on the string.

Complete.

67 ¢

42 ¢

31.2A

Complete.

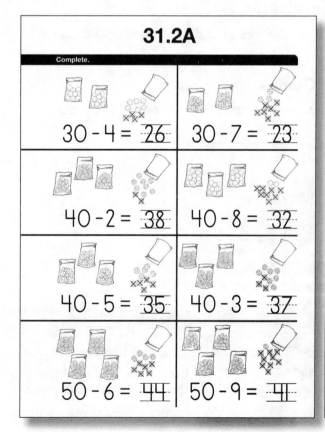

$30 - 4 = 26$

$30 - 7 = 23$

$40 - 2 = 38$

$40 - 8 = 32$

$40 - 5 = 35$

$40 - 3 = 37$

$50 - 6 = 44$

$50 - 9 = 41$

31.2B

Use a ruler to measure the sticks in inches.

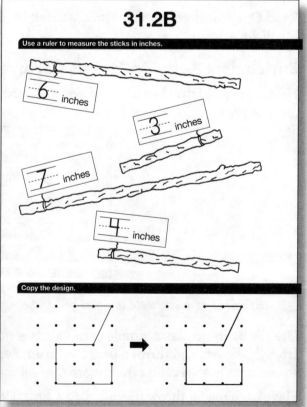

6 inches

3 inches

7 inches

4 inches

Copy the design.

Week 31 Answer Key

31.3A

Complete. Look for a pattern in each column.

10 - 5 = 5	10 - 1 = 9
20 - 5 = 15	20 - 1 = 19
30 - 5 = 25	30 - 1 = 29
40 - 5 = 35	40 - 1 = 39
50 - 5 = 45	50 - 1 = 49
60 - 5 = 55	60 - 1 = 59
70 - 5 = 65	70 - 1 = 69
80 - 5 = 75	80 - 1 = 79
90 - 5 = 85	90 - 1 = 89
100 - 5 = 95	100 - 1 = 99

31.3B

Complete the equation and sentence to match the word problem.

12 children are playing soccer.
5 are girls. The rest are boys.
How many are boys?

12 ⊖ 5 = 7

There are 7 boys.

Match.

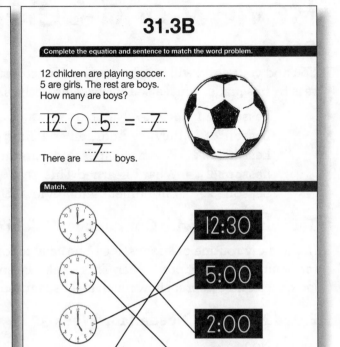

12:30

5:00

2:00

9:30

31.4A

Complete. Look for a pattern in each column.

40 - 1 = 39	90 - 1 = 89
40 - 2 = 38	90 - 2 = 88
40 - 3 = 37	90 - 3 = 87
40 - 4 = 36	90 - 4 = 86
40 - 5 = 35	90 - 5 = 85
40 - 6 = 34	90 - 6 = 84
40 - 7 = 33	90 - 7 = 83
40 - 8 = 32	90 - 8 = 82
40 - 9 = 31	90 - 9 = 81
40 - 10 = 30	90 - 10 = 80

31.4B

Celia made a bar graph of what kinds of books she read.
Use the bar graph to answer the questions.

Books I Read

Story books	▦▦▦▦▦▦
Information books	▦▦
Poetry	▦▦▦▦▦

How many story books did she read? 6

How many information books did she read? 2

How many poetry books did she read? 5

How many more story books than information books did she read? 4

How many more story books than poetry books did she read? 1

How many more poetry books than information books did she read? 3

Week 32
Review and Celebrate

Overview

You and your child will look back at how much your child has learned and celebrate the progress he has made. You'll also review some of the skills he has learned this year.

Lesson 32.1   Review Numbers to 100
Lesson 32.2   Review Addition and Subtraction
Lesson 32.3   Review Shapes, Measurement, Time, and Money
Lesson 32.4   What I Learned This Year
Lesson 32.5   Enrichment and Review (Optional)

Teaching Math with Confidence: Celebrating Progress

In the daily routine of lessons, it can be easy to forget how much progress your child has made since the start of the year. This week's lessons give both you and your child a chance to look back and celebrate how much he has learned.

Extra Materials Needed for Week 32

- None

Your child can choose his favorite math picture books to reread in Lesson 32.5, so you may want to gather these in advance.

Lesson 32.1
Review Numbers to 100

	Purpose	Materials
Warm-up	• Count by 5s to 150 • Practice memory work • Review missing addend problems in which the sum is a multiple of 10	• None
Activities	• Review the numbers to 100 with your child's favorite activities	• Varies, depending on the activities you choose
Workbook	• Review numbers to 100	• Workbook pages 32.1A and 32.1B

Warm-up: Counting, Memory Work, and Review

- Have your child count by 5s to 150.

- Have your child rhythmically recite the Time Chant. See Lesson 24.1 (page 376) for the full chant.

- Have your child solve the following missing addend problems.

  × 55 + _5_ = 60.
  × 79 + _1_ = 80.
  × 36 + _4_ = 40.
  × 47 + _3_ = 50.

Activity: Celebrate What Your Child Has Learned About the Numbers to 100

You have learned so much in math this year! This week, we'll celebrate how much progress you've made. Today, we'll look at how much you've learned about the numbers to 100.

At the beginning of the year, we started with the numbers to 10. With your child, flip through the Unit 1 workbook pages.

Then, in Unit 5 you learned about the numbers to 20. Page through the Unit 5 workbook pages.

In Units 6 and 11, you learned all about the numbers up to 100. Look over the Unit 6 and Unit 11 workbook pages.

If you tore out the workbook pages and no longer have them, flip through the matching lessons in the instructor's guide and have your child look at the workbook page answer keys instead.

Briefly discuss any concepts that were especially difficult for your child, and remind her of how far she has come in her math learning. For example: **Remember how hard it was at first to count by 10s starting at different numbers. Now that you've practiced so much, you don't have any trouble!**

Activity: Review Numbers to 100 with Favorite Activities

Today, we'll review some of your favorite activities with the numbers to 100. Have your child choose a few of her favorites from the following list and do them together.

- Memory (11-20) (Lesson 12.2)
- Make 20 Memory (Lesson 13.4)
- Multiples of 10 Go Fish (Lesson 15.4)
- Make a Heads and Tails Tally Chart (Lesson 14.1)
- Make a Number Race Bar Graph (Lesson 14.2)
- Make a Real-Life Bar Graph (Lesson 14.3)
- Two-Digit War (Lesson 17.1)
- Guess the Secret Number (1-100) (Lesson 17.2)
- X-Ray Vision with Sums of Tens and Ones (Lesson 16.4)
- Pretend to be a Counting Robot (Lesson 17.4)

Workbook: Review Numbers to 100

Have your child complete workbook pages 32.1A and 32.1B.

Lesson 32.2
Review Addition and Subtraction

	Purpose	Materials
Warm-up	• Count by 10s to 150 • Practice memory work • Review adding a one-digit number to a two-digit number	• Bags of 10 counters assembled in previous lessons • Counters
Activities	• Celebrate what your child has learned about addition and subtraction • Review addition and subtraction facts	• Workbook • Varies, depending on the activities you choose
Workbook	• Review addition and subtraction facts	• Workbook pages 32.2A and 32.2B

Warm-up: Counting, Memory Work, and Review

- Have your child count by 10s to 150.

- Have your child say the days of the week. **How many days are in a week?** *7.*

- Have your child find the answers to the following addition problems. Have your child model each problem with bags of counters and loose counters, and encourage him to complete a 10 or use related addition facts to find the answers.

  × 37 + 5 = *42*
  × 49 + 3 = *52*
  × 28 + 4 = *32*
  × 85 + 8 = *93*

Activity: Celebrate What Your Child Has Learned About Addition and Subtraction

In the last lesson, we reviewed what you learned this year about the numbers to 100. Today, we'll celebrate how much you've learned about addition and subtraction.

At the beginning of the year, we started with the addition facts to 10. With your child, flip through the Unit 2 workbook pages.

Then, in Unit 4 you learned how to subtract numbers up to 10. Page through the Unit 4 workbook pages.

In Units 8 and 10, you learned how to add and subtract numbers in the teens. Look over the Unit 8 and Unit 10 workbook pages.

Finally, in Unit 11, you learned how to add and subtract with numbers up to 100. Look over the Unit 11 workbook pages. **You'll learn a lot more about adding and subtracting the numbers to 100 in second grade.**

Briefly discuss any concepts that were especially difficult for your child, and remind him of how far he has come in his math learning. For example: **Remember how hard it was for you to subtract 9 at first? Now that you've practiced it so much, it's no problem!**

Activity: Review Addition and Subtraction Facts

Today, we'll review addition the addition and subtraction facts with some of your favorite games. Have your child choose a few of his favorite games and play them together.

- Make 10 Go Fish (Lesson 3.3)
- Make 10 Pyramid (Lesson 3.4)
- Addition Climb to the Top (Lesson 5.1)
- Subtract from 10 Memory (Lesson 9.3)
- Subtraction Tic-Tac-Toe (Lesson 10.1)
- Subtraction Climb to the Top (Lesson 11.1)
- Adding 9s Bingo (Lesson 20.1)
- Adding 8s Crash (Lesson 21.1)
- Addition Tic-Tac-toe (Lesson 22.1)
- Addition War (5-10) (Lesson 22.4)
- Subtraction Roll and Cover (Lesson 26.1)
- Subtraction Bingo (-9) (Lesson 27.1)
- Subtraction Bingo (-8) (Lesson 27.3)
- Connect the Boxes (Lesson 28.1)

Workbook: Review Addition and Subtraction

Have your child complete workbook pages 32.2A and 32.2B.

Lesson 32.3
Review Shapes, Measurement, Time, and Money

	Purpose	Materials
Warm-up	• Count by 5s to 150 • Practice memory work • Review subtracting ones or tens from two-digit numbers	• Bags of 10 counters assembled in previous lessons • Counters
Activities	• Celebrate what your child has learned about shapes, measurement, time, and money • Review shapes, measurement, time, and money	• Workbook • Varies, depending on the activities you choose
Workbook	• Review shapes, measurement, time, and money	• Workbook pages 32.3A and 32.3B

Warm-up: Counting, Memory Work, and Review

- Have your child count by 5s to 150.

- Have your child say the months. **How many months are in a year?** *12*.

- Have your child find the answers to the following pairs of subtraction problems. Have your child model each problem with counters, and encourage her to use place-value thinking to find the answers.

$$44 - 2 = 42 \qquad 63 - 3 = 60 \qquad 85 - 4 = 81$$
$$44 - 20 = 24 \qquad 63 - 30 = 33 \qquad 85 - 40 = 45$$

Activity: Celebrate What Your Child Has Learned About Shapes, Measurement, Time, and Money

In the last lesson, we reviewed what you learned this year about adding and subtracting. Today, we'll celebrate what you've learned about shapes, measurement, time, and money.

At the beginning of the year, you learned how to categorize and identify shapes. With your child, flip through the Unit 3 workbook pages.

Then, in Unit 7 you learned how to measure length. Page through the Unit 7 workbook pages.

In Unit 9, you learned how to read a clock and count coins and paper bills. Look over the Unit 9 workbook pages.

Briefly discuss any concepts that were especially difficult for your child, and remind her of how far she has come in her math learning. For example: **Remember how hard it was to tell time to the half hour at first? You worked really hard at that, and now you can do it!**

Activity: Review Shapes, Measurement, Time, and Money

Today, we'll review these topics with some of your favorite activities from the year. Have your child choose a few of her favorite activities from the following list and do them together.

- Copy a Pattern Block Design (Review, Lesson 6.1)
- Guess My Category (Lessons 7.1, 7.2, 7.3, 7.4)
- Make a Symmetric Design (Review, Lesson 9.2)
- Estimate and Measure Throws (Lesson 19.3)
- Tell Time to the Half Hour (Lesson 23.4)
- Money War (Lesson 24.2)
- Race to 100¢ (Lesson 25.2)

Workbook: Review Shapes, Measurement, Time, and Money

Have your child complete workbook pages 32.3A and 32.3B.

Lesson 32.4
What I Learned This Year

	Purpose	Materials
Warm-up	• Count by 10s to 150 • Practice memory work • Review subtracting 1-digit numbers from multiples of 10	• Bags of 10 counters assembled in previous lessons
Activities	• Reflect on the year and look ahead to second grade • Revisit favorite activities	• Workbook page 32.4A • Varies, depending on which activities your child chooses
Workbook	• Celebrate completing the workbook	• Workbook page 32.4B

Warm-up: Counting, Memory Work, and Review

- Have your child count by 10s to 150.

- **Name the even numbers in order to 20.** *2, 4, 6, 8, 10, 12, 14, 16, 18, 20.* **Name the odd numbers in order to 19.** *1, 3, 5, 7, 9, 11, 13, 15, 17, 19.*

- Have your child solve the following subtraction problems. Have him model each problem with bags of counters (as in Lesson 31.2), and encourage him to use reasoning rather than counting to find the answers.

  × 30 − 5 = *25*
  × 40 − 2 = *38*
  × 50 − 1 = *49*
  × 60 − 3 = *57*
  × 70 − 5 = *65*

Activity: Reflect on the Year

This week, we've looked back on all you've learned this year. Today, we'll reflect on the year and do a few more of your favorite activities.

Read the sentence starters on workbook page 32.4A to your child. Have your child complete the sentences, or scribe his answers for him.

Then, have your child draw a picture of his favorite math activity from the year at the bottom of the page.

Activity: Choice Review Activity

Have your child choose a few of his favorite activities from the year to revisit. Look at the lists in Lessons 32.1, 32.2, and 32.3 for suggestions.

Workbook: Complete Certificate

Complete the certificate on workbook page 32.4B and present it to your child.

Lesson 32.5
Enrichment and Review (Optional)

	Purpose	Materials
Warm-up	• Count to 100 by 1s and 2s • Count to 150 by 5s, and 10s • Review memory work	• None
Picture Book	• Reread your child's favorite math picture books	• Varies, depending on which books you choose
Enrichment Activity	• Revisit your child's favorite enrichment activity	• Varies, depending on the activities you choose

Warm-up: Counting and Memory Work

- Have your child count to 100 by 1s and 2s, and have her count to 150 by 5s and 10s.
- Quiz your child on the full memory work list. See page 499 for the list.

Math Picture Book: Child's Choice

Reread some of your child's favorite math books from the year.

Enrichment Activity: Child's Choice

Repeat one of your child's favorite enrichment activities from the year.

Week 32 Answer Key

32.1A

Complete the missing numbers on the 100 Chart.

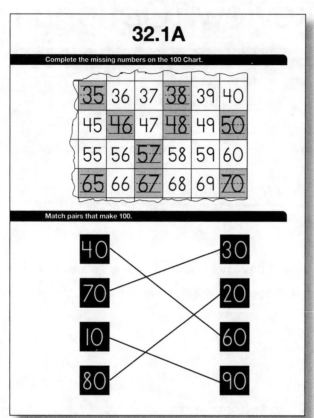

Match pairs that make 100.

32.1B

Match.

Complete the number patterns.

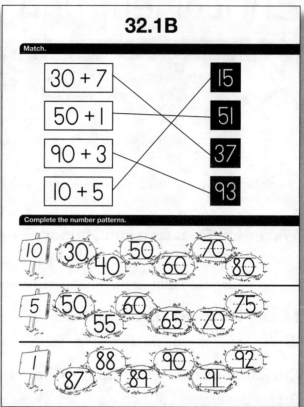

32.2A

Match.

Complete.

$8 + 8 = 16$ $5 + 6 = 11$

$9 + 9 = 18$ $4 + 8 = 12$

$6 + 6 = 12$ $8 + 9 = 17$

$3 + 9 = 12$ $9 + 7 = 16$

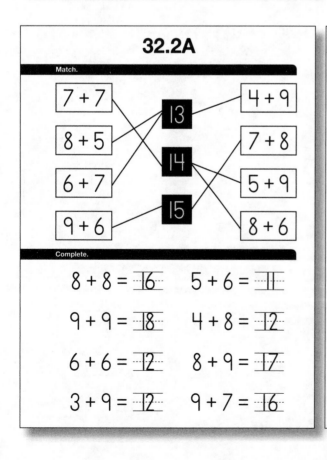

32.2B

Match pairs that make 20.

$8 + 7 = 15$
$7 + 8 = 15$
$15 - 8 = 7$
$15 - 7 = 8$

Color the subtraction facts that equal the number in the star.

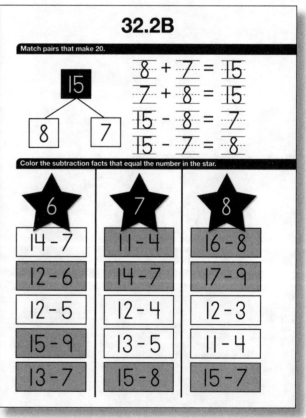

Week 32 Answer Key

32.3A

Use a ruler to measure the ribbons in inches.

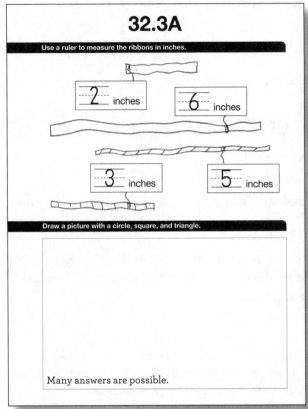

2 inches   **6** inches

3 inches   **5** inches

Draw a picture with a circle, square, and triangle.

Many answers are possible.

32.3B

Complete.

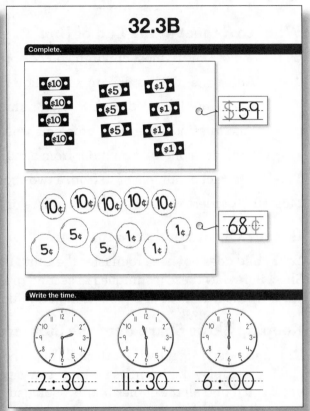

$59

68¢

Write the time.

2:30   11:30   6:00

32.4A

Complete each sentence.

My favorite math activity this year was

The most interesting thing I learned in math this year was

I worked hard to learn

Next year in math, I hope to learn

Draw a picture of your favorite math activity from this year.

Many answers are possible.

32.4B

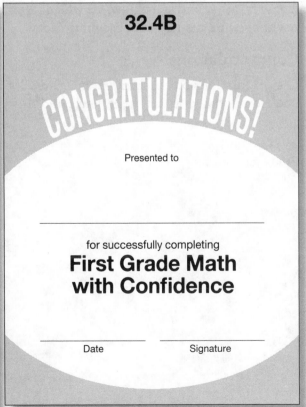

CONGRATULATIONS!

Presented to

for successfully completing

First Grade Math with Confidence

Date   Signature

Unit 11 Checkpoint

What to Expect at the End of Unit 11

By the end of Unit 11, most children will be able to:

- Add a one-digit number to a two-digit number.
- Add a multiple of 10 to a two-digit number.
- Find missing addends in problems with a multiple of 10 for a sum (like 38 + ___ = 40).
- Subtract a one-digit number from a multiple of 10.
- Subtract a multiple of 10 from a two-digit number.

Most first-graders will need to use counters or the Place-Value Chart to solve these problems.

Is Your Child Ready to Move on?

Your child does not need to master the Unit 11 mental math skills by the end of first grade. She will review these techniques in second grade as she deepens her understanding of place value and learns more about multi-digit addition and subtraction.

Keeping Skills Sharp over the Summer

Children often forget their math skills over the summer. If you'd like to keep your child's skills sharp, play math games a couple times per week to review what your child learned this year. You'll find all the games in this book listed on page 506 for easy reference.

If you'd like to do a methodical review of the addition or subtraction facts over the summer, check out *Addition Facts That Stick* or *Subtraction Facts That Stick*. You'll find many games (some familiar and some new), as well as workbook pages to help your child further increase her speed and fluency with the math facts.

Congratulations!

Congratulations on finishing *First Grade Math with Confidence*! Give yourself a pat on the back for all that you've taught your child this year.

Complete Memory Work List

Week	Memory Work
2	• **Raise your left hand.** *Child raises left hand.* • **Raise your right hand.** *Child raises right hand.*
4	• **How much is a penny worth?** *1 cent.* • **A nickel?** *5 cents.*
6	• **Name the days of the week in order.** *Sunday, Monday, Tuesday, Wednesday, Thursday, Friday, Saturday.* • **How many days are in a week?** *7.*
8	• **How many sides does a triangle have?** *3.* • **A square?** *4.* • **A rectangle?** *4.*
10	• **Name the months in order.** *January, February, March, April, May, June, July, August, September, October, November, December.* • **How many months are in a year?** *12.*
12	• **Say the "10 and Some More" Chant from 11 to 20.** *10 and 1. 11. 10 and 2. 12. 10 and 3. 13. 10 and 4. 14. 10 and 5. 15. 10 and 6. 16. 10 and 7. 17. 10 and 8. 18. 10 and 9. 19. 10 and 10. 20.*
14	• **Name the even numbers in order to 20.** *2, 4, 6, 8, 10, 12, 14, 16, 18, 20.* • **Name the odd numbers in order to 19.** *1, 3, 5, 7, 9, 11, 13, 15, 17, 19.*
16	• **Say the Tens Chant.** *1 ten. 10. 2 tens. 20. 3 tens. 30. 4 tens. 40. 5 tens. 50. 6 tens. 60. 7 tens. 70. 8 tens. 80. 9 tens. 90. 10 tens. 100.*
18	• **How much is a dime worth?** *10 cents.*
20	• **How many inches equal 1 foot?** *12.*
22	• **How many cents equal 1 dollar?** *100.*
24	• **Say the Time Chant.** *12 months equal 1 year. 7 days equal 1 week. 24 hours equal 1 day. 60 minutes equal 1 hour. 60 seconds equal 1 minute.*
26	• **How much is a quarter worth?** *25 cents.*

No new memory work is introduced after Week 26 so your child has enough time to memorize all of these items before the end of the year.

Scope and Sequence

Unit	Objectives
Unit 1 Numbers to 10	• read, write, and compare numbers to 10 • represent the numbers from 0 to 10 with counters on the ten-frame, tallies, coins, and paper bills • recognize the numbers from 6 to 10 as combinations of "5 and some more" • split quantities into parts (for example, split a group of 5 into 2 and 3) • join parts to find a total (for example, join 4 and 3 to make 7)
Unit 2 Addition to 10	• write addition equations with the + and = signs • find answers to addition facts with sums up to 10 • identify missing addends in equations with a sum of 10 (for example, 7 + __ = 10) • solve simple addition word problems
Unit 3 Shapes	• identify, describe, and categorize circles, triangles, rectangles, and squares • divide shapes into halves and fourths • find lines of symmetry in shapes • recognize pairs of congruent shapes
Unit 4 Subtraction to 10	• write subtraction equations with the − and = signs • use related addition facts to solve subtraction problems • write addition and subtraction fact families • find answers to subtraction facts in which both numbers are 10 or less • solve simple subtraction word problems
Unit 5 Numbers to 20	• read, write, and compare numbers to 20 • understand numbers from 11 to 20 as combinations of "ten and some more" • identify even and odd numbers to 20 • identify combinations that make 20 (for example, 13 and 7) • create and interpret simple tally charts and bar graphs

Unit	Objectives
Unit 6 Numbers to 100	• read, write, and compare numbers to 100 • understand place value in two-digit numbers • add 1 or 10 to two-digit numbers • add and subtract multiples of 10 (for example, 30+40 or 50–20)
Unit 7 Length	• compare lengths directly, indirectly, and with units • know the approximate length of an inch and a foot (or a centimeter and a meter) • estimate lengths in inches and feet (or centimeters and meters) • use a ruler to measure in inches and feet (or centimeters and meters)
Unit 8 Addition Facts to 20	• solve addition facts up to 10 + 10 • solve addition word problems with numbers up to 10 + 10
Unit 9 Time and Money	• identify the date and day of the week on a monthly calendar • tell time to the hour and half hour on a clock with hands • know common time equivalents • count combinations of ten-dollar, five-dollar, and one-dollar bills • count combination of dimes, nickels, and pennies • count quarters by 25s • solve word problems involving money
Unit 10 Subtraction Facts in the Teens	• solve subtraction facts up to 18 – 9 • use the relationship between addition and subtraction to solve subtraction problems • solve subtraction word problems, including take-away, take-apart, and comparison problems
Unit 11 Mental Math with Two-Digit Numbers	• add a one-digit number to a two-digit number • add a multiple of 10 to a two-digit number • find missing addends in problems with a multiple of 10 for a sum (like 38 + ___ = 40) • subtract a one-digit number from a multiple of 10 • subtract a multiple of 10 from a two-digit number

Complete Picture Book List

Reading math picture books together is a fun, cozy, and delightful way to simply enjoy math. Most of these books relate to what your child will learn each week, but some expose your child to other interesting or fun math topics. **These picture books are not required.** You do not need to buy every book or track down every book in your library system. It's also perfectly fine to use a book on a similar topic as a substitute.

Week	Book
1	*Missing Math: A Number Mystery*, by Loreen Leedy. Two Lions, 2008.
2	*Two Ways to Count to Ten: A Liberian Folktale*, retold by Ruby Dee and illustrated by Susan Meddaugh. Square Fish, 1990.
3	*Anno's Counting Book*, by Mitsumasa Anno. Crowell, 1977.
4	*Albert Adds Up!*, written by Eleanor May and illustrated by Deborah Melmon. Kane Press, 2014.
5	*Domino Addition*, by Lynette Long. Charlesbridge, 1996.
6	*Math Fables: Lessons That Count*, written by Greg Tang and illustrated by Heather Cahoon. Scholastic Press, 2004.
7	*The Greedy Triangle*, written by Marilyn Burns and illustrated by Gordon Silveria. Scholastic Paperbacks, 2008.
8	*Captain Invincible and the Space Shapes*, written by Stuart J. Murphy and illustrated by Rémy Simard. HarperCollins, 2001.
9	*Handa's Surprise*, written by Eileen Browne. Candlewick Press, 1999.
10	*Splash!*, by Ann Jonas. Greenwillow Books, 1995.
11	*Applesauce Season*, written by Eden Ross Lipson and illustrated by Mordicai Gerstein. Roaring Brook Press, 2009.
12	*Can You Count to a Googol?*, by Robert E. Wells. INDPB, 2000.
13	*Missing Mittens*, written by Stuart J. Murphy and illustrated by G. Brian Karas. HarperCollins, 2000.
14	*The Best Vacation Ever*, written by Stuart J. Murphy and illustrated by Nadine Bernard Westcott. HarperCollins, 1997.
15	*Let's Count to 100!*, by Masayuki Sebe. Kids Can Press, 2011.
16	*Chicka Chicka, 1, 2, 3*, written by Bill Martin Jr. and Michael Sampson and illustrated by Lois Ehlert. Simon & Schuster Books for Young Readers, 2004.

Week	Book
17	*Only One*, by Marc Harshman and illustrated by Barbara Garrison. Scholastic, 1993.
18	*Measuring Penny*, by Loreen Leedy. Henry Holt and Company, 1997.
19	*How Big Is a Foot?*, by Rolf Myller. Yearling, 1990.
20	*12 Ways to Get to 11*, written by Eve Merriam and illustrated by Bernie Karlin. Aladdin, 1996.
21	*What's New at the Zoo? An Animal Adding Adventure*, written by Suzanne Slade and illustrated by Joan Waites. Sylvan Dell Publishing, 2009.
22	*100 Snowmen*, written by Jen Arena and illustrated by Stephen Gilpin. Two Lions Publishing, 2013.
23	*Game Time!*, written by Stuart J. Murphy and illustrated by Cynthia Jabar. Great Source, 2000.
24	*A Chair for My Mother*, by Vera B. Williams. Greenwillow Books, 2007.
25	*The Penny Pot*, written by Stuart J. Murphy and illustrated by Lynne Cravath. Scholastic, 1998.
26	*Ready, Set, Hop!*, written by Stuart J. Murphy and illustrated by Jon Buller. HarperCollins, 1996.
27	*Math for All Seasons: Mind-Stretching Math Riddles*, written by Greg Tang and illustrated by Harry Briggs. Scholastic Paperbacks, 2005.
28	*Counting on Frank*, by Rod Clement. Gareth Stevens Publishing, 1991.
29	*Pigs Will Be Pigs: Fun with Math and Money*, written by Amy Axelrod and illustrated by Sharon McGinley-Nally. Aladdin, 1997.
30	*What's Faster Than a Speeding Cheetah?*, by Robert E. Wells. INDPB, 1997.
31	*One Hundred Hungry Ants*, written by Elinor J. Pinczes and illustrated by Bonnie MacKain. Houghton Mifflin, 1993.
32	Reread favorite books from the year.

Materials List

What You'll Need in Your Math Kit

You'll use the following materials regularly in *First Grade Math with Confidence*. Stash them in a box or basket and always keep them ready for your next lesson. (See page 8 in the Introduction for more detailed descriptions of each item.)

- 125 small counters
- Pattern blocks
- Coins (20 pennies, 20 nickels, 10 dimes, 4 quarters)
- Play money (10 one-dollar bills, 10 five-dollar bills, and 10 ten-dollar bills)
- 2 packs of 100 blank index cards
- 2 packs of playing cards
- 2 regular, six-sided dice
- Clock with hands
- 1-foot (or 30-centimeter) ruler
- Blank paper
- Pencils
- Binder with about 20 plastic page protectors (recommended but not required)

Other Supplies

Besides your Math Kit, you'll also need the following household items. You'll only need most of them once or twice, so you don't need to gather them ahead of time or store them separately. Check the weekly previews for the specific household items you'll need for each week's lessons.

Items marked with an asterisk are needed for the optional enrichment lessons (the fifth lesson each week).

- Small ball or beanbag
- *Construction paper or posterboard
- Real five-dollar bill and one-dollar bill
- 5 small toys
- *Chalk, tape, or 10 sheets of paper (for making a hopscotch course)
- *Small beanbag, stone, stick, or other hopscotch marker
- Plastic plate, optional
- *Natural objects, such as leaves, acorns, rocks, or sticks
- *Glue, optional
- *Dominoes, optional
- *Classic card game (like Skip-Bo or Uno), optional
- Printed wall calendar

- *10 plastic cups or empty water bottles
- Scissors
- *Toothpicks, craft sticks, or narrow strips of paper
- Food items that can easily be broken or torn in half or fourths, such as a banana, cookie, or slice of bread
- Round object for tracing (such as a cup or small bowl)
- Small plastic zip-top bags
- *10 blocks, boxes, or rolls of toilet paper
- *String
- *Can
- *Applesauce ingredients
- Tape
- *100 small craft items, such as stickers, pompoms, dried beans, beads, or small paper squares
- *Old magazines or newspapers
- *Weather forecast for your area, either printed or electronic
- Yarn
- Small toy animal, doll, or figurine
- 5 "skinny" household items such as a toothpick, pencil, screwdriver, fork, or comb
- 5 writing utensils of varying lengths (pens, pencils, colored pencils, crayons, etc.)
- *Bathroom scale or kitchen scale
- Beanbag, crumpled wad of paper, or soft, unbreakable toy
- Tape measure
- *20 items from your child's favorite collection, such as stuffed animals, rocks, toy cars, ponies, toy trains, or plastic figurines
- *Pudding, shaving cream, or fingerpaint
- *Large washable tray, clean counter, or fingerpaint paper
- 3-5 eating utensils of different lengths (such as forks or spoons)
- Digital clock
- *Materials for creating an obstacle course
- *Stopwatch, phone with a stopwatch app, or clock with a second hand
- *Toy catalog or access to a website with items your child would like to buy
- *Coins to spend
- *Play food, optional
- *Car speedometer
- *Large piece of posterboard (or 9 sheets of paper and tape)

Game List and Extra Game Boards

Below is the full list of games included in *First Grade Math with Confidence*, along with the lesson number where you can find their directions. All of the games are scheduled in the lessons, but you can also use them for review, extra practice, or days you don't have time for a full lesson.

Games marked with an asterisk require a printed game board. You'll find full-color versions of these game boards on the corresponding workbook pages in the Student Workbook. However, paper game boards sometimes have a way of disappearing, so black-and-white versions are provided on the next pages just in case. You will only need these if one of your full-color game boards from the workbook goes missing.

Game	Math Skill Focus	Directions
War (1-10)	Compare numbers to 10	1.2
Guess the Secret Number (1-10)	Compare numbers to 10	1.3
Race to 10	+1 and +2 facts	2.1
Make 10 Go Fish	Pairs that make 10	3.3
Make 10 Pyramid Solitaire	Pairs that make 10	3.4
*Addition Climb to the Top	+3 and +4 facts	5.1
Addition War (1-5)	Mixed addition facts	6.4
Race to 0	-1 and -2 facts	9.2
Subtract from 10 Memory	Subtract from 10	9.3
*Subtraction Tic-Tac-Toe	-3 and -4 facts	10.1
*Subtraction Climb to the Top	Mixed subtraction facts	11.1
Memory (11-20)	Read numbers to 20	12.2
War (11-20)	Compare numbers to 20	13.1
Guess the Secret Number (1-20)	Compare numbers to 20	13.2
Make 20 Memory	Pairs that make 10	13.4

Game	Math Skill Focus	Directions
Multiples of 10 Memory	Read multiples of 10 (10, 20, 30, etc.)	15.1
Multiples of 10 Go Fish	Pairs that make 100	15.4
Two-Digit War	Compare two-digit numbers	17.1
Guess the Secret Number (1-100)	Compare two-digit numbers	17.2
*Adding 9s Bingo	+9 facts	20.1
*Adding 8s Crash	+8 facts	21.1
*Addition Tic-Tac-Toe	+6 and +7 facts	22.1
Addition War (5-10)	Mixed addition facts	22.4
Money War	Count and compare paper money combinations	24.2
Race to 100¢	Count coin combinations	25.2
*Subtraction Roll and Cover	-2, -3, -4 and -5 facts	26.1
*Subtraction Bingo (-9)	-9 facts	27.1
*Subtraction Bingo (-8)	-8 facts	27.3
*Connect the Boxes	-7 and -6 facts	28.1
Make 20	Add several small numbers	29.1

Addition Climb to the Top

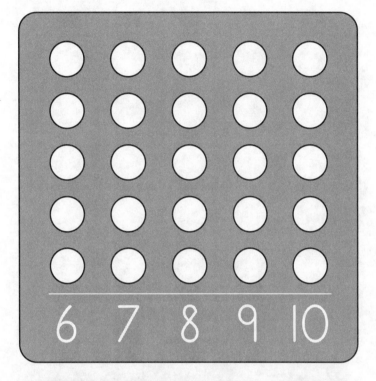

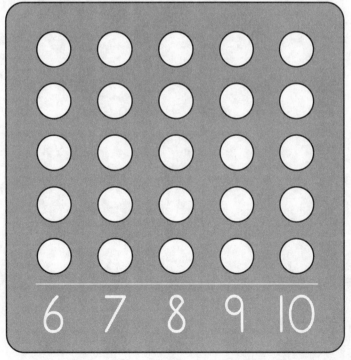

Subtraction Tic-Tac-Toe

4	3	5
6	5	6
7	4	3

Subtraction
Climb to the Top

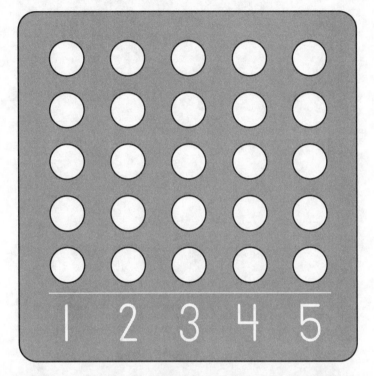

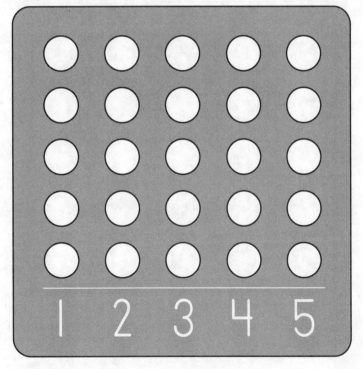

Adding 9s Bingo

B	I	N	G	O
13	14	17	16	12
16	11	15	12	17
18	15	FREE	11	10
11	18	12	14	13
14	10	13	17	15

B	I	N	G	O
10	13	11	16	17
15	11	16	10	14
13	14	FREE	12	15
17	18	13	14	12
16	12	15	13	18

Adding 8s Crash

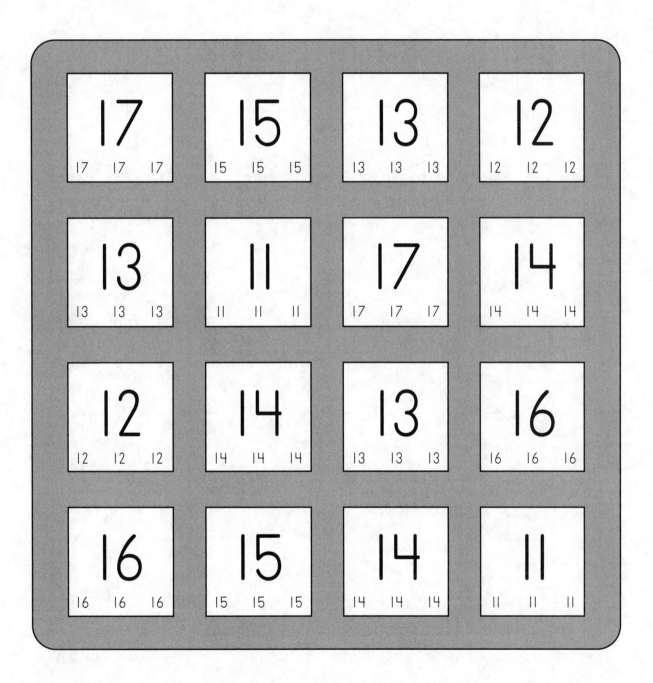

Addition Tic-Tac-Toe

11	12	14
13	12	11
14	13	12

Subtraction Roll and Cover

Subtraction Bingo
(-9 and -8 facts)

B	I	N	G	O
4	5	7	3	6
6	2	8	4	9
9	7	FREE	8	2
3	5	6	5	7
8	4	2	9	3

B	I	N	G	O
5	3	8	7	3
8	2	7	4	6
4	6	FREE	9	5
7	9	3	8	2
2	4	6	5	9

Connect the Boxes

7	11-6	16-7	4	13-7
12-7	8	6	14-6	9
5	15-6	7	15-7	8
6	6	13-6	5	11-7
13-7	14-7	8	9	12-6

Double Ten-frames
(Blackline Master 1)

Number Examples
(Blackline Master 2)

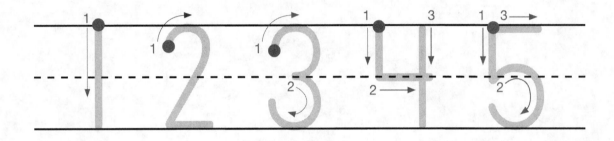

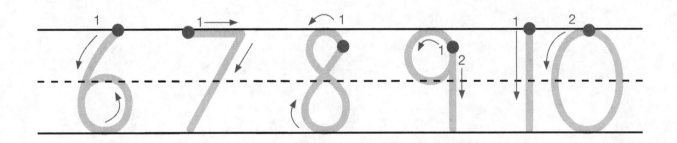

100 Chart
(Blackline Master 3)

1	2	3	4	5	6	7	8	9	10
11	12	13	14	15	16	17	18	19	20
21	22	23	24	25	26	27	28	29	30
31	32	33	34	35	36	37	38	39	40
41	42	43	44	45	46	47	48	49	50
51	52	53	54	55	56	57	58	59	60
61	62	63	64	65	66	67	68	69	70
71	72	73	74	75	76	77	78	79	80
81	82	83	84	85	86	87	88	89	90
91	92	93	94	95	96	97	98	99	100

Part-Total Mat (Blackline Master 4)

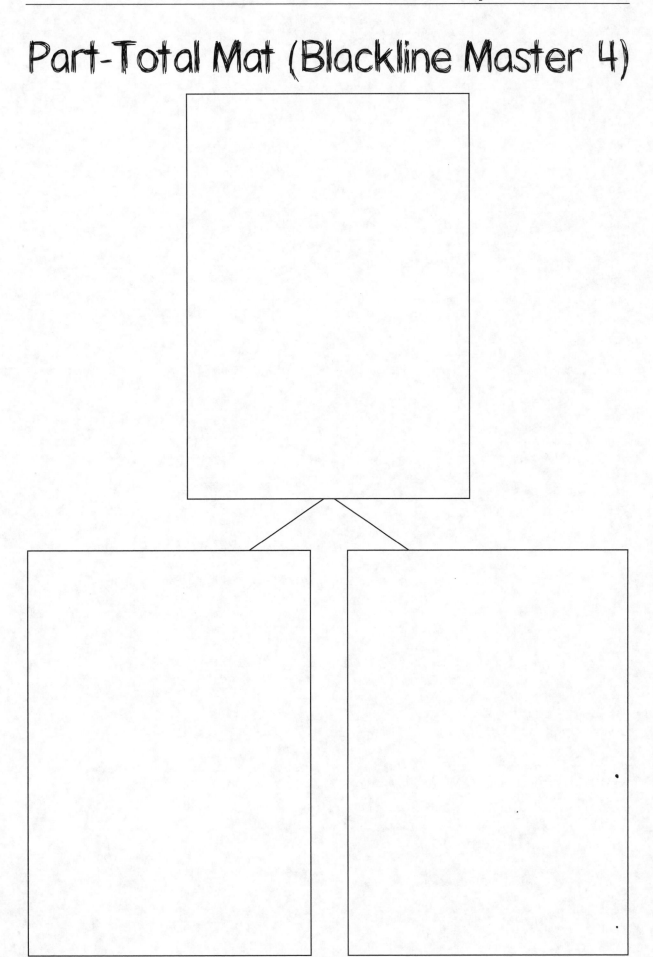

Shape Cards
(Blackline Master 5)

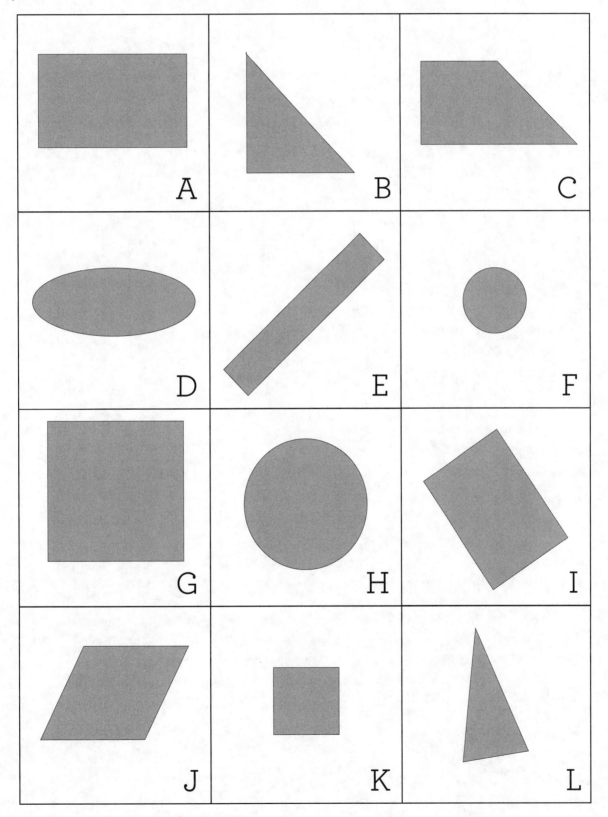

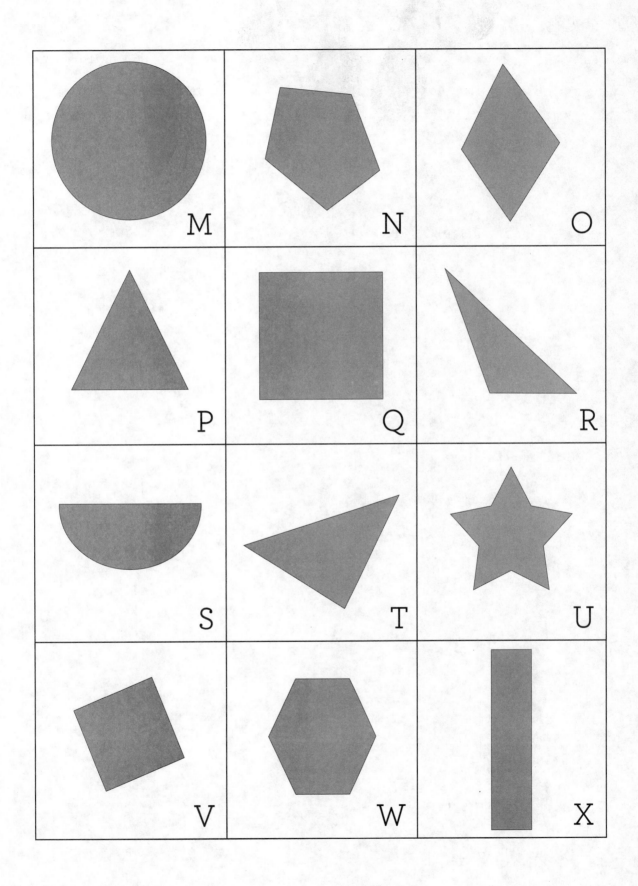

Simplified Tangram
(Blackline Master 6)

Place-Value Chart
(Blackline Master 7)

tens	ones

Paper Rulers, Inch Squares, and Centimeter Squares (Blackline Master 8)

Cut out and use the paper ruler that matches your family's measurement system.

If you use the U.S. Customary system: You only need to cut out the inch squares if your pattern blocks are not one-inch wide. See Page 290 for more information.

If you use the metric system: You only need to cut out the centimeter squares if you do not have centimeter cubes. See Page 285 for more information.

Centimeter Ruler

Inch Ruler

Inch Squares

Centimeter Squares

150 Chart
(Blackline Master 9)

1	2	3	4	5	6	7	8	9	10
11	12	13	14	15	16	17	18	19	20
21	22	23	24	25	26	27	28	29	30
31	32	33	34	35	36	37	38	39	40
41	42	43	44	45	46	47	48	49	50
51	52	53	54	55	56	57	58	59	60
61	62	63	64	65	66	67	68	69	70
71	72	73	74	75	76	77	78	79	80
81	82	83	84	85	86	87	88	89	90
91	92	93	94	95	96	97	98	99	100
101	102	103	104	105	106	107	108	109	110
111	112	113	114	115	116	117	118	119	120
121	122	123	124	125	126	127	128	129	130
131	132	133	134	135	136	137	138	139	140
141	142	143	144	145	146	147	148	149	150

Pattern Block Templates (Blackline Master 10)

You do not need these if you already have pattern blocks. If you do not have access to wooden or plastic pattern blocks, you can use this paper version instead.

Directions: Cut out the shapes and color them according to the following key:

- Hexagons (large, 6-sided shape): yellow
- Trapezoids (4-sided shape with 3 shorter sides and 1 longer side): red
- Triangles: green
- Squares: orange
- Wider diamonds: blue
- Narrower diamonds: tan

Play Coins for Families Outside the US (Blackline Master 11)

You do not need these if you use American coins. If you live outside the U.S. and your local currency does not come in units of 1, 5, and 10, you can use these generic coins in place of American coins in the lessons. (See page 28 for more details on how to substitute other options for coins.)

Directions: Copy this page on sturdy paper and cut out the coins.

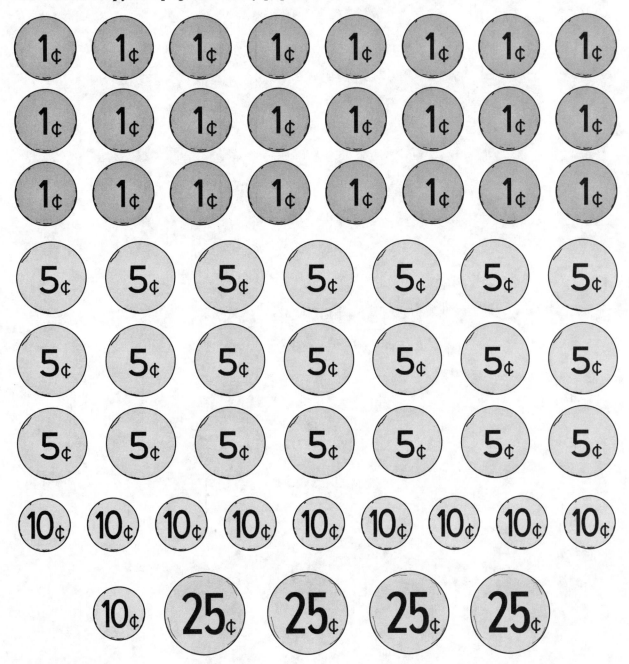

Play Paper Bills for Families Outside the US
(Blackline Master 12)

You do not need these if you have other play money, either from a toy cash register or board game.

Directions: Copy this page on sturdy paper and cut out the paper bills.

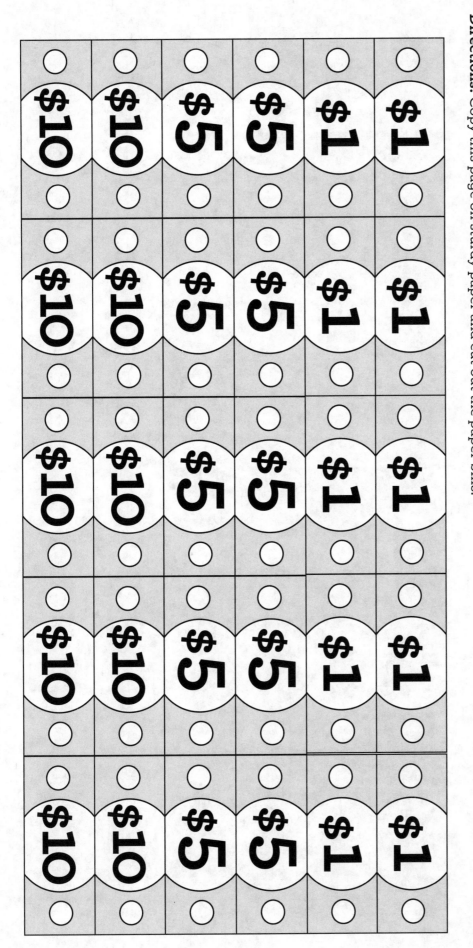

Acknowledgements

Thanks to Itamar Katz, whose design and illustration skills transformed my Word document and sloppy sketches into this clear, easy-to-read *Instructor Guide* and colorful, whimsical *Student Workbook*.

To Bethany Lake, whose close reading and thoughtful suggestions helped me find the balance between mathematical rigor and developmental appropriateness. To Shane Klink, who designed the wonderful covers for the series. And, to Rebecca Fields, who fixed all my typos and made sure that every i was dotted and t was crossed.

To Susan Wise Bauer, for her guidance and advice as I honed the vision for the Math with Confidence series. To Justin Moore, for his thoughtful clarifying questions and indefatigable copy-editing. And to Melissa Moore, not only for her expert project management but also for her support, encouragement, and friendship. Thanks for walking with me through 2020's many worries and challenges, Mel.

Finally, many thanks to the members of the *First Grade Math with Confidence* pilot-test group. Thank you for finding the activities that didn't work, the lessons that went too long, and the workbook pages that were too complicated. This program is better because of you, and I appreciate all the time you spent giving me feedback, answering my questions, and helping me understand how your kids responded to the lessons. Beyond these practical matters, thank you for your overall encouragement and support as I wrote *First Grade Math with Confidence*. Your commitment to giving your kids an excellent math education motivates and inspires me, and it is an honor to be part of that journey with you.

Meghan Akridge	Jami McCreary
Megan Anderson	Kate Nicolaus
Jacquelyn Beaumont	Katie O'Farrell
Nettie Black	Jenna R.
Bettina Gentry	Heather Reynaldo-Casanova
DeDi Goss	Ashley Scofield
Janelle H.	LuAnn Simons
Lisa Healy	Lynna Sutherland
Joanna Guiao Hidalgo	Jennifer Tierney
Rhebeka Hyland	Lindsay Toth
Alexis Jaeger	Amanda Troxell
Jane Kim	Monique Tyson
Rachel King	Duski Van Fleet
Emily Kuhl	Allison vanKlinken
Amy Lerner	Sara Watson
Melissa Mackey	Elizabeth Wenzel
Rebekah Martin	Valerie Winkley
Sarah McCormick	Amanda Yeary